DATE DUE			
Jul 7'82			

Teaching Literature

Designs for Cognitive Development

Teaching Literature
Designs for Cognitive Development

Deborah Elkins

Queens College
The City University of New York

CHARLES E. MERRILL PUBLISHING COMPANY
A Bell & Howell Company
Columbus, Ohio 43216

Published by
Charles E. Merrill Publishing Company
A Bell & Howell Company
Columbus, Ohio 43216

This book was set in Times Roman.
The Production Editors were Debbie Worley Payne and Jan Hall.
The cover was designed by Will Chenoweth.

International Standard Book Number: 0–675–08653–1

Library of Congress Catalog Number: 75–23891

1 2 3 4 5 6 7 8 9–81 80 79 78 77 76

Printed in the United States of America

To my sisters,
To Helen Hall Jennings
and
In memory of Hilda Taba

Preface

Teaching Literature: Designs for Cognitive Development is a curriculum book for both inservice and preservice teachers of English. To the prospective   teacher   offers assistance in solving day-to-day and long-range problems. For the experienced teacher the book attempts to stimulate thought about curriculum building; it is the teacher who must ultimately be the curriculum builder. For teachers of teachers it hopes to help open the door which may some day lead to the development of curriculum theory in literature, which is at present in its most rudimentary stages.

The theoretical framework of the book is based largely though not solely on the work of Piaget. Piaget studied the structures through which the human species acquires knowledge. For the most part the practices described in this book are the result of the author's interpretation of Piaget's theories. Piaget offers no suggestion for the educator, no instruction for action by the teacher, no procedures to be carried out in the classroom. As the author worked with small groups of teachers, new practices were evolved in concert and tested in the classroom. The many years of experience teaching in the secondary school gave the author a store of ideas to modify and test again in the classrooms of a new generation of teachers and students.

This book is based on the conviction that there exists a body of knowledge not yet put to use for building curriculum theory. This body of knowledge holds vast potential, and the enhancement of curriculum theory is seriously blocked by classroom practices which are too discrete to encourage curriculum building.

The influence of Piaget and his colleagues and followers is already being felt in many classrooms, especially in the elementary school. His work, particularly those aspects of his theory dealing with the emergence of formal thought and with egocentrism of the adolescent, has much to offer the secondary school. The thinking of the adolescent is of an altogether different order from that of the child. The emergence of formal thought means that for the most part classroom practices can be adopted which would have been impossible in the elementary school.

The first chapter explores the theories of Piaget and others which form the theoretical basis for the succeeding chapters. In the second chapter, the author discusses curriculum building in general and in particular as it relates to the teaching of literature.

Chapters three through seven develop ideas for teaching the major genre. Each genre is explored for its potential in contributing to the intellectual growth of students. The suggestions for particular practices are precisely that—suggestions; they are not meant to be prescriptions or recipes. The last chapter probes the role of evaluation, its ways and means.

No practice is suggested which does not promise to enhance cognitive functioning. In the course of testing out ideas, many efforts proved fruitless and were discarded. Many failures were experienced; most of them have not been recounted here for lack of space. Ideas that were adopted were scrutinized for the degree to which they were judged harmonious with the cognitive theory examined in chapter one. They were evaluated on the basis of evidence, however informal, that students' cognitive performance was affected in a positive manner. Cognitive development is closely related to the affective domain, that is, interest of the student, motivation and enjoyment, feelings of mastery, and values held. Any practice which ran counter to the possibility of positive affective consequences was discarded. The conviction that literature's potential is a stimulus for reshaping cognitive structures is evident in these pages.

Grateful acknowledgment is made to the scores of teachers whose questions stimulated the writing of this book and whose ideas are represented here. They shared their thoughts, tested out concepts in the classroom, and gave their time in working through the sequence of experiences which are a key feature in the teaching of each genre. Four of those teachers shared in the writing of several sections of the genre chapters; they are Marlene Maxwell Garnett, Alice Fritsch Stollman, Elinor Weinreich Joseph, and Lola Lee Cronacher. In each case, the sections on which they collaborated with the author are indicated in the text.

Very special gratitude is owed to five people: Dóris Vorwold, Queens College education librarian, for her assistance in ferreting out references essential to this work; the two reviewers who were sharp in their criticism and most helpful in their suggestions; to my sister Gertrude Elkins who persisted in the onerous task of typing the manuscript and somehow managed to read the handwriting that was no longer legible to anyone else; and to Emily L. Philpott for checking bibliographical data.

Deborah Elkins

Contents

Chapter One

Cognitive Foundations for the Study of Literature

"Critical thinking" has been a recognized goal of education for a long time. The activities said to foster the attainment of this goal are legion; they range from memorizing the "times tables" to evaluating a given set of criteria. In fact, there is little that the schools are consciously doing that isn't at one time or another surrounded by the aura of the critical-thinking claim.

Yet, few teachers have been educated to understand what is involved in the thought process. The thinking about thinking has been bungling perhaps because there are so many theories about the development of this most crucial aspect of human life, perhaps because the pendulum of educational goals in the past decade or two has swung so violently as to create confusion, perhaps because education generally has not focused on the relationship between cognitive processes and some of education's most trying problems. Whatever the cause, the questions besetting teachers who are sincere in their attempts to foster cognitive development have not received adequate attention. Many teachers are aware that now is the time when all the resources of every human being are needed to cope with the drastic, all-encompassing changes taking place with lightning speed. Man can move forward or annihilate himself. The technological developments in our society have created snow-balling problems in the lives of every human being. We have experienced the tensions of the energy crisis. Our adolescents have seen turmoil in Vietnam, Cambodia, the Middle East, and our cities. Children and adolescents grow up with a pervasive sense of fear, of the perils of life, the turmoil, confused beliefs and values they see about them, the alienation they and others feel, and the powerlessness of the individual unprepared to cope with a power structure he cannot even comprehend.

A new type of education is needed with cognitive development at its *heart*. There is no dichotomy between the cognitive and the affective domains, as will be discussed later in this chapter. Education for cognitive development includes the examination and establishment of values and beliefs by which men live, so that the insecurity nurtured by the destruction of old beliefs and values may be reduced and so that meaning may be restored to man's existence, reestablishing a sense of his own individual importance.

Appropriate cognitive experiences enhance the development of sensitivity to the human condition. Never has the world been more interdependent; never before has the behavior of one individual or group had such crucial consequences for others. A new education is called for to deal with the situation. That education places man at the center of its study, helps the student search for understanding in an age when understanding is obscured by upheaval, opens to him a range of alternatives, makes possible the comprehension of the forces that impose themselves upon him, and encourages him to examine those forces and evaluate and change them if necessary. Such education must be based in meaningful cognitive development.

Searching is a cognitive act imperative in an age of upheaval. Examination and evaluation are cognitive acts equally crucial. Knowing that even in a world in which the individual seems powerless there are some choices open to him, knowing there is freedom to make decisions about those areas of choice, knowing what forces to grant authority over him and what forces to reject are all cognitive acts. It is the cognitive process which brings order out of chaos and encourages a sense of autonomy. It is this process which connects the individual meaningfully to his world.

It is within the power of the school to increase cognitive ability. During the present era in human life maximum intellectual functioning including the affective domain is imperative. By focusing on intellectual and affective development, the school can help cushion the shock of increasingly rapid and unpredictable change.

The new education must come offering the wherewithal for creating a sense of harmony, of order, of sheer joy of living, thus freeing man from the overwhelming odds of an impersonal society; it must also provide a modus operandi for each person to build a sense of his own power as an individual. It is literature which casts man in the role of protagonist, which places him at the heart of its study. Inherent in this study is a rich store of resources for cognitive development, aesthetic pleasure, and an abundant affective life.

The Cognitive Process

There exist a number of theories of cognitive development. Some appear to be more pertinent to the teaching of literature than others. This book focuses largely but not exclusively on limited aspects of Piaget's theory; however, it is not claimed to be an educational design for even a large portion of his theory. His theory is a very complex system; no one attempt to interpret and apply his philosophy can possibly do justice to the intricate elements of cognition he has explored. This work deals with an interpretation of certain select aspects of his theory which appear to help the teacher enrich the teaching of literature.

Piaget is a prolific writer. Several of his books are now available in English translation. Increasingly, there appear on the market books which attempt to interpret his research for the English-speaking educator. The materials in this section are credited largely to four books by Piaget, *The Origins of Intelligence in Children* (1952), *Biology and Knowledge* (1967), *Six Psychological Studies* (1967), and *The Growth of Logical Thinking from Childhood to Adolescence* (Inhelder and Piaget, 1958) and to the work of Flavell (1963), Furth (1969), and Wadsworth (1971).

A brief review of Piaget's four main stages of human development from infancy to adulthood will serve as a background for some of the concepts explored in this book and will alert the reader to the fact that the thought of the adolescent is from a different order than that of the younger child. The intellectual development of the adolescent is founded in infancy and childhood. In *Six Psychological Studies,* Piaget refers to four stages of mental development; in other works, he groups them into three or sometimes six periods. Whichever the case, the changes occur on a continuum of intellectual development.

THE MENTAL DEVELOPMENT OF THE CHILD

The Neonate and the Infant: Sensorimotor Assimilation (0–2 years).   Piaget says that the period of infancy (from birth to the acquisition of language) is "marked by an extraordinary development of the mind."[1] At birth, the infant's mental activity is restricted entirely to reflexes. These reflexes may be sensory or motor. They are active. It is these active reflexes which permit intellectual development. At first, the infant "grasps everything to . . . his own body"[2] and sucks anything he encounters. He can grasp because the grasping reflex is there; he can suck because the sucking reflex is active. He is not compelled to learn to suck or to grasp. With practice, those reflexes become more precise. Through his haphazard movements he arrives at something he wants again. Soon he is able to repeat the act, without having to wait for a random movement to make contact. It is through these reflexes that the infant learns (assimilates) something of his world. The neonate has no other schemata but the sensorimotor. This period ends with the acquisition of language and the beginning of thought. Intelligence appears before language, as manifested by the child's manipulation of objects prior to the acquisition of language. For example, he wants a toy beyond his reach, and he pulls a string and gets it. He experiments with objects to see what happens to them. The fact that he comprehends the connection between a particular means and an end is the evidence of practical intelligence.

Early Childhood: Preoperational Thought (2–7 years).   This is the period of language development. At first, the child's use of language cannot be described as real communication. He talks to himself in the presence of other people. At age six or seven his speech is socialized, for he uses it to share ideas. As indicated earlier, the child manifests the beginnings of intelligent behavior before he develops language. But with the acquisition of language, there is increased intellectual prowess because his thought is no longer dependent on immediate activity. His thought can go beyond that when he has language. In addition, his intellectual prowess is increased because language facilitates the development of concepts. One can work faster with concepts than with sensorimotor events, yet it must be remembered that language cannot develop without sensorimotor development.

The young child is egocentric. He talks to himself; he plays in the presence of others but by himself. He cannot see another person's point of view because he thinks everybody's thoughts are identical to his. He does not question his ideas. At age six or seven, he plays by the rules; he plays to win. These are manifestations of real social behavior.

His ideas then may come in conflict with the ideas of others, and he may try to confirm them. These social behaviors move him away from egocentricity.

Childhood: Concrete Operational Thought (7 to 11 years).   In this period, the child frees himself from total dependence on perceptual operations to solve problems. He can solve them by using logical operations, if the problems are concrete. He displays cooperative social behaviors; he is aware that others have ideas different from his. He can note several different properties of an object or event, arrange things according to size, and classify objects and events. But he is still unable to deal with hypothetical situations, fails in efforts to place events in order, and lacks the power to handle problems that are solely verbal. He still needs real objects in order to solve problems.

Adolescence: Formal Operations (11 to 15 years).   At the conclusion of this period, the young person's cognitive structures are mature; his cognitive potential is at a maximum. After age fifteen, any cognitive structural changes are quantitative. The qualitative changes are at an end. This means the qualitative structure of intelligence can no longer be changed, but the function of intelligence can be changed. All through life, changes in schemata continue to be made by assimilation and accommodation. The fact that adult thought is different from adolescent thought is one indication that the function and the content of thought are still subject to change.

Formal thought is less limited than concrete thought which depends on the present and upon the tangibility of problems. Now the young person can deal with hypothetical and purely verbal problems. He can now use general theories and is able to handle several operations at one time to solve one problem. He can build and test hypotheses, and he can understand cause and consequence on a purely verbal level.

The changes that have been traced here are gradual. The structure does not change overnight from concrete to formal at the conclusion of the eleventh year of life. Each new structure builds upon previous structures and incorporates the previous ones. With formal operations, the young person is able to make hypotheses about the future, and his thoughts can encompass all of mankind.

How Cognitive Structures Are Constructed

Cognitive development has its origin in the infant's interaction with his environment and his *adaptation* to it. This adaptation, according to Piaget, involves two processes: *assimilation* or intake, and *accommodation* or output in the sense of extending oneself to the environmental objects or events.

The infant makes contact with the parental index finger. As he sucks it, which is an assimilation process, the process of accommodation takes place at the same time while he learns that the finger is not food. With each thing that goes into his mouth, he learns to *differentiate* the edible from the inedible and to *categorize* objects according to their edibility. The learning takes place because he actively seeks and because there is an environmental stimulus present to which he can respond.

Central to the cognitive process is the act of classification. This starts in infancy and originates in the active behaviors of the infant as he sucks and grasps and gropes. As the child interacts with his environment and learns to differentiate and categorize objects and events, he creates schemata. Wadsworth compares a schema such as the grasping schema or sucking schema to an index card or a concept or a category.[3] Infants have few "cards on file." Adults have many which are continuously being modified. Eventually, the cow the child sees is no longer a dog. His dog schema is sufficiently differentiated to distinguish a dog from a cow. At first, a cow fits into his dog schema. If the child is to be able to comprehend his world in some kind of order, he must learn to group details and he must learn to classify them. Stauffer emphasizes the function of categorizing; "Virtually all cognitive activity of conceptualization, inference, and so on, is dependent on the process of categorizing."[4]

The operation of classification originates in the process of assimilation. The tendency to assimilate is progressive, thus permitting the child to gain more and more knowledge. The child assimilates an object or event and comprehends it. His schema is enlarged by that newly assimilated object or event. Then comes another object or event, and the process is repeated. As he assimilates each object, he notes the similarities. He is classifying when he isolates the *common* criteria, or resemblances, and notes the differences.

If the child has an available "kitty" schema when he notes a squirrel for the first time, he acts. If the new squirrel stimulus qualifies for his kitty schema, this indicates that he noted the similarities between the squirrel and the kitty and assimilated the squirrel into the existing schema. Through assimilation as well as accommodation the cognitive structures, the schemata, change. Assimilation causes *quantitative* change as the new stimulus is blended into the existing schema.

Not all objects can serve as a stimulus. Furth uses the grasping structure to illustrate this fact.[5] Since an individual's structure tends to pull into itself the "environmental events," the body grasps things that can be grasped. If an object cannot be grasped, the existing grasping schema cannot incorporate it. Therefore, it cannot be assimilated; and if it cannot be assimilated, it is not a stimulus. It might just as well not be there.

This is a very important concept for the teacher of literature, for even though the thinking of the adolescent is different from that of the young child, it is based upon it, for assimilation and accommodation still go on. Despite the great changes that have taken place in the literary works selected for adolescents to study, there still exists the problem that the works selected are not a stimulus for all students in the same classroom at the same time. For the student whose literary novel schema is not ready for Knowles' *A Separate Peace,* that novel is no stimulus. It will not be assimilated; it will have no effect upon the existing schema, and the student will not learn. This is, of course, an oversimplification, for the literary novel schema is a very complex thing involving schema for subtleties of language, metaphor, characterization, etc.

As has been indicated earlier, the affective factors are part and parcel of the cognitive domain. Parents who raise objections to their offspring's reading of Thomas' *Down These Mean Streets* are caught up in the "bad language," the homosexual scene, and the violence. For them, the full import of the book is lost. They cannot cut through the "foul language" to the heart of the matter; they cannot accept those words as an intrinsic part of the life being portrayed. Therefore, they cannot assimilate the biography as an entity. They have no existing schema that can assimilate ideas about the human condition surrounded with "dirty words." Nor is accommodation likely, because that process involves changing existing schema.

In some cases, however, accommodation is an alternative to the "no stimulus" reaction. When the child fails to assimilate a new stimulus into his available schemata, due to the fact that he has no schemata that are suitable, he is forced to alter an old schema to accommodate the new stimulus. He may even have to create a new schema. If he succeeds, then the growth is qualitative. He forms new cognitive structures. Now, the child attempts anew to assimilate the stimulus. With the new or the modified schema or cognitive structure, he succeeds. Assimilation is the aim of the cognitive structure.

The processes of assimilation and accommodation can be illustrated in the study of literature, even though such study involves much more complex behavior. The student has an available happy-ending schema for stories. The teacher reads to him Maltz's "Afternoon in the Jungle," the story of thirteen-year-old Charles who is reared in the jungle of New York City's streets. The teacher stops reading at the climax and asks the student how he thinks the story will end. The student concludes the story with Charles as the winner of the coin over which he and an unidentified man have struggled. Charles becomes the benefactor, splitting the coin with the man. However, there is nothing in the story to indicate that everything will end happily ever after. Charles loses the coin as does the man. The elements are against them, for darkness approaches, the ice and bitter cold are deterrents, and the jungle behavior of both characters makes failure inevitable.

The student, upon his subsequent reading of the Maltz ending, cannot assimilate the failure consequence into his happy-ending schema. The teacher mediates: See how many times Maltz warns us that darkness is descending? Why does he do that? It's a cold, gray day. Why didn't Maltz make it a nice bright, sunny day? Let's look at the two characters. Are they doing anything to make it possible to bring up that coin? Through such mediation, some students' schemata will be altered so that the new failure consequence can be accommodated: Stories are not necessarily concluded happily; they may even terminate on a note of frustration; they may end in a draw; the protagonist may go through an experience that makes him a lesser human being rather than a better one. It takes many experiences over a long period of time for appropriate schemata to develop. Literature is there to offer the experience; the teacher is there to mediate.

Flavell explains that "the structures are *generalized* to assimilate the new object" and that "cognitive structures are not only *generalized* to the new object but are also *differentiated.*" He uses the illustration of a child sucking a ring for the first time. He cannot suck this in the same way that he uses the nipple. He tries again and learns that the ring and the nipple cannot be sucked in the same way. He learns that the ring feels different and looks different. "The important consequence of the structural changes wrought by this generalization and differentiation is, of course, the fact that this change makes possible new and different accommodation to future objects encountered."[6] Thus, the intellectual organization becomes increasingly modified by each new accommodation. By permitting the organism to generalize, the schemata also permit transfer of learning. By finding similarities, the schemata permit transfer to new situations, thus encouraging learning.

Balance of the two processes, assimilation and accommodation, is essential. When they are in balance the organism attains equilibrium, which Wadsworth describes as "a necessary condition toward which the organism constantly strives."[7] When the stimulus is assimilated, a state of cognitive equilibrium is attained. Flavell calls that state of equilibrium between assimilation and accommodation "the ideal norm towards which intelligence moves," for "intelligent functioning, when equilibrium obtains, is made up of a balanced recipe of about equal parts of assimilation and accommodation."[8]

Schools often fail to provide balance between assimilation and accommodation. Wadsworth points out that where assimilation activities take up an major part of the school day, the learner develops too few schemata. The learner fails to "detect differences in things."[9] The student who hears or reads only happy-ending stories fails to detect the differences in the clues offered by the authors of happy and unhappy stories. It takes alertness to differences to make intrinsic modification of the schema. The student fails also to detect the clues in the lives of people he meets in daily life or in the media. On the other hand, Wadsworth says that if exclusive doses of accommodation experiences are offered to students, miniscule schemata are developed.[10] This impairs the student's ability to detect similarities, which means he cannot find common elements and therefore cannot develop the power to generalize. Thus, if the teacher wishes to help develop the generalization that the individual's personality is affected by the people, objects, and events surrounding the life of an individual, he must give the student appropriate experiences through literature and perhaps in life. The student can observe these experiences in Maltz's "Afternoon in the Jungle," Heyert's "The New Kid," and Deasy's "The High Hill."

Although Piaget and his interpreters separate assimilation and accommodation in order to explain the dual process, they really occur simultaneously. These processes of structuring make up the acts of intelligence; they constitute *knowing*. Knowledge cannot be transmitted from the teacher to the student; it must be *constructed* by the student.

Motivation and Cognition

The most important concept for understanding motivation is centered around intrinsic motivation. As Stauffer explains, "Once cognitive structures have been generated by functioning, they tend to perpetuate themselves by more functioning. . . . The organ has to 'nourish' its cognitive schemas by repeated assimilation, the basic fact of intellectual life."[11] This does not mean that the teacher has no role to play in motivating the student to learn. Rather, it means that his role must take into consideration the basic one provided by the tendency of schemas to assimilate whatever is assimilable in the environment. It serves little purpose for teachers to devise attention-getting gimmicks unless intrinsic motivation is operating. Extrinsic motivation such as report cards, grades, and stars for neat papers cannot be effective when intrinsic motivation is weak and when the cognitive structure cannot exercise its tendency to assimilate, perhaps because the stimuli are not assimilable. While there is no question that an outside stimulus is critical, whether it be provided by the teacher, the classroom setting, the other students, the appearance of the principal, a toy, a book, or a new machine, the fact remains that there is simply more to the process. Furth recognizes that the "reaction of an organism . . . is always and at all levels also the response of the underlying structure within the organism."[12]

THE TEACHER AS MEDIATOR

What is the teacher's role in motivating functional cognitive development? Basically, the teacher is a mediator, an interpreter, as well as one adult who provides appropriate stimuli which might not otherwise be available to the learner. As the student manipulates the stimulus which the teacher provides or which is provided by other elements in the environment, the teacher helps him interpret what is happening. For example, the student who read *A Bend in the Road*[13] by Raymond and who concluded, "It shows that teenagers are not understood by parents and if they run away from home, they'll make it some place else," certainly needed a mediator. For the teacher to say, "Oh no, that's not at all what the author is telling us," would be futile if not detrimental. Questions which help the student examine each incident are far more likely to succeed, especially when considered with a small group of peers who can lend a variety of points of view to any one incident. In this case the teacher mediated through questions and by arranging a peer group situation. The student had already been motivated to read the book because it was about an adolescent who ran away from home. The student was engaged in manipulating the environmental event, but the teacher was needed to help interpret the events that were taking place.

The abstractions and the generalizations of which the adolescent is capable are based in the manipulation of concrete objects and events that take place mainly, though not exclusively, in the early years. It is those manipulations of concrete objects which make later abstractions possible. On the surface this appears to be a paradox, yet it is not. The child observes the consequences of his own actions as he manipulates objects, and the teacher as mediator helps him interpret the results. There can be many interpretations and many meanings; the teacher helps him find these. In discovering these meanings, the child's curiosity is increased, as is receptiveness to new knowledge which he acquires through his own activity. Thus, the environment becomes ordered as concepts and abstractions are formed, for these help the child's world move from its trappings of the confusion and chaos into an ordered universe.

The adult mediator, in helping to provide appropriate stimuli and in helping the child to interpret the environment, shares experiences with him. As he talks over a shared experience and thus helps the student to remember, he is developing the student's capacity to remember; he is developing memory. Remembering is in itself motivational. The student who remembers feels a sense of mastery. He knows he has in his possession some power which opens up new worlds. Thus, he approaches the next accommodation-assimilation experience with more energy and vigor than might otherwise be present. That new sense of mastery is in itself motivational.

THE ROLE OF VARIETY IN MOTIVATION

Hunt sharpens the close relationship between motivation and cognitive development in Piaget's theory by emphasizing the overt activities of the child: "The more new things a child has seen and the more he has heard, the more things he is interested in seeing and in hearing.[14] The bare walls of the ghetto, the sheer dearth of objects in the home, the single pot for cooking all foods offer few things to be seen; the bareness thus impairs the child's early motivational and cognitive development. The single textbook parallels that one and only pot. One literature anthology for the entire class, in some cases used for a whole semester, constitutes a dearth of objects in the schoolroom. "Moreover," Hunt adds, "the more variation in reality with which he [child] has coped, the greater is his capacity for coping."[15] Variety has motivational power. Piaget makes strong argument for variety of situations, objects, and events in the intellectual development of children. A lack of varied objects and events of an appropriate nature retards development. A variety of available books and other objects related to literature (e.g., tape recorder, costumes, music, paintings, films for film making and viewing) is an insurance that the student will find something of interest with which he will cope, thus making it possible that the coping will occur again and again.

A similar point can be made for variety in teaching-learning procedures. The same old developmental lesson will not suffice in the face of Piaget's findings. The events in the classroom must be varied to encourage coping. Dramatizing poetry where this is appropriate, re-creating it orally, writing poetry, setting it to music, or representing it in an art form are a very few of the various procedures through which students can become involved sufficiently to permit them to cope. Availability of a variety of stimuli alone will not do the job of fostering the coping. The mere presence of a variety of attractive books on poetry will bring some students to that shelf who would otherwise not "play" with poetry. However, the poetry schema of many students will not be modified and enlarged enough so that they take the initiative in seeking it out; then it is the role of the teacher to mediate, that is, provide ways and means for students to re-create the poems of the great writers and to engage in creating their own. Then the students will increasingly use available stimuli. They will notice more. They will cope and will enjoy coping. Through his acts of mediation, the teacher has provided opportunity for systematic interpretation of the student's environment. When a student is interested in seeing and in hearing, there exists the motivation to learn. Curiosity increases. If he is curious about many things, he takes the initiative in finding out about them, thus setting in motion the essential process of accommodation with its attendant modification and expansion of the appropriate schema. Then he moves on to assimilate new events and situations. This initiative provides the necessary *energy* to learn.

THE SOCIAL GROUP AND MOTIVATION

The social group, the peer group, is a motivating force often not recognized sufficiently by the school. It provides an exceedingly fruitful means of cognitive and affective development, particularly in the literature class. When schools confront the task of developing concepts or schemata that do not have physical referents (e.g., "integrity" as against "cat"), social interaction is necessary. Wadsworth explains that "the interchange of ideas between people" takes the place of acting upon concrete objects. This is especially so in cases where concepts are socially defined. For the child, social interaction is central to the "construction and validation of his concepts."[16]

Although the adolescent still needs some concrete experience for learning abstractions, his need for the concrete is far less than that of the younger child, if he has had sufficient, appropriate concrete experiences earlier in life. For the adolescent, social life becomes crucial. Thus, class discussions in large and small groups about experiences in literature and in life are motivational. They lend breadth to interpretations, since few readers gather all the innuendos inherent in a good piece of literature. Sigel as well as Ginsburg and Opper stress the implications of social life. "The significance of social life for cognitive development rests on the conceptualization of social interaction as a necessary condition for transition from one developmental level to another . . . social-ization creates stress that induces cognitive transformation."[17] Social interaction adds pressure because it forces the student to examine other points of view and to broaden his sights. "As he comes to understand another person's point of view, then he gains a more objective knowledge of reality. . . . Interaction inevitably leads to conflict and argument. The child's views are questioned. He must defend his ideas, and he must justify his opinions. In doing this he is forced to clarify his thoughts."[18]

Literature offers a focus par excellence for such interaction; this is revealed in discussions which are attuned to the interests of adolescents and which are centered on a controversial issue inherent in the piece of literature. Such an issue might be, Why does the author decide to have Marty in "The New Kid" take the initiative in torturing the new kid? Marty himself knew what it meant to endure such suffering.

SURPRISE AND MOTIVATION

There is an increasing body of literature on the role of surprise as a motivational force in cognitive development. Charlesworth comments that "surprise may well play an important role in the processes controlling cognitive development."[19] The child meets the unexpected and accommodates to and assimilates the unexpected event. Surprise is motivational because suddenly new relationships come to light, relationships that were not apparent earlier. There are new ways of assembling and grouping things. Bruner calls "an act that produces *effective* surprise . . . the hallmark of a creative enterprise."[20] Charlesworth explains that surprise is different from startle, which is quick and sharp and uncomfortable. Infants possess the capacity to be startled, but surprise is a capacity that takes much longer to develop. "The capacity to be surprised . . . requires an ability to recognize a signal and anticipate or expect the event the signal signifies."[21] As the student puzzles over a problem, there may occur without warning a misexpected event. The individual literally stops whatever he is doing because his attention is focused sharply on the new event. Berlyne uses repetition in music to explain the role of surprise and how it is created. "By repeating some feature a number of times in succession, the composer can encourage the expectation that the feature will continue, enabling him to create surprise and uncertainty by rudely disappointing this expectation. . . .The repetition of exactly the same sounds over and over again . . . is . . . regularly used to build up excitement. . . . There is a mounting expectation that the repetition cannot go on much longer, but it is not clear exactly when it will come to an end and what will replace it."[22]

Since surprise is thus highly motivational, it has a place in the study of literature. Students conclude their first reading of Jackson's "The Lottery" with a sense of shock and disbelief. In some cases, the initial reaction is rejection of the entire story. In other instances there is no awareness that Mrs. Hutchinson was stoned to death. "No, they didn't kill her! Where do you see *that?* They just stoned her. It doesn't say they killed her." The way in which the author dwells upon apparently harmless neighborly talk, the setting of a nice sunny day on the village green, and the antics of the children are part of what constitutes the backdrop for an horrendous occurrence. The clues which foreshadowed went unnoticed. The surprise experienced by the students makes it possible for the teacher to lead them to examine vestiges of such events in our society and in the world today. Then it is possible for the students to examine the subtle clues in the story and the way in which Jackson achieved surprise by building up certain expectations. Students experience still another surprise. How could we have missed all of those clues? Thus, the teacher uses the motivation of surprise to help them through the process of accommodation by means of comparison with the familiar. Then they achieve final assimilation of the events as well as of the whole literary work. Some students who reject the death and the violence experience shock rather than surprise. For them, the element of surprise cannot be motivational.

EMOTIONS

As was indicated earlier, emotions are closely related to the way in which intelligence functions. Piaget offers repeated illustrations of the fact that emotion is required to bring about the completion of an act of intelligence because emotions perform the motivational function of that act of intelligence. One example concerns the cumulative role of emotion in intellectual activity. "The [emotional] need set in motion the act and its functioning, but this functioning itself engenders a greater need which from the very first goes beyond the pure satisfaction of the initial need."[23]

Elkind examines the relationship between emotions and intellectual activity from another point of view. "Every affective experience . . . presupposes some form of cognitive structuring . . . the ability to recognize and label one's emotions requires the capacity to discriminate amongst the many possible emotions, and this in turn must engage cognitive structures."[24] Pulaski concurs, noting that emotions have the power to direct: "Emotion is what makes intelligence dynamic, directed, ever seeking a better equilibrium."[25] It is in the context of the social group that emotions can be educated and that sensitivity to the human condition is built. Dewey notes that "sense" functions in a broad context. It includes "the sensory, the sensational, the sensitive, the sensible, and the sentimental, along with the sensuous." Furthermore, "It cannot be opposed to 'intellect,' for mind is the means by which participation is rendered fruitful through sense . . . ."[26]

Social values consist of emotional as well as intellectual components; they cannot be learned by the individual in isolation. Values and feelings are learned; they are not usually learned directly from the words of the teacher. When students are engaged in the cognitive and emotional experience of social interaction, they do not set out consciously to learn values. However, this, by and large, is precisely the way a sizable portion of our values is learned. Here again, teachers are needed to help interpret what is happening so that the process of value education can become a conscious one. Values are all around the student in every phase of his life. He is unaware of them and their role. They need to be brought to the awareness level so that he and his peers can understand the many contradictions that exist and understand the emotional impact that is carried by a value.

Few if any values are taught simply by "telling." Nor will mere social interaction for its own sake achieve the end. Students need to live through experiences. Such learning requires the kind of social interaction which is purposeful for all participants, in which decisions are made that are important to those participants, and in which the feelings that are evoked become the subject of conscious examination. Literature study is a particularly effective vehicle for value education and sensitivity development. In itself, literature contains the necessary ingredients: emotional experiences to which students can respond, an array of values to which characters are responding with feeling, and an intellectual sequence which directly or indirectly explores the impact of those values. These values are something less than subtly portrayed in "The Test" by Angelica Gibbs, explored with the drive of a parable in Björnson's "The Father," and poignantly drawn in Haycox's "A Question of Blood" and in Mansfield's "Miss Brill." The list is endless. Literature study is effective also because it engenders emotions in the reader, listener, or performer. Students' emotional reactions in themselves are the fruitful object of intellectual consideration.

The Thinking of the Adolescent

A brief glance at two or three areas of difference in the cognitive functioning of the adolescent and the child will highlight for the literature teacher the distinctive features of the adolescent's abilities. Perhaps the most important difference between the cognitive functioning of the child and that of the adolescent is that the child functions in the real world only while the adolescent can function in the world of the possible. Flavell comments, "What he (the child) does not do (and what the adolescent does do) is delineate all possible eventualities at the outset and then try to discover which of these possibilities really do occur in the present data. . . ."[27] The younger child is unable to do this, for there is a tremendous development that must take place from the time he is quite unable to repeat the events of a story in sequential order to the time he is able to think in hypothetical terms. Before he can hypothesize, he must learn how to think back over events without concrete objects to help him. His ability to classify must reach new heights, progressing from the classification with one criteria to categorization using more than one and then on to increasingly generalized criteria.

Sensitivity Training.   Literature's power to accomplish the task of sensitivity training for academically superior students as well as for the academically undiscovered is still untapped. The range in sensitive responses to literature is certainly as great in a gifted class as it is in a deprived one. To perceive this range, teachers need simply to note the variation in students' sensitivity to problems, in their ability to identify, and in their insightfulness as evidenced only by verbal response to behaviors and situations described in a work of literature. In one class of academically gifted twelfth graders the following responses to "Miss Brill" were recorded; the range is worthy of note:

> I cannot sympathize with her loneliness; she's a useless busybody whose only enjoyment is eavesdropping. She loves nothing but her fur piece.

> This is a marvelous portrait of a pathetic figure. The author drew exquisite cameos in a few short spare strokes, such as the crude young couple. The author's descriptions are as complete as a work by Monet, yet have the same dreamlike touch.

The difference between a great piece of literature and a merely good one lies largely in the accuracy and the degree of sensitivity with which the human condition has been drawn. This being the case, the role of literature in sensitivity training is implicit.

Sensitivity training through literature can be an initial motivating force for increasing cognitive abilities. It can plunge students into a direct concern with intellectual problems; it can nourish the energy for learning concepts and other cognitive elements. For example, as students read individually selected stories around the theme, "Social class barriers tend to cause problems with which individuals find great difficulty in coping," they meet stories which occur in various times and places. They begin to gain a sense of the continuity of time and place as they compare notes about how the theme is handled by their author. They see how the events and the treatment of the theme are different because of difference in time and place. They see the universality of the theme through the facts that so many authors have chosen to deal with it and that it is repeated in so many eras and geographic locations. Flexibility is the key. It must be developed so that students can surrender their stereotyped notions of life and look anew at an old situation through the eyes of another, more insightful person possessing greater wisdom than they.

Sharing the emotions, desires, and aspirations of others helps the student make a part of his own life the people he meets in distant places or the people who are removed from him in personal characteristics.

When we study a piece of literature, we are free to attend to what the author implies, to the details he draws and the finer differentiations he makes. We are free because the situation is not ours; we do not have to face it in real life. We can reflect upon it, examine it carefully, and decide upon a response according to the details we discover important to the situation. The freedom and reflection develop flexibility and the ability to seek differentiation. We can discriminate because we have time to do this; we need not respond on the spot.

Some of the activities English classes have traditionally engaged in actually encourage stereotyping and discourage a flexible approach. For example, enumerating the traits of characters is not only a difficult thing to do but may have a stultifying effect. Once the student has labeled the character as "gay," "stupid," or "lazy," he no longer feels the need to probe for reasons, underlying factors in the environment, or motivational factors which have influenced the behavior of the character. Human behavior is too complex to be dismissed so peremptorily and so simply, and the student must learn the complexities. The student constantly searches for something more about the character than he already knows. He observes carefully, tests his hypothesis, and as new facts enter the picture, reformulates his hypothesis and tests again.

Sensitivity training and cognitive development support each other. Sensitivity training creates an environment which nourishes the learning of cognitive skills. Where the teacher aims to form generalizations, literature provides specifics needed for their formulation; then the generalizations are used in turn to examine other specifics in literature and in life. Since the generalizations about the study of literature are concerned with human beings, they are the focus of sensitivity training. It is the literary work itself which provides the emotional experience that is necessary for the education of attitudes.

Sensitivity training includes placing peers in situations which foster mutual ego fulfillment; it means creating or taking advantage of situations to gain maximum involvement and identification. Experiences which have emotional content are necessary for building attitudes; role playing can be such an experience. It has much to offer as a sensitivity training activity. Role playing intensifies the literary experience. It can be used most successfully after reading a story to its climax; students can role play the ending rather than write it. The teacher then reads the author's ending and encourages discussion about which conclusion seems more appropriate and why. This is followed by a number of new role-playing experiences in which the students' ideas of how the story should end are given new emotional and cognitive dimensions. The discussion following the enactments is as important as the opportunity to become the characters. During the discussion students perceive many clues which they missed on the first reading and often are inspired to read the story on their own to see why they missed these particular clues. It is important for the teacher to help them understand that no one picks up all the clues at the first reading, that we learn much from each other during a discussion because each one of us notices something ignored by others. Then the rereading becomes an enlightening engagement. Thus, a heightened awareness is gained from the fully expanded role-playing experience.

Many teachers have used the technique of confidentially prearranging with two students to role play an unexpected scene, such as an altercation with a monitor. This technique can be extended to serve an important purpose of setting students at ease about the fact that they failed to observe everything about a short story on the first reading. Academically superior students are specially prone to resistance when they discover their inability to note all details. The unanticipated role playing can be used to help them understand that not only did no one observe everything but there was little unanimity about the details they did observe.

Questions and activities must be specifically aimed at sensitivity training. For example, the question, "What would you do to make things better if you were the father?" is aimed at nudging identification. Identification is aided by activities such as having a student interview another who plays the part of one of the characters. One student takes the part of the mother in Porter's "He" and is interviewed by a second student who asks, "Why did you let him do such a dangerous thing?" To give further encouragement to the identification process and to help students perceive the short story as a slice of life, students write a follow-up scene to a story such as "Charles" by Jackson. "What will happen the next day?" is the focus for the writing; "What made you think so?" is the focus for the discussion which follows.

At first, students tend to be judgmental in their reaction to a character. Jody in Rawlings' "Mother in Mannville" "shouldn't have told a lie;" Mr. Gooby, the director of the Indian school in Courtright's "Yours Lovingly," is "responsible" for the death of Julius. Behavior is evaluated mostly on the surface; there is little search for complexity of motivation or deeper understanding. Also, there is the problem of taking stories quite literally. Students may decide the plot of Chekhov's "The Bet" is "unrealistic," for no one would make such a bet and sacrifice fifteen years of his life to incarceration; the prison situation is unreal because prisoners can not leave jail any time they choose. Later in the sequence there is evidence that the degree of identification increases, with a number of attempts to explain behavior. When teachers record discussions at given intervals during the year and then analyze their contents, they can determine to some extent the degree to which their objectives are being achieved.

Sensitivity training helps students learn those aspects of the art which are caught, not taught. When the students' feeling for human life is increased and when they become more sensitive to the complexities of human existence, they gain an appreciation of the work of art as art. The qualities of a work, its style, its form, and its uniqueness are intimately related to the feelings it produces in the reader or listener.

Because the adolescent can make high level abstractions, he can give definitions that are quite complete, taking in a variety of instances. The younger child concentrates on one aspect which has caught his attention. The adolescent can grasp double meanings. This is what makes it possible for him to deal with metaphor at this stage, and not before. Elkind explores further the phenomenon of double meanings: "The grasp of metaphor presupposes the ability to recognize parallels between quite disparate things such as political parties and donkeys and elephants. It also presupposes that the figure can be separated from its literal representation.[28]

When the adolescent is confronted with a problem in literature, he tries to project all the possible situations into which each character could be thrown. In examining Kjelgaard's "Code of the Underworld" and Steinbeck's "Flight," such a problem might be, which of the main characters in these two stories would have had a better chance of success in life had they lived? In making his projections the adolescent uses the data presented by the authors, and then he experiments with the possibilities as he combines each possibility with the data given in an attempt to determine which one would be the most likely. That is, he can perform this intricate process. It is not to say that he does do it in the study of literature. When teachers know what he can do cognitively, they can help him develop these cognitive functions. The cognitive structures of the younger child are not adequate for this task, even with appropriate training and suitable literature.

The adolescent's ability to go beyond the here and now means he also has the potential to think logically about people and situations that are not present. He does live in the present, as does the child, but he can also project into the future, which the younger child cannot do to any appreciable degree. Not only that, but the adolescent can take a false statement and work it through to its logical end as if it were a fact. This ability is a function of the liberated capacity to deal with the possible. Elkind stresses that "the capacity to deal with the possible means that the future is now as much of a reality as the present and is a reality which can and must be dealt with.[29]

The adolescent's ability to make hypotheses is what, in part, carries him through a novel. The teacher of literature can ascertain this by exploring with students their notions of the destiny of one character at two or three intervals in the novel or drama. Those who have been encouraged to exercise this ability can change the particulars of an hypothesis as more and different data appear. The student uses a combination of factors in his analysis and can make logical deductions. This is a kind of scientific reasoning which is a manifestation that the adolescent has a very real understanding of causation. As Flavell points out, "Much more than the younger child, the adolescent moves boldly through the realm of the hypothetical. . . . To try to discover the real among the possible implies that one first entertain the possible as a set of hypotheses to be successively confirmed or infirmed.[30]

Elkind emphasizes that an individual at this developmental stage is able to "take his own thought as an object which is to say that he can now introspect and reflect upon his own mental and personality traits.[31] He need not depend entirely on concrete objects. Ability to think about thinking is a capacity he possesses. "For the first time, the adolescent can take himself as an object and evaluate himself from the perspective of other people with respect to personality, intelligence, and appearance."[32] This competency is crucial for the study of literature, for now the student can compare the thoughts, feelings, and behavior of a character with his own. It is the ability to think about thinking which makes it possible for him to identify with the thoughts of persons that are not present. As he absorbs the thoughts of the main character in Tolstoi's "How Much Land Does a Man Need" he can understand them because his own thoughts and desires about possessions are not entirely devoid of greed. As he reads Steinbeck's "Flight," he comprehends the horror because though he hasn't killed a man, he knows what it means to take flight. Identification with literary characters and situations is a necessary ingredient in the humanizing process.

The competency to introspect also permits the adolescent to see the viewpoints of other people, viewpoints that may be sharply different from his own.

The adolescent's newly developed ability to generalize and to abstract permits him to direct his thoughts and his emotions to abstract ideals. He can be concerned not only about people he knows but also about justice and integrity. But his new "naive idealism" which develops because he is now able to live in a world of the possible and hypothetical and to abstract is really a new advanced form of egocentrism. Flavell expands upon the consequences of the adolescent's new idealism. It can result in "intemperate proposals" for reform and "an immoderate belief in the efficacy" of his thought "without regard for the practical obstacles"[33] that may have to be faced. He often feels everything can be achieved by thought alone. He has not yet taken on the adult roles such as making a living and entering into the responsibilities of marriage and rearing a family. Eventually, he must consider the realities of life. Then, egocentricity is reduced as the adolescent accommodates the systems of reality. The egocentric self having been submitted to discipline makes way for the true personality with its essential ingredient of cooperation. Piaget draws intricate relationships between formal thought, adolescent affectivity, development of personality, and equilibrium. At one point he states, "Equilibrium is attained when the adolescent understands that the proper function of reflection is not to contradict but to predict and interpret experience. This formal equilibrium surpasses by far the equilibrium of concrete thought because it not only encompasses the real world but also the undefined constructions of rational deduction and inner life."[34] When he tries to test his ideas about reform, it is the contact with reality that helps him to regain equilibrium and to move into adulthood. His formal thought begins with his ability to deal with possibility and then moves toward reality.

Egocentrism appears because even while the adolescent attempts to adapt his ego to the social environment, he also tries to adjust the environment to his ego. Egocentrism appears at various stages of development when new thought structures make their debut. Structuring formal thought is one of those stages. The intensity of egocentrism disappears when, through his social contact, the adolescent discovers the fragility of his own theory of reform. It is when he discusses his ideas endlessly with friends that there is an intellectual decentering, and his thought and experience are reconciled. Inhelder and Piaget point out that "feelings about ideals are practically nonexistent in the child" because the child does not possess an available operation which would enable him to "elaborate an ideal which goes beyond the empirically given." The authors elaborate, "The notions of humanity, social justice (in contrast to interindividual justice which is deeply experienced at the concrete level), freedom of conscience, civic or intellectual courage, and so forth, like the idea of nationality, are ideals which profoundly influence the adolescent's affective life; but with the child's mentality, except for certain individual glimpses, they can neither be understood nor felt."[35]

The people in his environment constitute the child's ideals, but the adolescent's ideals are autonomous. The adolescent's personality is the consequence of submitting the ego to an ideal, adhering to a scale of values, and adopting a social role. Inhelder and Piaget expand the idea that "this scale of values is the affective organization corresponding to the cognitive organization of his work which the new member in the social body says he will undertake." Now the adolescent has a life plan which "is also an affirmation of autonomy," and he "judges himself the equal of adults." This is another "affective feature of the young personality preparing himself to plunge into life,"[36] a feature for which the younger child is not equipped.

Aesthetic Pleasure

The previous exposition seemingly to the contrary, the prime function of the study of literature is pleasure. This goal in itself poses a number of knotty questions for teachers. One set of problems is embedded in the kinds of frustrations experienced by teachers. One such teacher's outburst came in protest against the notion of greater autonomy on the part of the student in selecting a larger number of the works he reads. "But he doesn't like to read even for enjoyment!" A few of the questions aroused by such a reaction are, Whose enjoyment is at stake? What book gives pleasure to whom? What factors other than an inappropriate choice of literary work inhibit pleasure? Just what are the ingredients of that pleasure? This section deals with the last of these questions, since the others are discussed later in this book.

Several things are certain. One is the fact that helping students gain deeper insights into literature need not block the enjoyment to be derived from it. On the contrary, when properly conducted at the appropriate time, such assistance enhances enjoyment.

The student can enjoy listening to a poem for the pleasure of the sounds themselves. He gets a "feeling" from the sound of the words and the way in which the words are assembled in Browning's "My Last Duchess." When he understands the Duke's role in the fact that the former Duchess was his "last," and when he realizes the implications for the next Duchess, the listener has something at stake which increases his pleasure.

Rarely can students on any level explain what they feel when they say they enjoy a book or a poem. This is true even with those students for whom life without the literary experience is almost unthinkable. Aesthetic pleasure is a complex concept. It is different from the joy of riding a bicycle or the pleasure of passions. Students can give illustrations of literature that meant a great deal to them. One fifteen-year-old tells of copying the poem "Résumé" by Parker on a scrap of paper and keeping it hidden for days under her pillow, during a long period of despair in her young life. "But was that enjoyment?" she later asked. Was the poem of sufficiently good quality to evoke an aesthetic experience? Perhaps Dewey would argue that having come "after a phase of disruption and conflict" in her life, the experience bore within itself "the germs of a consummation akin to the esthetic."[37]

Another student described her twelfth summer which was spent almost exclusively lying in a hammock reading every issue of "True Romance" that she could borrow from the ladies at the beach. There was also Alcott's *Little Women.* "When that summer was past and school began again and there was Rawlings' *The Yearling* and Rolvaag's *Giants in the Earth* and a poem called "Loneliness" by Jenkins, that was the end of "True Romance" forever. But that summer and those stories were a landmark. . . . My mother was a smart woman; she let me do it, knowing what those stories were." There are complex ingredients here: the needs of a girl experiencing the first and startling changes into womanhood, the satisfaction of discovering safely some of the great unknowns, the opportunity to taste forbidden fruit, to fantasize, and to indulge in those fantasies. Shoemaker would probably call it "mere indulgence."[38] Aesthetically, in the long run, the important thing is that there were great contrasts in what the child was ingesting as manifested by her reading *Little Women.*

Do scholars agree about what constitutes aesthetic pleasure? To a great extent they do, but there are elements which appear to defy agreement. For example, is delight an ingredient of aesthetic pleasure? Gilbert rejects this notion; Krutch incorporates it with other factors. Gilbert maintains that "the beauty of art is to remind rather than to delight";[39] Krutch believes that "some part of the delight which we receive from all novels is the delight of widening knowledge."[40] However, both agree that there is a strong relationship between aesthetic pleasure and cognitive development. "Aesthetic savor fulfills its function when it becomes a support for contemplation,"[41] is Gilbert's stand, and Dewey concurs, "The essential thing esthetically is our own mental activity of starting, traveling, returning to a starting point, holding on to the past, carrying it along. . . ."[42] Smith makes the point that works of art may "provide a special form of knowledge" and that such knowledge can "intensify original feelings of enjoyment because analysis would reveal the object to possess more aspects than perfunctory acquaintance had disclosed."[43] This revelation can be illustrated by the following excerpts from a discussion of Hansberry's "A Raisin in the Sun" which a tenth-grade class had read. At first the discussion consisted of comments such as

Reuben: A Negro going into a neighborhood is going to change the neighborhood.

Susan: Hate prevents them from living peacefully and happily, from living where they want to live.

Later, there came other ideas:

Isabel: I think it's more about a lack of understanding between generations doing the squelching.

Joe: Walter wants to be someone, an identification of his own. He thinks he can get there only through money. It's only when he learns to accept and be proud of his heritage that he becomes a man.

Ronald: Lack of opportunity does inhibit people and makes them turn to violence and do things that cause self-destruction.

Jean: But trust in people can be a risk because you can sometimes be hurt.

Beth: We once talked about the self-image of Walter Mitty. Well, Beneatha will find her self-image through intellectual and cultural pursuits. She wasn't interested in the money, but in what a person had to offer.

Jean: Dreams can often cloud the issue, the realities.

▸─◦─◦━◦━━◦━━◦━◦━━◦━━◦━━◦━◦━◦━◦━◦━◦━━◦━━━━◦━◦━━■

Teacher: What were some of the events of the play that hit you the hardest?

Catherine: That the family remained together despite all the different characters. There *is* a development in Walter that makes him make a success of himself. He's not all a flop. This is not a story of devastating failure; he's *changed.* He develops.

Mildred: There's a change in his values. Before, it was money before anything else. But now when there's a threat to breaking up his family, he shows pride in his family.

Mary: He allows his mother to fulfill her dream, also to implement her dream. That's how he fulfills *his* dream.

Isabel: You have to help a man when he's down, help him *be* a man. That's the whole play there.

■━◦◄

Linda: The mother didn't love only those who made things simple for her.

Ruth: She has an insight into human beings. In her own uneducated way, she's very perceptive; she really is.

Madeline: Seeing the love she felt her husband had for the children and his attachment to the children, she'd come to see the lack of what she had in her family. She doesn't like what she sees. She sees what this family is missing. She misses it for this family.

Then came evidence of Smith's hypothesis: "Thus art not only gives vent to the free play of man's mind, it also augments his consciousness of the world."[44]

Steve: It's the language of the play that makes it so good. It's so warm. You can sing it, like we once did and they do on Broadway. "Mama, you don't understand." I can hear that, a song. He's objecting, but it's still warm.

Ira: And "Whatcha gonna do tonight, daddy," and "Ain't that sad, ain't that cryin' sad." I like that!

Beth: What's the matter with "Get your mind off money," and "Mama, look at me."

Gene: I don't think there's *any* play that couldn't be a musical. There's nothing in the world that some people in some place don't have in music. There's music to everything—life, death, whatever it is.

Ron: If this play ended in tragedy, you couldn't make a musical comedy. But as it is, the scenes are really funny.

Teacher: When we say "musical" and mean "comedy," aren't we limiting ourselves?

Gene: "Musical" is such a broad term. What about a Catholic high mass, where they sing the whole thing?

Madeline: With this I was thinking of "Porgy and Bess" and real soul music, because it had the drama of "Porgy and Bess," but it also had the soul of today.

Aesthetic pleasure may be more important in a chaotic world than it would be otherwise, particularly because such pleasure derives in part from a sense of order and harmony. Order and harmony are born of events that are consistent, even when those events in a work of art are violent or tragic. The artist leads us to certain emotional expectations and then satisfies the desires, the cravings, he has aroused. In daily life, things do not seem so rational; events often just happen without reason and direction. Therefore, the emotion that is called forth tends to lack unity. Both Dewey and Krutch stress the same need for order. Krutch comments that "The world of imagination is delightful because it is so much less stubborn than the world of fact."[45] Dewey illustrates the impact of order on the emotions: "The irritable person . . . sets to work tidying his room . . . putting things in order generally . . . as he puts objects in order his emotion is ordered . . . if his original emotion of impatient irritation has been ordered and tranquilized by what he has done, the orderly room reflects back to him the change that has taken place in himself. . . . His emotion as thus 'objectified' is aesthetic."[46]

A spark of this sense of order, this lessened stubbornness, and this direction can be seen in Beth's and Catherine's comments above. Beth senses that "Beneatha will find her self-image;" Hansberry systematically planned for that. Catherine knows that "there is development in Walter," a development that just might not happen in the stubborn, real world.

Furthermore, aesthetic pleasure comes in the postponement of the release of tension. An author builds up tension through the order and direction of the events he creates. When the release of tension is sudden or immediate so that an overwhelming emotion is released, the effect is not aesthetic. Dewey concludes, "When complete release is postponed and is arrived at finally through a succession of ordered periods of accumulation and conservation . . . the manifestation of emotion becomes true expression, acquiring aesthetic quality—and only then."[47]

Aesthetic pleasure is a humanizing reaction to comprehensible patterns of life, behavior, values, and beliefs. The threat of disorder in the world about us is thus vanished for the time being and passions are tempered. The sudden disruptive confusing events that come without warning, the great responsibilities individuals must bear, the staccato evocation of first this emotion and then that one at last give way. Now there is sustained and tempered emotion, consistent order of events, and a freedom from crushing responsibility. From these elements, come the delight. We can be entertained even by vicious scenes because we are not responsible for them and because we are free of them; they are not really happening. Frye, in discussing the scene from Shakespeare's *King Lear* in which Gloucester's eyes are put out, makes clear that "what the imagination suggests is horror, not the paralyzing sickening horror of a real blinding scene, but an exuberant horror, full of the energy of repudiation. This is as powerful a rendering as we can ever get of life as we don't want it."[48] Frye continues to develop his thought that these are not the things we are enjoying but rather "the exhilaration of standing apart from them and being able to see them for what they are because they aren't really happening." It is this kind of experience that gives literature its humanizing quality.

"The more exposed we are to this, the less likely we are to find an unthinking pleasure in cruel or evil things ... literature refines our sensibilities."[49]

NOTES

1. Jean Piaget, *Six Psychological Studies* (New York: Vintage Books, 1968), pp. 8–9.
2. Ibid.
3. Barry J. Wadsworth, *Piaget's Theory of Cognitive Development* (New York: David McKay Co., 1971), p. 11.
4. Russel G. Stauffer, *Directing Reading Maturity as a Cognitive Process* (New York: Harper & Row, Publishers, 1969), p. 309.
5. Hans G. Furth, *Piaget and Knowledge: Theoretical Foundations* (Englewood Cliffs, N.J.: Prentice-Hall, 1969), p. 14.
6. John H. Flavell, *The Developmental Psychology of Jean Piaget* (Princeton, N.J.: D. Van Nostrand Co., 1963), p. 51.
7. Wadsworth, p. 18.
8. Flavell, p. 65.
9. Wadsworth, p. 18.
10. Ibid., p. 17.
11. Stauffer, p. 316.
12. Furth, p. 13.
13. Out of print.
14. J. McVicker Hunt, *Intelligence and Experience* (New York: The Ronald Press, 1961), p. 259.
15. Ibid., p. 256.
16. Wadsworth, p. 30.
17. Irving Sigel, "The Piagetian System and the World of Education," in *Studies in Cognitive Development*, eds. David Elkind and John H. Flavell (New York: Oxford University Press, 1969), p. 470.
18. Herbert Ginsburg and Sylvia Opper, *Piaget's Theory of Intellectual Development: An Introduction* (Englewood Cliffs, N.J.: Prentice-Hall, 1969), pp. 227–28.
19. William R. Charlesworth, "The Role of Surprise in Cognitive Development," *Studies in Cognitive Development*, eds. David Elkind and John H. Flavell (New York: Oxford University Press, 1969), p. 264.
20. Jerome S. Bruner, *On Knowing, Essays for the Left Hand* (Cambridge, Mass.: Harvard University Press, 1966), pp. 18–19.
21. Charlesworth, p. 272.
22. D. E. Berlyne, *Conflict, Arousal, and Curiosity* (New York: McGraw-Hill Book Co., 1960), p. 248.
23. Jean Piaget, *The Origins of Intelligence in Children* (New York: W. W. Norton & Co., 1963), p. 170.
24. David Elkind, *Children and Adolescents: Interpretive Essays on Jean Piaget* (New York: Oxford University Press, 1970), p. 72.
25. Mary Ann Spencer Pulaski, *Understanding Piaget: An Introduction to Children's Cognitive Development* (New York: Harper & Row, Publishers, 1971), p. 90.
26. John Dewey, *Art as Experience* (New York: G. P. Putnam's Sons, 1958), p. 22.
27. Flavell, pp. 203–4.
28. David Elkind, "Quantitative and Qualitative Aspects of Cognitive Growth in Adolescence, in *Readings in Child Development*, eds. Irving B. Weiner and David Elkind (New York: John Wiley & Sons, 1972), p. 408.
29. Elkind, *Children and Adolescents*, p. 76.
30. Flavell, p. 205.
31. Elkind, *Children and Adolescents*, p. 76.
32. Ibid., p. 78.

33. Flavell, p. 224.
34. Jean Piaget, *Six Psychological Studies* (New York: Vintage Books, 1968), p. 64.
35. Barbel Inhelder and Jean Piaget, *The Growth of Logical Thinking from Childhood to Adolescence* (New York: Basic Books, 1958), pp. 348–49.
36. Ibid., p. 350.
37. Dewey, p. 15.
38. Francia Shoemaker, *Aesthetic Experience and the Humanities* (New York: Columbia University Press, 1943), p. 43.
39. Katherine Gilbert, *Aesthetic Studies: Architecture and Poetry* (New York: AMS Press, 1970), p. 128.
40. Joseph Wood Krutch, *Experience and Art: Some Aspects of the Esthetics of Literature* (New York: Collier Books, 1962), p. 27.
41. Gilbert, p. 128.
42. John Dewey, *Art as Experience* (New York: Minton, Balch & Co., 1934), p. 102.
43. Ralph A. Smith, "Aesthetics and Humanities Education," in *Teaching the Humanities: Selected Readings,* ed. Sheila Schwartz (New York: The Macmillan Co., 1970), p. 62.
44. Ibid., p. 59.
45. Krutch, p. 97.
46. Dewey, p. 78.
47. Ibid., p. 156.
48. Northrop Frye, *The Educated Imagination* (Bloomington, Ind.: Indiana University Press, 1964), p. 99.
49. Ibid., p. 100.

References

Alcott, Louisa M. *Little Women.* Boston: Little, Brown and Co., 1915. Also, New York: Thomas Y. Crowell Co., 1955.

Berlyne, D. E. *Conflict, Arousal, and Curiosity.* New York: McGraw-Hill Book Co., 1960.

Björnson, Björnstjerne. "The Father." In *75 Short Masterpieces,* edited by Roger B. Goodman. New York: Bantam Books, 1961.

Bruner, Jerome S. *On Knowing, Essays for the Left Hand.* Cambridge, Mass.: Harvard University Press, 1966.

Browning, Robert. "My Last Duchess." In *Tales in Verse,* edited by Lewis G. Sterner and Marcus Konick. New York: Globe Book Co., 1963.

Charlesworth, William R. "The Role of Surprise in Cognitive Development." In *Studies in Cognitive Development,* edited by David Elkind and John H. Flavell. New York: Oxford University Press, 1969.

Deasy, Mary. "The High Hill." *Harper's Magazine* 196 (February 1948):128–35.

Dewey, John. *Art as Experience,* New York: G. P. Putnam's Sons, 1958.

Elkind, David. *Children and Adolescents: Interpretive Essays on Jean Piaget.* New York: Oxford University Press, 1970.

———"Quantitative and Qualitative Aspects of Cognitive Growth in Adolescence." In *Readings in Child Development,* edited by Irving B. Weiner and David Elkind. New York: John Wiley & Sons, 1972.

Flavell, John H. *The Developmental Psychology of Jean Piaget.* Princeton, N.J.: D. Van Nostrand Co., 1963.

Frye, Northrop. *The Educated Imagination.* Bloomington, Ind.: Indiana University Press, 1964.

Furth, Hans G. *Piaget and Knowledge: Theoretical Foundations.* Englewood Cliffs, N.J.: Prentice-Hall, 1969.

Gibbs, Angelica. "The Test." In *75 Short Masterpieces,* edited by Roger B. Goodman. New York: Bantam Books, 1961.

Gilbert, Katherine. *Aesthetic Studies: Architecture and Poetry.* New York: AMS Press, 1970.

Ginsburg, Herbert, and Opper, Sylvia. *Piaget's Theory of Intellectual Development: An Introduction.* Englewood Cliffs, N.J.: Prentice-Hall, 1969.

Hansberry, Lorraine. "A Raisin in the Sun." New York: The New American Library of World Literature, 1961.

Haycox, Ernest. "A Question of Blood." In *75 Short Masterpieces,* edited by Roger B. Goodman. New York: Bantam Books, 1961.

Heyert, Murray. "The New Kid." In *Pleasure in Literature,* edited by Egbert W. Nieman and George E. Salt. New York: Harcourt Brace Jovanovich, 1949.

Hunt, J. McVicker. *Intelligence and Experience.* New York: The Ronald Press, 1961.

Inhelder, Bärbel, and Piaget, Jean. *The Growth of Logical Thinking from Childhood to Adolescence.* New York: Basic Books, 1958.

Jackson, Shirley. "The Lottery," *The Lottery.* New York: Avon Books, 1965.

Jenkins, Brooks. "Loneliness." In *Reflections on a Gift of Watermelon Pickle,* edited by Stephen Dunning, Edward Lueders, and Hugh Smith. Glenview, Ill.: Scott, Foresman and Co., 1966.

Kjelgaard, Jim. "Code of the Underworld." In *Best Short Shorts,* edited by Eric Berger. New York: Scholastic Book Services, 1967.

Knowles, John. *A Separate Peace.* New York: Dell Publishing Co., 1962.

Krutch, Joseph Wood. *Experience and Art: Some Aspects of the Esthetics of Literature.* New York: Collier Books, 1962.

Maltz, Albert. "Afternoon in the Jungle." In *Modern American Short Stories,* edited by Bennett Cerf. Cleveland: World Publishing Company, 1945.

Mansfield, Katherine. "Miss Brill." In *Great Modern Short Stories,* edited by Bennett A. Cerf. New York: Random House, 1942.

Parker, Dorothy. "Resumé." In *Reflections on a Gift of Watermelon Pickle,* edited by Stephen Dunning, Edward Lueders, and Hugh Smith. Glenview, Ill.: Scott, Foresman and Co., 1966.

Piaget, Jean. *Biology and Knowledge: An Essay on the Relations between Organic Regulations and Cognitive Processes.* Chicago: The University of Chicago Press, 1974.

———. *The Origins of Intelligence in Children.* New York: W. W. Norton & Co., 1963.

———. *Six Psychological Studies.* New York: Vintage Books, 1968.

Pulaski, Mary Ann Spencer. *Understanding Piaget: An Introduction to Children's Cognitive Development.* New York: Harper & Row, Publishers, 1971.

Rawlings, Marjorie. *The Yearling.* New York: Charles Scribner's Sons, 1938.

Raymond, Margaret T. *A Bend in the Road.* New York: Longman's, Green & Co., 1934. (Out of print.) Suggested alternative: Zindel, Paul. *My Darling, My Hamburger.* New York: Bantam Books, 1971.

Rolvaag, Ole E. *Giants in the Earth.* New York: Harper & Row, Publishers, 1929.

Shakespeare, William. *King Lear.* In *The Complete Plays and Poems of William Shakespeare,* edited by William Allan Neilson and Charles Jarvis Hill. Cambridge, Mass.: Houghton Mifflin Co., 1942.

Shoemaker, Francia. *Aesthetic Experience and the Humanities.* New York: Columbia University Press, 1943.

Sigel, Irving. "The Piagetian System and the World of Education." In *Studies in Cognitive Development,* edited by David Elkind and John H. Flavell. New York: Oxford University Press, 1969.

Smith, Ralph A. "Aesthetics and Humanities Education." In *Teaching the Humanities: Selected Readings.,* edited by Sheila Schwartz. New York: The Macmillan Co., 1970.

Stauffer, Russel G. *Directing Reading Maturity as a Cognitive Process.* New York: Harper & Row, Publishers, 1969.

Steinbeck, John. "Flight." In *Short Story Masterpieces.,* edited by Robert Penn Warren and Albert Erskine. New York: Dell Books, 1954.

Thomas, Piri. *Down These Mean Streets.* New York: Signet, 1968. Alfred A. Knopf, 1967.

Tolstoi, Leo. "Now Much Land Does a Man Need?" In *A Book of Stories,* edited by Royal A. Gettmann and Bruce Harkness. New York: Holt, Rinehart & Co., 1955.

Wadsworth, Barry J. *Piaget's Theory of Cognitive Development.* New York: David McKay Co., 1974.

Chapter Two

Curriculum Patterns

Mrs. Kine

I been absent about 26 day and I know I am going be left back the 26 day absent my mother did not know about it those day I just didn't know what I was doing.

I think the work is to hard.

I tolded Mr. Carol but just siads to try hardest but I can't I think they put me in Room 216 thats were I should be and want to be last year I didn't pass they just put me in 8th grade then were my marks 7th = L.A-55, S.S. 70-math 65-sci 65-tal. 60 - shop 75 -gym 70 - H.Ed. 75/54

I wrote to you Mrs. Kine because you understand people like me I would run away but my mother is ill. Please don't think bad about me

Roberto

P.S. at a hideout away from school

Roberto, who is in the eighth grade, delivered this note by messenger to his favorite teacher in an urban school. What are Roberto's needs? What can the school do for him? What shape shall the literature curriculum take so that literature can be a vehicle through which it is possible for him to learn? In our schools there are many Robertos whose lives have been merely brushed lightly by what the school has offered them thus far. Such students have never known the meaning of success, yet the goal of the school is to mold successful human beings. Continuous failure never breeds success. Every student has the basic need for achievement. Every student has the *right* to experience a feeling of success. But in Roberto's life that need is rarely if ever fulfilled. The miracle is that he still wants to return to school.

Schools do not have the right to determine who will be the failures and who will be the successes in life. Yet, a school has made and is continuing to make this decision about Roberto. Every student can be a winner. Our society has a crying need for winners. The school should make an effort to make every student a winner; else, it plays a devastating role in rearing increasing numbers of misfits. We have many too many misfits as it is in our mental hospitals, reform schools, and jails. This is not to intimate that the school has created the misfits. It is to say that the school has not done what it is capable of doing to alleviate the situation. Somehow, every child must learn to be a success. The school is the only institution outside the family that touches the lives of all children in one way or another. Educators must assume the responsibility for helping to rear children who can be raised aloft by success.

It matters not one whit when Roberto fails to learn that the Julius Caesar of Shakespeare and the Julius Caesar of history were related. It is a life and death matter that he learn someone, somewhere, does care about him, that he learn he has the capacity to learn, that he begin to realize he already knows much, and that he sense deeply there is a place and will be a place in this world for him. The fact that he still wants to communicate with the school is a great plus; the fact that there is a teacher in whose class he wants to be is a real bonus; the fact that he can make himself understood in writing is a third and that he cares about what his mother and his teacher think of him is a fourth. He cries for help, and he directs his cry to the only institution he still believes can help him, despite all the blows it has inflicted upon him. In a few weeks he may no longer care, and then the school will lose its chance to save a life for Roberto and for an already too crippled society.

It is not possible to hold teachers accountable for whether the students in grade nine read the same material with the same understanding at the same time. It is not possible to hold them accountable for this any more than they can be held responsible for making two novices equally fine musicians by giving them the same number of lessons using the same pieces of music; the two students will not attain equal status as musicians. The human factors are too complex. However, teachers can be held accountable for one important thing: the degree to which each one makes it possible for each student to inherit his right to achieve.

Roberto complains that the work is too hard. Translated in terms of learning theory, he is telling the school, "The material you present to me is no stimulus for learning; the cognitive schema I possess cannot assimilate that stimulus." It is the obligation of the school to make available the kind of stimuli that Roberto's cognitive structure can assimilate.

While Roberto is in his hideout, Betty who is a student in Mrs. Kine's English class is writing her diary in school.

Dear Diary:
Yesterday I got up at 7:30 and washed up and got ready for school. Left at 8:30. When I arrived me and my friends played handball and won games. Then went into school. I worked hard and then came the 2nd period and I had to *teach* for shop. Getting the kids quiet was a hard job. They talked continuently and chewed gum and would not listen. But foundly I got them quiet and we read and talked and discussed child care.

Then we changed classes and went to lunch. I had 2 ice creams 3 cakes and 2 containers of milk and a tray of 2 hero sandwiches and desert. Then the school day ended for us. Then I walked home very very fast as usual because I had to teach children on the block.

So I went in the house. My father had cooked, so I cleaned my room and left for outside. I taught 3 classes from 3:30 to approprately 5:00 o'clock, then came in the house and taught my little sisters and brothers their A,B,C. Then I went to the store and bought a soda and cake and sat down to rest. Then it was 7:30 and I made sure I had my house work done.

I ate dinner at 8:00 and then got the clothes to wear for the next school day and went to the store with my mother, and when we came back, my baby sitter lady came for me.

I baby sitted from 9:30 till 11:00 I got paid a second time $7.35¢, and put it with the money I received for teaching that was $3.00 from my mother and $5.00 from 2 neighbors. Then I went to bed after reading a story, cause I read every night, cause it's good for you.

Then I slept and was ready to get up the next day, and start it the same but better so I got dressed ate breakfast and went to school met my cousins and we played handball and ate potato chips and went in school and went to class. Then I went to shop class to teach the 8th graders, cause they have no teacher they *weren't* bad today as they was yesterday they were good but hard to get quiet. Their was a substitute man teacher watching me teach. He watch the way I ask the children to stand up and read loudly and clear, and he watch the way I wrote on the board and gave the sentences and test. The two periods were over and he took my home room class. I think he will discust the matter of my teaching with official teacher or maybe the princible.

Then I went home rushed outside. Inside, ate. Dinner and went to bed.

Betty's diary reveals much. First of all, she is comfortable with school, herself, her family, neighbors, teachers, and peers. She has goals. She knows success; she experiences a sense of achievement. By no means is her academic ability the highest in her grade, if that ability is measured by standardized tests, but for her, school life is meaningful; there are many stimuli for learning and for achieving. She knows she is regarded as an individual; and school is not too hard for her. There is little question that her cognitive development will continue and that the school has played and is playing an important positive role in her life.

Both Roberto and Betty attend an inner-city school, virtually segregated. There are both black and Caucasian teachers. The school suffers from a high turnover of faculty; many of them have had little if any previous professional training. This last fact is not well publicized; rather, it is kept as quiet as possible. Too little professional training makes doubly difficult the problem of how to plan curriculum for students like Roberto and Betty who have vast differences in background, ability, interests, and aspirations. Even with much experience, planning curriculum to meet the needs of students as individual learners is a complex task.

Students reared in middle-income homes also have a great range of aptitude and affinity for academic participation. By no means does the school serve all middle-class students equally well. However, the values of the school are middle class, a fact which makes it possible for a significantly larger proportion of middle-class children to adjust to school expectations than can ghetto children.

When ninth graders in suburbia wrote about "Things That Make Me Angry," only nine out of sixty-eight mentioned school. Most students were concerned about parental, sibling, and peer relationships. Their tales were of parents who blamed them for something they didn't do, made them look after their little sister, or failed to respect their rights to ownership. A typical gripe against the school when students did mention it was written by a ninth-grade boy.

One thing that make me angry is English. Because we have to read book that I don't like. And some of the book we read are boring. And then there is Spelling. Sometime we don't have to spell those words in our life time. And now there is vocabulary some teacher would expect you to know all the definitions for that word when I look up. The definition in the dictionary the teacher still is not satisfied. When we are told to write these words in a sentence using them as adjective or verbs etc. it is hard as we never heard of the words. I have never heard our teachers using these words when they speak to one another. Why must we have to write compositions with a given number of words in it. After reading a book most times it can be sumed up in a few sentence. Why should we get a low mark if the teacher dosen't like our thought or what we think the book about.

When ghetto students wrote on the topic "The Thing That Makes Me Maddest," they revealed disappointments everywhere—at home, in school, and on the street. Parents often were a source of disappointment, largely because they did not know how to communicate their own inadequacies and problems to their children.

It was on a Friday morning my [mother] was cleaning up she said hey Sam let's take out today. . . . So he OK. Then my mother came in the kitchen hurry up and finish your work because we going other Aunt Mamie house. So when we finished we got dress. We got upstairs and outside. My [father] said wait right here I'll be right back because I'm going to the gas station. We waited for half hour. . . . So my [mother] told me to tell my brother's to unddress. And they could go out and play. Soon as everyone is unddress and comfortable my father comes walking in. So he [says] why aren't you dress. . . . Thats what makes me my father always says he coming right back and never does.

Also apparent in middle-income schools were students on the other end of the spectrum, for whom school meant the joy of intellectual challenge. Verbalizing was easy for them; they read and wrote voluminously. They were secure in the knowledge that teachers liked and appreciated them. It was often these same students who were involved in a number of school-related activities—the music club, drama club, and student government. Their parents lent encouragement to their activities and offered them large amounts of freedom. Not at all surprisingly, often these students were liked by peers and were considered outgoing. Further, they managed to find the time to be *nice* to others. In short, they contributed to the community image and status of the school, and the school offered its rewards to them. They were the ones who enhanced the self-esteem of teachers and of whom teachers were prone to remark, "He makes teaching worthwhile."

Most of the examples and procedures described in this book are from schools serving chiefly middle-income students. Within recent years, a vast number of publications[1] have been geared to teaching the underprivileged child; relatively few have given attention to the aspirations and needs of the middle-income student.

Learning about Students

In the past few years, more thought has been devoted to curriculum theory than ever before. Without theoretical design, the everyday problems of teaching, and particularly of teaching literature, are haphazardly solved. Yet, curriculum theory as it is related to the field of literature is still in its infancy. It is imperative that teachers, with a good background in literature and a thorough knowledge of human development including learning theory, be encouraged to develop curriculum, for curriculum is essentially a plan to aid learning.

Curriculum design includes detailed unit planning, not merely a bare content and activity outline. Curriculum design includes not only theory but also practical suggestions and models for putting theory into practice. It is the teacher who needs experience creating models for plans of teaching and learning. It is through this complex route of developing models that teachers learn how to state objectives so that these objectives give real direction to the learning activities that must be created. It is through the creation of learning sequences that teachers discover what it takes to provide for individual differences and what it means to plan experiences which build upon previous ones.

HETEROGENEITY OF SCHOOL POPULATION

If the school is serious about making it possible for every student to learn, then teachers systematically use diagnostic techniques that reveal those aspects of a student's makeup which bear upon his motivation and capacity to learn. Diagnosis is especially necessary today when almost 100 percent of America's children are in school. Interestingly enough, many of the school's problems are directly related to this achievement in a democracy: the attainment of educational opportunity for all its children. Since the educational system in America no longer caters solely to the elite 30 percent and since greater numbers of the remaining 70 percent now stay in school for longer periods of time, the secondary school draws from a population previously unfamiliar to that institution. At one time, the secondary school taught only the academic upper-third of the population, those highest in ability and in motivation to learn what the school determined they would learn. Now, the school population includes those who are not so well motivated, so capable, so well adjusted. Thus, the once relatively homogeneous school population has become one characterized by extreme heterogeneity.

This heterogeneity in urban cultures has been accentuated by special problems of children uprooted overnight in great waves of migration from the rural South and Puerto Rico to the cities of the North and Southwest. The bewilderment of children who are forced to make an adjustment in a cultural milieu which is at least 100 years more complex than the previous simpler one is a fact of their lives which schools must consider as they plan curriculum. While they are learning to survive in a new society with all the stresses and strains of the acculturation process, they are asked to learn the difficult tasks of speaking a new language or abandoning their regional dialects. Simultaneously, they are asked to learn to read and write and to acquire an endless list of new modes of behavior. When we add to all of these burdens the impoverished condition of most of the migrating families, with the uncertainty of employment and the consequent threat to a family's very existence, we can gain a sense of some of the pressures and frustrations that lay waste a student's energy to learn. Also, consider the impersonal urban existence which breeds anonymity and alienation as contrasted with the warm face-to-face contacts of people in a community of a simpler culture, people who are supportive of values being learned and who reinforce them in many aspects of personal life.

With such a background of conditions in the lives of many students, equal opportunity cannot mean the same curriculum for every child, the same mode of instruction, the same content, or the same objectives. Sameness makes for unequal opportunity when the needs and backgrounds are so totally different from middle-class students whose families have been able to offer what inner-city children have not yet known.

Poverty stricken children lack a background of variety of concrete objects in the home. Such physical deprivation is cause enough for deficiency in cognitive development; but if one adds to that the often poor diet, the lack of educational models which cripples early motivation that is so dependent on identification with models, and the lack of adult mediators, then the burden of deprivation becomes clearer. Cognitive development is dependent upon environmental conditions. With the meager conditions of ghetto life, children cannot develop the early perception of relationships that middle-class children do.

This is not to say that middle-income students are free from the effects of being uprooted. In general, the families of students discussed in this book moved from crowded urban areas into less crowded ones, and still later, into suburbia as the family fortunes became greater. Students' feelings about being uprooted were mixed; their problems, diverse. Often they found moving to be a frustrating experience. Their responses stressed anxiety about a new school, loss of old friends, difficulties making new friends, nostalgia for familiar surroundings. Others students found satisfaction in finally possessing a room of their own, enjoyed the excitement of the move, expressed happiness at leaving a dirty crowded urban neighborhood, and basked in the status of owning a private swimming pool. The range of reactions is evident from the following written responses.

> Moving into this new home gave my family many pleasures. First of all the house is brand new and has never been lived in before. It was also bigger in size and much roomier. So in the long run buying this house payed off. There were no more overly crowded neighborhoods. There were no more dirty streets, and houses. Also the people my family met were much more friendlier and nicer than the people they had known. (Boy, grade 9)

> Saying good-bye to our friends was one of the biggest problems of the whole affair. My cousin and myself would not leave each other and my sister sat in a circle holding hands with her friends. It took my father twenty minutes to separate us. After being in the new house for about three days, my sister and I started our first day in school. I was afraid of that day because I was worried that I would not meet up to the level of the others. But to my surprise I did meet up to the level of the others and was accepted by everyone. (Girl, grade 9)

A number of students missed the teeming streets, were shocked by the barrenness of the suburbs, found the people quite as empty as the streets, and felt cooped up with no place to go to escape family tensions. A simple thing like securing a candy bar meant a three-mile walk, and there were no easily accessible teenage hangouts. They would readily exchange their great green lawn for the dirty sidewalks of the city and the availability of people.

> The first problem I met up with is that I had to eat by myself during lunch which embarassed me. I also had nobody to hang around with after lunch. It was not a very good start. . . . (Boy, grade 9)

When we found our house it looked so big. It had four bedrooms, three bathrooms, a giant kitchen, livingroom den and basement. It wasn't in good condition but my father said we could fix it up. We had no livingroom furniture so the house looked really empty. We had lots of problems with the house. We didn't have any heat in my bedroom. The kitchen cabinets were falling apart and the shingles on the house were falling off. About three days after we moved in my father had to go into the hospital for an operation. When he got out he was putting in a boiler in our basement and he cut his hand. He had to go back to the hospital for thirty stitches. . . .

We didn't go out because even though we made friends they weren't allowed to stay with us because their mother felt that if we came from the city we had to be bad. . . . I liked living (in the city) because I had so many friend, and I could walk to any place I want or take the bus or train. I would still like to live there. . . . Here it is boring. (Girl, grade 9)

A substantial number of middle-income students experienced uprootedness more than once in their lives. They did not take lightly the frustrations implicit in the changes.

In October of last year, 100 Great Aircraft employees were scheduled to go to Southern California for a contract which was to last from four to six months. Our family was one of the 100. We were given two weeks to move out, and that meant pulling four kids out of school. I hated the idea and so did my older brother. We both had our roots in Friendship Village; *friends,* activities, goals and jobs.

When we first arrived in California the smog gave us eye problem for 3 days. I hated it. My school was in "free-school" style, which I wasn't accustomed to, which made adjusting very hard. In about three weeks I started getting involved in school, and the kids were really great. I had friends like I never had before.

About six months later, I realized that I didn't want to go back to New York. Then in our twelfth month there we had to leave. Again I was crushed. I was leaving my friends all over again. When I was back in New York in October of this year I really hated the place I used to love. The people, the places, the weather and everything really bugged me. (Girl, grade 9)

A substantial number of middle-income students who reported initial negative feelings about the family move ultimately were able to make a positive emotional adjustment to the new environment.

We lived in Brooklyn in the aerea of 18th Street. It was a quiet neighborhood there were no holdups or shootings or anything like it is now. We lived in a house, that was surrounded by stores and shops. The streets were always crowded with people and car's, all you herd was the honking of horns and the laughter and talking of people.

I felt really bad about leaving, because I loved my house, and had many friends. I also missed Saterday nights' at the candy store, this man Frank owned this candy store, he had so many selections of soda, and candy you would not believe. I also felt bad about leaving, because I always went to the movies every Saterday afternoon's. . . .

I felt strange living in a new house in an urban [sic] aerea without honking of horns and people shouting and talking. I met new friends, went to school and after a while I got used to it and I felt glad that we moved. The one thing that bothered me was the singing of the birds, and the noise of crickets, because I was not used to the sounds, and now I have a beotiful house, with a built in swimming pool, and a big room that I share with my brother. . . . (Boy, grade 9)

The students' feelings of hope and despair are reflected in their academic performance as well as their social and emotional development. The school must be concerned about what is happening to students because their experiences provide tremendous motivational power and meaningful focus for learning. Students' experiences serve as rich resources to aid the school in achieving its goal of providing universal education.

STUDENT RESPONSES TO OPEN-ENDED QUESTIONS

From students' responses teachers can gather a number of important pieces of information: the level of the students' concept development, the feelings which dominate their experiences, the insights they already have acquired, and the range of experiences which affect their learning. Open-ended questions furnish much fruitful information when a good relationship has been established between the students and the teacher, and when students feel comfortable in the classroom. Responses may be written; if so, the writing should be done in class, not for homework. In some instances, students may converse with the teacher or use a tape recorder.

Some initial topics which teachers found fruitful were "The Time I Moved," "My Worries," "My Wishes," "Things That Make Me Afraid," "My Neighborhood," "The People I Live With," "The Thing That Makes Me Maddest," and "The Person I Love Most." All of these topics brought such revealing responses that teachers were able to analyze them and use them for ideas in curriculum building. Meantime, students were engaging in the act of writing or talking about events of importance to them; the school was already playing a role in reassuring students that school was not separate from life outside of it. These papers were not corrected for syntax, spelling, or punctuation. Students were invited to mark their papers "private" if they did not want anyone except the teacher to see them. They were invited to ask for any help they needed as they wrote —how to spell a word, where to put a period, when to capitalize. This invitation in itself was very reassuring. Students were not forced to worry about mistakes. At first some teachers extended another invitation: the privilege of anonymity. In actual practice, more than half the students did sign their names; they wanted to be identified. Teachers offered those who had signed their names an opportunity to talk about their papers if they cared to do so; most did!

The responses to a series of open-ended questions were not written or discussed in one week. They were presented over a relatively long period of time. All papers were saved in students' folders held by the teacher but open to students' perusal if they felt the need. Most did not.

Teachers who received the greatest response were those who were "open" with students. These teachers revealed something of their own wishes or worries; They told in detail some joys and frustrations of family living.

In one class the students wrote responses about emotional words: "Happiness is_____," "Jealousy is_____," "Anger is_____," etc. The overwhelming number of inner-city students who mentioned that "Happiness is passing to the next grade" gave teachers food for thought. It is one thing for teachers to be told that students fear failure; it is another to read it in students' language as it appeared over and over again. It was especially poignant in light of the fact that the question was open ended and happiness could have meant a hundred different things. Several students who did not mention this factor under happiness did highlight its opposite under causes of sadness. Physical hurts were the second most important grounds for sadness while boy-girl relationships were almost unanimously the cause of jealousy.

When students wrote about fears, they had little difficulty finding words, but the initial discussion in one school fell flat. Some students whispered to the teacher that they'd prefer to write anonymously. They wrote, and the teacher saw the crux of the problem. Patrol guards, students selected by the administration to patrol corridors, stairwells, and the school yard intimidated others who did not dare to mention this fact aloud. The guards were feared because not only did they threaten and carry out threats of extortion but they involved themselves physically in violent fights between two students and they were known to have instigated the violence. They cued in their friends to annoy certain students, molested some students on the way home, and in general terrorized the student body. Fear of fighting and violence was on almost every page— fighting in the cafeteria, the corridors, the back of the room when the teacher wasn't looking. A feeling of helplessness and lack of protection was a recurrent theme. Several mentioned this as a reason for their absences. If they stayed in the house they felt safer, but the locks on the door weren't very secure, on second thought. A second fear was of fire. The fears of ghetto students were all too real. "Things That Scare Me" was a topic that did not end with one discussion or one writing session. When the teachers succeeded in setting a comfortable tone about revealing one's fears and when students lost their fear of revealing inner weaknesses, there came responses such as the following:

When I went South last week when my grandmother died I was scared because down there they bring the body to the house in the afternoon and they stay until the next morning. I remember when my mother was in an accident and the ladies on her job called the house and told me what had happened and told me to call my father on his job, I was so scared that I couldn't dial his number. (Girl)

The thing I'm telling you about is rats. When I see a rat I get scared because I think that might bite me. If I get bit I can die and I think if I meet a rat I will faint.

Another thing that scares me is drunk people. When they say something to me I feel like I'm going to jump out of my skin. If they touch me my skin crawls. (Girl)

What really scares me is when I can't sleep. I lie awake think what it's like to be dead because when you're alive and you look at a casket it looks kind of small but when you're dead I guess it makes no difference. (Boy)[2]

When teachers recognize the fear-ridden existence of the ghetto student, they can begin to comprehend many things: the violence and rough fighting that takes place in the ghetto and the nervous reactions of so many students who want to obey and sit down but who can't. One student said, "It's better to stand up; if you sit down, someone can come along and hit you on the head."

In middle-income schools, the incidence of fear of failure was minimal when compared with students in ghetto schools. The fears most frequently reported by students in suburbia related to family health and economic status.

Students need to understand that fears are universal. Many had no concept that adults have fears, that people fear many of the same things, that many fears vanish as time passes, that some fears are an advantage in that they cause people to protect themselves, and that fears manifest themselves in overt behavior. Students had never noticed that people in books had fears too, and certainly some had no idea that it was possible to cope with fears. Teachers who decided to work out a sequence on fears, used a format similar to the one on Elkins' "Man on the Move " (see pp. 39–41).

Students also needed to understand why they felt so mad or why other people disappointed them. They looked at the disappointments of other people in their class, in books, and in the lives of adults around them. They saw how others reacted to anger, and they viewed a continuum of reactions to disappointments. It was a giant step forward when students saw the relationship between the frustrations of people in their own lives and the way in which people beyond their horizon, for example, labor unions, grouped themselves to deal with those frustrations.

The responses to open-ended questions gave teachers new leads to content of curriculum. There were topics such as "Boy-Girl Relationships," "Human Emotions," "Things People Want," "Things People Worry About," "How Problems Get Solved," and "When People Move." Around these topics content and learning activities could be developed that were appropriate for the class at large and for individual students.

Curriculum Sequences

Concepts, content, and activities are elements basic to curriculum design, and units of work are an integral part of the design. When teachers plan a unit, they engage in all the processes necessary for curriculum design except for the broader pattern involved in a full year of work or in the full six-year secondary sequence. When teachers have had three or four experiences with unit building, they are usually ready for the task of working with others to create the larger design. Taba asserts that "curriculum development should be an inductive process, beginning at the grass roots and with natural small units and proceeding into the more general problems of overall organization."[3] There are many kinds of units, but they have in common a statement of objectives, content, and learning experiences. "Because planning such units brings into play all considerations and principles important in curriculum development, the decisions made in planning pilot units and the ways of making them should provide important insights into curriculum development in general."[4]

The planning of units by several teachers working as a team proved effective. The team planning of units proved to be a good laboratory for building larger curriculum design. Teachers had taken the first step in curriculum planning; they had learned something about the background, needs, capacities, interests, skills, and attitudes of the student. Although there were ready-made units of work already available, they seemed to have little bearing on what teachers had discovered about students; even the objectives of the ready-made units seemed far fetched. The teachers formulated objectives based on their findings resulting from the diagnostic devices they used. Now the problem became how to create a curriculum that was student centered and yet had structure. Daigon raised the question, "Where do we find an English that is committed to important ideas yet is not narrowly 'relevant,' that is student centered without giving up the special qualities of our subject, that reconciles openness with structure, affect with discernible outcomes, and creativity with the basic skills?"[5] Teachers tried to deal with the issues implicit in Daigon's question. They succeeded in varying degrees.

The problem in curriculum building is how to plan ahead of time to insure that objectives are clear, important, and possible to achieve. Teachers need a feeling of security; planning ahead is an essential way to implant this feeling. Furthermore, students also need a feeling of security. This is transmitted when they gain a sense that the teacher knows what he is doing. Part of the teacher's knowing is the ability to use students' ideas.

It was comforting to most teachers to realize that an open curriculum does not necessarily mean every student does what he wants to do at any given moment. An open curriculum is one that is open to the students' ideas, the students' responses, and their needs and interests.

It is difficult to create a completed unit in advance and still maintain openness and student centeredness. A preconceived unit tends to be rigid. A unit should be a flexible thing; it should grow and be modified with each use, as it responds to the particular students and teachers who are working with it. Curriculum sequences were built for flexibility. Sequences are designs for constructing units; they are models for organizing procedures, materials, and content. Those models must be characterized by continuity of student experience. Each new experience is dependent upon the previous one and grows naturally out of it. Each sequence varies in accordance with the learning objective. When students experience a sequence, they have a feeling of completeness. Sequences are relatively short when compared with a full unit, but when several sequences are related, they can cumulatively have the same sustained effect as a unit. For students with a short interest span, short sequences seem to be in harmony with their developmental level. After teachers had the experience of creating several models, they were able to make the changes necessary to meet the needs of individuals or groups. The models encourage activities which serve both as learning experiences and diagnostic procedures. This dual role in turn encourages flexibility.

For example, teachers who worked on the sequences developed for "People on the Move" used students' ideas which were brought forth during the diagnostic procedures described above. They sensed that their students needed a chance to talk in a safe and protected environment. The school could give them this through the literature class. They had much to talk about, and the teachers had much to learn. They discussed questions such as, how did their families decide to move? Why? How did they feel about leaving the old place? How did the new place "hit" them?

The population of middle-income schools in New York and surrounding communities frequently consisted of students from Japan, Korea, Turkey, and India as well as upward mobile students from the outskirts of the inner city. These discussions permitted all students to share experiences; thus it was from the information offered by students and gleaned from observations of students that teachers formulated objectives, concepts, content, and learning experiences. Their observations were reinforced by their study of the sociological and psychological scene.

Discussions around questions such as those described not only were diagnostic but also were geared toward achieving other objectives. Curriculum planning involves learning for multiple objectives: thinking, knowledge, skills, attitudes, and values. Students need appropriate experiences in all areas in order to formulate generalizations, acquire new attitudes toward themselves and others, and learn values and skills, both social and academic. Content is related to learning information. Content alone does not develop thinking, skills, or attitudes. It is experience which does these things. Because schools are concerned with the multiple objectives, curriculum includes both content and experiences. Thinking, an active process, develops with active experiences. Learning new attitudes also requires emotional experience and materials such as the literary world has to offer. To acquire skills one must repeatedly practice in different contexts; however repetitious, monotonous drill is counterproductive. A sharing session such as the one described above can be an experience in which a number of these objectives begin to be achieved.

Teachers who planned and carried through a sequence found that limiting coverage of content the most difficult task. The school day is limited. Coverage of content must be weighed against the necessary depth study, which is important for all students but especially for those whose reading and language skills as well as concept formation show a deficit. Therefore, a curriculum should emphasize important, significant, and enduring concepts, relate the specific details to be learned to those important concepts, but also limit those details. Students can learn more from procedures which permit them to study a few instances of an idea in depth than they can by lightly covering many instances.

Depth study is a crucial factor in the learning of middle-income as well as deprived students. Often middle-income students have already had a variety of experiences in depth study as a result of their home environment. Bronfenbrenner points out that in a study completed by Coleman it was found that

> home background was the most important element in determining how well the child did at school, more important than any of all aspects of the school which the child attended. This generalization, while especially true for Northern whites, applies to a lesser degree to Southern whites and Northern Negroes, and was actually reversed for Southern Negroes, for whom the characteristics of the school were more important than those of the home. The child apparently drew sustenance from wherever sustenance was most available. Where the home had most to offer, the home was the most determining; but where the school could provide more stimulation than the home, the school was the more influential factor.[6]

Perhaps the opportunity for depth study was a factor in the positive environment of middle-income children. For example, many of them had studied road maps on trips, learned the relationship between a map and the geographic terrain, perceived how ratio and proportion worked in the real life of travel, and gained a sense of the relationship between time and space. Their hobbies were the focus of real in-depth study; it was not unusual for them to possess a chemistry set. Further, their reading habits often followed in-depth patterns when they found an author they liked and read his books, one by one. Experiences such as these made it possible for them to encompass the various dimensions of a particular situation and to enrich and extend their perception of an instance or event. They were able to enfold many ramifications far beyond the immediate. Unless the curriculum emphasized depth study, they would be deprived of the opportunity to engage in the divergent level of thinking they were able to attain.

Depth study which is centered around concept development has other advantages. It permits individualization of instruction through small-group activity and self-selected activity, while retaining the advantages of full-class membership. For example, if students are examining the concept, "There are many different ways in which fears manifest themselves in human behavior," and each student is reading a different book, they can use the instances in their books to help contribute to the large group understanding of the concept. Such a procedure uses the special knowledge of each student. Possessing special knowledge is a decided advantage not only for the ego development of each student but also for his social as well as his intellectual development. He does not need to display hostility to receive attention from his peers or from the teacher; he learns to gain it in a positive context. Further, the procedure provides experience in another aspect of social development: The student is helping others learn; he is communicating knowledge only he or a small group possesses. Thus, he is a contributing member of a group. Individualization does not mean isolation. It means learning what each student is ready to learn and needs to learn, even while he uses his new knowledge for the benefit of the group. In turn, he can use the group's new knowledge because his own experience with his self-selected book, film, or recording which is appropriate for him has so altered his cognitive schema as to prepare him to assimilate the new knowledge peers have to offer. The interaction is a critical aspect of the socialization process; human beings cannot be socialized without a group. Further, individualization for depth study takes from the teacher the frustrating burden of trying to hold the attention of thirty-two or thirty-five adolescents.

A change in the traditional role of the teacher was essential. That was no small feat, nor was it accomplished overnight. Teachers could no longer be information givers. They were organizers, mediators or interpreters, motivators, suggestors of books and materials, providers of materials, encouragers, ego builders, arbiters where necessary —in essence, mature human beings who could provide a rich environment in which students could learn. The many roles teachers had to play demanded flexibility as a key to behavior. Hamachek emphasizes this characteristic:

> The good teacher is flexible. By far the single most repeated adjective used to describe good teachers is "flexibility" [sic]. Either implicitly or explicitly (most often the latter), this characteristic emerges time and again over all others when good teaching is discussed in the research. In other words, the good teacher does not seem to be overwhelmed by a single point of view or approach to the point of intellectual myopia. A good teacher knows that he cannot be just one sort of person and use just one kind of approach if he intends to meet the multiple needs of his students. Good teachers are, in a sense, 'total' teachers. That is, they seem able to be what they have to be to meet the demands of the moment.[7]

The teachers had to become familiar not only with students' needs but also with a wealth of materials. For this purpose, teachers banded together to create curriculum sequences and became acquainted with appropriate materials on a wide range to suit the needs of those adolescents who read at third-grade level as well as of others who could handle adult books. For example, the teachers who plotted curriculum on the topic "Fears" each read three books and shared them: for example, *His Own Where* by Jordan for students reading at a fourth-grade or fifth-grade level and who needed a "love story" while considering the topic of fears, *Bless the Beasts and the Children* by Swarthout for those who were on an eighth-grade level and were able to handle a short psychological novel, *J.T.* by Wagner and Parks for students who needed photos and few words with which to contend, almost any one of the sports books by Tunis for sports fans with an ability to handle sixth-grade material; *The Stepford Wives* by Levin with its deceptively simple language and subtle concepts rolled up in a "skinny book;" *A Choice of Weapons* by Parks for students reading at eighth-grade level. The list is endless. Universal concepts such as those intrinsic in a universal topic like fear attract to themselves dozens of books suitable for reaching students who read on any level of interest and ability. Also, the greater the number of appropriate books teachers know, the better they are able to use the contents for purposes of comparison.

Concentration on durable concepts with greatly reduced coverage permits time for contrasting examples of the concept which can be studied in depth so that ideas and understandings are sharpened and cognitive development advanced. Such depth study gives time for connecting concrete illustrations from literature and life to the generalization under consideration and encourages hypothesis making and prediction.

Thus, the central concept selected must be one that is durable and significant, universal enough to have appealed to many literary men, and so close to students that it is capable of involving any student regardless of his ability. There are aspects of life that do have such universality and still possess diverse elements in which each student can find his niche. The learning sequence or group of learning experiences which are organized in such a way that each step provides the foundation for the next one furnishes the means for finding that niche. The learnings may be complex and take a long period of time to acquire as, for example, attitudes which cannot be communicated in one lesson or even in one whole sequence.

In all sequences, the learning experiences begin with the ones that are the most concrete and the most familiar to students. Thus, in considering "Man on the Move," the students discuss and pool their own experiences about moving. Then they move on to new experiences: They listen to an excerpt from Courtright's "Yours Lovingly" to compare the experiences with those they know or with Dwyer's "The Citizen" or Estes' *The Hundred Dresses.* They read to find out for themselves how people in other places are affected by the problem of moving; they interview someone who has moved a whole generation ago; they listen to people who are considering moving; they watch a film; and they make up skits and poems. They are examining the focusing idea from several points of view and expanding it so that insights into it are enriched.

In most sequences there is ample provision for student discussion. Real conversation is the aim, but this takes time to achieve, especially with students who find it difficult to await their turn. Brief discussions are held around things they read and write. When students view films, dramatize, engage in related art media, hold interviews, and make observations, these activities become the focus of other brief conversations. They learn the skills they need to master; they learn to work together instead of in conflict with each other. They work at multiple objectives. Understanding the reason for what they are learning is crucial; it must make sense to them in order to nourish a self-concept.

Hope tends to be a very scarce commodity among children in the ghetto. They desperately want people not to forget them. Therefore, creating a class book to contribute in perpetuity to the school library is a reminder to others that they once learned here, and it is the kind of task that sustains effort. Writing brief book reviews to be filed in the class library for use by other students is a second such remembrance. This type of activity also contributes something to society and helps students acquire a feeling of belonging. Similar activities are appropriate for the middle-income student, though the materials used may be totally different and the discussions and conversations may be more sustained.

The chief differences between activities for the academically able and disabled is not in structure but in function. For example, the educationally disadvantaged student may need many more introductory and concrete experiences than his able counterpart. A role-playing session is concrete in a sense; a film can provide a concrete experience. Other concrete activities may be collecting projective pictures and responding to them in writing; matching descriptions of events to photos; making a cartoon from a story students have read; sharing, pooling, and thus bringing to the fore experiences students have had. The act of telling the events of a story in sequence is concrete and should precede attempts at comparison, prediction, or generalization. Academically able students may need only a sampling of such activities; the disabled need a substantial amount. For the able, these activities are necessary catalysts; for the disabled, they may make the difference between enhancement of ability to learn and intellectual stagnation.

An example of a sequence for the study of "Man on the Move" illustrates some of the principles for curriculum building.

Man on the Move

Concepts:

> People everywhere are on the move, all over the world. People move for a great number of reasons. The experience of moving may affect people positively or negatively, or both.

Content:

> This consists of specific instances from stories the teacher reads to students, books students are reading, and experiences in their lives.

Learning Activities:

> (The verb in each case describes what the *students* are doing.)

1. *Discuss* a time you moved. How old were you? With whom did you go? What happened before you left? on the way? when you arrived in your new place? Why did the family make that move? Do you think they'd do it again if they had a choice? How did you feel upon leaving the old place? upon arriving in the new one?

2. *Write* about "A Time I Moved." It can be in the form of a poem, story, or skit. Try to remember to tell about the things we talked about (see questions above). A list is on the board to help you remember.

3. *Categorize* and *tally* experiences (e.g., pleasant and unpleasant) or reasons for moving or incidents that happened.

4. *Listen* to the teacher read parts of "The New Kid" by Heyert.

5. *Read* the rest of the story. Use of the tape recorder is acceptable.

6. *Discuss* what happened, why Marty tortured the new kid, how things might possibly turn out for the new kid in the near future, how the new kid felt, what *you* would do if you were the new kid or Marty.

7. *Make* a chart of all the things that Marty did and all the things that the new kid did.

8. In small groups, use your chart to help you compare Marty and the new kid so that you can *write* a skit about them. (Note to teacher: The class may be divided so that some groups create a skit with Marty as the center of attention while the second half does the same for the new kid. In such case, comparisons between characters should be made after the skits have been performed.)

9. *Examine* carefully the rexographed sheet summarizing the tallies of our own accounts of the time we moved (see activity 2). Were any experiences universal? Did the pleasant ones outweigh the unpleasant ones?

10. *Add* to the tally these experiences of the new kid that have not been included in our list.

11. *Select* a book *to read* from the bibliography or one of your own choosing that tells the story of a character who moved from one place to another.

Arnothy, Christine. *I'm Fifteen and I Don't Want to Die.* New York: E. P. Dutton & Co., 1956.
Bonham, Frank. *Durango Street.* New York: Dell Publishing Co., 1972.
Buck, Pearl. *The Big Wave.* New York: The John Day Co., 1952.
_____. *The Good Earth.* New York: Pocket Books, 1949.
Cather, Willa. *My Antonia.* Boston: Houghton Mifflin Co., 1954.
Jordan, June. *His Own Where.* New York: Thomas Y. Crowell Co., 1971.
Lane, Rose Wilder. *Let the Hurricane Roar.* New York: Longmans, Green and Co., 1933.
Levin, Ira. *The Stepford Wives.* Boston: G. K. Hall & Co., 1973.
Parks, Gordon. *A Choice of Weapons.* New York: Harper & Row, Publishers, 1965.
Platt, Kin. *The Boy Who Could Make Himself Disappear.* New York: Dell Publishing Co., 1972.
Richter, Conrad. *The Light in the Forest.* New York: Alfred A. Knopf, 1953.
Rölvaag, Ole. *Giants in the Earth.* New York: Harper & Row, Publishers, 1929.
Sommerfelt, Aimée. *The Road to Agra.* New York: Abelard-Schuman, 1961.
Steinbeck, John. *The Grapes of Wrath.* New York: The Viking Press, 1939.
Yates, Elizabeth. *Amos Fortune, Free Man.* New York: Dell Publishing Co., 1971.

(Note to teacher: A list of thirty annotated books can be gathered by ten teachers within a short time. If students engage in the search, it takes a much shorter time. The ability and interest range of the selections should be wide.)

12. *Write* an hypothesis after you read the first chapter of your book. Do you think the main character's experiences will be harder or easier than yours? than the new kid's?

13. *Read* an exciting part of your book to the students in your group. Which book seems to be the most interesting so far?

14. When you finish, please *rewrite* the annotation to be rexographed for next year's class, making it as attention catching as you can. Please sign your name to your annotation.

15. *Present* in a panel the findings about the effects of moving upon the characters involved in your book. Audience responds with their findings.

(Note to teacher: If students need more experience and can stay with the same topic, the following activities are suggested.)

16. *Prepare* to interview an adult you know who will tell you about his experiences with moving. Examine the questions we used in Activity #1 and decide if the character in your book would be able to answer them.

17. Keeping the same questions in mind, *role play* an interview such as you will have with the person you plan to interview. Discuss.

18. *Hold* interviews with the adult. Take notes.

19. Class *discusses* the interviews. What did you discover? Did the interviewer seem comfortable? What did you do to achieve this? etc. (Note to the teacher: Conduct additional practice in role-play sessions as needed).

20. *Rewrite* your original account (see Activity #2), or write a book review, an account of your interview, a poem, or a play to enter into the class book on "Man on the Move." You may use enlarged photos entitled *Man on the Move* by Elkins. Collect your own portfolio of photos and tell their story. (This may require several students working together.)

21. *Read* the play *Thunder on Sycamore Street* by Rose and *dramatize* the scene that shows best how the people in the community affected the lives of the newcomers.

22. After the dramatization, *compare* the behavior of the adults in *Thunder on Sycamore Street* with the behavior of the boys in "The New Kid."

23. *Make up* a short play based on an experience of one of the people we interviewed.

Thus, the sequence is a way of plotting concepts, content, and learning experiences to carry out the promise inherent in the multiple objectives the schools hold. It is no rigid formulation; it can be remolded daily to the needs of students. Yet, it offers a guide with which teachers can prepare to meet the needs of individual students. The activities are diverse; not all students engage in every one; students themselves suggest others. The key is flexibility.

Learning More about Students: Diaries and Sociometric Interviews

While students engaged in learning experiences which resulted from the first set of diagnostic procedures, the teachers planned new devices which would furnish leads to the next areas of study. As indicated earlier in this chapter, students' diaries can give clues to the content of peer relationships, relationships with adults, and communication on the neighborhood scene. They can indicate which students have other human beings with whom they can communicate and which ones seem relatively isolated. Sociometric tests help to complete the picture.

Maria, age fourteen and one-half, Caucasian, living in a factory neighborhood of a large city in the northeastern section of the country regarded the diary as an opportunity to unburden herself. She was living temporarily at the detention home run by the juvenile court.

Dear Diary,
   I got up today at 6:30 then I woke Millie [roommate] up. She was mad but not too mad to laugh it off. I got dressed brushed my teeth comb my hair, and made my bed. Then it was time for me to go down stairs and eat my breakfast. I set the table and ate. Then I left for school. I got on the bus at 8:15 and I went home had a cigarette and went to school. Went through the same rueteen. Ate at the drugstore went home to see my father. Left for school later went back to the detension. Ate supper washed dishes and went to played outside then went up stairs did my homework and then to bed.

Saturday

Today I got up early again because it was another day at home. I was home by 8:00 today. Millie [roommate] was kind of hurt because I went home so much so I called her mother and told her to go down to see her. When I got home I washed the kitchen floor then I went upstairs to look at my room because my father just finished fixing it over. I was very pleased the way he and my mother fixed it up. I didn't think they could. Besides I couldn't stay in it till I got out. I think (I said) I'll wash the hall floor my sister-in-law blew up, "you can't do the work now because you don't live here." I felt kind of bad. So I left earlier than I'm suppose to. My father was hurt and cried when I left but I left at 5:30. . . . I didn't feel like talking so went right to bed.

The diaries of economically disadvantaged children led to the tentative hypothesis that disadvantaged children of any race too often do not have access to adults who can serve as mediators except in limited situations. There were almost no dinner-table conversations recorded, a time when families can share experiences of the day and when parents can help serve as mediators. Most mediation that students recorded was performed by an older sibling for a younger. Students rarely perceived that there was a relationship between the anger of adults and their own behavior, between their own aggression and the feeling of loneliness, and between their disappointments and parental lack of resources to give them what they had been promised. Diaries were full of instances of disappointments, as in the case of Maria who "felt kind of bad" at her sister-in-law's rejection and whose father seemed incapable of helping her. Frustration was heaped upon earlier frustrations, in every area of their lives, until it seemed as though they could bear no more. Their day appeared to consist of disconnected hit-and-run activities. An appalling number of diaries was filled with tales of after-school hours being spent going from drug store to corner lot to public park to street corner looking for a chance meeting with a friend. Teachers were baffled by what students implied as a definition of a friend, and these implications were confirmed in sociometric interviews.
   On the other hand there were economically disadvantaged students who described warm and satisfying family as well as peer relationships. Those students who were blessed with both were by no means in the majority. It came through very clearly to the adult readers of their papers that they were learning the values of the groups to which they did belong and that belonging was a key factor in their adjustment at home, at school, and with their peers. When teachers analyzed responses, they found that the students with serious problems in any one of these areas of their lives were often having

difficulty finding a comfortable niche for themselves in other areas. For the students who had good home and peer relationships, the school environment was one in which learning was more comfortable than it was for the others. Those students who lacked a sense of belonging often displayed values not accepted by the larger group. Values have an emotional as well as a cognitive component. Human beings learn them through communication with other human beings. Where communication and belongingness are lacking, students have little recourse but to adopt the values of groups who will enfold them.

Teachers reported to students, in very general terms and anonymously, their findings gleaned from diaries submitted to them. They were as follows:

1. Most students spent from two to three hours in front of TV each day of the two days we kept a diary.
2. By far, most parents expected teenagers to be in the house by 8:30 P.M. on weekdays.
3. Only a few teenagers had no household duties to perform, etc. etc.

Students were eager for the teachers' reports. They were intrigued by the authenticity of the findings. In one middle-income school, students used the basic findings to create a questionnaire to be administered to adult relatives, their own friends, and younger children. They collected the data and drew their own generalizations from responses to questions such as:

1. How long does it take you to get ready for school or work?
2. Do you eat breakfast?
3. What is your favorite TV program?
4. What is your favorite food?
5. How many different people do you talk to in one day?
6. What is the greatest length of time you talk to any one person?
7. What is your favorite topic of conversation?
8. What is your favorite hobby? How much time do you spend on it?
9. Do you have anything to do with the neighbors?

The students did not limit their questions to the study of communication patterns. The teacher had not yet determined the precise area of study. Rather, he was interested in the students' questions, how they would fare during their data-gathering sessions with other people, and what they wished to do with the data. Later, the communications questions could be pinpointed as an introduction to the particular area of communications to be studied.

The sociometric test gave clues to the teacher about the particular students who were in the greatest difficulty as far as peer relationships were concerned and gave a picture of the structure of communication, or lack of it, in the full classroom. Those students whose families moved frequently or who were placed with one foster family and then another had difficulty establishing positive peer relationships.

Administering the sociometric test takes little time. It simply consists of asking students to record on a card their first three choices of classmates for a particular enterprise, such as making up a skit, that has a social component. The students' choices are tabulated to determine 1. who are the leaders, or the most-chosen students upon whom the teacher can depend for help in incorporating others into group activities; 2. who are the unchosen whom no one notices; 3. who are the rejected ones with whom other students do not associate; 4. what the network patterns are (e.g., Are there cliques? Is the line of communication from one student to another a long one, or does it break in short sharp lines after every four or five students? Are there cleavages between dark and light black students? along racial lines?)

Sociometric interviews follow the administration of the test. The interviews may be written, but for most students the opportunity to talk alone with the teacher is a distinctive advantage. This can be done only after students have learned routines and experiences which are absorbing and which permit them to carry on without the constant attention of the teacher. For example, while the rest of the class is reading self-selected books to determine how fears affect the behavior of the character, the teacher can be conducting interviews in the corner of the room. At first teachers feared students would "clam up," but an interested expression or a word of encouragement was sufficient to keep most students talking. As a matter of fact, after the first session in which seven or eight students had been interviewed about "How they happened to choose . . . ," the others clamored for their time to have a confidential talk. The teacher reassured them that no one would be forgotten.

Interviews tended to confirm teachers' hypotheses, drawn from diaries, that the relationships involved in being friends were tenuous in inner-city schools. Some relationships were strong reminders of Francie and her best friend Sukie in *Daddy Was a Number Runner* by Meriwether: Francie's need for Sukie's companionship forced her to submit to Sukie's beatings so they could be best friends again. Typical of some of the unstable peer relationships are those described in the following excerpts from an eighth-grade girl's interview:

Choice 1
I chose her 'cause she's my friend and she's always treating me nice. We git along together all right, so I figure we could git along all right in a different class. . . . She doesn't live near me. I don't know where she lives at. . . . We have fun. At three o'clock we have fun. One time I went over to her house, but I didn't get far 'cause it was too late and I had to turn back.

Choice 2
She's my bes' friend. We always runnin' around in the class and hittin' each other and havin' fun; like today, we had some fun. . . . She don't live near me. She's just a class friend.

Choice 3
She was my first friend. She introduced me to the girls in the classroom, and that's how I got to be her friend, 'cause we always jokin' around about each other. . . . I don't see her after school, just every time we get ready to dismiss at three o'clock. . . . Yes, I have friends on my block. Judy, I can't remember her last name, and Delene and Paula. I have more but I can't think of 'em.

Often, the reasons given for a second and especially a third choice sounded more like a reason for rejection. Teachers compared notes and became aware that almost universally a third choice was not needed by students living in a highly mobile area. Therefore, they reduced the number of choices to two. Many students who were frequently on the move had difficulty making even one close tie. Excerpts from one eighth-grade boy's interview gives a sense of the quality of relationships.

> Jeffrey is not like the rest of them. He controls himself. Kevin and Donald are not my first choices because they don't know how to control themselves. That is why I picked Kevin and Donald *less,* because if we were playing in the yard or something like that, or tapping someone on the shoulder or running around, Kevin and Donald would look to start a fight, but Jeff he could control himself. He wouldn't go over there and say, "Ah, man, who are you? I'm gonna beat you up." We live far away. I only see him in school, in the lunch room and school yard. . . . Kevin is jumpy. He gets into fights. I told him he'd better sit down. He don't pay back his debts. He don't give us nothing. Donald gave him an ice cream sandwich. He hits people and then he runs. . . . He just wants to mess around with somebody.

High priority reasons for choice were willingness to lend money, willingness to share food, ability to engage in sports, and attraction to the opposite sex. Causes for rejecting others were violence, "picking on people," "bothering people," "fooling around," and unwillingness to share food and money. An excerpt from the explanation of a boy's second choice illustrates a common phenomenon:

> A lot of people, if they ask you to lend me a dime or somethin', they say ya don't have it. They gonna git engry an' they not gonna do you any favors, but if you tell Tryon you don't have a dime, he'll say, 'Alright,' but if he has a dime, he'll give it to you.

There was a higher incidence of rejection by girls than by boys.

> She threw my math book on the floor; she hit me; she took my book and stepped on it.

> I don't think we would get along together. I would've chose her if I had enough room. She's all right, but I wouldn't want her in my class. First time I didn't like her, but now I do.

> I dislike her because she's always pickin' on people and she's got some names to call somebody, and somebody call her 'Dump face' she don't like it. I stay far apart from her as I can.

> The boys talk about you and all that, you know, about what you do and about what they want and all that stuff. They say things, like if they get mad, they talk about your mother and father and all that stuff.

Teachers again summarized responses anonymously for their students, with such comments as, "People in this class seemed to want to be with people who do not start fights, who are generous," etc. Based upon the sociometric interviews, one topic such as "People Need People," "Growing Up," or "Be Yourself" was selected for class study.

By this time, teachers had gained some confidence in structuring a learning sequence and students had experienced at least one sequence. Teachers reviewed the various types of activities in which they had engaged, and now the students were able to make suggestions. For example, one activity for the sequence "Be Yourself" asked students to write about "Things I Like about Myself." There were great cries of protest: This was encouraging showing off; it was better to write what you didn't like; anyway, I don't like anything about myself. The final outcome was the decision that each student should choose whether to write about what he likes or doesn't like, or both.

One teacher read from *Crow Boy* by Yashima and "The Great Stone Face" by Hawthorne to furnish students with specific events and characters which would make it possible for them to grasp the meaning of self-concept. Students wrote their feelings about themselves—some humorously, some seriously. A few entitled their compositions "My Real Self," while others preferred "All about Me." The student who first protested against the topic "Things I Like about Myself" wrote the following excerpt:

My Real Self

I think of myself as a talker or a loudmouth and a fool. And a scaredcat, and a guy that can get himself in trouble without me doing it.

Students became increasingly aware that teachers were making positive use of their topics, for they could see the immediate results in what was being planned for and with them.

Among middle-income students the sociometric picture was often a more sustained one. The lifeline of communication tended to be long, connecting a large proportion of the students in one way or another.[8] There were students who gained early and held long the position of leadership among their peers. The reasons for the leadership were varied: "She's the life of the party;" "He doesn't let the others crush the underdog;" "People just enjoy her; she smiles and enjoys them;" "He helps everybody; no matter who you are, he helps in any way he can;" "He's a rebel and I'm a rebel too; lots of kids are. We don't do it too noisily, but we let it be known that some things that go on around here just aren't right."

The finding that surprised teachers most was the high percentage of rejected students in all schools. They had harbored the notion that since middle-income students were favored economically, this in turn meant they were favored in every respect. When they discovered that at least 20 percent of the students in their classes were rejected or unchosen, they realized that the problem of communication was a pertinent one for their students. The student who is a loner by choice is a rare find. Teachers discovered that loners by and large were unhappy with themselves, and these students demonstrated the effects of their isolation in a number of ways. The teacher had only to know how to read the signs, for most loners were forced into their position by the insensitivities and behaviors of others. In turn, peer reactions caused intensified, negatively regarded behaviors on the part of the isolated student. Students needed to be aware that to be alone by choice for long periods of time is the right of every human being; to be denied communication is wasteful and injurious to the human beings on both ends of the communication wire.

Individualizing Instruction

It is important to emphasize the need for individualization of instruction and to discuss its implications for curriculum planning. It means materials cannot be uniform except in cases where the teacher accepts the responsibility of bringing a short story or poem to the students via his own oral interpretations or through the media for a specific purpose. It means materials used by the students must match their individual abilities and interests. Further, pacing cannot be uniform, nor can performance.

It is not necessary—in fact, it is noneducative—to individualize by grouping students in the classroom according to reading ability. Groups should be formed in a number of real-life ways: because students want to be together, because each has a skill the others need, because interests are similar. When there is a common experience around which students are trying to make new discoveries, there is room for everybody to learn his own way. Students tend to be comfortable with the book they select and no one needs to be on the alert for snide remarks about the "dumb group." To individualize instructions is to accommodate heterogeneity; a great range of materials is needed on whatever topic is selected. Books, plays, poems, films, records, and pictures which tell a story should be among those materials. Learning experience must also cover a wide range (e.g., observing, interviewing, filming, recording, etc.)

Teachers who are aware of the importance of individualization of instruction must be aware of the role of pacing. Proper pacing dictates that most learning tasks be those which students can handle alone with minimal aid from the teacher. Every task is meant to be approached with a feeling of adequacy and concluded with a feeling of success and of *hope* for success in the next steps. A demanding task should not be approached before an easy one is mastered. For example, if students do not understand how dialogue is written, they cannot read a play. Therefore, the introductory steps must be sequential. Pacing is the series of small progressive steps that eventually build sufficient skill and knowledge to permit the learner to proceed to a higher level of endeavor. If teachers fail to pace experiences properly, students cannot learn. Schools tend to skip steps or to take certain skills and knowledge for granted. We fail our students when we do this.

The principle of pacing holds true for all students. However, a giant step for one group can be a dwarf step for another. Academically able students are often unaware that they are going through the steps intuitively, even as they arrive at a particular conclusion in one great stride. Sometimes a quick reminder or a new focus offered for brief consideration is all they need. For example, when they write creative scripts, the teacher may need to call attention to the fact that dialogue is the medium the playwright uses to move the action along. Students may find one or two examples from a play they know; then they are ready to turn their attention back to the task of scripting.

Open-ended learning tasks encourage contributions as students are able to offer them at different levels of advancement. Open-ended tasks enhance individualization. When one group of students considered the sequence "Walls Human Beings Erect," some were able to deal only with physical walls, while others grasped quickly the meaning of psychological walls between people. Each student responded on the level he knew, exploring the purposes of walls but meantime learning from the explorations of his peers who were functioning on a different level.

Role taking is another type of open-ended task, serving many purposes. Perhaps the greatest problem in individualizing instruction and planning for heterogeneity in inner-city schools is the intense need ghetto students, especially in the junior high school, have for the teacher's attention. If the teacher brings a tape recorder into the clasroom, everyone wants to be caretaker; if there are art materials to be distributed for puppet making, each student wants to do the honors. Role playing in which every student has a chance to play some role in a series of dramas in one class period is a great pacifier. Each student receives his share of attention not only from the teacher but more important from his peers. The advantages of role taking are equally great for the middle-income student. The teacher can have a word of praise for each student. Eventually, students will learn small-group skills so that they can gain positive types of attention from each other. One such role playing session is on conducting small-group meetings. They can role play ways of writing poetry and skits or of making decisions about booklets. They can do these things individually and role play how to use each other as sounding boards. Almost all sequences used role playing, whether those sequences were geared to an academically superior group, underachievers, or a heterogeneous group. Role playing is an activity of which students rarely tire. All students can participate if the problems selected are universal, because all students have lived through experiences which can be called readily to the fore. Students were never permitted to play themselves. Thus, personal problems could be aired, discussed, and considered thoughtfully, with no threats to the student and no hurt feelings.

Open-ended discussions encourage individuals to respond creatively and make way for the individualization of instruction. Teachers can raise questions that are large issues with which students have some familiarity, so that every student can respond. Thus, the manner of handling a discussion which may involve the whole class at the same time can concern itself with heterogeneity. Discussions that are open ended do even more: They bring out differences of opinion and feelings which sharpen perceptions of an issue; they become the medium through which students can learn to disagree without resorting to violence. Students learn that we all feel differently about certain issues because each of us is a unique person. It takes a long time for this concept to be internalized. Further, open-ended discussions are the vehicle for setting up a non-threatening atmosphere in which differences among students can be appreciated.

Individualization demands that there be in each sequence opportunity for rotation of experiences geared to assimilating information and expressing it in some way that is different from the way in which it was acquired. Some students may require more expressive activities than assimilative ones.

Teachers prepared individualized activity "banks" for each sequence they taught. The teacher made the initial "deposits;" students "withdrew" the ones they preferred. Before long, students were making deposits for other students to withdraw. The bank consisted of activities described on uniform cards, usually a letter-size or legal-size manila folder. The folders were colorfully composed and ranged from one solitary activity for students who were not prepared to cope with more to an entire sequence of activities. The activities ranged from invitations to "do it yourself" to opportunities to "do it with a classmate or group of classmates." It was possible to complete some activities in a short session; others were geared to long-term involvement. All of them were related to the particular topic being considered by the whole class. All of them, therefore, made it possible for each student to offer a unique contribution to the class. Teachers shared these "bank deposits" with each other so that each possessed a wealth of activities within a short period of time. A sample "bank deposit" was entitled "Carousel of Time," composed to accompany the sequence "Time in Our Lives."

Individualization demands that a large proportion of the materials carry emotional appeal. The most persistent problem lies in the fact that what makes an impact on one student may mean little to another. To handle the problem of widely differing interests and abilities, the teachers tried successfully to use a common experience as a catalyst for individualization. One teacher read the Triangle fire incident from Asch's *East River.* Every student in a usually unmotivated class was gripped by the sheer drama of it, related as it was to their own fear of fire. The topic was *"Protection;"* it emphasized how families protect, how laws serve as protectors, and how people band together for similar purposes. Any number of books and stories, with a wide range of interest and ability levels, play upon the theme of protection. The topic also lends itself to a wide variety of activities such as observing, talking with concerned people, reading, scripting, and collecting pictures and writing about them.

Literature offers the kind of emotional impact as well as concrete experience teachers seek. It also carries the ingredients necessary for various levels of abstract thinking so that all students can be served individually. Literature gives the English teacher a distinct advantage with a heterogeneous group, especially where the task of acculturation is present. Acculturation involves learning values, and values have an emotional ingredient. Since disadvantaged students often have been isolated, their families often find it extremely difficult to transmit values and behaviors that are necessary to survive in the cultural mainstream. Through reading literature students may obtain an aware ness of other values and behaviors. Middle-income students require acculturation in reverse. They need to examine values of people living in situations different from theirs, to understand whence these values come, and to reexamine their own. When the book and the student are matched literature helps the student to internalize values, to feel his way into someone else's shoes, and to give him new perspective.

Criteria for the selection of literature need to be carefully considered in the light of the heterogeneous groups in the schools. Books that are closely related to students' experiences make for important beginnings. Yet, they should not merely reflect those experiences; rather, they should broaden students' perspectives on them. The first books that academically deprived students use should be fast paced and contain rich sequences of incidents and character development through incident. There is available today a good selection of "skinny" books; students can gain a feeling of accomplishment by completing a book in three or four sittings. Further, an attractive layout of a page, with reasonably good margins and print that is clear and well spaced, encourages students to try a book. The problem to be developed by the author should be clear very early in the book, and the main character easily identified. Most important is that the student be given an opportunity to select a book *during class time* and to determine at least tentatively whether he wants to read it or return it to the shelves. Academically able students enjoy "skinny" books, too. However, they tend to read for a greater range of purposes. Books which often lie around the home are tasted, many times with gusto, by the adolescent.

Individualization of instruction is enhanced when activities as well as materials involve the student. Initial activities for any new study should be *overt,* and overt activities are dominant throughout any study sequence because these are the ones that have the greatest possibility of admitting students of all abilities. The students may dramatize a story incident, draw a stage setting for a play, interview each other, or plan and execute materials for a class book. Overt activity has motivational power. Students can put a literary character on trial for his deeds, make a series of cartoons about incidents in books, or use a projector to show a film relevant to a story.

All efforts at individualization will fail unless the learning experience results in rapid success. Once students know they can succeed, intrinsic motivation will take over. Contrary to the impression some students convey by blasé or hostile behavior, students do want to learn something. When they ultimately feel their way into a task that is meaningful to them, they will proceed with increasing independence. Success for each pupil demands that he find himself by losing himself in an involving activity.

Functions of Questions

The questions students and teachers raise have significant bearing on cognitive functioning and curriculum building. Questions that students verbalize are a critical key to curriculum flexibility. The questions teachers ask and the way in which they phrase them are also crucial. When students ask questions about a story, they can change the direction of the curriculum. Therefore, students need to know how to ask questions of the author, themselves, their peers, and the teacher. Traditionally, teachers have asked the questions, while students were expected to provide the answers; sound education dictates that the roles be reversed. Students' questions define what they do or do not understand and reveal where their interests lie.

There are times when a simple invitation to students to air the questions they'd like to raise about what happened in a particular story brings a delightful flow of questions. Teachers are often amazed both at the simple things some students fail to grasp and at the creative ways in which other students relate ideas. The perceptive students may unearth questions to which the teacher had never given a thought. With astonishing insights they arrive at issues such as one about Jackson's "The Witch." A student may conclude that "the little boy says at one time the witch is a 'she'; at another time a 'he.' Witches are usually women. Why does the little boy mix up his witches?"

Students' questions do not necessarily come in response to the teacher's query, Do you have any questions? Rather, they are more likely to become an integral part of a nonthreatening atmosphere encouraged by activities such as five-minute buzz groups formed to consider some of the puzzlements of "The Lottery" or "The Witch." Students' questions grow out of interaction among each other and with the teacher and the literature. They arise as a result of discovery activities. Whatever the specific methods teachers use, students should be encouraged to ask questions; students need to know that their questions are a part of their thinking process and that through their questions they contribute to the thinking of the entire group. During a class period in which one teacher read the scene about the Triangle fire from Asch's *East River,* a student asked, "How are we supposed to know what caused the fire and who was responsible?" The teacher became aware that he must offer more help in noting rich inferences in the story itself. Also, the student needed to be alerted to the many news items and TV programs citing causes of death by fire in buildings of large cities, so that he could begin to connect two diverse sources of enlightenment. When students were discussing "Yours Lovingly" by Courtright, one boy remarked, "That happened when Miss Canby took over." From another student came the challenge, "*When* did Miss Canby take over?" To this a third one replied, "From the very first sentence of a story the ending begins, and Miss Canby is right there in the beginning." Thus, the focus which originally was on the inadequacies of Mr. Gooby was shifted to the role of Miss Canby as students considered the question, Is she living a lie? At the same time, a new thought was introduced: Is it true that from the very first sentence of a story, the ending begins? Students examined, on their own, a number of their favorite stories in order to verify or refute the idea. This examination was not undertaken by the full class. Rather, it became a workshop activity for students to select from among a number of activities.

Students need to be educated to fruitful questioning. Without help, they often spend their efforts on relatively insignificant detail: How old were the children who were throwing stones? Can you name all the characters in the book? Students can search for the less than immediately apparent; they can act as detectives to uncover what is not yet on the surface. The training need in no way interfere with students' needs to ask whatever questions are of interest to them.

Questions advance learning and focus thinking. When teachers frame questions, it is essential that they predetermine the specific function of a question, since it is that function which decides the form and content of the question. For example, open-ended questions introduce a topic because they permit students to reply on their own terms using their own prior experiences. Further, open-ended questions lead to pooling and sharing information which provides a sturdy background for all to use. Examples of open-ended questions are: Do you think this story is true to life? If you were one of the characters, what would you do? Developmental questions follow the open-ended ones and consist of key questions which help focus the problems and advance the knowledge about new areas. The already pooled information is used for acquiring perspective wherever possible, as the questions lead the students into new territory. A third question category is geared toward encouraging the formation of generalizations. These questions appear on several levels, usually when students have already examined a number of instances which are illustrative of that generalization. Thus, when students have read and discussed three fables, they are ready to make some tentative generalizations about fables: What are the functions of fables? Why did the fables use animals so frequently rather than people? A fourth category of questions, application, is to help students make use of their newly found knowledge in other situations. The teacher might ask, "What newsworthy item this week would make a good subject for an Aesop fable? What present characters would be central in the fable? What moral would you want your fable to illustrate?"

Questions should be arranged in a sequential order, even though they usually cannot be used in this manner. Teachers need to be armed with such questions, but they should also be ready to relinquish them when they prove to be something less than useful. For example, when students grapple with an open-ended question, they may hit on a variety of points which are basic to the questions the teacher had planned to raise. Thus, they indicate the degree of their understanding of the main issue. Before the teacher uses sharpened questions, he should make certain that all points of view have been thrown into the hopper and that many feelings have been brought out in the open. The way in which a question series can move from being open ended to sharply focused can be illustrated from plans for a discussion of an incident from Brink's *Caddie Woodlawn*. The teacher was seeking to lead students to examine how people can break down emotional walls and build bridges of communication.

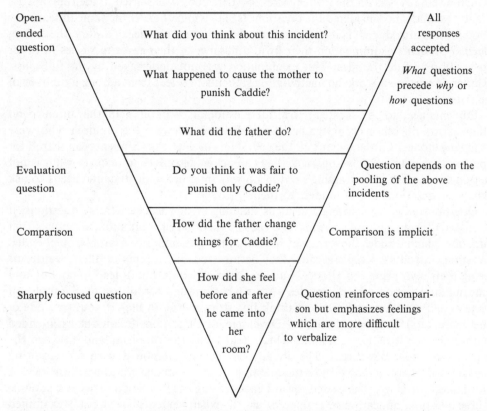

Through question sequences students learn models for examining literary works. When students can anticipate certain fundamental questions, they have at least a three-pronged advantage in the initial stages of the sequence. First, they can begin to appraise a new piece of literature independently and to deal with it on a higher cognitive level than if the questions planned were haphazard and demonstrated no model. Second, they can later work with peers on some common ground to discuss self selected, outside readings which pertain to the issues at hand. Third, they learn to pattern inquiry about significant questions. For example, why did Saki, the author of "The Open

Window,'' give Mr. Nuttel that particular name? Why did Shakespeare give us the first glimpse of the Friar in *Romeo and Juliet* when he was picking herbs?

A knowledge of the functions of questions helps eliminate the common practice by teachers of conducting a lesson with a bombardment of questions which call for insignificant and inconsequential answers. Such questions encourage a one-to-one response with the teacher rather than the development of conversation. They are not educative in that they prevent students from discriminating between the significant and the insignificant and in that they divert their attention from the crucial aspects of a piece of literature. When teachers learn to formulate questions that encourage divergent thinking, they enhance the opportunity of students to react as creative individuals.

Aids to Curriculum Planning

RESOURCE CENTERS

To achieve the learning environment necessary for accomplishing the goals of individualization of instruction and cognitive as well as affective development, a workshop atmosphere is fundamental. There are many kinds of workshops, each dependent upon the human and the material resources brought to it. Variety is a key when describing resources which support the workshop atmosphere. Resource or interest areas, when set up by students and teachers together, help to encourage and develop the workshop patterns.

The workshop class design is a more natural learning situation than the usual row-on-row arrangements or the rigid six-desk groupings. From early childhood on we live and learn in workshop situations. For example, the kitchen is such a design and provides a place where the young child learns countless skills and vast knowledge. The child learns as he interacts with his environment, while other family members proceed to carry out their daily activities and interact with him.

The interest areas in the classroom can be set up in a number of ways to meet the unique situations that exist in each school. Where teachers have a classroom of their own, the task is relatively simple. Where the rooms are shared with other teachers, cooperative arrangements of one type or another are necessary. For example, interest area materials can be stored and used on a mobile table which can be shifted from class to class. Better still, English teachers who plan curriculum cooperatively may request that certain classrooms be grouped for their use and that their schedules be adapted to the available space in their bay. Then, common basic materials can be gathered and made available. Cabinets can serve as a focus for interest areas, and when space in three or four classrooms is used cooperatively, a variety of materials for workshop design can be gathered.

The workshop areas should serve diverse interests. For example the "Books Waiting for Authors" center is an invitation to student writers. It is an uncomplicated affair since it consists only of a table and chairs, and attractively bound books constructed of assembled sheets of paper cut in different sizes and shapes. Included are "Books Waiting for Coauthors." Collaboration by students in a writing effort is often frowned upon by educators, yet it is acceptable in the business and professional world. For students who take a dim view of writing as well as for students who enjoy it, collaboration is one of the most sustaining motivations.

A writing center can be more comprehensive. It can include magazines, construction paper and other art materials, pictures, and objects that inspire writing. Both students and teacher may contribute ideas and a variety of conversation pieces, such as unique crafts. Generally, the school provides the "bread-and-butter" materials. Students use the center as their interest moves them. For example, one student was so intrigued with the sequence of human hands and their relationship to emotions that he mounted on colored construction paper pictures he found of human hands.[9] The hands manifested emotional content: praying, holding a gun, cuddling a baby, shaking a finger, pointing a finger, holding up the heavy head of a woman as she faced the window of a car in a funeral cortege. For each picture he wrote a brief essay or poem. When students happen upon pictures that say something to them, they are often able to respond in writing.

Another resource area holds props for dramatization and materials for creating those props. Costumes are produced by students. Cardboard swords and paper-bag helmets coated with silver paint are inspiration for creative one-act medieval plays. A nurse's navy blue cape becomes the distinctive garb of Cyrano, and a large straw hat decorated with paper flowers and waxed fruit contributes to the adolescent's transformation on stage.

Puppets warrant another interest center, with a stage all their own. Puppets are a versatile tool. They are a rich source of enjoyment and a motivation for learning. Further, they enable a shy student to hide behind the stage while putting his puppet's foot forward. The student who fears his own voice in the classroom comes through loud and clear by way of his puppet. Puppets range from simple hand-manipulated dolls to marionettes controlled with complicated string or wire arrangements. In the case of a number of students, creative drama with puppets is the activity which constitutes a landmark in the overt change of learning behavior. A shelf installed high above the usually used space can store the puppet stage when it is not in use.

The class library serves a function that cannot be served by the school or public library: the immediate availability of books. There are reluctant readers who do pick up attractive books that happen to be near them. It accomplishes little to argue that schools should educate students to use the library. Few educators will deny the importance of the aim, but students do not learn everything at once. First, the desire to read is nurtured; then the resources of the library become important. The class library should hold poetry, drama, and short story collections as well as novels. Novelettes, such as *His Own Where* by Jordan, that are fast-paced are as important as the full-length novel, not only for the slower reader but for any student who seeks to relax with a book in one, two, or three sittings. Poetry collections such as *Reflection on a Gift of Watermelon Pickle, and Other Modern Verse,* edited by Dunning, Lueders, and Smith, are attractive in title and format. One-act and other short plays should be available. Scholastic Book Services has published the Scope Play Series which includes *Twelve Angry Men, Teacher, Teacher, Dino,* and *Requiem for a Heavyweight.* They are relatively inexpensive paperbacks. The class library may include books created by previous students, individually or as a class. One teacher noted that these books are the first ones to be handled by students who find reading a burdensome task. Students are interested in what their peers have to say; they look for authors that are known to them and can even be caught smiling at something a friend has written or sharing the choice piece

with a classmate. Near the class library is a quiet reading corner, with a comfortable chair, area rug, and lamp. At first, this corner may present a problem when it is in constant demand. However, as students become involved in other projects, the quiet corner is no more in demand than are other areas. The class library may also include annotated bibliographies of young children's books, the result of a project by a group of students in a previous class.

The audiovisual resource center may outrank the other centers in popularity during the first weeks of the school year. It includes tape recorders with earphones; an annotated list of available filmstrips, movies, tapes, and recordings; a list of suggestions for projects needing slides or 8 mm film to be shot by students; forms to fill out for reserving the school projector; and slides, photos, and 8 mm film projects made by previous classes. There are taped dramatizations of literary works by students. There are tapes of student groups reading short stories in the dramatic vein. Students can listen to peers read a story before or after they read it themselves or simply enjoy hearing friends perform. Poetry readings to music are available on tape.

In a sense, the classroom itself and the people in it comprise a resource center. In a workshop atmosphere students soon learn that their peers have much to offer and that no one person is in possession of all useful and interesting knowledge. The room itself can be arranged so that in a very short time it can be a "circle in the square" for creative drama, a courtroom in which the trial of Brutus takes place, a forum for open discussion, or a production center for a class newspaper.

Resource areas achieve a number of objectives. Students enjoy working at them because the choice of area and project is theirs. Academically unmotivated students find them a pathway to involvement in school activities. The areas permit experiences to be structured so that the teacher does *not* have to try to hold full-class attention. The student gains independence in learning and knowing how to learn. The cognitive level at which learning is attempted tends to be the appropriate one because the level itself is more or less self-selected by each student. The interest areas grow and change with the students, since they are manipulated by them; in turn, the areas enrich the students' powers to learn.

THE ROLE OF MEDIA

Literature teachers generally have ignored the mass media as an educational tool. Yet, television's impact upon the way we think about politics, the world community, economics, and health has been almost incalculable. Kilpatrick stresses that "media create environments"[10] today just as Gutenberg's printing press did for another day. Hipple and Hook point up the facts that, whether we like it or not, the dramas on TV "serve as virtually the only literature for millions of adults,"[11] and that the mass media will constitute the teachers of our students when they leave the confines of the school walls. Nevertheless, teachers do little to educate students for the intelligent use of TV, nor do they give adequate attention to judging fact from opinion and to recognizing persuasion techniques. Schools must assume some responsibility for media literacy, the aim of which is, as Karl phrases it, a population "capable of judging whether electronic media are humanizing or dehumanizing contemporary civilization." Media literacy means students learn to "read media as they do print."[12]

Educators' neglect of the media is a dangerous act of omission in light of the fact that children acquire attitudes and modes of behavior from the screen without learning how to analyze what they see and hear. We cannot divorce ourselves from the powerful influences that affect our students, for while we continue to teach as we have taught for many years, the student is being manipulated. Fillion argues that "the film viewer must be liberated from such manipulation, and he should understand that he is not experiencing something necessarily 'truer than life,' but a very powerful expression of another man's view of life. . . ."[13]

Media can be an asset in achieving educational aims. Because film is such a concrete media, due to the fact that it involves the ear, the eyes, and the mind simultaneously, it is useful for teaching all students. Thus, it is a boon for the teachers of heterogeneously grouped classes as well as for teachers of academically advanced or academically undiscovered pupils. A film can evoke intense reactions and provoke stimulating exchange of ideas. Most students are acquainted with this media so that its particular language speaks to them. Because it speaks to everybody, the film, McGlynn assures us, is "thus a common ground and therefore of crucial importance in a world where means of human communication sometimes seem in very short supply."[14] Thus, the film involves students of diverse backgrounds, abilities, and interests. As teachers work with film, they realize that the mere viewing of it cannot achieve the communication implied by McGlynn's statement. Involvement includes activities such as discussion of keenly felt issues, sharing points of view, brainstorming, and using the film experience in subsequent related activities.

Because films possess the power to involve pupils and because they command sharp focusing of all the senses, they furnish stimulus material for cognitive development. Thus, not only have films the ability to speak to diverse individuals but their demanding nature makes them an ally in cognitive and affective development. Stern goes so far as to say that "no other art form" is so demanding.[15]

The film's potential as a cognitive stimulus is enhanced by the variety of ways in which the literature teacher can put it to use. The most obvious use is comparison, that is, the one-to-one relationship between a film based directly on a novel or short story and the story itself. "The Occurrence at Owl Creek Bridge" by Bierce is a case in point. Students who see the film and read the story or have it read to them learn an important concept explored by Deer:

> The film story is very different from the novel. Obviously, the film is not merely a motion picture recording of the black marks found on the pages of a book. Nor is it merely an acted out version of the novel. The camera is a performer too; it moves up and down, in and out, to one side or the other. . . . When we watch a film, we see what has been selected for us. . . . When we watch a stage performance . . . we are our own editors. We see the whole stage at once and choose to see whatever we like.[16]

Comparing a film as a unique art with literature as another particular art enables students to understand more deeply the meaning of both. Pupils gain this deeper insight when they understand that the film uses action to portray a thought at a certain point or arranges space in such a way as to denote time, while literature spells out time through the tenses of its verbs.

Comparisons between the films and literature can be stimulated by considering factors such as, Which scenes are the most touching in the story? in the film? What did the author or film maker do to achieve this reaction on your part? What do students notice through the eyes of the film maker that escaped them on the first reading of the story? How are time and space handled by the story maker? the film maker? When students are able to view the film more than once and read the story as many times as they need to do so, they can discover critical aspects of each art never apparent to them before. Equal in importance to their differences are the similarities between films and works of literature. Katz says that the purpose of both is to "make you see." He further states:

> Both literature and film are liberating arts . . . [they] present to us an artist's ordering of the chaos of human experience. . . . Literature and film are similar also in that both tend to be content oriented. . . . Both require cognitive participation in order to have the reader or viewer understand them. Finally, both film and literature frequently offer some form of entertainment.[17]

There need not be a one-to-one relationship between story and film. Teachers can use one of a number of beautiful very short films like "The String Bean" in conjunction with a number of short stories such as Mansfield's "Miss Brill." Just as poetry is read to music, each enhancing the other, the story and film each complement the other.

The experience of film making and radio script writing also stimulate cognitive development. When students write a script based on Jackson's "Charles," they use the skills of reading, writing, dicussing, and listening. The script may ultimately be performed on tape, or filmed using several film slides coordinated with the taped script or using Super 8 mm camera. More easily performed than a short story or novel is a documentary which is based, for example, on Mayerson's *Two Blocks Apart.* Since the documentary does not possess the complexity of a novel or even a short story and since it permits the filming of neighborhoods as they are, shooting the documentary is a much simpler activity. Slide films are easier for students to create than a movie film of a play. A roll of film consisting of twelve exposures can be purchased and developed relatively inexpensively and gives virtually as much satisfaction as a film.[18] Further, the process offers two-way and even six-way communication, as students involved in planning executing, and evaluating this activity consult each other, read, write, check for peer opinion, plan the shots, decide the length of the script, and determine how sight and sound will be coordinated.

TV commercials are valuable subjects for both film study and film making. Students, if taught or guided to do so, watch TV with a new insight in order to analyze the techniques of persuasion. If they film their own TV commercial with scripts of one-minute maximum length and use Super 8 mm film, they can use virtually all of their faculties and skills. Again, a script is required, so there is reading and rereading, writing and discussion and re-writing, plus teamwork on several levels. Students can engage in a research study of the programs they watch and the products they use. They can interview parents about the effects of TV commercials on the pressures of their children to buy certain products. This is not to say the school is teaching students not to buy, rather, only to examine and understand the consequences. In this way, the school recognizes its role in helping students understand the present, comprehend their environment, and hopefully cope with the future.

The excellent article entitled "*Now* Says: TV Commercials Insult Women"[19] can be the catalyst for all kinds of film study, especially commercials. It analyzes the inferior role of women as portrayed in a number of TV commercials. Students can use its content to observe commercials in a new light; then they can listen to a cassette repeat the commercials without the visual image in the classroom. The recording makes a startling contrast and *adds* a dimension even while it subtracts one. Then students can write their own script creating a new image of women. Of course, many perceive nothing awry with the present TV image and are very critical of the article. The difference of opinion among students makes the discussion especially important.

The literature teacher need not fear that print literacy will suffer as a consequence of the emphasis on multi-media. Morrow and Suid assure the teacher that "the multimedia approach does not in any way deny the importance of print; rather it provides a more realistic context in which the student can approach this medium in school . . . for all the supposedly nonliterary dimensions of media, there are very few movie or TV shows worth experiencing that did not begin as a written statement. . . . Writing is vital to every aspect of media production planning."[20]

Teachers who avoid the task of media literacy because they regard electronic media as inferior to print have been short changed by their professional schools. In contrast to the United States opinion, England, France, and Russia honor its film makers. Those countries recognize that true mastery of the medium requires an understanding of writing, photography, sound, music, optics, architecture, editing, and acting.

To pinpoint for the literature teacher the fact that a wealth of resources is at his command, there is a very brief list of films, cassettes, and recordings at the end of this chapter. In some cities, short films can be borrowed from public libraries. This resource is crucial where boards of education have not yet seen fit to acquire film resources.

Summary

This chapter has as its purpose the elevation of curriculum building to a classroom teacher level. Since no true curriculum can be built without regard for students and since teachers are the persons who can know the students better than educators on other levels, it is the teacher who must become, with his students, the curriculum creator. Therefore, it is he who must have ways and means at his command for learning about students; it is he who must know how to use his findings to create curriculum sequences; and it is he who must build an environment which is truly a learning environment.

NOTES

1. See Hilda Taba and Deborah Elkins, *Teaching Strategies for the Culturally Disadvantaged* (Chicago: Rand McNally & Co., 1966).
2. Ibid., pp. 30–32.
3. Hilda Taba, *Curriculum Development: Theory and Practice* (New York: Harcourt Brace Jovanovich, 1962), p. 345.

4. Ibid., p. 346.

5. Arthur Daigon, "English: A Three-Ringed Circus." *English Journal* 62 (1973): 1117.

6. Urie Bronfenbrenner, "The Split-level American Family," in *Learning Environments: Readings in Educational Psychology,* ed. William J. Gnagey, Patricia A. Chesebro, and James J. Johnson (New York: Holt, Rinehart & Winston, 1972), p. 10.

7. Don E. Hamachek, "Characteristics of Good Teachers and Implications for Teacher Education," in *Learning Environments: Readings in Educational Psychology,* ed. William J. Gnagey, Patricia A. Chesebro, and James J. Johnson (New York: Holt, Rinehart & Winston, 1972), p. 71.

8. This generalization was not applicable to all classroom groups, in particular suburban schools to which students came from isolated areas. Students in one of these schools were children of executives whose occupations required a high degree of mobility.

9. For a description of this sequence, see Taba and Elkins.

10. W. Kirk Kilpatrick, "McLuhan: Implications for Adolescence," in *Readings for Teaching English in Secondary Schools,* ed. (New York: The Macmillan Co., 1973), p. 250.

11. Theodore W. Hipple, *Teaching English in Secondary Schools* (New York: The Macmillan Co., 1973), p. 241. Also, on the same subject, see J. N. Hook et al., *Representative Performance Objectives for High School English* (New York: The Ronald Press, 1971).

12. Herb Karl, "Media Literacy: The Right to Know," *English Journal* 63 (1974): 9.

13. Bryant P. Fillion, "Turning On: The Selling of the Present, 1970," in *Readings for Teaching English in Secondary Schools,* ed. Theodore W. Hipple (New York: The Macmillan Co., 1973), p. 243.

14. Paul D. McGlynn, "Rhetoric in Fiction and Film: Notes toward a Cultural Symbiosis," in *Readings for Teaching English in Secondary Schools,* ed. Theodore W. Hipple (New York: The Macmillan Co., 1973), p. 277.

15. Adele H. Stern, "Using Films in Teaching English Composition." in *The Compleat Guide to Film Study* ed. G. Howard Poteet (Urbana, Ill.: National Council of Teachers of English, 1972), p. 171.

16. Irving Deer, "Mass Media and the English Teacher," in *Readings for Teaching English in Secondary Schools,* ed. Theodore W. Hipple (New York: The Macmillan Co., 1973), p. 229.

17. John Stuart Katz, "An Integrated Approach to the Teaching of Film and Literature," in *Challenge and Change in the Teaching of English,* ed. Arthur Daigon and Ronald T. Laconte (Boston: Allyn & Bacon, 1971), p. 149.

18. Lidstone and McIntosh dub still cameras "pale substitutes for working on one's own with a loaded movie camera." John Lidstone and Don McIntosh, *Children as Film Makers* (New York: Van Nostrand Reinhold Co., 1970), p. 15.

19. Joseph Fletcher Littell, ed., *Coping with Television* (Evanston, Ill.: McDougal, Littell & Co., 1973), pp. 178 181.

20. James Morrow and Murray Suid, "Media in the English Classroom," *English Journal* 63 (1974): 38–39.

References

Arnothy, Christine. *I'm Fifteen and I Don't Want to Die.* New York: E. P. Dutton & Co., 1956.

Asch, Sholem. *East River.* New York: G. P. Putnam's Sons, 1946.

Bierce, Ambrose. "The Occurrence at Owl Creek Bridge." In *Understanding Fiction,* edited by Cleanth Brooks, Jr. and Robert Penn Warren. New York: Appleton-Century-Crofts, 1943.

Bonham, Frank. *Durango Street.* New York: Dell Publishing Co., 1972.

Boyer, Ernest L. "A New Liberal Arts Crucial to Survival." *New York Times* 124 (January 15, 1975):57, 98.

Brink, Carol R. *Caddie Woodlawn.* New York: The Macmillan Co., 1935.

Bronfenbrenner, Urie. "The Split-level American Family." In *Learning Environments: Readings in Educational Psychology,* edited by William J. Gnagey, Patricia A. Chesebro, and James J. Johnson. New York: Holt, Rinehart & Winston, 1972.

Buck, Pearl. *The Big Wave.* New York: The John Day Co., 1952.

_____. *The Good Earth.* New York: Pocket Books, 1949.

Carroll, Ellison. "Teacher, Teacher." *Teacher, Teacher and Other Plays.* Scope Play Series. New York: Scholastic Book Services, 1971.

Cather, Willa, *My Antonia.* Boston: Houghton Mifflin Co., 1954.

Courtright, Eugene. "Yours Lovingly." In *Adventures in Appreciation,* edited by Luella B. Cook, H. A. Miller, and Walter Loban. New York: Harcourt Brace Jovanovich, 1947.

Daigon, Arthur. "English: A Three-Ringed Circus." *English Journal* 62 (November 1973): 1115–22.

Deer, Irving. "Mass Media and the English Teacher." In *Readings for Teaching English in Secondary Schools,* edited by Theodore W. Hipple. New York: The Macmillan Co., 1973.

Dunning, Stephen; Lueders, Edward; and Smith, Hugh, eds. *Reflections On a Gift of Watermelon Pickle, and Other Modern Verse.* Glenview, Ill.: Scott, Foresman and Co., 1966.

Dwyer, J. F. "The Citizen." In *Reading for Appreciation.* Book 2, Part 1, edited by W. E. Grady and Paul Klapper. New York: Charles Scribner's Sons, 1935.

Elkins, Deborah. "Man on the Move: 16 Visual Teaching Pictures and Teacher's Manual." New York: Franklin Watts, 1969.

Estes, Eleanor. *The Hundred Dresses.* New York: Harcourt Brace Jovanovich, 1944.

Fillion, Bryant P. "Turning On: The Selling of the Present, 1970." In *Readings for Teaching English in Secondary Schools,* edited by Theodore W. Hipple. New York: The Macmillan Co., 1973.

Hamachek, Don E. "Characteristics of Good Teachers and Implications for Teacher Education." In *Learning Environments: Readings in Educational Psychology,* edited by William J. Gnagey, Patricia A. Chesebro, and James J. Johnson. New York: Holt, Rinehart & Winston, 1972.

Hawthorne, Nathaniel. "The Great Stone Face." In *Reading for Appreciation.* Book 2, edited by William E. Grady and Paul Klapper. New York: Charles Scribner's Sons, 1936.

Heyert, Murray. "The New Kid." In *The Study of Literature,* edited by Edward J. Gordon. New York: Ginn and Co., 1964.

Hipple, Theodore W. *Teaching English in Secondary Schools.* New York: The Macmillan Co., 1973.

Hook, J. N. et al. *Representative Performance Objectives for High School English.* New York: The Ronald Press, 1971.

Jackson, Shirley. "Charles." *The Lottery.* New York: Avon Books, 1965.

_____. "The Lottery." *The Lottery.* New York: Avon Books, 1965.

_____. "The Witch." *The Lottery.* New York: Avon Books, 1965.

Jordan, June. *His Own Where.* New York: Thomas Y. Crowell Co., 1971.

Karl, Herb. "Media Literacy: The Right To Know." *English Journal* 63 (October 1974):7–9.

Katz, John Stuart. "An Integrated Approach to the Teaching of Film and Literature." In *Challenge and Change in the Teaching of English,* edited by Arthur Daigon and Ronald T. Laconte. Boston: Allyn & Bacon, 1971.

Kilpatrick, W. Kirk. "McLuhan: Implications for Adolescence." In *Readings for Teaching English in Secondary Schools,* edited by Theodore W. Hipple. New York: The Macmillan Co., 1973.

Lane, Rose Wilder. *Let the Hurricane Roar.* New York: Longmans, Green & Co., 1933.

Levin, Ira. *The Stepford Wives.* Boston: G. K. Hall & Co., 1973.

Lidstone, John, and McIntosh, Don. *Children as Film Makers.* New York: Van Nostrand Reinhold Co., 1970.

Littell, Joseph Fletcher, ed. *Coping with Television.* Evanston, Ill.: McDougal, Littell & Co., 1973.

McGlynn, Paul D. "Rhetoric in Fiction and Film: Notes toward a Cultural Symbiosis." In *Readings for Teaching English in Secondary Schools,* edited by Theodore W. Hipple. New York: The Macmillan Co., 1973.

Mansfield, Katherine. "Miss Brill." In *Story and Structure.* 2d ed., edited by Laurence Perrine. New York: Harcourt Brace Jovanovich, 1966.

Mayerson, Charlotte L., ed. *Two Blocks Apart.* New York: Avon Books, 1971.

Morrow, James, and Suid, Murray. "Media in the English Classroom." *English Journal* 63 (October 1974), 38–39.

Parks, Gordon. *A Choice of Weapons.* New York: Harper & Row, Publishers, 1965.

Platt, Kin. *The Boy Who Could Make Himself Disappear.* New York: Dell Publishing Co., 1972.

Richter, Conrad. *The Light in the Forest.* New York: Alfred A. Knopf, 1953.

Rölvaag, Ole. *Giants in the Earth.* New York: Harper & Row, Publishers, 1929.

Rose, Reginald. "Dino." *Dino and Other Plays.* Scope Play Series. New York: Scholastic Book Services, 1971.

———. "Thunder on Sycamore Street." *Dino and Other Plays.* Scope Play Series. Scholastic Book Services, 1971.

———. "Twelve Angry Men." *Twelve Angry Men and Other Plays.* Scope Play Series. New York: Scholastic Book Services, 1971.

Saki. [pseud. for H. H. Munro]. "The Open Window." *Humor, Horror, and the Supernatural: 22 Stories by Saki.* New York: Scholastic Book Services, 1965.

Serling, Rod. "Requiem for a Heavyweight." *Requiem for a Heavyweight and Other Plays.* Scope Play Series. New York: Scholastic Book Services, 1971.

Shakespeare, William. "Romeo and Juliet." In *The Complete Plays and Poems of William Shakespeare,* edited by William A. Neilson and Charles J. Hill. Cambridge, Mass.: Houghton Mifflin Co., 1942.

Sommerfelt, Aimée. *The Road to Agra.* New York: Abelard-Schuman, 1961.

Steinbeck, John. *The Grapes of Wrath.* New York: The Viking Press, 1939.

Stern, Adele H. "Using Films in Teaching English Composition." In *The Compleat Guide to Film Study,* edited by G. Howard Poteet. Urbana, Ill.: National Council of Teachers of English, 1972.

Swarthout, Glendon. *Bless the Beasts and the Children.* New York: Doubleday & Co., 1970.

Taba, Hilda. *Curriculum Development: Theory and Practice.* New York: Harcourt Brace Jovanovich, 1962.

Taba, Hilda, and Elkins, Deborah. *Teaching Strategies for the Culturally Disadvantaged.* Chicago: Rand McNally & Co., 1966.

Tunis, John R. *His Enemy, His Friend.* New York: William Morrow & Co., 1967.

———. *Yea! Wildcats!* New York: Harcourt Brace Jovanovich, 1944.

Wagner, Jane, and Parks, Gordon. *J. T.* New York: Dell Publishing Co., 1971.

Yashima, Taro. *Crow Boy.* New York: The Viking Press, 1955.

Yates, Elizabeth. *Amos Fortune, Free Man.* New York: Dell Publishing Co., 1971.

Suggested Films, Cassettes, and Records

Most of the following films were selected because they are short and can therefore allow for discussion during one forty-five-minute period into which so many secondary school schedules are divided. They were also chosen because they are relatively recent productions. This is not to imply that older and longer films are to be forgotten; it is to say that the existence of older films is generally known to teachers, principals, and boards of education. For additional selections, *The English Journal* and *Media and Methods* are among the literature teacher's best friends.

A C T Films, Inc.
35 West Forty-fifth Street
New York, N.Y. 10036

Garden Party, 24 min., based on story by Katherine Mansfield.

Avi Associates, Inc.
825 Third Ave.
New York, N.Y. 10022

Asian Fables, 35 mm filmstrip, series.
Cesar Chavez, 35 mm filmstrip

B F A Educational Media
2211 Michigan Ave.
Santa Monica, Calif. 90404

Four Views of Caesar, 23 min.
Henry IV, Part 2: Act V, Scene 5, 8 min.
I Have a Dream: The Life of Martin Luther King, 15 min.
Paul Laurence Dunbar: American Poet, 14 min.
Paul Revere's Ride (Henry Wadsworth Longfellow), 10 min.
Romeo and Juliet: Act II, Scene II, 9 min.
Shakespeare Primer, 28 min., excerpts from several plays.
The Wave: A Japanese Folktale, 9 min.
What Is Poetry? 9 min., news report about an auto wreck compared to Karl Shapiro's poem entitled "Auto Wreck."

Centron Educational Films
1621 West Ninth Street
Lawrence, Kansas 66044

Poetry for Fun: Dares and Dreams, 12 ½ min.

Chelsea House Publishers
70 West Fortieth Street
New York, N.Y. 10018

*I Have a Dream: Martin Luther King, Jr. and the
Nonviolent Crusade,* 8 mm. motion cartridge.

Contemporary Films
330 West Forty-second Street
New York, N.Y. 10036

> *Adventures of an* *, 10 min., animated satire
>
> *The Hand,* 19 min., animated satire
>
> *Hangman,* 12 min., may be used for comparison with Shirley
> Jackson's "The Lottery."
>
> *The House,* 32 min., technique of flashback.
>
> *The Leaf,* 20 min., about poetry.
>
> *Occurrence at Owl Creek Bridge,* 28 min., based on Ambrose Bierce's short story.
>
> *The String Bean,* 17 min., can be used to compare with Mansfield's "Miss Brill."
>
> *Very Nice, Very Nice,* 7 min., about poetry.

Coronet Instructional Films
65 East South Water Street
Chicago, Ill. 60601

> *African Folktales,* 35 mm. filmstrip, series.
>
> *Paul Bunyan, Lumber Camp Tales,* 11 min.
>
> *Miss Habisham,* 25 min., Tales from Dickens' Series.
>
> *Rolling Rice Ball* 11 min., Japanese fairy tale.
>
> *Understanding Shakespeare: His Stagecraft,* 25 min., episodes from several plays.

Doubleday Multimedia
1370 Reynolds Ave.
Santa Ana, Calif. 92705

> *International Folk Stories,* 14 min. series, 8 mm. motion cartridge.

Educational Record Sales
157 Chambers Street
New York, N.Y. 10007

> *Ozymandias,* 35 mm. filmstrip

Encyclopedia Britannica Educational Corporation
425 North Michigan
Chicago, Ill. 60611

> *Bartelby* (Herman Melville), 28 min.
>
> *Charles Dickens Christmas, A.,* 17 min., adapted from
> *Pickwick Papers.*
>
> *Cherry Orchard—Comedy or Tragedy?* 22 min.
>
> *The Lady or the Tiger?* (Frank Stockton) 16 min.
>
> *The Lottery* (Shirley Jackson), 18 min.
>
> *Macbeth: The Themes of Macbeth,* 30 min.
>
> *My Old Man* (Ernest Hemingway), 27 min.

Eye Gate House
146-01 Archer Ave.
Jamaica, N.Y. 11435

> *Folklore and Legendary Heroes,* series (Mike Fink and the River Highways, etc.),
> filmstrip and cassette.
>
> *Image Makers,* series (Jackie Robinson, Gwendolyn Brooks, Marian Anderson,
> Dr. Ralph Bunche, etc.), filmstrip and cassette.
>
> *Myths and Legends of Ancient Greece and Rome,* series, filmstrip and cassette.

Films, Inc.
1144 Wilmette Avenue
Wilmette, Ill. 60091

> *Glass,* 11 min.

Guidance Association
Subsidiary of Harcourt Brace Jovanovich
41 Washington Avenue
Pleasantville, N.Y. 10570

> *The Boy Who Could Do Anything,* Mexican folktale 35 mm. filmstrip.

Halewyn Films, Ltd.
7 King Street West
Toronto 105, Ont.

> *Unknown Citizen* (W. H. Auden), 3 min.

Imperial Film Co., Inc.
4404 South Florida Ave.
Lakewood, Fla. 33813

> *American Indian Myths,* series, 35 mm. filmstrip.

International Book Corporation
7300 Biscayne Boulevard
Miami, Fla. 33138

> *Black Leaders of Twentieth Century America,* series, 35 mm. filmstrip.
>
> *Latin American Folktales,* 35 mm. filmstrip.

Janus Films, Inc.
267 West Twenty-fifth Street
New York, N.Y. 10001

> *The 400 Blows* (Francois Truffaut), 98 min.

Learning Corporation of America
711 Fifth Avenue
New York, N.Y. 10022

> *The Rug Maker: A Folktale of Africa,* 10 min.

Line Films
P.O. Box 328

Capistrano Beach, Calif. 92672

Walt Whitman's Leaves of Grass, 21 min.

McGraw-Hill Textfilms
330 West Forty-second Street
New York, N.Y. 10036

The Days of Dylan Thomas, 21 min.

Hangman, 11 min., based on Maurice Ogden's poem.

The Legacy of Anne Frank, 29 min.

A Tale of Two Cities, 14 min.

Twenty Thousand Leagues under the Sea (Jules
Verne), 10 min.

Macmillan Audio Brandon Film Center
34 MacQuestion Parkway South
Mt. Vernon, New York 10550

The Apple Thieves, 9 min.

The Bold Dragon (Washington Irving), 15 min.

The Boor (Anton Chekhov), 15 min.

The Canterville Ghost (Oscar Wilde), 15 min.

The Cask of Amontillado (Edgar Allen Poe), 15 min.

The Critic, 5 min., animated satire.

A Fable (Poland), 7 min.

The Game, 11 min.

The Occurrence at Owl Creek Bridge (Ambrose Bierce), 27 min.

The Pardoner's Tale (Chaucer), 15 min.

A Raisin in the Sun (Lorraine Hansberry), 128 min.

The Red Balloon, 35 min.

The Signalman (Charles Dickens), 15 min.

Silent Snow, Secret Snow (Conrad Aiken), 17 min.

The Tell Tale Heart (Edgar Allen Poe), 8 min.

A Unicorn in the Garden (James Thurber's animated satire), 8 min.

The Well: A Parable, 10 min.

A Work of Art (Anton Chekhov), 9 min.

Popular Science Publishing Company
355 Lexington Avenue
New York, N.Y. 10017

An Enemy of the People (Henrik Ibsen), 35 mm. filmstrip

Pyramid Films
Box 1048
Santa Monica, Calif. 90406

Concrete Poetry, 12 min.

The Legend of Sleepy Hollow, 13 min.

The Marble, 10 min.

Paul Laurence Dunbar, 23 min.

SL Film Productions
5126 Hartwick Street
Los Angeles, Calif. 90041

The Dolls' House, 17 min., based on Katherine Mansfield's story.

Society for Visual Education, Inc.
1345 Diversey Parkway
Chicago, Ill. 60614

Mary McLeod Bethune, phono record

George Washington Carver, phono record

John Fitzgerald Kennedy, phono record

Harriet Tubman, phono record

The Reverend Dr. Martin Luther King, Jr., phono record

Sterling Educational Films
P.O. Box 8497
Universal City
Los Angeles, Calif. 91608

Casey at the Bat, 8 min.

Orpheus and Eurydice, 10 min.

Teaching Film Custodians
25 West Forty-third Street
New York, N.Y. 10036

Shaw's Pygmalion, 18 min., excerpts from 1938 film.

Troll Associates
320 Route 17
Wahwah, N.J. 07430

John Henry and His Mighty Hammer, 35 mm. filmstrip

Universal Education and Visual Arts
221 Park Avenue South
New York, N.Y. 10003

The Red Badge of Courage—A Film Prologue
(Stephen Crane), 17 min.

Weston Woods Studios
Weston Woods Street
Weston, Conn. 06880

Mike Mulligan and His Steam Shovel, 10 min.

Chapter Three

Teaching the Short Story

A study of the short story offers numerous opportunities for creative thinking, acting, discussing, and writing. Too often, however, one story after another is read by a class, with no unifying force. For example, it is common for a story to be read for its humor; however, when the class analyzes the humor, that quality is left almost completely dried up. Another story may be considered for its mood; still a third, for some undefined thing called "style." Students conclude with episodic pieces of knowledge, which add up to very little that can be labeled *significant*.

Short stories are about *ideas*. When teachers decide what ideas their students need to explore, they have at least one set of criteria by which to select stories. The ideas not only permit but encourage depth study of the stories, and, in turn, literature helps students discover some underlying principle which illuminates an aspect of life. For example, literature deals with human conflict in a vast array of its ramifications. The short story is one genre which portrays conflict.

Because students examine ideas in depth through one instance after another and because ideas are the central focus around which other aspects of the short story are considered, students have an opportunity to examine and perceive their own experiences in a new light. Their explorations of stories as well as events in their own lives furnish materials with which to create their own stories.

This chapter describes how teachers used short stories to make it possible for students to place themselves in a great variety of situations and to project the consequences of the conditions inherent in the situations. There is no limit to the broad spectrum of vicarious circumstances short stories can offer. Students can identify with people in a wide range of positions, and they can experiment vicariously with many solutions and consequences.

The Role of the Short Story in Units of Study

Almost all units of study, whether they concentrated on drama, the novel, the short story, or sometimes even poetry, were initiated with at least one short story. The short story captures students' attention because of its brevity; thus the teacher does not need to be concerned about sustaining students' attention while they are being introduced to a new idea. Because the short story is narrative, it can be the medium through which the development of concepts and the discovery of generalizations are initiated. The familiar aspect of the narrative makes it valuable to the teacher. We all engage in narrative when we relate something that happened.

Using the short story helps the teacher plan for the heterogeneity among students. For example, what is often regarded as a simple act of uncovering and retelling in sequence the events that occur in a story is an intellectual feat for some students whose lives have not been characterized by any appreciable amount of order. Students who lack such experiences need many confrontations with sequential events. The brevity and the variety of the short story offer the teacher an opportunity to stimulate further learning, for "the more new things a child has seen and the more he has heard, the more things he is interested in seeing and in hearing."[1] Thus, a study of the short story offers as much to a student who is not academically inclined as to one who is.

Stories offer limitless concrete data upon which abstractions can be built. This happens, for example, when students attempt to explain why the author's order of events must of necessity be so. The process of building abstractions involves manipulating events and arriving at cause-and-effect relationships. For example, after reading "Mother in Mannville" by Rawlings, the students list the events and then consider why it is necessary for the wood-chopping sequence to come before Jerry's revelation that his mother lives in Mannville. Students begin to see reasons for sequence of events, grasp the intricacies of cause and effect, see the relationship of events to each other and to the characters. If Jerry had not revealed his integrity in the wood-chopping sequence, the narrator might not have left her dog in his charge and the intimate chats between her and the boy might not have developed.

Another advantage to beginning with the short story is that it is conducive to the development of divergent thinking. This kind of thinking needs to be emphasized early as a goal. When a student thinks divergently, he explores all kinds of possible connections and relationships between objects and events. The author must be so sparing in his use of details that the events he does select portray a sense of a whole life. Therefore, the reader must use the author's clues to furnish for himself those events which might have preceded the action of the story and those which are likely to follow. In other words, much of life has preceded the story's opening and much will go on when it is concluded. Why did the author select this particular slice to reveal so much? Why is it so crucial in the lives of the characters? There is no correct answer; convergent thinking is not appropriate for students grappling with these problems. Motivational power also lies in the rich confrontations with the emotions offered by short stories. Brooks and Warren write, ". . . the story gives a concrete instance of the generalizations, and furthermore, it recommends the abstract generalization to us by clothing it in emotional terms."[2] Finally, the wealth of short stories available to the teacher on every cognitive as well as emotional level makes it possible to experiment with matching stories to students and with building from the simple to the complex. The generalizations being evolved can thus become modified and enriched.

Selection of Stories

The selection of short stories is important both because of the scope needed and because the sequence must be appropriate to increasing cognitive ability. Lansu attempts an analysis of three levels of short stories: The first level is illustrated by Connell's "The Most Dangerous Game" with its concentration on plot; the next level includes Richter's "Early Marriage" which emphasizes character, setting, and theme as well as plot; the third is implicit in Steinbeck's "Flight" which is highly unified and includes complexities such as symbolism and ambiguities.[3]

For many students Jackson's "The Lottery" and Mansfields' "Miss Brill" are too difficult in the beginning of the sequence; for them, Hawthorne's "The Minister's Black Veil" is impossible. Some twelfth-grade students may not be ready to handle the Hawthorne story or even "Miss Brill," despite the fact that many stories have been read and concepts explored. To push the issue is to destroy the very things for which the school aims: enjoyment of literature, development of sensitivity, and development of cognitive abilities.

This chapter will not spell out a rigid sequence of stories for a particular grade. The more teachers worked with students and with each other, the more they realized that each of their classes needed different stories for different purposes. Only those which were found fruitful for use by a number of teachers for specific groups of students will be described here. The case is well stated by Malarkey, "Literature is not a science and cannot be made rigorously sequential the way mathematics or a science or even a foreign language can."[4]

However, teachers must consider a number of factors when selecting stories and developing scope and sequence. The story must be an instance of the concept under study. This means that the concept must be inherent in the story, so that the student does not have to distort the story to draw the generalization. It also must be capable of involving students emotionally and of advancing the cognitive level of students. Therefore, it is mandatory that the narrative be within their grasp as well as interesting to them. The teacher looks for elements that permit inference making when this is the ability he wishes to emphasize; he selects the tale that contains a sequence of events that can be analyzed when he wants the students to engage in analysis.

Furthermore, students can provide teachers with leads to selection. For younger adolescents, the presentation of a concrete problem which is truly problematic results in the pouring forth of an extensive list of items with which they are concerned. Such problems can be, "What do adolescents worry about the most?" "Why don't we put a stop to crime in the streets?" "Do you think our society is concerned with the lot of the individual?"

Selection of stories is also guided by spontaneous questions that arise as the study progresses and by the gaps in knowledge and understandings that become glaringly apparent from what students say and do. For example, during a discussion of de Maupassants "The Necklace" in an advanced ninth-grade class, this comment was made: "Her husband was a sucker because he didn't realize what she was. I don't know why he loved her. She hated him and was greedy. She deserved what she got." The expression, "She deserved what she got" was frequently heard and was a manifestation of the students' limitations in present understanding.

Students should be exposed to inferior stories as well as to the superior ones. Brooks and Warren advocate this practice "in order to give the student exercise in destructive analysis and criticism."[5] The student needs experience in comparing works. There is no evidence to support the notion that if we expose the student only to the best works and if we make the study rigorous, he will choose to read superior works and shun inferior works.

Abstractions must be obvious in the first stories selected for study. For example, suppose the element of *change* is to be considered. There is some kind of change in every story. Pannwitt writes, "This principle of change is what unites character and action to effect theme. Without the change of some sort, a narrative is merely a happening and not a short story."[6] For the student who needs to play with concrete events for a long time before the abstractions are possible, the change must be relatively obvious. Still another type of abstraction related to the concept of change must also be considered. While it is true that students need an opportunity to explore whether things would happen in real life, Pannwitt's caution that the change must be credible is worth consideration. "The believability depends not on whether these things could happen in real life but also on whether they might logically be expected to happen in the world of the story as the author has presented that world to us."[7]

Since the concepts to be taught offer a critical guideline to story selection, these concepts must be inherent in the meaning of the story selected. Teachers read widely to formulate a list of stories and then shared their findings so that those recommended by each teacher were read by all the others before final evaluations were made. Then they reviewed their own findings resulting from diagnostic procedures used with their classes and made decisions about those stories most appropriate for their particular classes. Thus, they freed themselves from the selections available to them only from the anthology selected by their board of education or by a committee in their own school. They were aware that no anthology can be adequate to meet the intellectual and emotional needs of any group of students.

Concept Development: Introductory Activities

Students who have not mastered the ability to perceive and retain sequence of events cannot be expected to grapple with cause and effect successfully. Most students need opportunities to list incidents in any order at first, but this pooling must be followed by the rearrangement of events in chronological order and by a discussion of reasons for the chronological order. Fenson and Kritzner advocate the practice of summarizing stories, even on the college level, because a good summary "indicates that we have understood what we have read, have a grasp of the essential details. . . . Without such mastery of details and such understanding of the central action of the story, all other discussions and evaluation . . . is sure to be misleading and inaccurate. It will be so because in a very fundamental and special way the story is *action*—a series of events happening to the characters in the work, dramatically presented and chosen and arranged by the author so that the reader will arrive at an understanding of the significance of these events, a significance which we generally call the author's theme."[8] In the light of this relationship between the action of a story and its significance, it is surprising that many teachers do not give students an opportunity to review the story before plunging into an analysis of the theme or other elements of the work.

The eliciting of central events takes on added significance when it is realized that the process is also the first step in concept development. This step constitutes differentiating the relevant details from the masses of details in which they are embedded. There are different levels in the process of differentiation. Students must differentiate when they pool resources about events that happen in a story or about things they fear most. They also differentiate when they isolate certain expressions used by Ross in "Cemetery Path" to build up tension in the reader and to give a sense of the rising terror in Ivan. Just as the young child learns that the words *cat* and *bat* have common elements, the secondary student learns to sense the common element in "senseless gurgling noises" and "nameless horror" and "massive dread."

The process of pooling ideas about a story serves not only as an early step in concept development but also as an important aspect of sensitivity training. In the first place, students discover that what they once considered their unique concerns are also the concerns of a number of peers. They also learn that their peers are thinking about issues which have thus far not occurred to them. The realization that each student has something unique to contribute which enriches the insights and knowledge of the whole group is an important element in the development of sensitivity.

CONCEPT DEVELOPMENT: COMPARING LITERATURE AND LIFE*

These introductory activities described develop the concept of values. One short sequence will demonstrate how teachers moved within the structured concept-development routines in such a way as to permit and encourage inference making and generalizing, and to advance growth in the sensitivity areas.

One class read Shaw's "Strawberry Ice-Cream Soda" in order to consider how members of the same family can have different values and how things they do and say show what they value. Students were amazed at the clarity with which values were evident in the characters' behaviors. They were asked to observe the same phenomenon among children they knew, preferably not in their own families. Their observations became the subject of their first major written assignment. In class the discussion centered around a comparison between their findings and "Strawberry Ice-Cream Soda." Questions were asked such as, Which characters showed their values more obviously, those in real life or in the story?

It was a common experience at this point for younger adolescents to use this discussion as a chance for expressing their own feelings about sibling relationships. They made statements such as "She's like my shadow," and "I hate my younger brother. He thinks he's a privileged character." It is fruitless to force the discussion in another direction until students have had an opportunity to share problems. Out of this, the teachers can lead them to understand, without telling them, that there are values underlying their reactions. It is the story itself which can help them gain perspective about their own problems and values. At first, even with the story as a lever, they resisted surrendering their evaluation of their own experiences but did permit the story to enter in a minor way. One student commented, "I have an older brother, but in the story the older one was harder to get along with. In my house, I'll have to admit, I'm a pain in *his* neck."

*This section was written with Marlene Garnett.

The discussion began to take on a different tone when, at this point, the teacher asked the following question, which led to a consideration of values: "In what way do these two brothers behave differently?" Responses to the question were as follows:

Boy: Lawrence seems to have more control over himself. He'll say, "Take it easy. Let's not get into a fight."

Rona: They have different outlooks on life, completely. Eddie is very brave; Lawrence is very timid.

Jessie: In the beginning, Eddie tries to push him and is ashamed of him. In the end Eddie treats him like a person his own age.

The students were asked to give a number of illustrations directly from the text to show that Eddie was ashamed of Lawrence. Only then was the teacher able to elicit a perceptive response to the questions. In such a case, what are the things that are important to Eddie? What does he value? What is important to Lawrence? What does he value?

Sue: Lawrence has his place in life. He knows what he's going to do. So it doesn't matter to him whether or not he fights the other boy. To Eddie it does matter whether Lawrence will stick up for his rights.

Robert: Lawrence values his hands, because if anything happens to them his career is ruined. Eddie doesn't want his brother to be chicken because that makes *him* feel cheap.

Jeff: To my surprise my sisters sounded just like the story. One seemed to value pride; the other seemed babyish.

Certainly, the results of this progression of activities were not startling. There was still little ability on the students' parts to explore with any depth the implications of human behavior. It takes many and varied experiences to build deep insights and awarenesses. The process of looking both at life and literature helps in achieving this difficult task. When students are guided in their application of new understandings to old relationships, the teacher prompts them to take a further step forward. The new understanding gleaned from literature help them to gain new perspectives in the old real-life relationships already taken for granted.

Steinbeck's "The Peppermint Candy," in which people's values are evident in their behavior, can be compared with "Strawberry Ice-Cream Soda." The softheartedness of the salesgirl in contrast to her crude brusque outward behavior is a favorite focus of discussion. Students are able to give ample specific instances of her generosity and to translate her behavior into the values she held. One class felt "The Peppermint Candy" gave them a greater chance to handle the difficult task of translation than did "Strawberry Ice-Cream Soda." They were more certain of people's values in the Steinbeck story. In "Strawberry Ice-Cream Soda" they were not sure of their judgments. For example, they didn't know if Lawrence was just a sissy or if he really cared about his hands or if he was using his hands as an excuse for not fighting. They wanted sharply delineated answers that could be categorized as right or wrong. Despite the assets inherent in "The Peppermint Candy," which teachers decided should precede "Strawberry Ice-Cream Soda," some teachers had serious objection to using an excerpt from a novel as a short story.

Examining the Conflict

Since conflict is the foundation of the story, its nature needs to be explored. Examining the conflict and its outcome helps one to arrive at the concept of the theme; it helps bring out the nature of human dilemmas and the complexities of the human condition as portrayed by the author. The manner in which students are led to uncover the conflict is determined by the story itself. As Moffett points out, "The essence of story is once upon a time; Once. Unique and unrepeatable events. . . ."[9] The short story cannot be handled as if it were a science. Thus, the shattered illusions in Mansfield's "Miss Brill," the stripping away of every fantasy, are inherent in the succession of crises through which the author takes her and in which lie embedded the conflicts within Miss Brill. Advanced students in high school can uncover the conflicts through this stripping away and these crises.

Dividing certain short stories into three or four possible scenes is helpful in analyzing the conflicts. When students read Björnson's "The Father," they decide Thord values status and prominence. Not the baptism nor the confirmation nor the engagement of his son change his behavior. Only his son's death brings enlightenment and causes his behavior to change with the awareness that he had been using his son as he had his money to gain the coveted prestige. The very fact that students may not be in accord about where the scenes begin and end provides a framework for fruitful discussion.

Another group of stories lend themselves to examination of conflict through analysis of their titles. The teacher may suggest that students change the title for one they prefer. Through examining Stephenson's "Leiningen versus the Ants," students become aware that there were more than one level of conflict. Through their discussion of alternative titles, the students' attention moved from the simple physical struggle so evident in the story to the more complex one of the inner struggle.

Joe: The conflict was him and ants. He was out to get them. Everyone else was conquered by them and he had to stand up to them no matter what it cost him.

Elaine: He realizes at last that this is no game, that he's really fighting for his life. He envied them for their amazing organization, their complete discipline, the precision. It was more a conflict of mind than of action. He doesn't want the men to get killed because he's responsible for keeping them there. He wanted to prove to the world that it is possible to beat these ants.

Ronnie: Leiningen valued pride and bravery. He wanted to prove he was not a coward and would not run. Men have brains and are therefore better. The peons were cowardly and I would be too. I'd be scared stiff.

Charles: He valued material things—that land. It cost him years of labor. He's willing to risk the peon's lives to save his land. The peons followed him like bugs. He was the great leader.

Ronnie: He was not willing to sacrifice them. He expected some to run and he didn't blame them. He felt himself higher. He felt his mind was better than theirs.

Changing titles is an intriguing activity which helps students grasp the entirety of a conflict in a story. For Benét's "By the Waters of Babylon" students rejected peer suggestions of "The Priest's Son," "O, Dad, Poor Dad," "I Go," "My Journey," "Forbidden Journey," and "After the Atomic War," and settled for Benet's title after much discussion of the heart of the story.

The fact that dialogue helps to portray character and to bring conflict and crisis to the fore needs special attention. When a new element is to be introduced, a relatively simple piece of literature serves best. "The Test" by Gibbs lends itself easily to this task, as does Jackson's "After You, My Dear Alphonse." To focus attention on dialogue, role playing is a remarkably good starter activity, for it assists students with interpretation as well as identification. It offers an opportunity for output when this is needed for activity balance; it reinforces the role of dialogue in the development of crises; it moves learning ahead by offering an awareness of dialogue's relationship to character development.

A number of conflict situations was improvised by the students as they sought one which offered the greatest flexibility needed for portrayal of different types of personalities. Most acceptable was the situation in which the Fuller Brush man tried to unobtrusively force entry into a house to sell something to a housewife. Several improvisations around this idea were role played. In one case the oldest son of the family, hippie style, came to the door. In another, the character was a belligerent old man. The audience was asked to observe carefully and take notes, as though it was seeking material for descriptions of behavior. The teacher elicited characteristics of the persons portrayed, building toward deep enough insights to make the generalization that speech and action not only play critical roles in crises but are important clues to character. Students experimented with writing dialogue to make the Fuller Brush man come alive in a crisis. The importance of using only that dialogue which serves the purpose is by no means simple to teach. Then students were sent back to reexamine the dialogue in the appropriate previous stories read and to role play the dialogue experimenting with tone of voice and gesture and stress on selected words to bring out the intended conflict and meaning.

Comparing Conflicts in Literature and Life*

Through stories such as Heyert's "The New Kid" the teacher can encourage students to compare conflicts in literature and life. At first, students may dismiss this story with expressions of disgust and frustration. They hate it. It is unpleasant and violent. They may say, "The kid who wiped his nose on his sleeve is vulgar, and Marty is a fink." There is little if any awareness that the position of an individual in a group does determine to some extent how he thinks and feels and that the question of personal power is basic to the conflict. Bright students do become concerned with the roles of

*This section was written with Marlene Garnett.

leaders and followers as a focus of conflict. This story serves as a catalyst for discussing these roles especially when the actions of the minor characters are questioned by a student who demands peer explanation of the problem, Why should anybody stick his neck out to help others?

This story encourages comparisons with current issues such as racial conflict in our society. For an appreciable period of time 'the issue of racial conflict rather than the story becomes the focus of attention. The teacher's task is to guide students' use of insights from life and literature to help one illuminate the other. One boy used his familiarity with "The Blacks" by Genet to bring him to the threshold of understanding; now it was the teacher's task to help him cross that threshold.

> I think the white people are taking the disadvantage of the Negroes to their own advantage. There's a play called "The Blacks" that shows how Negroes hate the whites, and they are going to give them what they got from them, only harder. And there are parts of the play that make you feel real guilty. A Negro man hands a plastic flower to the woman, and it leaves the impression on the viewer that the white really doesn't accept the Negro and doesn't take anything. After you see the play, it really bothers you, it really bothers you! It's a very disturbing thing.

When the students' exploration of the racial issue reaches the point of no new returns, it is time to take a new look at the literature which propelled the discussion. The transition back to conflict in the story may require some structure which encourages students to examine the issue with new perspective. The new perspective is especially needed if the story itself has been rejected on such a superficial level as disgust. Writing often induces a cooler examination as when students are asked to select three characters in "The New Kid" and to cite the needs of each, whence they come, how they are manifested, and how they are related to the conflict.

The comparison of newspaper events with short stories can demonstrate to students the difference between the purposeful order of the short story as it exposes conflict and the coincidence of everyday life. Students see, too, that while the newspaper is real in one sense, the short story's portrayal is real in the sense of being universal. They are able to compare reality and universality when they have read a number of short stories, and can then perceive that there is a relationship between the stories and the human experience as revealed by the newspaper. Students can also match headline and short story as an aid to writing the short story. Incidentally, such purposeful use of the newspaper is superior to a unit on newspaper in which the parts of the newspaper are dissected.

As students grow in ability to react to stories intelligently, teachers are tempted to raise the level of the literary works being used. When teachers are able to analyze the story and the maturity level of students accurately, the consequences are beneficial. For example, a study of Chekov's "The Bet" proved to be a wise choice for which adequate preparation had been made. The negation of the main character's responsibility toward society was disturbing. The man-against-society conflict was so strong and dramatic in the final letter written by him that it pinpointed the conflict for the student and caused it to take on something in the nature of a crisis. There was no dearth of newspaper material to use for comparison.

When "The Minister's Black Veil" by Hawthorne was selected by tenth-grade teachers for comparing conflicts in literature with those in life, the results were far less positive. In evaluating what occurred in the classrooms their decision was that "The Great Stone Face" by Hawthorne or "How Much Land Does a Man Need?" by Tolstoi would be preferred. The reasons were as follows: There is too much complicated symbolism in "The Minister's Black Veil" that is beyond the understanding of fifteen year olds, and to have a good understanding of the story, a certain knowledge of Calvinism is necessary. A number of attempts were made to relate the story to real or vicarious experiences. Despite these efforts only about four or five students in each class were able to do so. Further evidence that the story was not appropriate for the students lay in their inability to consider questions which on other occasions before and after this one brought about excited responses.

Teachers of twelfth-grade academically gifted students met with results equally deflating when they used this story. They recognized that when a work is too difficult, there can be no real cognitive experience, no enjoyment, and no development of sensitivity. One group did appreciate the story and grasped its significance but gave it a low rating on the enjoyment scale.

Making Generalizations and Drawing Inferences

If the preparation for drawing generalizations is inadequate, students tend to overgeneralize or fail to approach the level of generalization. For example, in examining Thurber's "The Secret Life of Walter Mitty," students may make comments such as "I don't see how he could stand his wife; she was such a nag." In such case they need first to examine precisely what it is she nags about. They may categorize Walter as "milktoast" and wash their hands of him. They need to examine his specific daydreams to feel a sense of his true nobility; this new sense in turn helps them see why he feels alienated from the real world.

Helping students arrive at generalizations is one of the most difficult processes for teachers to learn. Part of the problem lies in the fact that as students of literature, teachers were told too often what opinions to hold about a work; in turn, they tell their students what they learned in college and then center the remainder of the study on finding verification for these opinions. Many teachers fear that their students will arrive at doubtful conclusions. Stafford cautions us that "literature is not at its best when presented as achieved knowledge. The temptation is to instruct, but that violates what literature offers. . . . At its best literature provides an occasion for exploring and professing."[10] Suchman concurs for a different reason; he states, "When there is a premium placed on being 'right,' there is less willingness to run the risk of arriving at 'wrong' conclusions through the independent process of inquiry."[11] If it is assumed that there is one and only one correct interpretation of a given work, then the sharing of ideas becomes unnecessary. If it is recognized that each person must respond according to his own previous experience and that the response is truly an interaction between the individual and the work, then sharing is essential.

Each piece of literature constitutes a concrete event which illustrates a principle. The student must discover that principle through manipulating concrete details which are furnished by the author. Then the student can predict the phenomena and their consequences when he meets the next short story. However, the illustrative event must be studied in its many ramifications until the student can discover the principle that lies imbedded in it. The adult must help the student gain many interpretations and many meanings for any one object, event or series of events. One of the great powers of literature lies in its amenability to a variety of interpretations and meanings. Without an opportunity to explore a variety of interpretations, the student fails to develop intellectual flexibility. Even the students' curiosity may be at stake, and his receptiveness may easily be blocked by the practice of one-right-answer routines.

Does this mean any interpretation is acceptable? Not at all. Some interpretations cannot be defended; others can be justified to some extent; still a third group are capable of being clearly sustained. Students can see this only if they explore their own ideas related to the work and compare them with other students' ideas. For example, some academically gifted junior high students tend to regard Jody in Rawlings' "Mother in Mannville" as a liar because he claims to have a living mother with whom he is acquainted. Such students ignore all but one detail, they fail to recognize his integrity. Such students are not prepared to examine works with greater social implications. They need preliminary experiences with literature and with classroom exchange of ideas. Further, teachers are confronted by the fact that comprehension is affected by past experience. We comprehend words, such "religion," "mother," "chaste," and "home," differently because our emotional associations are different. When we expose the connotation these words have for us in the arena of peer opinion, and in the context of a literary work, we expand meanings.

As the student manipulates and interprets events, situations, and characters in the story, he acquires abstractions. It is the acquisition of abstractions which ultimately helps him order his world.

LEARNING HOW TO DISCOVER MEANING*

Students need to learn *how* to discover the meaning of a story. One of the most concrete procedures is for the teacher to read the story to the climax and have students write the ending. It is through the follow-up of this activity that the teacher can help students perceive how various elements such as plot, character, and setting help determine the central idea. The teacher can start with a very short simple story such as "Cemetery Path" by Ross; the reading is cut at the point at which Ivan thrusts the sword into the ground.

When students are asked to write the ending to a story the first time, many are shocked; they seem uncertain of themselves, what to do, and what is expected. This is understandable when the fact is considered that they usually have been told the ending. Questions often follow the statement of the assignment: Do you want us to write what happened or what you think should have happened? Do you want one sentence or an entire paragraph? Why do you want us to guess? Can't you just read the end to us? The teacher's instructions consist of little more than a statement that their guesses should be based on what the story has already revealed to them. The students write

_____
*This section was written with Marlene Garnett.

their own endings, maintaining the style of the author as much as they possibly can. This is another opportunity for students to express themselves in writing. Several are able to produce remarkable results, as is evident in the following one by a ninth grader:

> The words "Ivan the Pigeon" ran through his mind.
> "I'm no longer a pigeon," he resolved.
> Suddenly, the wind broke loose with a tremendous howl, and as it whistled it chanted, "Ivan pigeon, golden pigeons, rubles, Ivan! Five gold rubles!"
> He rose only to see on the mausoleum wall the shadow of Satan! Ivan's eyes froze: the frost-biting wind pierced Ivan's eyes and they started to tear. "Five gold rubles, pigeon." His eyes blurred; he could not see clearly. The devil's cloak waved on the mausoleum. Ivan stood fast, for a new object was flying over the devil's horns, a pitchfork!
> It struck hard and the wind cried. The blood rushed into his face while to the rhythm of his heart, came the lacerating cries, "Rubles, pigeon? PIGEON, Pigeon, pigeon, pigeon."
> As the sound died out, so did Ivan's pulse. The ground sank beneath Ivan. Five gold rubles!
> The rooster crowed and the sun blazed. They came after him. Oh, they found the sword. They found Ivan too; a branch shaped like a fork cracked his skull. And the early rising sun cast a shadow of Satan. It was but a thorn bush and a gravestone forming the image. Five gold rubles!

It was through a discussion of students' endings that the teacher was able to help them uncover the idea that the author has one purpose and everything else that takes place in the story must be fitting to that purpose and must help carry it out. Students need time to feel their way into this complex idea. The following excerpts are from a ninth-grade class discussion in which students explored the purpose of "Cemetery Path."

> Sam: If Ivan felt around a little he'd have realized that the sword was holding his coat and not a ghost from the grave. He was really scared because he thought he was being pulled down by some devil or something.
>
> Jeffrey: Fears conquer rationalizations.
>
> Rubin: I think he wrote this as a weird story for people to enjoy. It wasn't a story like "Peppermint Candy" or something like that to enlighten people. He was just trying to give enjoyment to someone who wants to read a weird story.
>
> Paul: He's saying man creates his own fears. Also he's saying people have a desire to be accepted by other people.
>
> Dena: I know that for all the stories about anything about human beings, you'll find they'll usually wind up doing something to be accepted because this is just what people do and the reason they do anything. It's the reason they go on to live. I don't think that's a fair purpose to say because this is what is always present in any story about something human.
>
> Joe: It's only human to want to be accepted. Like Marilyn Monroe. She committed suicide because she wasn't accepted. You have no reason for feeling like living.

There finally evolved some kind of consensus that the purpose of the story was to demonstrate the critical value people place on belonging, although some felt the greater emphasis was on the power of fear. The class considered whether or not the author's conclusion was well supported by the events and the setting he chose. Students made statements like, "The setting is just right. A cemetery is scary." Others said, "The inn was in a desolate place and the weather was perfect for what happened." With each factor being considered, the teacher referred the class to their own endings as well as Ross's. All students were not equally perceptive. Some were so deeply attached to their own versions that they refuted the poetic justice of a cemetery. Often their attachment to their own creations gradually disintegrated as they gained new insights.

Diane: Many of us realized it had to be Ivan who died.

Paul: The lieutenant says, "If you live." It foreshadows the ending. You expect something terrible or strange.

Rubin: The idea of cemetery in the story brings the idea of death. Also his whole background foreshadows it.

Paul: If we say the purpose is "Fear plays a potent force in our lives" or "Fear conquers the rational mind," then it's good. But if we say "acceptance" is the purpose, then any place will do—a camp, where such things happen, but, of course, no deaths.

Then they evaluated the author's choice of Ivan as a character to carry out this purpose; the class found him uniquely suited. Some said, "He's such a meek timid thing. If you say 'Boo!' he'd jump." Others noted, "He was pitiful right from the start—so bowing and scraping for a morsel of attention."

A consideration of the events in the plot as well as of the importance inherent in the order of events sharpened the view of Ivan as a suitable character for the author's purpose. Students mentioned the soldiers' mocking of Ivan, Ivan's circuitous route around the cemetery, the lieutenant's challenge, and Ivan's plunging of the saber through his coat. Once the events were exposed in their proper order, the remainder of the discussion centered around the author's reasons for selecting these and arranging them in this particular order. The difficulties inherent in the task of rationalizing the sequence of events are evident from the following excerpts:

Ronnie: Several items in this list are related. He's caught in his own fears.

Alan: Because Ivan was "chicken" and "pigeon-toed" all his life, he couldn't be clearheaded in the cemetery when he needed to be.

Ken: The author makes him go all around the cemetery to show us how scared he is.

Too often, plot is taught simply as a sequence of events. When this happens, teachers lose an opportunity to involve students in inference making, for as Burgan points out, "plot concerns mainly the *causes* of action."[12] thus furnishing the materials necessary for drawing relationships involved in inference making. In this process of discovering relationships, what the narrator reveals about the action may be as important as the character's motivation.

Making students aware of the specific use of high-tension words also can help illuminate the central meaning.

Teacher: Good authors use strategic words, to indicate mood or tone of voice. Jot down the words Ross uses which build up to great tension in "Cemetery Path."

Alfred: "Unyielding," "gasping," "tugged," "gurgling," "pounded."

Teacher: How do "gasping," "gurgling," "pounding" help to build tension?

George: He's so frightened

Teacher: What people "gurgle?"

Lola: A baby. He's losing himself so much that he's acting like a baby. He has no control over himself.

Paul: "Lonely shack," "bitter winds," "moistening his lips," "echoed," "howled," "massive dread," "nameless horror." There's a type of cruel desolateness to it. The wind is cruel; it brought him to his death because it blew his coat over.

The short sequence of activities described above is virtually a universal success partly because thinking and attitudes are developed from an active rather than from a passive process.[13] As a result of active procedures, a ninth-grade class was able to work with symbols in Cather's "Paul's Case" until they could see relationships between objects and events. For example, they decided the red carnation was grandness for Paul at the beginning of the story and then became one brief wonderful moment before it wilted, like his few days in New York. Then they discussed the role of the train in the story. The comment was made that the train represents the forces of evil in the ugly world which will destroy him. Another student said, "The train represents escape. At first it took him away from the ugly part of his life; then it took him from life altogether."

This natural flow of students' thoughts to a consideration of symbols runs counter to many teachers' view that the interpretation of symbols is the highest goal for which to reach in the teaching of the short story. Examination of symbolic meanings is certainly not to be ignored, if only to strengthen the cognitive development and lend deeper appreciation and enjoyment of a story. To delve into symbols means seeing relationships and making inferences. The study of symbolism is fruitful for the development of divergent thinking because what an object, character, or event symbolizes is not specifically stated and because the study permits students to stretch the imagination. One danger is inherent in the teacher's insistence that an event or object be considered a symbol for a particular thing because such insistence cuts off creative thinking. Another danger comes with pushing students beyond their own level of preparation and beyond what can be reasonably expected of the story itself. For example, Burgan emphasizes that even though the little lamp plays a critical role in Mansfield's "The Doll's House," this does not mean that it symbolizes truth, as some are wont to believe.[14] It is most important that symbolism be discussed for what it has to offer in arriving at central meaning. This is often ignored in the teacher's enthusiasm for the study of symbols themselves. However, when symbolism is not handled with restraint, we lose the student in the process of analysis.

Contrasting Stories*

Comparison and contrast are crucial processes in cognitive development. The short stories selected should offer opportunities for these processes, and there should be additional provision for comparison with other genre. For example, a comparison of Walter Mitty and Miss Brill, the alienated ones, as well as Walter Mitty and Holden Caulfield[15] can lead to sharpened perspective. Stories for comparison are not difficult to find when the teacher is a wide reader of stories or when several teachers work together and pool their resources. Students on a search for comparative stories are the best available resource. Together, teachers and students may discover that Chekov's "The Bet," DeMaupassant's "The Little Cask," and Tolstoi's "How Much Land Does a Man Need" have subtle as well as obvious similarities.

Contrast is necessary in depth study involving the use of only a few illustrations which help the student perceive a whole idea. Otherwise, his perspective is blunted. With the precise perception born of contrast, the student's cognitive functioning is sharpened. Contrasting stories also help the student to find the central meaning of a story. As a follow-up of "Cemetery Path," a very poorly written story entitled "It Happened to Me" by Johnson was used for contrast. It centers around a teenager who is dared to cross the cemetery on a rainy night and to plunge a ruler into the ground as proof that he has been there. As one teacher read this story, students began to call out possible endings amidst general laughter at recognition of the similarity of some events. "Oh no! He's not going to stick that ruler into his coat! It can't be. No grown-up author would do that." Some students were genuinely disturbed at what they called plagiarism. Others strongly denounced the author for using such a simple style and concluded that he should go back to school to learn to write. The achievement of the teacher's purpose in having the students compare the two stories is clear in the following comments:

> Patricia: In the story there were incidents that had nothing to do with the story. For instance, his friend jumped down the steps instead of walking. Everything in the first story was related to the plot and had meaning. This just came in.

> Micky: The jumping down the steps did have significance. It helped tell the age group; I don't see college kids jumping down the stairs that way.

> Izzy: He had a purpose, but he lost it somewhere along the way when he started making it out for teenagers. He steered us all over the place and lost the mood of the thing.

"The Peppermint Candy" and "Strawberry Ice-Cream Soda" were briefly reexamined for elements that reinforced central meaning. Most students were very perceptive. They gave substantial evidence that the diner in "The Peppermint Candy" was a microcosm of human experiences and agreed with the author that this was the only possible setting. The comments of one eighth-grade class about Steinbeck's setting demonstrated their appreciation of the diner on Route 66. "On a highway you meet

---

*This section was written with Marlene Garnett.

rich and poor." "They are en route to California. It's long and lonely. In the diner there are people to break the loneliness." "Everyone seems to be en route somewhere." "It's like an oasis in the desert because there are people as well as water and food." "People are as important to Mae and Al as to the father and children." On the other hand, their view of the importance of setting in "Strawberry Ice-Cream Soda" was another thing. They felt the kind of sibling rivalry portrayed in the story could take place anywhere. They not only felt it was unnecessary to place it in the country, but it would be even more effective in the city.

Examination of sharp contrasts *within* a story itself and the role these contrasts play is also essential. For example, there are sharp contrasts in "The Jockey" by McCullers. Students are able to discover these areas of contrast: the physical appearance of the men, the food they eat, the clothes they wear, their way of speaking. The sounds, smells, and colors serve as concrete details around which to build toward the meaning. What the jockey does and says and the manner in which he does these things contrasts with the setting and illuminates the values the author delineates. Uncovering these contrasts is especially helpful when high school students find themselves battling about whether the jockey is a man of sensibilities, a man to be pitied, or a boor.

Becoming Familiar with One Author

Reading several stories by one author encourages a high level of generalization. The reader's task is to try to catch a glimpse of the author's philosophy. This concentration on one author requires considerable experience because it involves not only making high-level abstractions but also using previously gained knowledge to explain new situations.

Twelfth-grade students who selected Hemingway were able to draw a number of insightful conclusions after reading "Snows of Kilimanjaro," "The Short Happy Life of Francis Macomber," "The Killers," and "A Clean Well-Lighted Place." The students concluded that Hemingway was very preoccupied with death, failure, and despair; that to him "everything is nothing and man is nothing"; and that he is sympathetic to people who are despairingly alone against deteriorating circumstances and concerned about people trapped by life. They decided that he selects characters who are either physical or mental cripples, that he is consumed with pity for his characters, that he understands their terror, and that he can make you feel how lost and alone people can be.

One group of students in the eleventh grade became intrigued with Saki's stories and read a number of them on their own. They drew the following conclusions: Saki concentrates on the perverse; he makes wide use of animals as symbols; his endings are sudden and unexpected; his paragraphs are often short ones of a single sentence; he lets the actions of the character reveal that character instead of permitting others to reveal him. Saki seems to laugh at how unimportant human beings are when compared with how important we think we are. Human foibles are mocked; the good things about people who seem quite ordinary are stressed. He thinks we should dig more deeply to find out what a given human being is really like and not be satisfied with what he seems to be. Saki seems to like the theme "Man sometimes traps himself." His humor is dead serious.

A tenth-grade group read Salinger's stories and drew a number of hypotheses about him. From "A Perfect Day for Bananafish," "Down at the Dinghy," "Pretty Mouth and Green My Eyes" and "Just before the War with the Eskimos," they hypothesized that Salinger is concerned with the individual's inability to cope with societal forces, the individual's conflict with society, his feeling of isolation and alienation, and the discomfort of children in the adult world. They found that Salinger seems to like the theme of the misfit in society and that he represents society as an evil force. He believes, they felt, that the exceptional individual must somehow escape society to avoid being corrupted. A comparison between the conclusions drawn by these tenth, eleventh, and twelfth graders seems to produce a commentary on the elements stressed by each teacher rather than a revelation of the difference between grade levels. Regardless of whether the reader agrees with the specific conclusions drawn by students, those conclusions furnish evidence of the degree to which students were able to cull meanings and formulate concepts from a group of stories by the same author.

Applying Knowledge

The aim of learning to formulate concepts and make abstractions is their usefulness in accommodating new knowledge, predicting events and consequences, and explaining new situations. Every new story is a new situation which lends itself to prediction and analysis, thus permitting the learner to use his recently gained knowledge. Though much of the work involved in this phase of study occurs at the end of a learning sequence, many students put this cognitive ability to work on an informal basis, even in the earlier stages of the sequence. For example, when a twelfth-grade class was reading "Miss Brill" and attempting to understand the milieu in which she functioned, they called upon their earlier analysis of Cather's "Paul's Case" to assist them with the more subtle situation in "Miss Brill."

When students wrote endings to stories, they were predicting consequences. Actually, the thoughtful reader uses the same prediction process even while he reads, accumulating and evaluating clues to formulate a number of possibilities. As students come to know a particular author through the reading of several of his works, they can learn to be predictors of consequence on a much higher level than in the first stages of attempting to decide only how an author will end his story.

To achieve a high level of prediction and generalization, students need an opportunity to assume responsibility for independent analysis of ideas in stories. At first they explore stories which embody a familiar concept such as, "Within every society there is an accepted range of values." This concept in itself is a universal idea which concerns the literary man in all eras and in all places. Crises are created when the elasticity of the range is worn out or when behaviors manifested extend beyond the given range. Crises are created for an individual when human values of that individual distort his perspective. "The Necklace" involves students in this issue through such questions as, What is your most treasured possession? Do you think other people value this as much as you do? More? What conflict have you known to be impelled by the very existence of a treasured possession? What potential do treasured possessions have for creating conflict? What gives them this power?

For independent analysis, students need relatively simple stories. "Without Words" by Merrick, "The Use of Force" by Williams, and "First Confession" O'Connor are possibilities for younger adolescents; "I'm A Fool" by Anderson, "Rope" by Porter, and "The Prussian Officer" by Lawrence are suggested for the more mature students. In general, teachers gave students a list of stories from which to select those they wished to read. Many teachers offered students the freedom to ignore this list and to search for their own stories.

Assigning Rank Order

An activity which proved to be fruitful for encouraging students to use knowledge in explaining new situations was the arrangement of stories in rank order by some predetermined criterion, such as intensity of the conflict or validity of changes that took place in the story. Other criteria were the degree to which the stories would affect a whole society if every member read them, the appeal of the stories, or the greatness of the stories. Students prepared a careful defense for the order they chose; the result was ample material for group application of knowledge gained. It is not so much the ratings themselves that concern the teacher; it is the level of thinking demanded by the activity itself, which is extended by the succeeding group attempts to resolve conflicts. To fulfill the objectives of using knowledge to explain new situations and of raising levels of abstraction, teachers must be exceedingly careful not to project or reveal their own evaluations of the stories under consideration. There is nothing that can deter student thinking as effectively as a gesture of distaste or astonishment at a conclusion drawn by a student. The gesture indicates to the student that his judgment is not the same as or equal to the teacher's.

For the very first attempts at assigning rank order, most teachers chose specific stories assigned to the whole class to read and evaluate. Later they encouraged students to make their own selections. Teachers tallied the number of votes for first, second, and third rank assigned to each story and found their classes very excited, applauding, or most upset by the results of each vote. The discussion then centered around the story that provoked the most glaring student conflict. Jackson's "The Lottery" often was the catalyst. Teachers by this time were generally experienced enough to permit students to voice their reactions before pushing for analysis. Students were shocked, taken aback, had to think twice to see if what they were reading was really written, and felt it too devastating to read. As one student listened to these responses, she attacked the group with, "I don't think Shirley Jackson ever meant this as a real situation; it never really occurred, so why are we all getting excited about it?" And then came the onslaught: "She wrote it in 1947. She was commenting on the Nazi holocaust." "Sure it's not real as it was written; but an author selects incidents that say what he wants to say, what he means." "She's commenting on life as she sees it, and the picture she sees isn't pretty." "The story isn't true, but what the author is saying is true." "Unless people can examine their traditions they will die—literally as well as figuratively." "She's saying we'd better examine some of ours. We stone people to death plenty, even today, emotionally if not physically." "We still have traditions of race hatred. They flare up all over the world, and they are as devastating as this story." "She wasn't trying to tell you nicely, now be good children and look at what you are doing and believing. She knew she has to hit us over the head to make us do it. And she did."

When students wrote their defense of the rank they assigned to stories, they gave evidence that they could discover central meaning in a number of ways and on a wide range of cognitive levels. One twelfth grader wrote about the "tinsel title" of Mansfield's "The Garden Party" as compared to the story's "harsh reality." A tenth grader called "Born of Man and Woman" by Matheson a "chilling picture of mutation," described the conflict between the child and parents who tried to hide him from the world "because he is a symbol of their shame," and hypothesized that the story "reveals the values of a society which rejects extreme differences."

Assigning rank order to stories lends itself to group work and to the exposure of one's ideas to peer scrutiny. Three or four stories were assigned to the whole class, divided into panel groups with each panel being held responsible for discussing the issues in only one of the stories. The other panels served as the audience which became not only the listeners but the challengers. Actually only one panel presented the issues: The others responded during the open participation period when students were invited to question, comment, discuss, and challenge. One teacher appointed three student judges with power to veto a question from the audience if judges felt that question required little thought, was poorly phrased and unclear, or was repetitious. They sat in the rear of the room and had the privilege of being recognized immediately by the moderator. The use of judges encouraged all groups to carefully prepare questions, to select the most stimulating and to eliminate the weak questions, to base queries on the heart of the story and eliminate questions such as, When did Paul buy his new clothes? Devising questions, like assigning rank to stories, demands high-level application of previously gained knowledge.

There are problems inherent in any procedure and teachers must learn to deal with them. For example, the teacher who used the three judges commented: "There were several children who were so anxious to express their own ideas that they did not listen to what other people were saying. Also, the questions were sometimes repetitious and the judges were hesitant at first to interfere. Later, the judges took a more active part in the discussion until, by the end of the period, they were a little too anxious to criticize the questions." Such problems may be due to a setup that is too elaborate for the activity, or the students may be inexperienced or too immature to handle the responsibilities inherent in such structure. It takes time and systematic preliminary training in sensitivity to prepare students to handle such complexities. The teacher modified the procedure by having students write out questions in advance; judges then selected those to be discussed.

In a twelfth-grade class, Porter's "He" was assigned top rank as well as bottom rank in a group of stories and therefore became the subject of a heated discussion following a panel presentation. Excerpts are revealing.

Tom: This is about man's inability to love, and it makes a deep impact.

Paul: It's hypocritical love.

Paula: Where did you get that idea?

Bernadette: The most obvious thing is that the mother never refers to that boy by his Christian name. Everything she does is out of the feeling, "What will the neighbors think," not out of love.

Tom: She feels guilty about not loving him and overcompensates by telling everyone that she does love him.

Bernadette: He's the fall guy for the rest of the family. When someone else is cold, she takes the blanket from him and says he won't feel the cold. And let him get the pig; he's the strongest. Oh, yeah! And what difference does it make anyway? *He* is always capitalized. There's the Christ symbol, where man is hypocritical to Christ.

Barbara: He's the simple fool who was used by everybody and eventually crucified. After he killed the pig, he became sick and he wouldn't eat before the fast.

Marion: He had a desire to die.

Tom: It's a poverty-stricken cotton farm in a small town where everybody knows what everybody else is doing. The neighbors think the child is the product of sin, and the mother reacts to that.

Rona: The contrast is good. The farm is a symbol of home and hearth and love which this whole situation is void of.

Paula: And the farm gives a chance for many things to happen—the pig episodes, for example.

Vivian: She's so terrified that her relations will go into the kitchen and see she's put the boy there to eat. She's terrified that people will think she doesn't love this boy, which she doesn't love. Because if she did, she wouldn't have guilt feelings about what people think. They would just know she loves him.

Marion: Her whole lack of protection for her son.

Karen: I don't feel as strongly against her as the others do. Her whole situation: she's poor, and her pride. Really, the conflict is within her—between pride and love. Her pride makes her so aware of the neighbors and brings out the guilt. The pride prevents her from loving. You have to ask what even a mother could love under the circumstances. And the father: He seemed pretty inadequate in handling, not the situation with the son because you might say he was at least realistic—he could face the situation—but he wasn't the one who had the pig killed; it was the woman. They reversed the parts they played, and that shouldn't have been. That's another thing she had to cope with.

Rona: The personality of the father is in sharp contrast to the suffocating warmth of the mother. And actually she was the cold and ruthless one. He took a more accepting view of the child. I don't think he was that inadequate. He made it quite clear he would not kill that pig. His views are based in reality. She thinks of what life should be.

Karen: If he's the man of the house, he could have said, "Let's keep the boy right here." But he didn't. So why condemn the mother more than the father?

Lola: But he made no bones about it. He never said, "I love my child." It was, "He's my child; he was born; that's it; finished!"

Vivian: This was not a selfless mother. She didn't really care about the child. She kept saying, "I care, I care," but she took the blanket from him to give to another child. Why didn't she give the child her blanket? Her coat? This is not a selfless mother. She definitely wouldn't make mother of the year.

Karen: But why did she cry in the end?

Paul: She realized he was human and she was guilty.

Vivian: And she didn't turn back, either.

Karen: The author said she loved that child better than her two other children put together. The author herself makes that comment, not through the mother.

Chris: She wasn't cruel. She felt it didn't bother him to be cold. She almost felt he was a superhuman character, that he wouldn't be harmed by the pig because he had this gentleness about him.

Constance: But you know that's not so because she herself has such a fear of going after this bull.

Richard: And then she fears the situation into which she had placed him, because she does love him.

Lola: The boy didn't need the coat; he wasn't going to school. The others were. He was warm enough without it. But when he got sick, she did give him the blanket.

Vivian: When he was sick the blanket was being washed because the doctor was coming. She left him uncovered while he was sick.

Susan: She said that the blanket was being washed because she was ashamed to tell the doctor it wasn't on his bed because she had given it to another child.

Lucille: The blanket wasn't being washed. It was on the other child's bed, and she was ashamed to have the doctor know that because he'd think she was mistreating the child.

Karen: The author states without compromise that she loves the child. Guilt feelings are not out of the ordinary for a parent of a retarded child. And you have this compounded with the fact that she is an ignorant person who feels God will protect the innocent, that he is almost an animal in his strength, and nothing will hurt him. . . .

Gail: I can't find the passage where the mother takes the blanket from the boy to give to another child. I don't remember it.

Teacher: Will two or three people help look while we go on?

Vera: My question is, did she kill him in the end?

Charlene: Oh, no!

Don: She says at the end, Don't feel so bad, you don't feel so bad, do you? He seemed to be accusing her of something. This is what she feels. She knows she doesn't love him. And then she says, "Maybe he knows they were sending him away for good, and all because they were too poor to keep him."

Paul: There! The point isn't that she says she loves him; it's what's behind those words. The author says she was forever saying she loved him, more than the other two put together, and then she'd throw in her husband and her mother for good measure when she was talking to neighbors. When neighbors tell her not to let him do certain things, she almost screams at them. When others look at things she's doing objectively, this appearance of her caring turns out to be not caring. . . . And she says, "He gets enough to eat and wear, don't he. . . . "

Vivian: When the doctor leaves, she takes her blanket and puts it on his bed and puts his bed near the fire. Then she says, "They have to be cold on his account. . . . " A loving parent doesn't even think of this as a sacrifice for a sick child.

Gail: We found the blanket business. He did have one blanket. The blanket in question is an extra one which they took off because they thought he wouldn't need it.

Paul: You simply cannot take these things literally. You have to consider the tone. It's ironic —that she loved him as best she could! The general tone of the story must be considered. The author is saying, This is what we label love. The question is, Is it really love?

Vera: Besides, there's just too much evidence that she doesn't. Look at the facts: She subjects him to all kinds of dangers, she neglects him; she dresses him up and he gets dirty so she boxes him and says, "People will say I don't keep you clean."

Karen: That's perfectly normal. A normal intelligent mother would feel the same way.

Paul: You can't just say she loves her child. Something in the story must tell you that. Specifically, what leads you to that conclusion? What is the author trying to say about this human relationship?

Karen: She does wish he had never been born.

Several pieces of evidence can be gathered from the above excerpt:

1.   There is a great range of cognitive as well as sensitivity levels on which students function even at the end of a sequence of study experiences.
2.   Students are able to make use of previously gained knowledge, such as interpretation of symbols.
3.   They are willing to exchange ideas and to permit their ideas to be enriched by what their peers are able to uncover about a story.
4.   They can make some relationships between literature and life.
5.   They still have a long way to go; one sequence cannot bring results that require years of maturation.

Conducting Discussions

To help students gain satisfaction from art requires that they react to it and *examine* their response to it which in turn means exchanging ideas and sharing points of view. Reflection is a necessary ingredient. One of the huge problems teachers face is how to focus the discussion so as to enhance the enjoyment by helping students to uncover the meanings inherent in the story, people's behavior, and their own feelings. Feeling compassion for a character enhances the enjoyment of a story. Feelings of compassion are in no sense divorced from understanding.

The student imbibes human values, aspirations, and attitudes about the social order from the literary experience which includes sharing ideas. The teacher's activities are directed toward advancing social understanding, developing ways of thinking about human concerns and behavior, generating ideas, and helping students know how to use literature for the maturation of those ideas. The teacher is aware that attitudes are not changed by telling students what attitudes they should adopt.

Discussions may be diagnostic or instructional. Actually, these two purposes cannot be separated. If the primary aim of discussing the conflict in a story is diagnostic, then the questions must be open-ended. Discussions around open-eneded questions make it possible for the teacher to judge the level of concept development and the students' ability to relate cause and effect. Discussions can be used to push forward the level of abstraction; in this case, there will be a difference in the way they are conducted and in the questions which serve to focus the thinking.

Encouraging Student Writing*

Writing short stories has a number of important educational values for students. The first is enjoyment that the student experiences when he creates, expresses something that lies within, and communicates. Second, writing creates an awareness of the tremendously complex process involved in the endeavor of creating a short story; the awareness in turn results in an enriched appreciation of other works. Third is the opportunity to apply some of the understandings gained from the reading and study of the short story. Discussions of students' works are constantly interwoven with discussions of literary works for appreciation and clarification. Also, there is the benefit which accrues to cognitive development, for the student must explore a situation about which he has strong feelings and explore it in depth so that a fundamental idea comes out of it. Writing aids verbalization which is essential for optimum development of intelligence. Ausubel claims that "Even the seemingly simple act of making a choice of words in developing an idea involves complex processes of categorization, differentiation, abstraction, and generalization; the rejection of alternative possibilities; and the exclusion of less precise . . . meanings."[16]

Hiatt rejects the practice of preliminary exercises such as observing and describing a person, to gain skill in writing a short story. She claims, "The story is the first thing," though she points out that the student must be "made aware of the material for a story within himself and within the world about him. Once the wealth of material is opened up, the impulse to tell a story should be developed and not aborted by too much practicing of the scales beforehand."[17] A long training period makes the student anxious about his ability to write.

Methods of assisting students with the writing of their short stories need careful consideration. First is the task of helping students explore situations about which they have strong feelings. Reading and discussion of stories can achieve a large measure of this goal. A "secret notebook" is a valuable asset because it prevents excessive exercise assignments by the teacher and permits the student to record his notations of the world around him in his own creative manner. It should be an ongoing activity in which

*This section was written with Marlene Garnett.

students record the numerous things they see and hear, feel, and learn about people from real life, the mass media, and literature. Thus, they are engaging in daily writing that amounts to much more than mere finger exercises.

Students need opportunities to record their own observations for future use. The fact that students must record forces them to observe more acutely; the fact that they may use their observations creates high motivation. Excerpts from one boy's secret notebook will be quoted at some length in order to illustrate the thinking that went into the task and the seriousness with which the work was regarded. This same eighth-grade boy is the author of the story which appears at the end of this chapter. The reader can see the relationship between his earlier thinking and the final product.

Nov. 18 entry
From reading several short stories I have found that when people tell their problems to others, they are relieved.
People create their own fears. Fear suppresses reasoning. Men find a scapegoat for their fears. Many times men will refuse to admit their fears to others.

Nov. 19
I want a dramatic story about hate and fear. A man is painting a picture of a man, and into it he is painting all his hate. The picture is a symbol for his hate. . . . The portrait comes to life and has a great battle with the painter to the death, and the painter overcomes the painting.

Nov. 20
Setting: The turn of the century in Norway. A man's private study.
Theme: To have fears is human and natural: everybody has fears.
Purpose: I want people not to be ashamed of their fears.
Mood: Terror—tense excitement.
Characters: Klor Stober (painter) and boatman (painting).
Plot: Stober grabs his knife and stabs wildly. He is free of his fears.

Nov. 21
I'm not sure who Stober stabs. If he stabs the painting, then the painting actually does come alive for him—man vs. man. If he stabs himself, man vs. himself idea. . . . The painting is a composite of all his fears; if the painting or boatman is dead, he is free of his fears. If he stabs himself, he will die, and thus have no more problems or fears.

Nov. 22
My purpose isn't clear. It is to make people not be ashamed of their fears, for the simple reason that fear is a very part of human life; *everybody* has fears. . . .

Nov. 23
My friends still think this is not clear. . . . For this reason, I will have to continually stress the point that everybody has fears. . . .

Dec. 1
I have been told that my story represents "The Portrait of Dorian Grey" (not sure of spelling or exact title) but because of the fact that I have never heard of nor read the story before I began to lay down the basics for my story, I will write my story.

Dec. 2
A description of the characters, dress, and accessories. Stober—navy-blue chapeau. . . .

Dec. 3
Several comments have been made about my story: overdescriptive . . . why is Stober dead?
(unclear). . . .

Some students were delighted with this routine because now there was real impetus
to write a diary, which they did not have enough discipline to begin by themselves or
which they couldn't begin for a lack of focus or purpose. The teachers were delighted
because they saw students make real attempts to refine and sharpen their powers of
observation and because students devoured one short story after another, each seeking
an answer to his own specific problem of the moment.

However, there were students who wanted the teacher to tell them specifically the
things that should go into the secret notebook. Still others felt that the notebook
was not really secret because the teacher read it eventually; they felt it should be
called a cooperative notebook. Whatever the name, the activity made a deep impression:

> I also found that this notebook had become a type of diary for me. I wrote many things
> that have happened to me personally and my friends in school. Though it was difficult, I
> tried basically to give fact and reaction, not my own personal, slightly partial viewpoint.
> I assure you that it felt good to express my feelings to someone, somewhere.

Students read many stories with a wide range of content and quality. This phase of
story writing—independent reading to prepare before and during writing—offers innu-
merable opportunities for the meaningful teaching of any number of related skills and
appreciations. For example, the words and phrases which are savored and recorded are
expressions which at one time would have been passed over lightly. Now, it is meaning
that is sought, and the way the author conveys the meaning becomes important.
Students select phrases such as "lay enveloped in darkness" and "the dull panting of
the motor." Students' entries often reveal what they think they need to know; teachers
take clues from these entries to assess gaps in learning.

It is through writing their own short stories that students can learn to appreciate the
full importance of a number of factors such as repetition in the stories they read.
Mirrilees instructed professional writers on this point: "What is to impress a reader
must be repeated and re-repeated, ground into his mind by repetition. And yet each
repetition, though it must be like the rest in kernel, must differ in outer shell."[18]

Writing a short story helps students become conscious of the importance of elements
such as the setting. When students have decided on a situation about which they feel
deeply, a series of photos in different lands or in different rural or urban settings[19] can
become the focus of discussion to help them extend their view of the possibilities
inherent in their situation.

Using a series of four or five phrases that have inherent in them the possibility of
story creation is another encouraging device. Examples are

"discarded can of sardines;"
"sharp cry in the night;"
"screech of a car turning the corner on two wheels."

Once students perceive the potential in these phrases, they can begin collecting the expressions from their reading, TV, and their own informal lunchroom conversations to see who can come up with the most appealing or hair-raising ones.

Exploring endings before beginnings appeals to students, especially after the experiences they have had with creating the endings of stories read to them. Knowing how things ended helped students firm up a theme and make decisions about characters and events.

Writing activities that take place as part of the reading of short stories are often helpful in focusing students' ideas about their own short stories. For example, in connection with Sudermann's "A New Year's Eve Confession," students wrote about an event in their lives on which they could now look back with some perspective and evaluate it in a manner enriched beyond what they were able to do at the time it occurred. When teachers gave the class the same skeleton of details as those in a specific short story and asked students to construct a story around that skeleton, they were providing an experience not only in noting sequence of events but in gaining a sense of complexity of plot. Of course, this activity was followed by reading the original story and by a usually heated discussion.

A productive device for encouraging students to examine the clues they have included in their stories is for the teacher to read a short story to the class during which time students record clues as they detect them. They may not go back to pick one up after the completion of the story, because the whole purpose of this activity is to note the clues and what they achieve as the story progresses. As might be anticipated, their lists become the subject of excited interchange. Later, when students are paired for work on their own stories, they use the same device with peers who help them test their clue building for adequacy. High school teachers do not read aloud enough to students. Reading aloud has many advantages: It brings the members of the class in close emotional touch with the teacher, the author, and each other. It has high motivating power. It teaches students to listen for tone of voice of the author.

By no means should it be assumed that students are waiting all this time for the teacher to assign the writing of the story. Most students have written at least one. What the teacher and peers are helping them do is to gather more ideas and to assess the events in everyday life, so that each contact offers some new perception to bring to the creation awaiting fulfillment. Excerpts from comments by pupils in the same eighth-grade class mentioned above reveal something of what happens during this process:

Arnold: The end of my short story is very twisted. As a matter of fact, I thought about the ending first and then I built the whole short story around the ending. The theme is, "Things don't always turn out the way you want them to and fate has a hand in everything." And I can foreshadow the last event by having little things happen to him, all along the way.

Paul: When I read "The Great Stone Face" I said I didn't find much of a purpose. Then you [teacher] commented on it, and I went home and actually got the true meaning out of it. The meaning was so great . . . that I want to draw on the story. . . .

Jeffrey: I'm going to have a murder or a monster. I noticed in the candy store yesterday, a man came in and said, "I have a box of cigars stashed away for you. You can have it if you want." I put this in my notebook. I can use this in another way. I can have someone say, "I have a revolver stashed away. You can use it." You can exaggerate on all these things you see in everyday life.

Rubin: My story is the person. It's someone I know. He's the story. I've been observing him and others. It will take about twenty people to make this one. Every week I observe a different person and I write about him. Take something like fear. You have it in your secret notebook and you write it into your story.

It must be remembered that the finest lessons in the technique of writing will never create the short story. As Glickberg reminds us, there are "no authoritative texts" on how to write diction because there are "no technical secrets" to be taught.[20] Confidence-building procedures are essential. Confidence can quickly be destroyed during a creative activity simply by the way in which teachers handle correction. Authors offer teachers the best clues for correcting students' papers. For example, Mirrielees discusses the problem of "polishing." "It is usually wise to leave intensive polishing till the story is entirely on paper. In the course of writing, that much praised 'infinite capacity for taking pains' degenerates readily into mere piddling, till what the writer believes to be a struggle towards perfection becomes no more than a delaying action against the effort of further invention."[21]

Important devices that the teacher can use to encourage students' writing include the use of constructive questions or comments and the elimination of any grades from students preplans. Such procedures help create a feeling of freedom to disagree with the teacher's ideas. One such comment by a teacher written in the student's notebook and the student's reply illustrate this quality of freedom:

You have an interesting idea that you have developed carefully. One of the things we admire in art is economy of words, motion. There is something to be said for clear, sparkling images and large vocabulary, which you have attempted. It is important, however, to make sure that these analogies and descriptive words are appropriate to the context and subject matter. If they are not, other more suitable expressions should be found. Otherwise, your style becomes pompous and pretentious and loses directness and clarity.

The student wrote in response what other teachers call "sheer impertinence;" this teacher's relationship with each individual protected her and her students from any such value judgments.

There are many corrections in my short story that I do not agree with. I have encircled them. I had my reason for writing them all in. I would like to hear your reason for correcting them (after school).

Some teachers used the questioning technique as a constructive device for helping students in the process of writing their original stories. In one case, the relationship of the characters to each other was not clear. The teacher queried on a strip of paper attached to the student's work:

Is Mr. Devon fond of Durwood in the end? How does Durwood feel about him? After learning about his mother and the gifts that she buys, would Mr. Devon leave without saying good-bye—only to leave money? Is this in keeping with the story and the characters? Does this succeed in making your purpose clear to the reader?

Teachers gave help by referring students to other authors and by suggesting specific models:

> It seems that you have been influenced by the style of Hawthorne and Poe. You have attempted to use symbolism and have succeeded fairly well for a first try. You have, however, become too much involved with a style that is not really your own. . . . Perhaps this would be a good time to read some stories by Hemingway or Steinbeck to get an idea of the beauty in *simple* writing as well as that which is more ornate.

Comments, questions, and suggestions of all kinds ranging from a direct idea to a literary model may come from peers as well as from the teacher. Often students take peer criticism more seriously than they do teachers' statements. Therefore, the teacher must create a climate in which students can interact constructively. This may be done by using small groups whose function from the start towards classmates is to help, not to destroy.[22] The small group is an important aspect of sensitivity training. Students understand that by aiding each other to improve their written work, they are also making the teacher's time available to all for assistance with other aspects of the work; thus they are contributing to an atmosphere of mutual concern. They soon learn that by teaching other people and by discussing ideas with peers, they themselves benefit. Writing is a massive effort requiring all available help; many of the writers they have read once sought the assistance of knowledgeable and respected peers. Perspective is needed on our own work; it is only other human beings who can give it to us. None of us can see everything there is to see, alone and unaided.[23]

Not only can individual assistance be offered, but a workshop atmosphere takes hold. The classroom becomes a place where small groups gather to test one's ideas and to gain the attention of a respected peer. In some instances, these sessions are so stimulating that teachers have been induced to join the creative fray and to try their own hand at writing. They can be assured of a helpful and critical literary circle. Once the spirit of creativity and involvement grips the class, there is an endless demand made upon the teacher's time. If open office hours are available a few minutes before and after school, students and teacher find the contacts beneficial. To illustrate the grip of enthusiasm and involvement comes this tale from one teacher: Several religious holidays caused the absence of most students from school. Nonetheless, a number of students appeared for the block period in order not to be cheated from their time with the teacher and classmates, time that was scheduled for working on stories. Others arrived before and after school so that their attendance would not be recorded on the holidays and to prevent teachers in other classes from looking for them. It is apparent that students felt the teacher's willingness to organize his day around their needs. This willingness built a feeling of the importance of the task and a sense of students' own importance to their teacher.

There were other bits of evidence that students were experiencing a deep involvement. One homeroom teacher remarked that the only thing students talked about was the story they were writing or some activity related to it. Here was evidence that school can provide something worthwhile as a subject for students' conversation, both in and out of school. Parents were generous in their expressions of pleasure (even those who declared openly that math, science, and grammar were the only worthwhile subjects for school study); a few had become so engrossed in what their offspring were achieving that they even felt the thrill of offering an idea of their own for passing consideration. Two fathers began to join in the endeavor, but on their own terms; they wrote their own short stories and dared to subject their offerings to the critical adolescent eye.

Some will say that the greatest piece of evidence of achievement lies in the final products of the students. The importance of this is not minimized here, and one product will be presented. However, the chief purpose of this activity—the new and deeper appreciation of the art itself, the development of power to think and feel about the human condition, the examination of ideas and values with which human beings are concerned—must be kept in the forefront. The following story by a ninth-grade boy was among those that were printed in the school magazine.

THE BOATMAN

The bright beam from the large overhead lamp sliced the silent darkness of the chamber, revealing a stocky figure painting in the center. He wore a crisp, navy blue chapeau and a matching cravat and shirt. Painting vigorously, Stober forced his brush swiftly over the canvas.

Irritated, he blew his nose with a large handkerchief and quickly replaced it in his dark green pantaloons, already stained with paint from his incomplete work. In the picture was a heavyset boatman with a dark, salt-covered sweat shirt, and an old sea cap, covering thick, sun-bleached hair. His beard, sprinkled with silver, was rough and grizzly. The sneer on his face was accented by a laceration scar over his left eye. Photographic in detail the eyes followed the observer to all corners of the studio.

This was Stober's gallery; one of the many rooms of the large country house in which he displayed his well-known and unequaled collections. On the walls of the room that he occupied were several antique weapons: eight pistols, several knives, and a crossbow.

Stober was not a happy man, for he was cursed with many irrational fears. He feared the loss of his life; he feared the loss of his works; he feared the loss of his family. Possessing a talent in the arts, it was his desire to use the medium to rid himself of his fears. The painting he was working on was actually a composite of all his fears; he was painting them out, just as a child runs and kicks a can to relieve himself of his anxieties. This painting was truly the most challenging. To him, it was the most important.

Pivoting toward the canvas, he clumsily knocked his paintbrush to the floor, spattering magenta on the white tile. He frowned. Grabbing a spare chamois cloth, he dipped it into a can of turpentine, fell to his knees, and immediately began to scrub the floor free of the oil paint.

Instead of rising, he froze. Before him he saw a pair of dirty, seaweed-stained sneakers. Looking upward slowly, a figure was revealed to him. First his eyes traveled up to a pair of wet red pants to a belt with a large tarnished silver buckle, past a black sweat shirt, and finally rested on a sneering face—that of a seaman. Sun-bleached hair protruded from under a blue sea cap. Stober recoiled from the intruder. "Hello Lars," said the boatman seriously. Stober did not reply. He was frozen in panic. "It is no use," continued the boatman, "to try to rid yourself of me. Everybody has fears, Lars. To have fear is to be human. You must learn to live with me and to cope with problems." The boatman extended his large, calloused hand.

All that could be heard was the gurgle issuing from Stober's throat. His horrified eyes widened as the boatman approached and his damp hand clung desperately to the wall.

"Come Lars, come and greet me on my arrival!" The gallery echoed with the sound of the challenge.

Stober got up and stood his ground. Bravely, he charged at the boatman. The arm muscles tensed and twitched as Stober, with one sweeping blow, hurled the boatman through the air, his back suddenly smacking the wall as he landed. Fear had given Stober his strength and motivated him to take action.

He saw his weapon . . . it was on the wall not more than three feet away. But, alas, what a three feet! He tried to move but his fear held him fast as he saw the boatman approach with his hand extended again. With a defiant scream, Stober leaped for the knife, and succeeding, grabbed the deadly weapon tightly in his fist. The boatman began to run towards Stober. Leaping to his feet, Stober crazily plunged the knife's keen edge into the heavy, tough folds of the boatman—in and out, in and out—he stabbed wildly, wildly, unable to control himself. Stober felt a sudden surge of victory as the entire chateau echoed with the laughter of a madman. Certainly, he had conquered fear!

A huge crowd was gathered at the gallery the next morning, concentrated in the chamber of antique weapons. There on the floor, before a painting entirely ripped to shreds, lay Lars Stober, dead, without a mark on his body.

Teaching about Values through the Short Story

One group of teachers in charge of grades seven through twelve selected their large concepts or ideas around the topic "Values by Which Men Live." Literature deals with values, and these teachers judged their adolescents not only to be capable of examining their own values in relation to others but also very much in need of such examination in light of the changing values that were in conflict with society's values. Parents expressed little concern to these adolescents about school matters except for high grades leading to admission to colleges. Their contacts and goals were restricted. They were highly intelligent, had much potential, but were rigid in their ways of looking at life.

THE NEED FOR STUDYING VALUES

The need that students have for values is thoughtfully placed before us by Martin who discusses the "social vacuum created by an absence of shared norms and values" through which students can test their own experiences. This does not mean that the teacher should preach his values. Rather, an examination of them through the literary artist's work helps students begin a "philosophy of the quest," for "to live is to choose. . . . In some way, by certain values, we affirm life or deny it. We must begin here, and this gives us our foundation."[24]

Literature reveals men in revolt against certain societal values. Because the adolescent is in the process of rebellion against the values of authority figures, he is ready for this study. In this era of the value crisis, reflection upon values as well as behaviors through literature helps to liberate the student from those values that are detrimental to the whole society's progress. These detrimental values may be found in his own newly created subculture or in the establishment. Reflection on values gives him something tangible with which to grapple. It does not permit him merely to reject the old, leaving nothing to fill the gap. Rather, such examination gives new directions, new ideals, and goals for building his own world.

Schools have the obligation to help students view cultural standards not as something apart but in the setting of the fundamental values of society. Rosenblatt reminds us that "the individual will be liberated from blind subservience to the norms of his group, not by throwing overboard all standards, but by seeing them in relation to the whole complex of attitudes and values into which they fit."[25] We are so imbued with the values and attitudes of the society into which we are born that we take them for granted and tend not to subject them to any kind of scrutiny.

Schools have the obligation to help students perceive that though man is influenced by the society in which he is reared, he is not a helpless pawn. An individual grows and matures by interaction with his environment. He can modify that environment just as it modifies him. Interaction is a two-way process. If this were not so, there would never be any cultural change.

When students have an opportunity to study a great many varied situations and to contrast social conditions in many stories, they will not fall into the trap of settling for values that are alive in only one. They have a chance to make choices and decisions when they consider carefully the ideals of our society as against those of other societies. They can then investigate the degree to which the various societies permit people to meet those needs and to achieve the societies' values.

When a topic like "Values" is the focus of attention, it must be kept constantly in mind that the study is not a sociological or psychological one. It is the work of art that is to be considered. Though the emotions explored by the artist are examined, the exploration takes place with a focus on emotions as an element in the acquisition and expression of values. Along with this inquiry comes the examination of how the artist manipulated our emotions and managed to pull our empathy toward one character and our feelings of rejection toward another.

Summary

For all teachers who worked on the procedures described in this chapter, the experiences were new. They were learning as they taught. The usual routine for handling a short story before the group of teachers began to work together on new procedures is described by one teacher:

> Although I had taught "The Lottery" three times previously, I had approached it by reading a section with the students and then having them finish it for homework, followed by a class discussion of the text questions. That way I could keep the discussion from going on tangents . . . safe but not very lively.

In the light of this situation, the achievement of students was appreciable in terms of their cognitive and sensitivity development, appreciation of an art form, and increase in writing ability.

NOTES

1. J. McVicker Hunt, *Intelligence and Experience* (New York: The Ronald Press, 1961), p. 259.
2. Cleanth Brooks, Jr. and Robert Penn Warren, *Understanding Fiction* (New York: Appleton-Century-Crofts, 1943), p. 286.
3. Helvi Lansu, "The Shape of Literature," *English Journal* 54 (September 1965): 520.
4. Stoddard Malarkey, "Sequence and Literature: Some Considerations," *English Journal* 56 (March 1967): 394–400.
5. Brooks and Warren, p. xiii.
6. Barbara Pannwitt, *The Art of Short Fiction* (Boston: Ginn and Co., 1964), p. 25.
7. Ibid., p. 27.
8. Harry Fenson and Hildreth Kritzer, *Reading, Understanding, and Writing about Short Stories* (New York: The Free Press, 1966), pp. 6–7.
9. James Moffett, *Teaching the Universe of Discourse* (Boston: Houghton Mifflin Co., 1968), p. 121.
10. William Stafford, *Friends to This Ground* (Champaign, Ill.: National Council of Teachers of English, 1967), p. 27.
11. J. Richard Suchman, "Inquiry and Education," in *Teaching Gifted Students,* ed. James J. Gallagher (Boston: Allyn and Bacon, 1966), p. 196.
12. Mary Alice Burgan, "On Teaching Short Stories," in *On Teaching Literature,* ed. Edward B. Jenkinson and Jane Stouder Hawley (Bloomington: Indiana University Press, 1967), p. 47.
13. For other activities see Robert Whitehead, *Children's Literature: Strategies of Learning* (Englewood Cliffs, N.J.: Prentice-Hall, 1968).
14. Burgan, p. 56.
15. In J. D. Salinger, *The Catcher in the Rye* (New York: The New American Library of World Literature, 1953).
16. David P. Ausubel, *The Psychology of Meaningful Verbal Learning* (New York: Grune & Stratton, 1963), p. 148.
17. Mary Hiatt, "Teaching the Writing of a Short Story," *English Journal* 54 (December 1965): 810.
18. Edith R. Mirrielees, *Story Writing* (New York: The Viking Press, 1962), p. 32.
19. For a photo sequence with implications for story-writing material see Deborah Elkins, "Man on the Move" (New York: Franklin Watts Publishing Co., 1969).
20. Charles I. Glicksberg, *Writing the Short Story* (New York: Hendricks House, 1953), p. 19.
21. Mirrielees, p. 192.
22. Sociometric grouping makes peer assistance more acceptable.
23. Moffett explores additional ideas for encouraging students to write. See James Moffett, *A Student-Centered Language Arts Curriculum, Grades K–13: A Handbook for Teachers* (Boston: Houghton Mifflin Co., 1968), chapters 12–16.
24. Warren B. Martin, "An Answer for Anomie," *Teachers College Record* 68 (October 1966): 21–32.
25. Louise Rosenblatt, *Literature as Exploration* (New York: Appleton-Century-Crofts, 1938), p. 178.

References

Anderson, Sherwood. "I'm A Fool." In *Great Modern Short Stories,* edited by Bennett A. Cerf. New York: Random House, 1942.

Ausubel, David P. *The Psychology of Meaningful Verbal Learning.* New York: Grune & Stratton, 1963.

Bailey, Matilda, and Leavell, Ullin W., eds. *World to Explore.* New York: American Book Co., 1960.

Benét, Stephen Vincent. "By the Waters of Babylon." In *Great Short Stories,* edited by Wilbur Schramm. New York: Harcourt Brace Jovanovich, 1950.

Björnson, Björnstjerne. "The Father." In *75 Short Masterpieces: Stories from the World's Literature,* edited by Roger B. Goodman. New York: Bantam Books, 1961.

Brooks, Cleanth; Purser, John; and Warren, Robert Penn. *An Approach to Literature.* New York: Appleton-Century-Crofts, 1952.

Brooks, Cleanth, Jr., and Warren, Robert Penn. *Understanding Fiction.* New York: Appleton-Century-Crofts, 1943.

Burgan, Mary Alice. "On Teaching Short Stories," In *On Teaching Literature,* edited by Edward B. Jenkinson and Jane Stouder Hawley. Bloomington: Indiana University Press, 1967.

Cather, Willa. "Paul's Case." In *Great Modern Short Stories,* edited by Bennett A. Cerf. New York: Random House, 1942.

Chekov, Anton. "The Bet." In *Short Stories,* edited by H. C. Schweikert. New York: Harcourt Brace Jovanovich 1934.

Connell, Richard. "The Most Dangerous Game." In *Stories,* edited by Frank G. Jennings and Charles Calitri. New York: Harcourt Brace Jovanovich, 1957.

Courtright, Eugenie. "Yours Lovingly." In *Adventures in Appreciation,* edited by Luella B. Cook, H. A. Miller, and Walter Loban. New York: Harcourt Brace Jovanovich, 1947.

Daudet, Alphonse. "The Last Lesson." In *38 Short Stories: An Introductory Anthology,* edited by Michael Timko and Clinton F. Oliver. New York: Alfred A. Knopf, 1968.

Deasy, Mary. "The High Hill." *Harper's Magazine* 196 (February 1948):128–35.

DeMaupassant, Guy. "The Little Cask." *The Complete Short Stories.* Vol. I. London: Cassell & Co., 1970.

———. "The Necklace." In *Stories,* edited by Frank G. Jennings and Charles J. Calitri. New York: Harcourt Brace Jovanovich, 1957.

Elkins, Deborah. "Man on the Move." New York: Franklin Watts Publishing Co., 1969.

Fenson, Harry and Kritzer, Hildreth. *Reading, Understanding, and Writing about Short Stories.* New York: The Free Press, 1966.

Ford, Corey. "Snake Dance." In *Stories,* edited by Frank G. Jennings and Charles J. Calitri. New York: Harcourt Brace Jovanovich, 1957.

Genet, Jean. *The Blacks: A Clown Show.* New York: Grove Press, 1960.

Gibbs, Angelica. "The Test." *75 Short Masterpieces: Stories from the World's Literature.* Edited by Roger B. Goodman. New York: Bantam Books, Inc., 1961.

Glicksberg, Charles I. *Writing the Short Story.* New York: Hendricks House, 1953.

Hawthorne, Nathaniel. "The Great Stone Face." *Reading for Appreciation.* Book Two, edited by William E. Grady and Paul Klapper. New York: Charles Scribner's Sons, 1936.

———. "The Minister's Black Veil." In *Stories,* edited by Frank G. Gennings and Charles J. Calitri. New York: Harcourt Brace Jovanovich, 1957.

Hemingway, Ernest. "A Clean Well-Lighted Place." In *The Story,* edited by Mark Schorer. New York: Prentice-Hall, 1953.

———. "The Killers." In *Thirty-Eight Short Stories,* edited by Michael Timko and Clinton F. Oliver. New York: Alfred A. Knopf, 1968.

————. "The Short Happy Life of Francis Macomber." *The Short Stories of Ernest Hemingway.* New York: Charles Scribner's Sons, 1953.

————. "The Snows of Kilimanjaro." In *Great Modern Short Stories,* edited by Bennett A. Cerf. New York: Random House, 1942.

Heyert, Murray. "The New Kid." In *The Study of Literature,* edited by Edward J. Gordon. New York: Ginn and Co., 1964.

Hiatt, Mary. "Teaching the Writing of a Short Story." *English Journal* 54 (December 1965), 810–18.

Hunt, J. McVicker. *Intelligence and Experience.* New York: The Ronald Press, 1961.

Jackson, Shirley. "After You, My Dear Alphonse." *The Lottery.* New York: Avon Books, 1965.

————. "Charles." *The Lottery.* New York: Avon Books, 1965.

————. "The Lottery." *The Lottery.* New York: Avon Books, 1965.

Johnson, Harold. "It Happened to Me." In *Teen-Age Tales.* Book I, edited by Ruth Strang and Ralph Roberts. Boston: D. C. Heath & Co., 1954.

Lansu, Helvi. "The Shape of Literature." *English Journal.* 54 (September 1965). 520–24.

Lawrence, D. H. "The Prussian Officer." In *Great Modern Short Stories,* edited by Bennett A. Cerf. New York: Random House, 1942.

Malarkey, Stoddard. *"Sequence and Literature: Some Considerations"* English Journal 56 (March 1967), 394–400.

McCullers, Carson. "The Jockey." In *Fifty Years of the American Short Stories.* Vol. I, edited by William Abrahams. Garden City, N.Y.: Doubleday & Co., 1970.

Mansfield, Katherine. "The Doll's House." In *Stories,* selected by Elizabeth Bowen. New York: Alfred A. Knopf and Random House, 1956.

————. "The Garden Party." In *Stories,* selected by Elizabeth Bowen. New York: Alfred A. Knopf and Random House, 1956.

————. "Miss Brill." In *Story and Structure.* 2d ed., edited by Laurence Perrine. New York: Harcourt Brace Jovanovich, 1966.

Martin, Warren B. "An Answer for Anomie." *Teachers College Record* 68 (October 1966), 21–32.

Matheson, Richard. "Born of Man and Woman." *75 Short Masterpieces: Stories from the World's Literature,* edited by Roger B. Goodman. New York: Bantam Books, 1961.

Merrick, Elliott. "Without Words." In *Twenty Grand Short Stories,* edited by Ernestine Taggard. New York: Bantam Books, 1941.

Mirrielees, Edith R. *Story Writing.* New York: The Viking Press, 1962.

Moffett, James. *A Student-Centered Language Arts Curriculum, Grades K–13: A Handbook for Teachers.* Boston: Houghton Mifflin Co., 1968.

————. *Teaching the Universe of Discourse.* Boston: Houghton Mifflin Co., 1968.

O'Connor, Frank. "First Confession." *Points of View: An Anthology of Short Stories.* New York: The New American Library, 1966.

Pannwitt, Barbara. *The Art of Short Fiction.* Boston: Ginn and Co., 1964.

Perrine, Laurence. *Story and Structure.* New York: Harcourt Brace Jovanovich, 1966.

Porter, Katherine Anne. "Rope." In *Twenty Grand Short Stories,* edited by Ernestine Taggard. New York: Bantam Books, 1941.

Rawlings, Marjorie K. "A Mother in Mannville." In *Twenty Grand Short Stories,* edited by Ernestine Taggard. New York: Bantam Books, 1941.

Reisman, David; Glazer, Nathan; and Denney, Reuel. *The Lonely Crowd.* New York: Doubleday & Co., 1953.

Richter, Conrad. "Early Marriage." In *Out West, an Anthology of Stories,* edited by Jack Warner Shaeffer. Boston: Houghton–Mifflin Co., 1955.

Rosenblatt, Louise. *Literature as Exploration.* New York: Appleton-Century-Crofts, 1938.

Ross, Leonard Q. "Cemetery Path." In *Worlds to Explore: The Mastery of Reading,* edited by Matilda Bailey and Ullin W. Leavell. New York: American Book Co., 1951.

Saki [pseud. for H. H. Munro]. "The Easter Egg." *Humor, Horror, and the Supernatural: 22 Stories by Saki.* New York: Scholastic Book Services, 1965.

————. "Laura." *Humor, Horror, and the Supernatural: 22 Stories by Saki.* New York: Scholastic Book Services, 1965.

————. "The Open Window." *Humor, Horror, and the Supernatural: 22 Stories by Saki.* New York: Scholastic Book Services, 1965.

Salinger, J. D. *The Catcher in the Rye.* New York: The New American Library of World Literature, 1953.

————. "Down at the Dinghy." *Nine Stories by J. D. Salinger.* New York: Bantam Books, 1953.

————. "Just before the War with the Eskimos." *Nine Stories by J. D. Salinger.* New York: Bantam Books, 1953.

————. "A Perfect Day for Bananafish." *Nine Stories by J. D. Salinger.* New York: Bantam Books, 1953.

————. "Pretty Mouth and Green My Eyes." *Nine Stories by J. D. Salinger.* New York: Bantam Books, 1953.

Shaw, Irwin. "Strawberry Ice-Cream Soda." In *Adventures for Readers.* Book Two, edited by Egbert W. Nieman and Elizabeth O'Daly. New York: Harcourt Brace Jovanovich, 1958.

Stafford, William. *Friends to This Ground.* Champaign, Ill.: National Council of Teachers of English, 1967.

Steinbeck, John. "Flight." In *Understanding Literature,* edited by Elizabeth White, Joan Wofford, and Edward Gordon. New York: Ginn and Co., 1964.

————. "The Peppermint Candy." In *Worlds to Explore: The Mastery of Reading,* edited by Matilda Bailey and Ullin Leavell. New York: American Book Company, 1951.

Stephenson, Carl. "Leiningen versus the Ants." In *Pleasure in Literature,* edited by Egbert W. Nieman and George E. Salt. New York: Harcourt Brace Jovanovich, 1949.

Suchman, J. Richard. "Inquiry and Education." In *Teaching Gifted Students,* edited by James J. Gallagher. Boston: Allyn & Bacon, 1966.

Sudermann, Herman. "A New Year's Eve Confession." In *Great German Short Novels and Stories,* edited by Bennett Cerf. New York: Random House, 1933.

Taggard, Ernestine, ed. *Twenty Grand Short Stories.* New York: Bantam Books, 1963.

Thurber, James. "The Secret Life of Walter Mitty." *The Thurber Carnival.* New York: Dell Publishing Co., 1962.

Tolstoi, Leo. "How Much Land Does a Man Need?" In *A Book of Stories,* edited by Royal A. Gettmann and Bruce Harkness. New York: Holt, Rinehart & Co., 1955.

Whitehead, Robert. *Children's Literature: Strategies of Learning.* Englewood Cliffs, N.J.: Prentice-Hall, 1968.

Williams, William Carlos. "The Use of Force." In *Thirty-Eight Short Stories,* edited by Michael Timko and Clinton F. Oliver. New York: Alfred A. Knopf, 1968.

Suggested Short Stories

Blue, Cecil. "The 'Flyer'." In *The Negro Caravan,* edited by Sterling A. Brown, Arthur P. Davis, and Ulysses Lee. New York: Arno Press, 1970.

Bontemps, Arna. "A Summer Tragedy." In *American Negro Short Stories,* edited by John Henrik Clarke. New York: Hill & Wang, 1966.

Buck, Pearl S. "The Old Demon." In *Great Modern Short Stories,* edited by Bennett A. Cerf. New York: Random House, 1942.

Chinn, Laurence C. "Spelling Bee." In *Best Short Shorts,* edited by Eric Berger. New York: Scholastic Book Services, 1958.

Chute, B. J. "A Really Important Person." In *Prose and Poetry: Adventures,* edited by William J. Iverson and Agnes L. McCarthy. Syracuse: The L. W. Singer Co., 1957.

Clarke, John H. "The Boy Who Painted Christ Black." In *American Negro Short Stories,* edited by John Henrik Clarke. New York: Hill & Wang, 1966.

Collier, John. "Thus I Refute Beelzy." In *Story and Structure.* 2d ed., edited by Laurence Perrine. New York: Harcourt Brace Jovanovich, 1966.

Crane, Stephen. "The Upturned Face." In *75 Short Masterpieces: Stories from the World's Literature,* edited by Roger B. Goodman. New York: Bantam Books, 1961.

Dwyer, James F. "The Citizen." In *Reading for Appreciation.* Book 2, Part I, edited by W. E. Grady and Paul Klapper. New York: Charles Scribner's Sons, 1935.

Edmonds, Walter D. "Judge." In *Prose and Poetry for Enjoyment,* edited by J. Kenner Agnew and Agnes L. McCarthy. Syracuse: The L. W. Singer Co., 1955.

Faulkner, William. "Barn Burning." In *Stories,* edited by Frank G. Jennings and Charles J. Calitri. New York: Harcourt Brace Jovanovich, 1957.

————. "Wash." In *A Book of Stories,* edited by Royal A. Gettmann and Bruce Harkness. New York: Holt, Rinehart & Winston, 1955.

Fessier, Michael. "That's What Happened to Me." In *Prose and Poetry for Enjoyment,* edited by J. Kenner Agnew and Agnes L. McCarthy. Syracuse: The L. W. Singer Co., 1955.

Gale, Zona. "Bill's Little Girl." In *Stories,* edited by Frank G. Jennings and Charles J. Calitri. New York: Harcourt Brace Jovanovich, 1957.

Galsworthy, John. "Quality." In *Prose and Poetry of England,* edited by Delmer Rodabaugh and Agnes L. McCarthy. Syracuse: The L. W. Singer Co., 1955.

Halper, Albert. "Prelude." In *Twenty Grand Short Stories,* edited by Ernestine Taggard. New York: Bantam Books, 1963.

Hawthorne, Nathaniel. "The Birthmark." In *Understanding Fiction,* edited by Cleanth Brooks, Jr. and Robert Penn Warren. New York: Appleton-Century-Crofts, 1943.

Haycox, Ernest. "A Question of Blood." In *75 Short Masterpieces: Stories from the World's Literature,* edited by Roger B. Goodman. New York: Bantam Books, 1961.

Himes, Chester. "Mama's Missionary Money." In *American Negro Short Stories,* edited by John Henrik Clarke. New York: Hill & Wang, 1966.

Jackson, Shirley. "The Witch." *The Lottery.* New York: Avon Books, 1965.

Jacobs, W. W. "The Monkey's Paw." In *Understanding Literature,* edited by Elizabeth White, Joan Wofford, and Edward Gordon. New York: Ginn and Co., 1964.

Jones, Paul. "The Shanahan Strad." In *Best Short Shorts,* edited by Eric Berger. New York: Scholastic Book Services, 1958.

Kjelgaard, Jim. "Code of the Underworld." In *Best Short Shorts,* edited by Eric Berger. New York: Scholastic Book Services, 1958.

Kleihauer, Lois D. "The Cub." In *Best Short Shorts,* edited by Eric Berger. New York: Scholastic Book Services, 1958.

Lardner, Ring. "Haircut." In *Stories,* edited by Frank G. Jennings and Charles J. Calitri. New York: Harcourt Brace Jovanovich, 1957.

———. "I Can't Breathe." In *Twenty Grand Short Stories,* edited by Ernestine Taggard. New York: Bantam Books, 1963.

McNeely, Marian H. "The Horse." In *Best-Liked Literature.* Book 3, edited by Angela M. Broening, A. Laura McGregor, Leonard V. Koos, and Grayson N. Kefauver. New York: Ginn and Co., 1947.

Maltz, Albert. "Afternoon in the Jungle." In *Modern American Short Stories,* edited by Bennett Cerf. Cleveland: The World Publishing Company, 1945.

O'Flaherty, Liam. "The Sniper." In *75 Short Masterpieces: Stories from the World's Literature,* edited by Roger B. Goodman. New York: Bantam Books, 1961.

O. Henry. "After Twenty Years." In *Stories,* edited by Frank G. Jennings and Charles J. Calitri. New York: Harcourt Brace Jovanovich, 1957.

———. "The Last Leaf." In *Adventures for Readers.* Book 2, edited by Egbert W. Nieman and Elizabeth C. O'Daly. New York: Harcourt Brace Jovanovich, 1958.

Parker, Dorothy. "The Standard of Living." In *75 Short Masterpieces: Stories from the World's Literature,* edited by Roger B. Goodman. New York: Bantam Books, 1961.

Porter, Katherine Anne. "He." *The Collected Stories of Katherine Anne Porter.* New York: Harcourt Brace Jovanovich, 1966.

Reynolds, Quentin. "A Secret for Two." In *Prose and Poetry for Appreciation,* edited by Elizabeth F. Ansorge, Harriet M. Lucas, Raymond F. McCoy, and Donald M. Tower. Syracuse: The L. W. Singer Company, 1942.

Salinger, Jerome D. "Uncle Wiggily in Connecticut." *Nine Stories by J. D. Salinger,* New York: Bantam Books, 1971.

Saroyan, William. "The Shepherd's Daughter." In *75 Short Masterpieces: Stories from the World's Literature,* edited by Roger B. Goodman. New York: Bantam Books, 1961.

——— "The Stolen Bicycle." *The Man with the Heart in the Highlands and Other Stories,* New York: Dell Publishing Co., 1968.

Steinbeck, John. "Over the Hill." In *75 Short Masterpieces: Stories from the World's Literature,* edited by Roger B. Goodman. New York: Bantam Books, 1961.

Stephenson, Carl "By the Waters of Babylon." In *Great Short Stories,* edited by Wilbur Schramm. New York: Harcourt Brace Jovanovich, 1950.

Stevenson, Robert Louis. "Markheim." In *Prose and Poetry of England,* edited by Delmer Rodabaugh and Agnes L. McCarthy. Syracuse: The L. W. Singer Co., 1955.

Stuart, Jesse. "Split Cherry Tree." In *Twenty Grand Short Stories,* edited by Ernestine Taggard. New York: Bantam Books, 1963.

Updike, John. "Should Wizard Hit Mommy?" *Pigeon Feathers and Other Stories.* Greenwich, Conn.: Fawcett Publications, 1962.

Vonnegut, Kurt, Jr. "D. P." *Welcome to the Monkey House,* Dell Publishing Co., 1972.

Vontver, May. "The Kiskis." *Adventures for Readers.* Book Two, edited by Jacob M. Ross, Mary R. Bowman, and Egbert W. Nieman. New York: Harcourt Brace Jovanovich, 1947.

Wood, Frances Gilchrist. "Turkey Red." *American Short Stories,* edited by Lewis G. Sterner. New York: Globe Book Co., 1966.

Yerby, Frank. "The Homecoming." In *American Negro Short Stories,* edited by John Henrik Clarke. New York: Hill & Wang, 1966.

Chapter Four

Teaching the Novel

. . . in a novel there is always a clock.
E. M. Forster

Because both the novel and short story are narrative forms, the earlier study of the short story should have prepared the ground for the novel. However, the differences between the two genre are great. Just sheer length is the most obvious difference. Because the novel stresses change, time is a critical ingredient. In this genre, the author's purposes may be manifold rather than single and character development is much more complex. The novel permits the reader to view the main character in a wide variety of situations and experiences. Hale reiterates the importance of time and society in the novel and concludes that it "preserves the illusion of life as it really happened" while the short story has a tempo which "is not that of real life but that of inner decision: the tempo of crisis."[1] Plot is more intricate in the novel than in the short story. As Forster points out, causality is given emphasis in plot—this to differentiate it from mere tale.[2] Plot offers new opportunities for students to explore cause and consequence and to become aware of relationships not previously known to them. When we add to these opportunities for exploration the fact that there are main theme and various minor themes woven into the novel, it can be seen that the task of uncovering the meaning is broad in scope.

Developmentally, the adolescent is ready to enjoy the novel if he makes contact with the appropriate works. As mentioned in an earlier chapter, his thinking is different from the child's. He has entered the stage of formal operations which means, among other things, that he can deal with the realm of possibility. The ability to deal with the possible is especially important to the study of the novel because of the novel's intricate network of relationships including characterization, themes and subthemes, plot and subplot; its viewpoints and motivations for behavior; its web of opposing forces and conflicts; its host of meanings; and its design. The more complex the relationships, the wider is the range of possibilities. The reader who is ready for the novel makes hypotheses continuously as he pursues the author's unfolding of character and events. He makes predictions and revises them as he progresses through the work and gains new facts and insights. His manipulation of possibilities is influenced by innuendos, by the covert as well as the overt, and by his own ability to observe the "multiplicity of possible links." In the words of Inhelder and Piaget, he can "select the combinations which occur from the total number of possibilities." He is able to "make use of a combinatorial system"[3] so essential to comprehending the complex novel.

The adolescent's recognition of the multiplicity of possible links means that he is able to select appropriate factors from the many available to him and to eliminate inappropriate ones. Inhelder and Piaget explain that "unless he tries to select the combinations which occur from the total number of possibilities, the subject would not feel the need to go beyond the empirically occurring associations to separate out the variables. Rather, he would be limited to accumulating new associations." The younger child can accumulate new associations, but he cannot use a combinatorial system; he cannot *multiply* those associations, a process which is required in using a combinatorial system.

Because of its elaborate structure, the novel offers tremendous opportunities for cognitive development and for the development of social sensitivity. The multiplicity of motifs, for example, is inherently rich in possibilities for concept development, if the teacher is aware that abstractions require a solid concrete base.

When a teacher asks, "What events in this story stand out in your mind?" and students pool their recollections until a composite list is formulated, they are engaging in a differentiating process and preparing the data for combinatorial functions. The same data is needed for building generalizations. As is true of formulating concepts, generalizing implies pulling together concrete events and includes rendering reasons for particular events and shaping a generalization or inference. When several novels are selected around a common issue, or theme, or problem, generalizing can become a high-level function. For example, literature deals with the insistent problems of the generation gap. If the class is comparing the role of adults in the lives of the young as portrayed in Golding's *Lord of the Flies,* Knowles' *A Separate Peace* and Salinger's *Catcher In The Rye,* it is essential that students examine the events in which the adults do participate in each novel. When reasons are given for certain selected events and for adult roles in them, students can compare, contrast, and then make inferences or generalizations about the roles of adults in relation to the maturation process of adolescents. As one teacher noted, "The three novels seem to state that communication and real understanding between the generations are not easily achieved."[4] In the three novels mentioned above, the sharp contrast offered by the literature dealing with the problem of relationships between generations permits students to perceive the complexity of the problem and to study it in depth. Hypothesizing about possibilities is a crucial aspect of depth study.

In this chapter, systematic suggestions for exploring the novel will be offered. Teachers need to be prepared for the demise of many time-honored methods. For example, teachers traditionally spend too much time on aspects such as the point at which the climax is reached. This point is relatively insignificant, and school time needs to be spent on far more germane issues. Hunt puts it sharply: "If by climax you mean the point where the reader's pulsebeat and respiration was fastest, then where it appeared is a medical question. But what produced that emotional climax is important. What hopes met what fears?"[5]

The teaching of the novel can be divided into two major parts which permit and encourage the systematic development of concepts and divergent thinking as well as generalizations and productive transfer of knowledge. The first part consists of a series of experiences which constitute the initial reading. These activities are geared to mustering the concrete events necessary for concept development. They are systematic; each is a natural outgrowth of the previous one; most offer opportunities for divergent thinking and for rotating the assimilation and accommodation tasks. The second part consists of a series of activities, quite different in nature and purpose, because it is assumed the novel has been read in its entirety. Now the emphasis is on generalizing as well as extending divergent thinking with opportunities for interpreting data, making inferences, transforming events to ideas, comparing and contrasting events and discriminating between the relevant and irrelevant events. It is at this point that the combinatorial functions can be performed optimally.

Usually, teachers who have not been introduced to alternatives handle the novel by assigning specific chapters to be read independently or requiring that the whole novel be read by a specific date. They give one or more quizzes to ascertain whether the student has completed the assignment or in some cases to assess the student's level of understanding. Class time is spent talking about the chapters read, with the teacher doing most of the talking or asking questions which often require one-word answers. There is little to commend this process. For most students it holds no motivational power for reading, instills no energy for learning, and offers little in the way of systematic experiences with comparison and contrast. The process fails to take advantage of the literary work's power to perform its roles as a sensitizing agent and transformer of events into ideas and fails to recognize the fact that the novel has been selected by the teacher and imposed on students regardless of their interests or abilities. Thus, there is a need to explore at least a few of the processes which will enrich the teaching of the novel.

Selection of the Novel

For junior high school students especially, and also for most high school students, it must be kept in mind that when the school impels them to read a novel which has been selected for them and when they have no decision-making power in that selection, the students and the teacher begin the study with two strikes against them. Since it is highly unlikely that the students' interests and levels of sensitivity are identical, the enjoyment of the novel by many of them is in jeopardy. Certain compensatory situations must take place if any novel is to be read by a whole class.

First of all, if the teacher selects the earlier novels, he should choose short ones. There do exist good short novels, which permit highly complex activities without the danger of the reading and the discussions becoming toilsome. The activities described in this chapter are as suitable for short novels as for long ones. Further, a short novel permits the teacher to help students uncover with relative rapidity certain truths in the work. The reinforcement of knowledge gained from the short novel can be achieved as the student reads a longer work which he selects. Thus, when the class is discussing dramatic moments in Steinbeck's *The Pearl* those students who finish reading the book and begin a book of their own choice can bring enrichment to the discussion. It must be remembered, too, that schools have to recognize the continuing lure of TV which offers programs that can be completed in one sitting. A book that students can read in two hours or so can be an equal competitor. Later, when students have formed the habit of picking up a good book, the teacher need not be concerned about length. The precise time when students form this habit is a purely individual matter. It may already be a part of the student's life when he enters grade seven; it may not yet be attained at the conclusion of grade twelve. The fact remains, however, that the development of the "love of reading" is clearly a high-priority aim of the literature teacher.

The earlier books selected might profitably contain concrete incidents which take place at a relatively fast pace. Again, students who have been reared on the speedy diet of TV are not geared for the slow winding pace of some novels. The teacher's aim is to make the students aware of the richer aspects of those novels, but to begin at a point far beyond the level attained by the student achieves nothing but frustration. The school must have the time permitted by the short novel to help students sense, feel, and perceive the richness of the artist's work as it is read.

Teachers should not neglect to consider "teen-age" novels such as those by Tunis, Jordan, Cavanna, Daly, Felsen, Stolz, Sherburne, Blume, Hinton, Hamilton, and Summers. These books serve an invaluable purpose for the adolescent who is not prepared to reach great literary heights and for the more intellectually inclined student who needs time to relax with reading. It is fascinating that some literary men have long recognized the importance of common and current publications. Chesterton explored their value in an essay entitled "A Defense of Penny Dreadfuls." One of the strangest examples of the degree to which ordinary life is undervalued is the example of popular literature, the vast mass of which we contentedly describe as vulgar. The boy's novelette may be ignorant in a literary sense . . . but it is not vulgar intrinsically—it is the actual centre of a million flaming imaginations.[6] . . . "Ordinary men will always be sentimentalists: for a sentimentalist is simply a man who has feelings and does not trouble to invent a new way of expressing them. These common and current publications have nothing essentially evil about them. They express the sanguine and heroic truisms on which civilization is built; for it is clear that unless civilization is built on truisms, it is not built at all."[7]

Opinions differ over the use of the junior novel and literature for the adolescent. Rouse puts in "a few words not only in defense of trash, but in praise of it." He praises "cheap fiction, the kind of thing your high-school English considered unfit for frivolous young minds in need of serious fare." He maintains "that popular fiction has more value and usefulness in the typical high-school classroom than the books generally taught there." The classics taught are often not the best of the author's works (e.g. *Ivanhoe* and *Silas Marner*). He classifies as *good* "that book which gives the student a meaningful emotional experience." Rouse chastises teachers for selecting books which "satisfy their own needs and not those of the students." Included among the teachers' needs are "academic respectability" and "the need to keep students at a distance." A book which deals with students' "discomforting questions" and "unsatisfied yearnings" would loosen the barriers. Teachers fear that loosening, according to Rouse.[8] Jennings, who feels the teen-age novel is an improvement over *The Rover Boys,* nonetheless finds such novels are trivial. Yet, he reminds us that "the readers of *The Rover Boys* have gone into the world, died on some of the battlefields, grown old enough to have teen-age children themselves, and have even learned to vote the cautious slate."[9] Burton believes "the junior novel has come of age" and performs a significant "transition function" to the adult novel. It does this by "illuminating the *now*" and permitting relatively easy identification with characters. He admits, "The great majority do lack literary attributes; the great majority do present a gumdrop, pastel world. But there are the true artists among the junior novelists." Further, "The fact that young people find naturally in the junior novel immediate rewards is vitally important, regardless of the quality of the genre. Unless students have come to the realization that the reading of imaginative literature *can* be rewarding, the serious *teaching* of literature will be plowing in sterile acres."[10]

The Initial Reading

It cannot be mentioned too many times that literature is primarily for enjoyment, and activities geared to the development of cognitive functions and sensitivity can enhance enjoyment. One of the chief causes of student complaint is the seeming endlessness of the study of a particular work. When the initial reading of the novel is dragged out over a long period of time, the wholeness of the work is destroyed for the student, momentum is lost, and stimulation for reading it is dimmed.

How can the student read every word and not have the novel drag? The expression, "read every word," needs analysis. In the first place, when a reader is gripped by a story, he permits his eye to scan across the lines. In the second place, one role of the teacher is to read to students certain critical parts in order to highlight those events, to give all students a common focus, and to permit the events and ideas in the novel to increase the momentum of involvement. In the third place, some students profit from reading every page and chapter; others benefit more from concentrating on particular ones, learning about the ones that presented difficult problems to them from comments of the group. One role of group discussion is to share experiences and findings. None of us brings the same background, feelings, and sensitivities to any novel; therefore, none of us can come away from any novel with the identical reactions and perceptions. A student who has missed a chapter can still contribute acute perceptions about events and characters in other chapters.

In the activities which follow, note that each step teaches another aspect of the novel while it assists the student in getting through the first reading. There is much to be taught about a novel, and permitting the student to learn by involving him in a relevant activity is generally superior to having the teacher lecture about a particular aspect under consideration. Although a number of the excerpts of class discussions in this chapter are centered around the same novel, this does not mean that any one class engaged in all of these activities. The excerpts are taken from a number of different classes. It is assumed that the teachers carefully planned the concepts to be taught so that these were guiding forces in all activities during and following the reading of the novel.

CONSIDERING THE TITLE

When the teacher introduces a novel, he need not say anything about the book. When the students have all received their copies, the teacher may write on the board, "Do you like that title?" or "How do you think you'll like this book just from the title? Don't open the book." The procedure may continue in the following manner: The teacher, without saying a word, hands the chalk to a student and sits down in a student's chair. The student usually goes to the board; on the other hand, he may refuse the chalk and sit dumbly. There may be dead silence as the student writes; in other cases, there may be restless undertones of "What's up?" The student writes, "The book looks stupid," and hands the chalk to the teacher or another student who indicates he wants it. The teacher may write "Why?" under the first student's comment or he may write nothing and simply give the chalk to another student. Soon there is a silent "discussion" with students reacting in writing for all to see.

What students have engaged in thus far is a form of pooling events and reactions. However, it is much more than that. It is a valuable sensitizing experience. Through this activity, students perceive how peers regard themselves and the world much more readily than through talk alone. After this experience, they tend to listen to each other more carefully and to interpret in greater depth what their peers say. More than that, they approach the actual reading of the book with greater curiosity as well as awareness, since they possess a wealth of reactions.

Teachers must not fear silence. We often dread awkward silence because we feel it is due to our inadequacy that students haven't been stimulated to talk. Silence can be comforting and comfortable, a refreshing interlude in the world of talk. Teachers and students need to learn to appreciate silence in a society and era that bombards us with noise. The silent activity described above helps make silence more acceptable. It is an essential ingredient for learning to think, but it need not spell a void. Silence needs to be a period in which much is taking place.

As usual in any group situation some responses are more relevant than others. The teacher accepts all responses and leaves them on the board. The teacher picks up clues from some comments to write questions or additional comments. For example, although the teacher has asked for reactions to the title, some students write about the format of the book, its cover, the size, the weight. The teacher can make beneficial use of such remarks. He writes, "Would you rather read another kind of book?" It must be remembered that the purpose of this kind of lesson is not to drive home a particular point. Rather, it is to open up curiosity about the book, to stimulate reading, and to motivate. Students usually request that it be done again and even suggest on-the-spot situations for which they consider it appropriate.[11]

MAKING HYPOTHESES

Leaving all comments on the board, the teacher reads the first chapter; some students may follow in their books, others just listen. Depending on the book, he may read more or less than the first chapter. The important thing is that he read to a point at which students are highly involved. That point must be far enough into the novel to offer sufficient data so that the students can entertain some preliminary hypotheses. Sometimes the nature of the novel and the class' abilities and interests demand that the first chapter or two be omitted; in such cases, the teacher's reading begins with a later chapter. With many novels, there is nothing sacred about beginning at the beginning. For example, W. Somerset Maugham in his introduction to *Of Human Bondage* wrote:

> A novel is not like a fugue, for instance, which if you cut, say, twenty bars from it, would be rendered meaningless, nor like the picture in which one element balances another to complete the composition. A novel is a very loose form of art. You can do almost anything with it. It is also a very imperfect form of art. . . . A writer is a fool if he thinks that every word he writes is sacrosanct and that his work will be ruined if a comma is omitted or a semicolon misplaced.[12]

To involve students, the teacher must do the initial reading. A recording of a professional actor's performance cannot serve the same function, nor is this a time for sight reading on the part of the students. The intimacy that only the teacher's reading can bring about between himself, the students, and the novel is essential at all times in the teaching of literature read in common, but it is even more so in the initial stages of the reading of a long work. The teacher's art of helping students become involved in the novel rather than assigning them a certain number of pages or chapters to read partly compensates for the students' having to read books that they did not select.

In general, teachers are sensitive to the point at which students become involved. Often, this point coincides with one which is suitable for the kind of hypothesizing inherent in the question, Given the situation thus far elaborated by the author, what are the possible outcomes? The fact that students must defend their hypotheses sets up a process uniquely suited for the development of cognitive functioning. Students are required to use data when they predict consequences, to uncover relationships between various events and people in order to make those predictions, and to perceive a multiplicity of possibilities. For example, after reading the first chapter of Steinbeck's *The Red Pony,* students in grade seven postulated ten possible hypotheses. Each student wrote a defense of the one he felt most plausible. The teacher supported the students' attempts with the comforting instructions to make the defense only from the facts presented thus far in the reading.

> Jody and the horse will run away. I believe this because he is forgetting his chores and they say they'll give him away so I think he doesn't do his chores and he runs with the horse because he's afraid they'll give him away.
>
> I believe that Gabilan will become ill in some way or another. Jody, being very attached to him, will be very brokenhearted. He will worry and he might even become ill. Of course, in the end Gabilan will become well again and Jody will be happy once more.
>
> I think Jody will mature greatly. His great admiration and thrill of having a pet has already shown its effects. The boy already has been working with exhilaration on the pony. . . .
>
> I think that the horse will run away, get sick, or get hurt. It would not die (in such stories it never dies) but almost die by natural causes.
>
> I think the horse will try to save Jody in some way and get hurt doing it.*

*Excerpts contributed by Alice Fritch Stollman.

In their first experiences with this kind of activity, students rarely offer a real defense for their hypotheses. Yet, they do demonstrate a degree of sensitivity to certain innuendos in the novelette. For example, two or three of the students feared the consequences of Jody's showing off before his peers. Steinbeck says Jody "felt the superiority of the horseman" and permits Jody to teach his peers what he has just learned from Billy Buck. The students sensed the mutual love and respect of the boy and the pony.

Few wrote irrelevant hypotheses, though a number gave as their defense the fact that "That's what usually happens in this kind of story." However, the teacher felt the difficulty lay with the fact that she did not read far enough; students had too few clues with which to work.

In the brief discussion which follows, the teacher focuses upon the clues offered by the author. Students learn the important fact that an author plants specific clues in particular places for definite reasons. These clues are critical in forcing us to make hypotheses as we proceed through the novel. At the same time, the teacher focuses on the feelings of the characters as well as those of the students.

INDEPENDENT ASSIGNMENTS*

Now the teacher faces the problem of the first independent assignment in connection with the novel. How much shall he expect of the students? Only some guiding principles can be set forth in answer to this question. First, the abilities and interests of the students as individuals determine what shall be expected; second, the novel's difficulty is a factor; and third, flexibility is essential since this is not a self-selected novel, though the genuine interest of many students may have already been captured.

One way to achieve flexibility and to recognize individuality is to open up decision-making power to the students. An assignment which builds on what has been taught during class time might be as follows: Read on until you come to a part in the novel which makes you want to change your hypothesis. State your new hypothesis and defend it. On the other hand, as you read, you may decide that the new events strengthen your hypothesis or give it a new twist. If so, defend that position.

At first, many English teachers object to such a "permissive" assignment. What are the problems as teachers view them? "Some students will read two pages and quit because they find something to change or to substantiate their hypothesis." "Other students will read the whole book and say, 'I knew it all the time," and they'll give away the ending to the others." "If he finishes the book the first day, what homework does he get?" Once teachers become interested in trying new ways to solve old problems, they conclude the following:

Many more of my students do *some* reading.

When they come to class the next day, the excitement of those who did read and did discover something new is catching.

---

*This section and the following two were written with Alice Fritch Stollman.

What is done the next day in the class follows naturally. Students discuss the changes they made and cite specifics from the novel to defend their new position. Students are interested in peer reactions and in comparing notes about judgments made, consequences predicted, clues detected, and clues previously unnoticed. New admiration grows for the student who exposes a clue which slipped by his peers.

When students in one ninth grade were making hypotheses about the events in *The Member of the Wedding* by McCullers, several changed their hypotheses after continuing the reading independently:

> At first I said that she'll change and be like the others, but she was jealous and she felt left out and she wanted to belong to all these clubs.

> Well, my first hypothesis was that Frankie would try to get revenge on the world because up to about page fifteen it describes her as being very withdrawn and lonely and jealous. But on page forty-three I changed my hypothesis because it says she finally admits that she has love for someone and she wants to live with her brother and his wife. And I wrote that no longer would she have to take revenge on the world.

Other students found reason to bear with their original hypothesis.

There are always unforeseen outcomes of the assignment upon which the teacher can help build new understandings. For example, one student's hypothesis of *The Red Pony* consisted of "Jody grows up with his colt and they love each other and go on adventures together." To this, another student blurted, "You can't write a book about only that. There has to be something more to it." There are a number of things to be done at this point: The teacher needs to uphold any student's right to maintain his own tentative hypothesis as long as he can defend it. What clues did this student use? Second, the teacher has in the student's encounter a ready-made opportunity to encourage students to discover as they read some ingredients, such as conflict, of a novel. What is the "something more to it?" Third, at some later point there needs to be a consideration of the ways in which those things we wish would happen can block our evaluation of what does happen.

Usually, there are several students who finish a book in one sitting, especially if it is a short one like *The Red Pony* or *The Pearl.* They have no ongoing hypotheses to write and defend. These students can now begin to grapple with trying to find out why the novel did not end as they thought it should. They can play the role of devil's advocate during the class discussion of student hypotheses, without revealing the ending. They can delve into shorter pieces of literature which will help illuminate some of the elements of the novel in question. For example, Steinbeck's "Flight" is a good choice, when *The Pearl* has been read.

THE DRAMATIC MOMENT

Another activity that is appropriate for the initial reading is the discovery of dramatic moments in the novel and the examination of their role. It is often the dramatic moments in life which help to sensitize us to the feelings of other people, an awareness of our own needs, and the universality of human conflict and emotions. An eighth grader related the following during a discussion of Forbes' *Mama's Bank Account* in which students were exploring whether everyone at one time or other had taken something not belonging to him.

> I stole dolls' shoes from the five-and-dime store when I was little. I don't know why I took them; they just looked so beautiful. And I hid them in the cellar so my mother wouldn't see. Well, she found them one day. And she screamed and screamed. And really, I didn't know what stealing was until then. Her excitement, her horror . . . I was frightened at her reaction.

Dramatic moments are inherent in the novel. They illuminate the characters, conflicts, motifs, and the relationship of characters to events. Within these moments are critical clues to the novelist's meaning.

By no means should the teacher offer a definition of "dramatic moment." Rather, a definition evolves from experiences with several such moments. The teacher reads to a dramatic event, picking up from a point at which the discussion of hypotheses was centered. This centering is usually an indication that most students have read at least to this point. It does not matter that some have gone beyond or that they have already read to the dramatic moment in question. The teacher is engaging them in a new experience with the material. Nor should there be too much concern about the few who have not read to the part where the teacher begins. From the preceding discussion, they should have gained a sense of what has occurred. There will be at least one student, in all likelihood, who will now be stimulated enough to catch up with what he feels he missed. Questions like, Who did what in this incident? and Why? become the center of interest in the discussion. The who-did-what sequence is concrete and prepares students for the more abstract question, What makes this incident dramatic? The specific responses are compiled and kept for future use.

Then the students are ready for their next independent assignment: Read until they come to an even more dramatic moment than the one read by the teacher. They must be prepared to defend the relative dramatic merits through discussion and enactment. The prospect of enactment usually causes the reading to take on a more profound quality. Students who agree upon a particular dramatic moment can form a group and portray the incident. This portrayal serves as the focal point of discussion to analyze reasons for considering that moment more or less dramatic than the one read the previous day or the ones selected by other students. The original list of ingredients of a dramatic moment are reexamined and modified or enlarged. By the time this process is completed, students have evolved their own working definition of a dramatic moment. Because there is rarely universal agreement about the most dramatic moment in any one section of a novel, the resolution of differences presents vast opportunities for creative rereading, thinking, and sharing ideas. Finding dramatic moments and comparing them makes demands upon thinking powers; comparing requires awareness and reflection upon what has happened up to a given point including the effect of these events upon the characters.

The question usually arises: Is dialogue necessary in a dramatic moment? After considerable exploration of specific incidents, students discover that this is not a basic criterion. For example, in *The Red Pony* there is Jody's desperate destructiveness when he kills and mutilates a little bird. On the other hand, there is dialogue in Jody's attempt to protect Gitano from Carl Tiflin's rejection and in Gitano's stealing of Old Easter with whom he disappears never to return, both to die in the land of their birth.

Anything can happen as a consequence of an enactment of a dramatic event. One ninth grade reenacted the scene from *The Member of the Wedding* between the monkey man and the soldier. The discussion moved away from the ingredients of a dramatic moment and centered on content which concerned students:

Nancy: Where do you get the idea that the monkey man was Italian? Where did you get it?

Bob: The organ grinder is almost always Italian.

Teacher: In the book does it specifically mention that he is Italian?

Jack: I don't think so.

Teacher: Let's check (she gives them time for this).

Here is a student-initiated opportunity to consider the motifs of the novel, which will be discussed later in more detail. Does the novelist seem to be concerned with the ethnic backgrounds of people? What evidence is there? It is also an occasion for a consideration of stereotypes, the various ones held by each member of the class, and of the ways in which stereotyping affects our behavior. Does anyone in the novel give evidence of stereotyped thinking? What is the effect upon him and others?

In a variety of ways, teachers can use the dramatic moment to help students appreciate some of the subtleties of character portrayal. For example, students may be asked to convert the dramatic moment to dialogue, if it is one which lends itself to this. One teacher worked with the class on the knife-throwing episode in *The Member of the Wedding*.

Teacher: What other directions can you give to Berenice? Do you want to give her more stage directions?

Robin: Well, she can have a teasing look in her eyes and an expression on her face that is like making fun of Frankie.

Jack: She started tapping her foot like to a tempo.

Cheryl: She talks faster and faster and tension mounts.

Concentrating on the concrete act of devising appropriate stage directions furnishes the basic material with which abstractions about character can be made. The dramatic events are among those they will transform to ideas.

CHANGES IN MAIN CHARACTER

A third means of enriching the initial reading is to fasten attention on changes that take place in the main character. The novelist has greater opportunity than the short story writer to explore change, and in many novels it is a critical force of which students must be made aware. They also need to examine the appropriateness of that character transformation; relationship between cause and effect is intrinsic and has much to do with the quality of the novel, that is, its greatness or its mediocrity. What caused the transformation of the character? Is the cause adequate? Is the change appropriate? Again, the teacher begins this exploration by reading a portion of the novel to a point where some change in the main character is evident. Before students can evaluate the changes, it is usually necessary to review with them the behaviors of the character as they first were introduced to him. This review sets the transitions in perspective.

One of the difficult problems teachers must conquer in developing a concept of characterization is the tendency to ask questions such as, What kind of person is Billy Buck? Students' tendency is to come up with a string of adjectives which are generalizations often unsupported. Rather, there must be a systematic search for what Billy Buck does and says and what others do and say to and about him before generalizations are warranted. Such a search is essential for at least three reasons:

1. To teach students the stuff of which personality is made.

2. To avoid the superficial answers academically bright students especially are wont to give without very deep thought.

3. To get all specifics out in the open so that when generalizations are made, there is a common understanding about what they mean.

The following excerpt is from a discussion in which students examined Frankie's behavior for evidences of change:

Nancy: "Frankie" sounds awfully immature and babyish. The new name sounded more sophisticated.

Vivian: "Frankie" is a boyish name too. She was a tomboy.

Carol: When you mature, it sort of comes naturally. But for Frankie, she didn't mature naturally. She had to put on an air.

Steven: Some of the girls she used to hate and yell at them. Now she doesn't yell anymore hoping they might accept her.

Denise: Berenice tells her to try to act grown-up. And now she's wearing a dress.

Diane: She took a cigarette and before that she'd have slapped her hand. So, Berenice is regarding her differently.

Marc: Frankie put something in her ear but not all the way, so she could hear Berenice's words. And I started to think about it. It shows she's not as close minded as she used to be. She's getting ready to listen to Berenice and to take her advice.

Robin: On page ninety-five it says the old Frankie would never have submitted to love, and here F. Jasmine was nodding at what Berenice was saying.

Bennett: She throws her costumes on the shelf and hangs up her wedding dress. She's throwing away her play clothes, her childhood.

Mickey: She becomes neat. She used to throw things around and now she's putting everything in its place.

Marie: But even with the dress on she was the same underneath—dirty. And her elbows have a yellow crust.

Robert: She still insists on leaving home; she doesn't want to stay with her family.

Howard: She says to Berenice, 'Hush up your old mouth.' She's still mean mouthed.

Kitty: She has the same type of material appreciation. When you enter into the adolescent stage, you begin to think more about emotional things and more deeply about all kinds of things. She's still thinking about cars and motorcycles.

Iris: When John Henry and Berenice are concerned about the death of Uncle Charles, she's still thinking about the wedding; that was the only thing in her life.

Kenneth: She says, "If not, I'll kill myself." She's still childish. She wants to go along and tag along. That's childish, threatening because you can't get your own way.

Teacher: Are these changes reasonable? Did something provoke them?

Jane: The wedding started the change because she began to act nice.

Mitchell: The soldier had something to do with it also, because when he asked her for a date, she felt grown-up and was thrilled and wanted to act nice for him.

Jack: Berenice. She kept trying to convince her to stop being a baby. She kept antagonizing her.

Roy: How about the club members when they called her a freak.

Eddie: When Uncle Charles died, it made her think of herself. She was afraid of nothingness.

Jack: It was more Ludy, the ex-husband of Berenice. Even though she never saw him, she still really saw and liked him better because Berenice was always talking about him. That's what made her understand death more, not just Uncle Charles. Berenice was close to Ludy. She realized that if a person is very close to you and they die, it's very bad.

To help students perceive change, it is often necessary to give specific aids. Questions can assist. For example, in Part Two of *The Red Pony* Jody refuses to leave the barn when Billy Buck orders him out. The question, Would Jody have reacted this way when we first met him? offers an opportunity to explore change as manifested in a particular event. When students can perceive specific concrete changes such as the one implicit in the question, they are later able to grasp the more subtle transformation. They can make the leap from Jody as "only a little boy, ten years old who obeyed his father without questions of any kind" to a Jody whose concerns began to be sharpened in the direction of other human beings.

Often it is helpful for students to rank order events that caused a change in Jody to determine whether the causes of change are adequate. Rank order procedure was described in the previous chapter. Through this means, such events as the death of Gabilan are examined for far-reaching effect. The death of Gabilan made Jody aware of forces beyond man and compelled him to see the fallibility of man, even of Billy Buck.

Students read on independently, this time until they find a crucial change in the main character. They are charged with the responsibility of being able to account for the change. Since they will not all select the same incident which portrays a transformation, there is usually an opportunity for comparison: Which situation chosen reflects the most critical change? Which change has the most justifiable causes?

It is fruitful in a study of maturation changes to compare ways in which minor characters are more or less mature than the main character. Students perceive that maturation is not a steady process, that it is accompanied by evidences of regression, and that no one matures equally in all respects. In one class students formed small groups to consider each character in *The Member of the Wedding* and to compare him with Frankie.

Kitty: We said John Henry is mature, but with some immature points. On page 136, he said, "They put old Frankie out of the wedding." He's teasing. But he should leave her alone. But later he says, "Don't cry. We'll have a good time tonight." That's mature. His physical appearance deceives his intellectual mind and his emotions. Even though he's only six years old, he's a thimble of wisdom and maturity. He's alone but he's not feeling alone. He's not sad or moody about staying by himself. Frankie is.

Marc: When she's going to meet the soldier and she tells John Henry to go home and he doesn't question her that much because he knows, he knows that she wants to be alone for some reason. It's maturity to be able to leave a person alone. It shows insight into that person.

Selecting a crucial event that caused the change and preparing to dramatize it is an alternative activity. In this case, the specific change is known and the emphasis is on the causes. Alternating emphasis on consequence and cause helps to implant the relationship between the two. At this point watching the performance of a child on TV can be useful. What events are important in the life of this child? What guesses would students predict about his behavior as an adult? What makes them think so? Can anything happen to break the chain of events that seem inevitable? While half the class watches the performance of a child, the other half may study carefully the behaviors of an adult on TV. They imagine what he might have done and said as a child and how others behaved toward him; then they give justification for their hypotheses.

It is beneficial to have adolescents evaluate at least two children's books for the changes inherent in the characters. Does the author portray change? If so, is it reasonable or is it unrealistic? In either case, which seems to be the better piece of literature? If a group of thirty students evaluate a total of sixty books, they can develop some cognitively high-level generalizations, and students can see the kinds of materials on which young children are being nourished. This is a highly popular activity about which students become excited. Some might argue that this activity carries the concentration away from the novel. Not necessarily. Rather, it can reinforce one of the most critical aspects of the novel. It is during this session that the teacher introduces the notion of examining books. The intense part of the evaluation and discussion may come later. The reading and evaluation of children's books sharpens the concept because the contrasts are so great not only between the young child's books themselves but also when compared with novels adolescents are reading.[13]

Activities such as those described in this section help students perceive what Bentley stressed about the novel. The novelist is "able to compress longer stretches of time, vaster stretches of space, into his work than any other kind of artist," and "his dual command of the specific and the integrated enables him to present *change,* change either slow or rapid, with an ease and power no other art form possesses."[14]

CREATING CHAPTER TITLES

When students are asked to entitle a critical chapter or to change the title if they think such modification is appropriate, they are alerted to the significance of titles. They must get at the central meaning of events in order to create a significant title. When the group has the opportunity to share their titles and their defense of them, they engage in an intellectual battle to determine which one is nearest to the heart of the novelist's meaning. Further, they learn that in the final analysis, the ultimate judgment must be delayed until the entire novel is read. It is difficult to hold judgment in abeyance, especially after a battle has been fought long and won hard. This is another activity, then, which carries over into the reexamination period. When eighth graders were asked to write titles for certain sections of *The Pearl* and to justify their selection, they presented titles and arguments such as:

"The Song of Evil"
  It foreshadows danger.
"The Conspiracy"
  There seems to be a plot against the family.
"Blessed or Cursed?"
  The pearl holds the promise of so much good and yet the result is tragedy.
"Cheated"
  Kino was being cheated and he was even cheating himself and his family.

By engaging students in a variety of activities during the initial reading, they learn much about the novel as a genre. They gather insights about the plot, the characters, and human emotions, specifically and in general. They learn how to read novels and what to look for. They gain a sense of how certain factors are interrelated and what significance lies in these interrelationships. Most of all, they enjoy literature and begin to think about the larger issues of life, as is evident in an eighth grader's response:

> I think that Steinbeck believes there never can be an ideal world. In his stories he shows the evil in people and by this I feel that he believes all people have some evil in themselves and will never be changed. In *The Pearl,* Steinbeck shows the evil in many people. For instance, the pearl buyers who tried to swindle Kino and even Kino himself showed his evil when he practically went mad to get the money for the pearl.
>
> Although I feel that Steinbeck believes there can never be an ideal world, I think he believes some small changes for the better can be made.

The Reexamination

The reexamination begins when the reading of the novel is completed. Now the students can react to the totality, emotionally and intellectually. At this point, the emotional response is first in importance. There is a kind of release brought about by the act of completion. If interest was sustained in the novel, there is usually a need for students to share responses with peers and teacher. These reactions provide the teacher with material which helps guide future action.

Following are excerpts from twelfth graders' reactions immediately after reading *The Red Pony*. Most students read it in one evening. It is fascinating to note the range of interests, sensitivity indicators, and the particular events to which individual students responded.

Renee: I didn't like *The Red Pony*. It was just about growing up. There wasn't enough action or drama for me. It took me long to get through it, because I couldn't maintain interest.

Sarah: I rated it higher than *The Pearl*. It has everything that life is all about in this short novel, including the birth of the colt and the death of the horse.

Marilyn: I found myself clutching my neck while I was reading—when Buck killed Nellie to get the colt out. It had a very great effect on me.

Sharon: It went from the old to the young in its four sections. It ranged the gamut of emotions from birth to death. I was very involved and couldn't put it down.

Winifred: *The Pearl* is more contrived. *The Red Pony* is much more real. I like the boy coming at odds with Billy because of the death of the pony. We all do this and get angry for things we can't help.

Sarah: That was part of the boy's growing up. He had to realize Billy is not omnipotent.

Susan: I like the fact that there wasn't only one story line. Not every experience in life is connected.

Ann: I saw a great similarity between his father and the one in *The Learning Tree*. . . . Men are taught to suppress their emotions to such an extent that they have a great deal of difficulty expressing love to the child because they associate love, tenderness, understanding with femininity.

Mary: But Billy was able to understand, and he was a male adult. . . . Was the title applied originally only to the first part? I was trying to see how those parts were related.

Sarah: The point is other adults sometimes understand us more than mothers and fathers do.

Marlene: The mother does understand; she understands the lemonade situation, for example, and when he doesn't do his chores once.

Sarah: But even she doesn't react overtly. She, too, doesn't like to show much of her emotions. She holds herself back.

Marlene: Whether she shows it or not is irrelevant, as long as it's brought across to him.

Marlene: When Jody killed the sparrow, Carl could feel the meanness in the boy. And Jody knew his father sensed his meanness. There's a relationship between the boy and his father there.

After such an open-ended discussion the teacher can follow one of a number of possible courses. He may pick up clues thrown out by students, clues such as the effect of sex roles taught by a society, the relationship between Jody and his father, the relationship among the four parts of the novel, and the changes that take place in Jody.

REVIEWING INDEPENDENTLY FORMULATED HYPOTHESES

There may have been sufficient enthusiasm generated about hypothesis making to consider at this point the hypotheses students formulated as they read the novel. For this consideration they need to examine the original hypothesis in light of the full novel. What were the questions raised by the novelist in the beginning of the book? How did he resolve the problems or answer the questions? In what ways did his progress (or regress) along the way toward resolution affect the hypothesis? Students now need an opportunity to discuss and/or write how they would have resolved those questions given those same major clues of the novelist. Discussion of basic meaning and intent can only be initiated here. Strategies for the discovery of these ideas will be discussed later in this chapter. Considering possible resolutions is of prime importance because the process requires a searching new view of the novel and offers opportunity to discover and consider concepts inherent in it. The discussion exposes to students their own values about life which can be shared and thus influenced. Also, the activity demands comparison and contrast, identification of relevant factors, and interpretation of the novelist's data. It encourages the making of sharp relationships between cause and effect, and it expands the ability to engage in divergent thinking.

REEXAMINING CHAPTER TITLES

Another opportunity for reexamination lies in the previously made but tentative titles of a crucial chapter. Recall that the teacher forced students to hold in abeyance the final judgment until the full novel was read. Students demand in many instances that they now reconsider the title proposed. Excerpts from a ninth-grade discussion of the book title *The Red Pony* follow:

Jimmy: I don't think the title was unified too good. If the pony's gonna die in the first chapter it doesn't have anything else about it in the rest of the book. It is the main part of the book but the book should have a different title.

Teacher: Would anyone like to comment on that? Robin.

Robin: Well I think that he's wrong because the red pony kept on going on in his mind for the rest of the book, like he used to sit under the trees and think about the pony. He always wanted a new pony and like it helped him bring up new experiences but he still kept it in his mind and that's why I think it's a unified creation.

Steven: Well I agree with what Robin said. The red pony even though it wasn't alive all through the book, its name and thoughts appeared.

Leonard: I disagree with Jimmy because actually that is the main idea. It shows that he's first starting to change when he gets the red pony and he's starting to face reality and it's showing that all of this is leading up to that.

Paul: Just because this change started is like saying that a boy starts changing and growing up as soon as he steps into the middle of the street, so he's supposed to have a book named *Middle of the Street* just because he started changing in the middle of the street. I agree with Jimmy. I agree with Jimmy because I don't think it should be named *The Red Pony*. I think it should be something like *Jody* because it's about Jody.

Ellen: I agree with Jimmy. I think that after the pony died that he didn't think about the pony anymore because he was too enthused about the colt. If you read the book, I don't think you'll find anything about him thinking about the red pony after the first book.

Whether students reach consensus or whether they arrive at conclusions that coincide with the teacher's are irrelevant factors. It is the process that matters.

Interpreting Meaning

Every literature teacher must eventually cope with the problem of various interpretations of the meaning of the novel. Which one is nearest to the intent of the author? How does a teacher handle his own biases about meaning when they conflict with students'? How can the teacher help students see that everyone brings his own biases to a piece of literature and that literature is a catalyst for examining them? How can students become aware that even the author's conscious intention may have been something less than—or more than—the final outcome? How can the teacher help the group make some decision about author's intent so that ultimately they come to understand that "any old interpretation" may be unwarranted? Schuster cautions, "If any interpretation is as good as any other, why bother to think? What is to prevent me from projecting my own set of problems and solutions on to every book I read? A student ought to yield himself to a book. He is not likely to do so if he carries with him the complacent notion that any interpretation is as good as any other."[15] Brooks takes a strong stand on the controversial issue of author's intention: "The formalist critic . . . assumes that the relevant part of the author's intention is what he got actually into his work; that is, he assumes that the author's intention *as realized* is the 'intention' that counts, not necessarily what he was conscious of trying to do, or what he now remembers he was then trying to do."[16]

One excellent example of the need for teaching students how to find the key to the author's intent lies in the extremely different interpretations critics offer of the two main characters in Knowles' *A Separate Peace*. Greiling[17] sees Phineas as having a "love of excellence," respecting others, incapable of hatred, delighting in giving pleasure to others, needing no rules to keep him good, and being incapable of hatred. Gene, she feels, is morally ugly, lacking in the humanity necessary to make the generous response to others. Yet, she does recognize there is goodness in Gene. On the other hand, Devine[18] regards Phineas as the villain. Phinny is not only an idler but a German spy; his name indicates "something fishy;" he burned the Greek classic with a furtive Nazi code on it; he "lulls the students of Devon into believing that there really is no war;"

he is deceitfully clever and decadent rich. As for Gene, he is a healthy, hard-working, all-American boy. He is a war hero because he impairs the effectiveness of a spy. Such extreme positions point up the need for caution on the part of the teacher who may feel inclined to play the role of the all-knowing interpreter.

Almost every novel used in the high schools has had its share of devastating criticism as well as unrestrained praise. Pelletier's reaction to Crane's *The Red Badge of Courage* is a good example.

> I became convinced that his diction, rather than advance, virtually impeded his high-minded theme of a youth's slow farewell to innocence and sudden plunge into experience ... there is throughout not only a touch of the poet but also a touch of the phony. .... If *Red Badge* does not blind the reader with its lush colors, if its smoke does not gag him, then the pulverizing blare of noises will deafen him."[19]

How can teachers help students engage in the process of finding keys to meaning? Students can learn some relatively simple aspects of structure as a consequence of attempting to deal with the problem of interpretation. By structure I mean something quite different from the usual classifications such as climax and dénouement. Rather, by structure I mean the keys to the novelist intention.

REPETITION OF MAJOR EVENTS

For example, one such key is the repeated *set* of happenings or events so closely related that the set constitutes one episodic thread even though it may run through the entire book. The situation is of such great moment that it appears repeatedly. The events which occurred as a consequence of Billy Buck's relationship to Jody constitute such an episode. It was Billy who told him that the red spot in the egg yolk would not hurt him, that it was "only a sign the rooster leaves;" it was Billy who explained (p. 11) how Jody's father bought the red pony, who offered to make a hair rope, who denied him the right to ride Gabilan to school but gave him the reason for such denial, who told Jody "a great many things about horses" (p. 15), and "gave him riding instructions over and over" (p. 19). It was Billy who was capable of making mistakes and yet could feel "bad about his mistakes," who let Jody take part in the highly emotional task of trying to save the life of Gabilan, and "held him tightly to calm his shaking" (p. 35). Billy on occasion "agreed with Jody's father" (p. 39) but defended the right of a beast of burden "to rest after they worked all their life" (p. 45); he defended the "old *paisanos*" (p. 48), yet expressed understanding of Carl's situation. It was he who warned Jody that he'll "get awful tired waiting" for Nellie's colt to be born (p. 57) but assured Jody that he could be present at the birth of Nellie's colt (p. 62).

Billy saved the colt and "laid it in the straw at Jody's feet" (p. 72), but he also struck out verbally at Jody when his own emotions were too much for him (p. 73). It was Billy whom he saw at work and who reminded him to ask his father for permission to do certain things (p. 75). When students gather together all these events, they are able to examine them for their relationship to each other and thus evolve central meaning; such sequences become the handles by which they can grasp the author's intention.

Once students have reexamined the novel for such repetitions and interrelationships, they gain a whole new perspective, for now they have much data with which to think and new foci around which to discuss interpretations and author's intention. Students learn that the judgments they make can have and must have a basis in the novel itself and that there are ways of discovering these bases. They become aware that any interpretation is not defensible merely because "I think so" and "That's my opinion." Thought requires making connections between given facts and arriving at conclusions beyond those data, but with serious consideration of them.

PROMINENT POSITIONS IN THE NOVEL

A second key which can unlock the author's intention and which adds enrichment to the study of the novel is an examination of the content that appears in decisive and prominent positions of the novel. For example, beginnings and endings of chapters are important; this is likewise true of the first and last chapters of the book or of sections of the book.

In *The Red Pony,* the very first sentence and paragraph give Billy Buck an impressive position and introduce him as a man with "contemplative eyes." No sooner does he emerge from the bunkhouse than he is seen "talking quietly" to the horses "all the time" he is currying them. When the red pony is given to Jody, the episode ends with Billy Buck explaining how he was purchased, getting a saddle for him, helping Jody name him, and sending him off to school without the pony. Part I, "The Gift," concludes with the last paragraph devoted to Billy Buck's response to Jody's father when the father tries to explain that the buzzard was not responsible for the pony's death.

> It was Billy Buck who was angry. He had lifted Jody in his arms, and had turned to carry him home. But he turned back on Carl Tiflin. " 'Course he knows it," Billy said furiously, "Jesus Christ! Man, can't you see how he'd feel about it?"

The second part, "The Great Mountains," and the third part, "The Promise," do not open with Billy Buck but rather with revealing descriptions of Jody's behavior. The author's intent is not merely to make a character study of Billy, but rather to reveal the growing up of a boy. Nor do these parts conclude with Billy, but rather with Jody: "He covered his eyes with his crossed arms and lay there a long time, and he was full of a nameless sorrow." And at the end of Part III, Jody's thoughts are of Billy. Part IV once more makes its beginning with a picture of Billy Buck working on the ranch but ends with a new perspective on Jody's level of maturation.

The Member of the Wedding opens with Frankie's overwhelming sense of disconnectedness and concludes with her triumph over alienation. In the beginning she is at ease with John Henry who symbolizes her stage of childhood, but at the close of Part II, she is uncomfortable with him, for she is leaving the world of childhood.

MOTIFS

Another key is the discovery of themes or motifs. When teachers ask students to find *themes* before they seek *a* theme, they are encouraging divergent thinking. For example, when reading *The Red Pony* one ninth-grade class found faith and disillusionment as one motif because "Jody has faith that Billy Buck can cure Gabilan" and "Billy Buck trusts himself but loses his faith when he fails to save Gabilan and must kill Nellie and realizes Jody's reaction to him." Further, "Gitano has trust enough in other human beings to make the long trip so he can die near his old home but is quickly rebuffed by Carl."

A second motif students are able to find is life and death. Gabilan dies, Nellie dies, the new colt is born, Old Easter and Gitano go off into the mountains to die, spring is born, violence kills all kinds of living things. There are the vulture, the black cypress where the pigs are killed, the destruction of the thrush, and the mice. A third motif is revolt. Billy Buck's name smacks of it, as do Jody's dreams. Gabilan revolts; and Gitano, old and facing death, makes a last gesture of revolt.

People's dreams are still another motif. Langston Hugh's "Dreams" can be compared here. There are Jody's dream of leadership, Billy's of infallibility, and grandfather's of westering. The mountains are there to enrich dreams. "For if dreams die/ Life is a broken-winged bird/ that cannot fly,"[20] whether those dreams be Jody's, grandfather's, or the people for whom Langston Hughs speaks. Students think Carl Tiflin is a harsh character until they realize even he has a dream.

In *The Member of the Wedding* the motif of belonging is strong and all-pervasive. Frankie is a "member of nothing in the world"; she is "unjoined" and very frightened. Escape is another motif here—escape from home, alienation, confusion that lies within her. Incompleteness is still a third movement in the novel. So many people and events are unfinished: Honey Brown, the octave of the piano tuner, the bridge game with the missing cards, Frankie herself and her relationships with the outside world.

All the motifs cited here were discovered by students themselves.

Uncovering Motifs.   How are motifs discovered? Often a motif can be unearthed by examining the recurring use of one word or one image, such as in Santiago's dream in Hemingway's *The Old Man and the Sea* or the letter *A* in Hawthorne's *The Scarlet Letter,* or by the repeated use of an object such as the conch in Golding's *Lord of the Flies* or the various animals in Steinbeck's *The Pearl.* All of these images or objects hold multiple or ambiguous meanings and offer opportunity for exercising divergent thinking to expose those meanings. Alerting students to repetitions of all kinds helps to make them aware of the significant underlying meanings of the novel.

The unfinished music in *The Member of the Wedding* repeats itself and stresses the agitation and turmoil into which Frankie is thrust. It also emphasizes that her awareness of herself is in no way finished or complete. The music is lost, as is Frankie. As in *The Pearl,* the music makes a sweeping change, simultaneous with Frankie's going out to connect with the town and repeatedly to inform that world of the miracle of the imminent wedding. The music changes again when her calloused elbows clash with the satin garment for the wedding. In the background there are snatches of notes made by piano tuning that break in upon the ear.

EXPLORING SYMBOLISM

The study of symbolism can be a part of the discovery of motifs. It should be studied for its own contribution, for it originally did have a real function in the creation of the novel. The letter *A* in *The Scarlet Letter* so artistically embroidered with "flourishes of gold thread" has many implications. Why did Hester adorn it thus? In what spirit?

Did the spirit match the branding for which it was intended? In Golding's *Lord of the Flies* there are Piggy's glasses, the conch, and the fire to be examined for their symbolic intent. There are other symbols, too, but by no means should the teacher attempt to exhaust the study of every symbol to be found in any novel.

Students cannot be expected to make the kind of analysis that is sometimes achieved by a scholar. For example, Morris quotes Steinbeck: " 'Kino awakened in the near dark.' " Then he adds that Kino's society "is in the dark or the near dark intellectually, politically, theologically, and sociologically. But the third sentence tells us that the roosters have been crowing for some time, and we are to understand that Kino has heard the cock of progress crow."[21] To push interpretation of symbols beyond the students' level of comprehension is to defeat the purpose of the study. They can only conclude that there is some great mystery behind all of this which they can never hope to unravel. However, arriving at the author's intent with the aid of symbols helps students understand the specific buildup he used to achieve his goal. For example, the characters must be built to fit the goal. Nagle illustrates: "If Kino is to be hunted, trapped, and physically defeated like an animal by the novel's end, then Steinbeck must bring out Kino's animal characteristic throughout the entire novel."[22] Kino acts impulsively, as do animals. He "glides," snarls, bares his teeth, "hisses" at Juana, kills a man; then he runs "for the high place, as nearly all animals do" when pursued.

Often the teacher must give specific aids for the understanding of a symbol. For example, the cypress tree in *The Red Pony* is such a case. Students need to examine and record with the teacher precisely what happened before and after each memtion of the cypress tree. At other times, a direct question is appropriate: Why did Steinbeck put the mountains so prominently into his novel? Students react:

> Barbara: On page thirty-eight, Jody's looking at the mountains. He's curious about them and doesn't have information about them. He thinks they are wonderful and gives them human qualities when he says they are "aloof" and "imperturbable." When he grows up he won't think it is all he thought it was.

> Teacher: What effect do mountains have on people?

> Marc: They make people feel small.

> Melanie: They protect people too. They guard. They don't let strangers through; they form a barrier.

> Robert: They keep Jody from going out. They form a box around him. He can't get out. They are all around him.

> Louise: He heard the mountains are endless, and he wanted to go. No one knows what's on the other side. He thinks it must be wonderful because no one knows about it. That was his dream—to find out what is on the other side. The mountains are hiding his dream's fulfillment.

Students need to explore their own notion of a particular symbol, and on their own terms, before they move to higher levels of abstraction.

> Ari: The Great Mountains symbolize a barrier. There are things to be discovered in this world, but there is something that stops us.

Howard: That's negative. I had a positive feeling about what the mountains meant. They mean greatness in Jody. He wanted to know what was beyond them. That was his purpose in life. So, I think they sort of symbolize a great purpose in life. He became the leader of the people, or he showed that he might be one some day.

The level of response implicit in the last two remarks might never have been attained if students had not been encouraged to explore "what mountains do" before they were expected to work with symbols as such.

Relating Ideas to Music.   Related to the study of symbols is the experience of listening to music and relating the novel to it. For example, Copeland's *The Red Pony Suite* is a case in point. Students first need an opportunity to explore the parts of the novel they think could be set to music. They then use these primary responses as a focus of comparison with Copeland.

Steven: When Jody's gonna kill the bird.

Teacher: Which one? The buzzard?

Steven: No. The second chapter when he killed the little bird with his slingshot.

Teacher: What made you pick that part?

Steven: It's suspenseful when he's creeping up. When he fired the shot, it was suspenseful.

Marc: I think it could be kind of soft in the beginning and then get faster and louder. Then, as soon as the bird gets shot, it quiets everything.

Teacher: *The Red Pony Suite* has six ideas. I'll put them on the board in scrambled order. As you listen, write which one you think is first, second, and so on. When we talk about it later, we'll try to give some kind of justification for our order.

Rosalie: I have a question about what we chose to put music to. Everybody chose the dramatic moments. I would disagree with using all dramatic moments because I think when Jody was just casual you could have music to show that he was dreaming or in a daze or when he came back to that spot near the tree, when he always walked by it. I don't think it's necessary to show very dramatic moments but casual ones.

Jimmy: I wrote "The Boy on the Ranch" as the first movement. It had music like waking up and having to start the morning off.

Teacher: The first movement according to Aaron Copeland is "Morning on the Ranch."

Danny: I think the fifth one was "Grandfather" because in the first part it was kinda slow and then I think he met the Indians and it became dangerous; and then it got calm again.

Jimmy: Well, I think it was Grandfather's story because gradually it was slow. It was like you were repeating something over and over, and then it got very loud like they were having a fight.

Danny: And also you heard bum, bum, the horses' feet touching the ground.

Linda: I think another reason why you can tell it's the ending because some of it is a repetition of some of the other parts of the music from the other movements. . . .

Teacher: It's like a summary. . . .

Linda: Yes. They all work together and take some of the music from the other parts, like the middle from the dream.*

ELIMINATING A MINOR CHARACTER

When students are grappling with basic meaning of a novel, there is another device which assists them in uncovering it. If they select a minor character to remove from the novel and then project the consequent changes that would be necessitated in plot, events, and relationships, they can come remarkably close to the author's meaning. John Henry in *The Member of the Wedding* is such a character, as is Gitano in *The Red Pony.*

Mark: I think John Henry was a very useful character. When he asked Frankie what happened when she went out with the soldier, she gave him a look that showed she understood it but he was too young. By seeing the difference between the two, we know how much Frankie is growing up.

Jay: The way she used John Henry brought out her loneliness; when she was lonely she'd say, "I'll keep you company because you're lonely."

Robin: She could take her feelings out on him. She told him he was ugly and lonely when really she was feeling ugly and lonely.

As in this case, it often happens that students wind up defending the existence of the character they decided to eliminate. In such instances, the teacher may or may not decide to push toward a consideration of how the novel would have to be changed. If the purpose is achieved without taking that step, there is no point in pursuing it. However, in the event that more probing is essential, the activity can be pursued profitably.

ROLE PLAYING THE CHARACTERS

Students often need help in identifying with characters. One fruitful activity is to ask two students to take the part of two of the characters in a novel and to tell what they think of one another. Using this performance as a focus, the rest of the class asks questions about the content of the interchange and the reasons for the players' reactions to and feelings about each other.

Simon (as Jody): After I realized that you [Billy Buck] could make such a mistake and everything, I felt that now I was on my own because I didn't trust you anymore and I think that it helped me to face my responsibilities because I realized you weren't perfect. I always felt you were perfect and as long as you were there, I would be OK, but now I had to face

---

*Excerpts contributed by Alice Fritsch Stollman.

my own problems and that helped me to learn to care for Nellie when she was expecting a colt.

Marc (as Jody): Grandpa, you were a major factor in my life, because I didn't change that much until you came along because then I learned not to be selfish.

At first, students find talking to each other as characters a difficult task. It is usually the questions and challenges of other students in the class that help them slip into the roles of these characters.

Ari: You made it sound as if Jody had tremendous respect for his father. I think he was scared of his father.

Valerie: It wasn't that Jody liked Billy Buck better than his father; his father was busy.

Paul: The father found it hard to be a real father because he couldn't act natural. In a way he was scared too. Really, Billy Buck was the spiritual father to Jody. How do you think Carl felt about that?

Jimmy: You could tell he wasn't such a tough person as he pretended to be. Once when the mother said something to him, he didn't act so tough.

COMPARING AND CONTRASTING NOVELS

Comparison and contrast help give perspective so that basic meanings can become sharpened. One way to encourage these processes is to use novels students select for comparison with a novel read in common. Usually, students select the novel they wish to read from an annotated list presented by the teacher. The list consists of books which have been read and annotated by previous classes in addition to those originally selected by the teacher. In general, the books focus on basic themes stressed in the novel which all students have read in common. When novels are to be individually selected by students, a wide variety must be available. The list of books must satisfy a wide range of interests and abilities, so all students can find one to which they are able to respond. This is necessary because the book selected is to be read independently.

Students do not make book reports in the traditional sense. Rather, they use the knowledge gained from their novel to elaborate on an idea shared with the class. Usually, this is done in an open discussion. Sometimes panels are conducted, especially in instances where several students have read one novel and discovered many differences of opinion among themselves. Teachers assist students with focusing questions and activities such as, "Read to the point where you feel the character is changing." Class time is devoted in part to a consideration of those changes. This kind of process in which each book is used to shed light on a universal problem is far superior to the standard book report. It reinforces the teaching already done; it assists those students who are unable to handle the complexity of a novel alone; it gives them an opportunity to elaborate upon the concepts already developed in their initial phases. They can now see those concepts in their manifold ramifications. The thematic focus enables all students to select a novel of their own choosing. Carlsen explores several thematic areas around which adolescents select books of their own choosing: *The Search,* "in which individuals are looking for a direction for their lives;" *Problems of the Social Order* for the adolescent who must come "to terms with where he will stand in relation to his society;" *The Bizarre, The Off Beat, The Unusual in Human Experience* for the young adult who "is curious about the fringes of human life;" and *The Transition* in which a book "details the movement of a character from adolescence into early adult life."[23] These are not the only areas of adolescent concern; others are defined by Carlsen. All of them move definitely in the affective area of adolescent existence and are therefore appropriate for sensitivity impact. Often one student introduces his discovery to others and before long five or six students have read the book. In such case, these students form a group to discuss the concepts already considered in the novel read in common. Students examine these same concepts through questions they raise about what has happened in the lives of the characters in their book. They present their findings and puzzlements to the class. Attempts are made to solve the problems by contributions from the class about how such things happened in their book, how the questions were presented differently by their authors and what answers their authors were projecting. The many ramifications of any significant problem are perceived; insights into the concept are extended. The enrichment occurs because the data are extensive. If thirty students read a total of twenty books, the simple concepts framed as a consequence of the book read in common are now greatly enhanced.

If, on the other hand, only one or two students read the same novel, all is not lost; small panel discussions and presentations are still possible. Students in the class may group themselves by some criteria other than a particular book. For example, several may read books about sports; others may read junior psychological novels like *I Never Promised You a Rose Garden, Bless the Beasts and the Children, The Catcher in the Rye, The Boy Who Could Make Himself Disappear, Tell Me That You Love Me, Junie Moon,* or *The Stepford Wives.* These students can function in a small group because they are considering a theme and concepts in common with novels read by the rest of the class. It matters not that some are reading junior novels and others adult ones. The concepts, questions, and issues are the focus, and every student has some unique contribution to make because the book he read is different from the others and furnishes him with facts, insights, and understandings to share.

Comparing self-selected novels with one read in common encourages divergent thinking. Divergent thinking as opposed to convergent thinking is productive of transfer of knowledge. It involves freedom to make new associations. Convergent thinking, on the other hand, involves an analysis of data given or recalled; it focuses upon one "right" answer for a problem's solution. Guilford suggests that "we need a better balance of training in the divergent-thinking area as compared with training in convergent thinking. . . ."[24] The gathering and processing of information in a number of novels are exciting and satisfying activities. Literature teachers must avoid placing high priority on right answers, for this diminishes independent search for data and conclusions.

Conducting Discussions

Discussions about the same topic or phase of a book, day in and day out, may become tiresome. Discussion needs to be alternated with other activities such as interviewing, roleplaying, and other experiences which stimulate divergent thinking. Teachers who have created a nonthreatening atmosphere can find out how students feel about their discussions simply by asking.

> Boy: I really liked reading *The Pearl.* It showed the greediness of some people, the love that some people have. . . . It is filled with things to stir up your emotions, like the time when Coyotito was shot to death (I actually cried when I read it). . . . But the discussions were very boring. To me, I did not get anything out of the discussions except for the definition of the songs (of Evil, Enemy, Family, etc.)

> Boy: I think the book was fair, but the discussion was always boring. We would always ask almost the same questions every day: Was the pearl evil? Was the pearl good?

Consideration of even the most hallowed novels must be achieved within reasonable periods of time which recognize developmental levels of students. Sauer pronounces *A Tale of Two Cities* unworthy of the customary six-week study period. "Why six weeks on a work for which the author spent part of his life apologizing?" He declares further, "It is difficult to think of any novel which would require more than ten discussion periods."[25]

In general, questions need to be carefully planned to reflect the purpose of the discussion. If the purpose is to focus on the differentiation process in order to prepare for inference making and generalizing, the questions must induce the necessary comparison and contrast. The relevant factors must be unjoined from the mass in which it is imbedded. As a mediator, the teacher helps students use the novel to bring new understandings into their lives. In *To Kill a Mockingbird,* for example, there are a number of neighborhood legends symbolizing the influences of society upon the children's lives. What were they? How did they come to be? What difference did they make in the lives of the children? In other words, why were they important? There may be legends in the students' neighborhoods which can be compared to those in the novel. It is the wealth of supplementary novels the students now possess collectively that makes it possible to explore legends in many of them, for comparative purposes and for contrast.

Activities Which Develop Social Awareness

There exists a wealth of novels which furnish content for expanding students' social awareness. However, the act of reading a novel in and of itself does not necessarily achieve the social awareness aim. Social awareness contains an affective as well as a cognitive component. Therefore, the activities selected for development of such awareness must be capable of performing a dual role.

MAKING OBSERVATIONS

Activities sharply related to the issue at hand as well as to the specific novels help to involve the student and make use of social interaction as a motivating force in the learning. When students are involved in a supporting experience such as observing a child, an adult, and/or a teenager—none in their own families—several aims are achieved. They are preparing to relate literature to life while they note the ways in which others behave as mature and/or immature individuals. In writing their findings to share with the class, they sharpen the experience. Through the experience they gain a new perspective on the human beings around them and on themselves; they engage in the process of data gathering which, when pooled, warrants significant consideration and usually has an impact on how students regard others. It is one thing to pass speedy judgment on Frankie as "abnormal;" it is quite another to know that among thirty young adolescents they observed, a substantial number appear to behave in an alienated and disconnected fashion, that these adolescents, too, feel the need for belonging. It is one thing to express scorn for Frankie because "She's such a baby but thinks she's so grown up;" it is quite another to compare notes about thirty adults who "are grown up but sometimes act like such babies."

An activity which focuses on students' observations of life about them sharpens the perceptions of the novel. It has the advantage of captivating interest by virtue of the fact that each student can record what captures his attention. It gives the teacher a means of assessing precisely what is attracting students' attention; it cues him in to the depth of understanding they bring to the observation. Such an ongoing "people watcher" activity provides a measure of evaluation with respect to the empathy a student brings to the human events around him.

INTERVIEWING

Another "social-being" activity is the interview. Students can interview each other about their goals, their dreams in connection with the reading of *The Red Pony*. Or, they can interview adults. After students have discussed what it is Jody wants out of life, how they know this, and what happened to him as a result of his dreams, then they can profitably discuss goals and dreams with adults or older adolescents. They see Jody's dream compared with grandfather's; they perceive where the elements of reality and unreality lay. Projections can be made about possibilities for the realization of Jody's or grandfather's dreams and for the dreams of the person they interviewed.

With some classes, teachers preferred that students interview individuals in a single age group. Others encouraged students to interview adults and older adolescents. The questions to be asked were planned in class, and the interviewing techniques were practiced in role-playing sessions to give confidence to students who had never engaged in this experience. Students were encouraged to interview their parents because it was felt that parents would appreciate having this kind of school-related contact. Teachers hoped this occasion would encourage communication and a measure of understanding between parents and offspring.

The next day in class, two or three students reported the results of their interview. The teacher demonstrated how to tally information, and students were placed in informal groups to compare notes and arrive at some tentative conclusions.

Lillian: My interviewee is a thirty-four-year-old male, a teacher. I asked him what he wanted to be when he was younger. He said, "A teacher and a Brother and join the seminary. When I asked him if he wanted the same things now, he said he's a teacher and enjoys being a teacher but doesn't want to be a Brother anymore. When I asked him what he wanted to do now, he said, "Go into politics." I asked him how close he was to attaining it, and he said he was studying for his law degree. I also asked who helped or hindered him? He said his parents hindered him, because they didn't want him to go to college.

Students tended to accept the quite universal, "My parents hindered me," until they met a number of interviewees who declared they hindered themselves by wasting time, indecision, etc. They reevaluated the maturity factors and came to the conclusion that people are mature in varying degrees and with respect to specific behaviors and values. In one class, students concluded that adolescents have a more "far-fetched outlook," "are in trouble," and "really want to get like a higher peck than an adult."

Cheryl: Most of the teen-agers were immature like Frankie Adams. She was selfish and inconsiderate. Adults want happiness for their family and achievements for their children.

Eddie: Younger kids don't usually realize that some things are harder to get, so they want everything.

Students repeatedly met the same kinds of problems while interviewing. Discussion in class helped to point out some of those problems and to bring out some possible solutions.

Roslyn: If I hadn't pushed him—I think that he was afraid to answer some of the questions, like he says to me, "You better not mention my name or anything like that." I tell him that I wouldn't, but I had to push him for many of the answers.

Robert: Mine gave me a hard time about everything I asked him. He gave me a whole story, and I was being polite and didn't want to say, "O.K. That's enough already."

Students were evidently not sufficiently mature to see human relations roles they could play. With the help of group sharing, they were able to understand to varying degrees how they could satisfy the needs of others which were beyond the confines of the assignment itself.

An interesting aspect of the discussion is the evidence it offers that a real-life activity connected with literature does make a "social-being" impact. Before the interviews most students had rejected Frankie as "plain crazy."

Nancy: I interviewed adults and adolescents. When I interviewed the adolescent, I expected her to say she wanted material things, and it surprised me that she didn't have any real goals in mind. She was like Frankie Adams; unsure of anything she wanted.

Martin: I had to give up on an adult because he thought the questions were so ridiculous (Laughter).

Jerry: Well, the problem I had was I wanted to make the person very calm so I asked him if he wanted anything to eat and he got a whole bowl of nuts and while I'm writing I turned around to see if he was calm and he was lying on the couch relaxed and playing with the dog while I was asking questions, so I think that he was more calm than I was.

Teacher: That was one possibility we anticipated yesterday which was well founded (Laughter).

Brian: I don't think Frankie was so different from the adolescents we interviewed or from us. All children have to have friends, and they all feel misunderstood.

Nancy: I think it was a big accomplishment for Frankie and hundreds of children to try to go on their own and be responsible and be something other than what is their own environment and try to have a more objective point of view. It showed a great deal of intelligence on Frankie's part to go out and try to find out more about Michelangelo. There's a difference between her and the kids in the class. We live in this environment, and we're always influenced by this kind of stuff. We were very lucky to be exposed to this and Frankie wasn't. It showed a great deal of maturity for her to want to go out and find out.

Richie: The adults not only want something for their children, but in their subconscious they want something that they've always wanted.

Sidney: I think they're very immature to say that they want to grow up and become rich, marry a guy who's rich. I think that they are marrying the guy for his money, not for love or anything. None of the men we interviewed said that.

Paul: If a man dies and the woman is left a widow, she has to go out and work and doesn't have time for both—to take care of her children and everything. That's very hard, so she tries to find security in a man.

Stuart: Our group found that many people are just like the characters in books; they dream a lot when they're younger and perhaps settle for something different when they are older.

Jack: But in our interviews there weren't any people who wanted to run away from their town or anything.

Teacher: Most people at some time or other do think of running away, whether they actually run or not.

William: About two years ago, I grabbed my coat and ran out of the house. I walked all over the park maybe about four hours, till my brother and mother came and got me and brought me home. I just, you know, pitied myself, and said, "You've got a rotten family; everyone treats you so cruel, and they're so mean."

Carol: But Frankie's been dreaming about it for a year already. We do it for about fifteen minutes.

Teacher: Often books do exaggerate to bring a point across.

In the discussion cited above, students were exploring the relationship between literature and life, and ultimately they raised the questions: When does the change start taking place as adolescents become adults? When did it start taking place in Frankie? In general, they found that adolescent goals were not occupation oriented and they wondered about this. Were there any seeds of occupational concerns in Frankie's life? Or were her immediate concerns too overwhelming to permit other considerations? Thus students, even as they raise questions and make comparisons, begin to perceive the universality of emotions.

USING NEWSPAPER ITEMS

Another supporting activity is to peruse human interest newspaper items and to compare them with the novel or novels being read. Students try to construct the framework of a novel as a particular novelist might handle it, using the human interest item as the catalyst. They can gain a number of benefits from such an experience. First of all, by considering a number of such articles, they can see the impact of society upon individuals; they can also assess the impact of individuals upon others and themselves, as well as on society. Second, they perceive how totally ignorant the news item can leave them of the real-life situation of the human beings involved. Third, they begin to appreciate how much the novelist does for them that the newspaper reporter is unable to do or simply not equipped to do. Fourth, they reexamine with Hamilton the meaning of "truth": "fiction at its best is much more true than such careless reports of actual occurrences as are published in the daily newspaper. . . . The newspaper may tell us that a man who left his office in an apparently normal state of mind went home and shot his wife . . . though the story states an actual occurrence, it does not tell the truth. . . . The incident itself can become true for us only when we are made to understand it."[26]

In conjunction with their reading of *The Pearl,* students selected articles stressing *good* and *evil,* shared them in class, set up the framework for a "Steinbeck novel" surrounding the article, and wrote a defense of their outline. Excerpts from one eighth-grade boy's response to this activity follow.

Polluted Water

I. The Family

   a. Father—strong, proud

   b. Mother—proud, follows husband

   c. Child—scared, hangs on to mother

   d. Poverty of family

II. Setting

   a. Run-down, three-story building

   b. Family lives in small cubicle

   c. Outskirts of town

   d. Yellow, polluted stream runs by

III. Action

   a. Ignorance. Water pipe breaks. Need for water

   b. Father brings water from polluted stream. Tells wife to boil it.

   c. Wife forgets.

   d. Child drinks it and becomes ill.

   e. No doctor; child dies.

   f. Investigation shows sewage in stream due to community carelessness.

An author like Steinbeck would believe that people are controlled by their environment. He sees only the worst part. He does not think it is possible for individuals to maintain ideals against odds. . . . In *The Pearl,* Kino seems to be an ideal man, providing for his family and seemingly content with his position in life. Juana is an ideal woman, obeying her husband and watching the baby. Yet, placed in other circumstances, Kino kills a man . . . and Juana disobeys her husband.

The issue is not whether the teacher agrees with the student's response to Steinbeck, but rather the way in which the student is responding to the characters created by Steinbeck and the situations and values explored by him.

DECISION MAKING

Students become very interested in the novelist's concern with society and its impact upon the individual. One of the sensitivity-training assignments was as follows:

Write down all the decisions you made this weekend.
Which ones were related to unwritten rules and regulations a society uses to control its members?
Which ones did you make on your own, without regard for society's values?

Later they compared their own "growing-up decisions" with Jody's in *The Red Pony.*

In the Great Mountains, his relations with adults have changed. He obeys because he feels the pressure of public opinion rather than a strong belief and respect. Also Billy can now say, "I'll try to make it turn out all right," not, "Yes, it will." And Jody can accept the fact that it's uncertain.

The first time he decided to disobey was when Billy ordered him out of the barn when Nellie was giving birth. Before that he obeys out of belief and respect.

To grow up you have to sacrifice something. Sacrifice was the means he used. He realized finally that to be an adult human being you must give without any thought of getting.

Through such processes students learn the import of Ryan's statement that "the student learns to sense what idea the consistency of the character's motivation in a sequence of choices implies; he begins to appreciate plot as the visible manifestation of theme."[27] When students are learning about consistency of motivation and individual choices, they are also becoming aware of the human being as a social being. In these sensitivity experiences, the student is involved in an activity of concern to him and the findings provide data for comparison and contrast with the novel; the activities provide the opportunity for identifying with characters in the novels. An illustration of such identification came from the response of an eighth grader:

The book brought on an inner fight within me while reading it. I wasn't sure whether Juana was right for not wanting to keep the pearl, or Kino for wanting to.

The decision-making process, for good or for evil, in anyone's life is far-reaching. Students are interested in Steinley's assessment of choice making by the central character:

"As the novella progresses, how does the central character choose to regard the value or meaning of the symbol and how does the central character himself change? . . . as the value (or meaning) of the central symbol does change in the eyes of each protagonist, it should be stressed that the symbol just doesn't happen to change but that the protagonist chooses to change it. . . . Kino could have accepted 1,000 pesos for his pearl; he chose to make it worth more . . . each man is creating values by his choices, and as he makes choices, he himself changes; and as he himself changes, he is in effect creating himself, for each man is different, almost a 'new man,' at the end of the novella.[28]

The novelist is mindful of the significance of role taking. In *To Kill a Mockingbird* Atticus counters Scout's tale of misfortunes in school with the advice that "you never really understand a person until you consider things from his point of view . . . until you climb into his skin and walk around in it." Atticus calls it "a simple trick for getting along a lot better with all kinds of folks." The trick may not be so simple but the process is one that can be learned. The walking around in someone else's skin not only enhances life for "all kinds of folks" but enriches that of the "walker" who senses a great new being within himself.

The need for awareness of self and creation of self is especially true of younger adolescents. We do not need to wait until adolescents reach the upper years of high school and college before permitting them to grapple with the artist's ideas even while experiencing the joy of his creation. The earlier a student begins to understand himself and to sense the vast resources he has within himself for deep feelings and rich thoughts, the better. The young adolescent cannot engage in self-examination as a discrete process and in this manner understand himself. He needs perspective with which to gain the essential insights; role taking in literature can give him that perspective. When he experiences with Jody in *The Red Pony* the death of a beloved mare, his own feelings about the awesome phenomenon of death become a subject about which he can talk. When he experiences with Jody the rejection of Guitano, he begins to empathize. This kind of role taking occurs inwardly. To help students arrive at a high level of proficiency in this process, role playing is, for many, a necessary step.[29] For example, there are a number of situations in *To Kill a Mockingbird* that lend themselves to this kind of exploration: Atticus arguing with Alexandra about the way Calpurnia brings up the children; Atticus explaining to the children why he took Tom Robinson's case; Calpurnia breaking the news of Tom's death to Helen.

Role playing is one way of providing a balance between input and output. It offers an opportunity to permit the artist to affect the human being; that affect is an active, not a passive, process. However, equally important is the discussion which follows the role taking. Was the student portrayal of Atticus in accord with the novelist's intent? What caused the players to interpret his behavior as they did? Almost inevitably, interpretations will be questions. In the process of arriving at some accord, the social interaction affects the emotional and cognitive content.

Summary

Strategies such as those discussed will enable the student to receive enjoyment, increased sensitivity, and higher-level cognitive functioning from reading the novel.

Equally important, the strategies make it possible for the literary artist to help an increasing number of adolescents capture a sense of the great potential that is lodged in themselves and in other human beings, emotionally as well as intellectually.

NOTES

1. Nancy Hale, *The Realities of Fiction* (Boston: Little, Brown and Co., 1962), p. 72.

2. E. M. Forster, *Aspects of the Novel* (New York: Harcourt Brace Jovanovich, 1927), p. 87.

3. Barbel Inhelder and Jean Piaget, *The Growth of Logical Thinking from Childhood to Adolescence: An Essay on the Construction of Formal Operational Structures* (New York: Basic Books, 1958), p. 277.

4. Sister M. Amanda Ely, O. P., "The Adult Image in Three Novels of Adolescent Life," *English Journal* 56 (November 1967): 1127–2231.

5. Kellogg W. Hunt, "Getting into the Novel," *English Journal* 50 (December 1961): 605.

6. Warner Taylor, ed., *Essays of the Past and Present* (New York: Harper & Row, Publishers, 1927), p. 438.

7. Ibid., p. 441.

8. John Rouse, "In Defense of Trash," in *Literature for Adolescents, Selection and Use,* ed. Richard A. Meade and Robert C. Small, Jr. (Columbus, Oh.: Charles E. Merrill Publishing Co., 1973), pp. 91–93.

9. Frank G. Jennings, "Literature for Adolescents—Pap or Protein?" in *Literature* ed. Richard A. Meade and Robert C. Small, Jr. (Columbus, Oh.: Charles E. Merrill Publishing Co., 1973), p. 96.

10. Dwight L. Burton, "The Role of the Junior Novel: The Teacher's Stake," in *Literature for Adolescents, Selection and Use,* ed. Richard A. Meade and Robert C. Small, Jr. (Columbus, Oh.: Charles E. Merrill Publishing Co., 1973), pp. 213–14.

11. For further suggestions on "the silent treatment," see Bud Church, "Silence Makes the Heart Grow Louder," *Media and Methods* 7 (October 1970): 32–34, 66.

12. W. Somerset Maugham, *Of Human Bondage* (New York: Pocket Books, 1954), pp. v and vii.

13. For a description of how this procedure was carried out by a group of students with reading problems, see Deborah Elkins, *Reading Improvement in the Junior High School* (New York: Teachers College Press, 1972).

14. Phyllis Bentley, *Some Observations on the Art of Narrative* (New York: The Macmillan Co., 1947), p. 28.

15. Edgar H. Schuster, "Discovering Theme and Structure in the Novel," *English Journal* 52 (October 1963): 510.

16. Cleanth Brooks, "The Formalist Critic," in *The Modern Critical Spectrum,* ed. J. Goldberg and Nancy Marmer Goldberg (Englewood Cliffs, N.J.: Prentice-Hall, 1962), p. 3.

17. Franziska L. Greiling, "The Theme of Freedom in *A Separate Peace,*" *English Journal* 56 (December 1967): 1269–72.

18. Joseph E. Devine, "The Truth about *A Separate Peace,*" *English Journal* 58 (April 1969): 519–22.

19. Gaston Pelletier, "*Red Badge* Revisited," *English Journal* 57 (January 1968): 24–25.

20. Langston Hughes, "Dreams," in *Reflections on a Gift of Watermelon Pickle, and Other Modern Verse,* ed. Stephen Dunning, Edward Lueders, and Hugh Smith (Glenview, Ill.: Scott, Foresman and Co., 1966), p. 129.

21. Harry Morris, "*The Pearl:* Realism and Allegory," in *Scholarly Appraisals of Literary Works Taught in High Schools,* ed. Stephen Dunning and Henry Sams (Champaign, Ill.: National Council of Teachers of English, 1965), p. 490.

22. John M. Nagle, "A View of Literature Too Often Neglected," *English Journal* 58 (March 1969): 402.

23. G. Robert Carlsen, "For Everything There Is a Season," in *Literature for Adolescents, Selection and Use,* ed. Richard A. Meade and Robert C. Small, Jr. (Columbus, Oh.: Charles E. Merrill Publishing Co., 1973), pp. 118–19.

24. J. P. Guilford, "Three Faces of Intellect," *American Psychologist* 14 (1959): 478.

25. Edwin H. Sauer, *English in the Secondary School* (New York: Holt, Rinehart & Winston, 1961), pp. 141–142.
26. Clayton Hamilton, *A Manual of the Art of Fiction* (New York: Doubleday & Co., 1937), p. 16.
27. Margaret Ryan, *Teaching the Novel in Paperback* (New York: The Macmillan Co., 1963), p. 52.
28. Gary Steinley, "The Contemporary American Novella: An Existential Approach," *English Journal* 59 (January 1970): 52–58.
29. Stanford analyzes some of the problems involved in initiating role playing with students. See Gene Stanford, "Why Role Playing Fails," *English Journal* 63 (December 1974): 50–54.

References

Bentley, Phyllis. *Some Observations on the Art of Narrative.* New York: The Macmillan Co., 1947.

Brooks, Cleanth. "The Formalist Critic." In *The Modern Critical Spectrum,* edited by Gerald J. Goldberg and Nancy Marmer Goldberg. Englewood Cliffs, N.J.: Prentice-Hall, 1962.

————; Purser, John; and Warren, Robert Penn. *An Approach to Literature.* New York: Appleton-Century-Crofts, 1952.

Buehler, Charlotte. "Basic Theoretical Concepts of Humanistic Psychology." *American Psychologist* 26 (April 1971):378–86.

Burton, Dwight L. "The Role of the Junior Novel: The Teacher's Stake." In *Literature for Adolescents, Selection and Use,* edited by Richard A. Meade and Robert C. Small, Jr. Columbus, Oh.: Charles E. Merrill Publishing Co., 1973.

Carlsen, G. Robert. "For Everything There Is a Season." In *Literature for Adolescents, Selection and Use,* edited by Richard A. Meade and Robert C. Small, Jr. Columbus, Oh.: Charles E. Merrill Publishing Co., 1973.

Church, Bud. "Silence Makes the Heart Grow Louder." *Media and Methods* 7 (October 1970): 32–33, 66.

Church, Joseph. *Language and the Discovery of Reality.* New York: Random House, 1961.

Clayton, Hamilton. *A Manual of the Art of Fiction.* New York: Doubleday & Co., 1937.

Crane, Stephen. *The Red Badge of Courage.* New York: Pocket Books, 1954.

Devine, Joseph E. "The Truth about *A Separate Peace.*" *English Journal* 58 (April 1969):519–20.

Elkins, Deborah. *Reading Improvement in the Junior High School.* New York: Teachers College Press, 1972.

Ely, Sister M. Amanda, O. P. "The Adult Image in Three Novels of Adolescent Life." *English Journal* 56 (November 1967):1127–31.

Forbes, Kathryn. *Mama's Bank Account.* New York: Bantam Books, 1947.

Forster, E. M. *Aspects of the Novel.* New York: Harcourt Brace Jovanovich, 1927.

Golding, William G. *Lord of the Flies.* New York: G. P. Putnam's Sons, 1962.

Gordon, Caroline. *How to Read a Novel.* New York: The Viking Press, 1958.

Green, Hannah. *I Never Promised You a Rose Garden.* New York: The New American Library, 1964.

Greiling, Franziska L. "The Theme of Freedom in *A Separate Peace.*" *English Journal* 56 (December 1967):1269–72.

Guilford, J. P. "Three Faces of Intellect." *American Psychologist* 14 (1959):469–79.

Hale, Nancy. *The Realities of Fiction.* Boston: Little, Brown and Co., 1962.

Hamechek, Don E. *Encounters with the Self.* New York: Holt, Rinehart & Winston, 1971.

Hamilton, Clayton. *A Manual of the Art of Fiction.* New York: Doubleday & Co., 1937.

Haslerud, George M., and Meyers, Shirley. "The Trasfer Value of Given and Individually Derived Principles." In *Selected Readings in the Learning Process,* edited by Theodore L. Harris and Wilson Schwahn. New York: Oxford University Press, 1961.

Hawthorne, Nathaniel. *The Scarlet Letter.* New York: Pocket Books, 1954.

Hemingway, Ernest. *The Old Man and the Sea.* New York: Charles Scribner's Sons, 1952.

Hughes, Langston. "Dreams." In *Reflections on a Gift of Watermelon Pickle, and Other Modern Verse,* edited by Stephen Dunning, Edward Lueders, and Hugh Smith. Glenview, Ill.: Scott, Foresman and Co., 1966.

Hunt, Kellogg W. "Getting into the Novel." *English Journal* 50 (December 1961):601–06.

Inhelder, Barbel, and Piaget, Jean. *The Growth of Logical Thinking from Childhood to Adolescence: An Essay on the Construction of Formal Operational Structures.* New York: Basic Books, 1958.

Jennings, Frank G. "Literature for Adolescents—Pap or Protein?" In *Literature for Adolescents, Selection and Use,* edited by Richard A. Meade and Robert C. Small, Jr. Columbus, Oh.: Charles E. Merrill Publishing Co., 1973.

Kellogg, Marjorie. *Tell Me That You Love Me, Junie Moon.* New York: Farrar, Straus & Giroux, 1968.

Knowles, John. *A Separate Peace.* New York: Dell Publishing Co., 1962.

Lathrop, Henry B. *The Art of the Novelist.* London: George G. Harrap and Co., 1921.

Lee, Harper. *To Kill a Mockingbird.* New York: Popular Library, 1962.

Levin, Ira. *The Stepford Wives.* Boston: G. K. Hall & Co., 1973.

McCullers, Carson. *The Member of the Wedding.* New York: Bantom Books, 1964.

Maugham, W. Somerset. *Of Human Bondage.* New York: Doubleday & Co., 1950.

Morris, Harry. "*The Pearl:* Realism and Allegory." In *Scholarly Appraisals of Literary Works Taught in High Schools,* edited by Stephen Dunning and Henry W. Sams. Champaign, Ill.: National Council of Teachers of English, 1965.

Nagle, John M. "A View of Literature Too Often Neglected." *English Journal* 58 (March 1969):399–407.

Pelletier, Gaston. "*Red Badge* Revisited." *English Journal* 57 (January 1968):24–25, 99

Platt, Kin. *The Boy Who Could Make Himself Disappear.* New York: Dell Publishing Co., 1972.

Rosenblatt, Louise. *Literature as Exploration.* New York: Appleton-Century-Crofts, 1938.

Rouse, John. "In Defense of Trash." In *Literature for Adolescents, Selection and Use,* edited by Richard A. Meade and Robert E. Small, Jr. Columbus, Oh. Charles E. Merrill Publishing Co., 1973.

Ryan, Margaret. *Teaching the Novel in Paperback.* New York: The Macmillan Co., 1963.

Salinger, J. D. *The Catcher in the Rye.* New York: The New American Library, 1953.

Sauer, Edwin H. *English in the Secondary School.* New York: Holt, Rinehart & Winston, 1961.

Schuster, Edgar H. "Discovering Theme and Structure in the Novel." *English Journal* 52 (October 1963):506–11.

Sheridan, Marian and the Committee on Intensive Reading. "How Should We Teach Novels?" In *Essays on the Teaching of English,* edited by Edward J. Gordon and Edward S. Noyes. New York: Appleton-Century-Crofts, 1960.

Stanford, Gene. "Why Role Playing Fails." *English Journal* 63 (December 1974):50–54.

Steinbeck, John. "Flight." In *Understanding Literature,* edited by Elizabeth White, Joan Wofford, and Edward Gordon. New York: Ginn and Co., 1964.

———. *The Pearl.* New York: Bantam Books, 1956.

———. *The Red Pony.* New York: Bantam Books, 1955.

Steinley, Gary. "The Contemporary American Novella: An Existential Approach." *English Journal* 59 (January 1970):52–58.

Stratemeyer, E. [Allen Winfield] *The Rover Boys, Winning a Fortune.* New York: Grosset & Dunlap, 1928 (circa).

Swarthout, Glendon. *Bless the Beasts and the Children.* Garden City, New York: Doubleday & Co., 1970.

Taba, Hilda. "Learning by Discovery: Psychological and Educational Rationale." In *Teaching Gifted Students,* edited by James J. Gallagher. Boston: Allyn & Bacon, 1965.

Taylor, Warner, ed. *Essays of the Past and Present.* New York: Harper & Row, Publishers, 1927.

Suggested Novels

Achebe, Chinua. *Things Fall Apart.* Greenwich, Conn.: Fawcett Publications, 1959.

Agee, James. *A Death in the Family.* New York: Bantam Books, 1971.

Aldrich, Bess S. *A Lantern in Her Hand.* New York: Pocket Books, 1947.

Anderson, Mary. *I'm Nobody! Who Are You?* New York: Atheneum Publishers, 1974.

Annixter, Paul. *Swiftwater.* New York: Hill & Wang, 1950.

Armstrong, William H. *Sounder.* New York: Scholastic Book Services, 1969.

Arnothy, Christine. *I Am Fifteen and I don't Want To Die.* New York: E. P. Dutton & Co., 1956.

Arundel, Honor. *Emma in Love.* New York: Thomas Nelson, 1972.

Babb, Sanora. *An Owl on Every Post.* New York: The New American Library, 1975.

Blume, Judy. *Are You There, God? It's Me, Margaret.* Scarsdale, N. Y.: Bradbury Press, 1970.

———. *It's Not the End of the World.* Scarsdale, N.Y.: Bradbury Press, 1972.

Bonham, Frank. *Durango Street.* New York: Dell Publishing Co., 1972.

Bontemps, Arna. *Lonesome Boy.* Boston: Houghton Mifflin Co., 1955.

Braithwaite, E. R. *To Sir, With Love.* Englewood Cliffs, N.J.: Prentice-Hall, 1960.

Buck, Pearl. *The Big Wave.* New York: Scholastic Book Services, 1965.

———. *The Good Earth.* New York: Pocket Books, 1973.

Burstein, Chaya. *Rifka Bangs the Teakettle.* New York: Harcourt Brace Jovanovich, 1970.

Cather, Willa. *My Antonia.* Boston: Houghton Mifflin Co., 1954.

Cavanna, Betty. *Going On Sixteen.* New York: Scholastic Book Services, 1972.

Clark, Ann Nolan. *Medicine Man's Daughter.* New York: Farrar, Straus & Giroux, 1963.

Clymer, Eleanor. *The Trolley Car Family.* New York: Scholastic Book Services, 1970.

Cone, Molly. *Dance around the Fire.* Boston: Houghton Mifflin Co., 1974.

———. *Number Four.* Boston: Houghton Mifflin Co., 1972.

Craven, Margaret. *I Heard the Owl Call My Name.* New York: Dell Publishing Co., 1973.

Daly, Maureen. *Seventeenth Summer.* New York: Dodd, Mead & Co., 1942.

DuJardin, Rosamond. *Wait for Marcy.* New York: Scholastic Book Services, 1963.

Ellis, Mel. *This Mysterious River.* New York: Dell Publishing Co., 1973.

Engebrecht, P. A. *Under the Haystack.* New York: Thomas Nelson, 1973.

Fast, Howard. *April Morning.* New York: Crown Publishers, 1961.

Felsen, Henry G. *Bertie Comes Through.* New York: Scholastic Book Services, 1972.

Forbes, Kathryn. *Mama's Bank Account.* New York: Bantam Books, 1947.

Gipson, Fred. *Old Yeller.* New York: Pocket Books, 1956.

Guareschi, Giovanni. *The Little World of Don Camillo.* New York: Grosset & Dunlap, 1950.

Haggard, Elizabeth. *Nobody Waved Goodbye.* New York: Bantam Books, 1971.

Hamilton, Virginia. *The House of Dies Drear.* New York: The Macmillan Co., 1968.

_____. *The Planet of Junior Brown.* New York: The Macmillan Co., 1971.

Hawthorne, Nathaniel. *The Scarlet Letter.* Boston: Houghton Mifflin, 1960.

Hemingway, Ernest. *For Whom the Bell Tolls.* New York: Charles Scribner's Sons, 1940.

_____. *Old Man and the Sea.* New York: Charles Scribner's Sons, 1952.

Hersey, John. *A Bell for Adano.* New York: Alfred A. Knopf, 1944.

Hilton, James. *Good-Bye, Mr. Chips.* Boston: Little, Brown and Co., 1934.

Hinton, S. E. *The Outsiders.* New York: Dell Publishing Co., 1968.

_____. *That Was Then, This Is Now.* New York: Dell Publishing Co., 1972.

Horgan, Paul. *Whitewater.* New York: Farrar, Straus & Giroux, 1970.

Hunt, Irene. *No Promises in the Wind.* New York: Grosset & Dunlap, 1970.

Jackson, Helen Hunt. *Ramona.* New York: Grosset & Dunlap, 1912.

Jordan, June. *His Own Where.* New York: Thomas Y. Crowell Co., 1971.

Kerr, M. E. *If I Love You, Am I Trapped Forever?* New York: Dell Publishing Co., 1973.

Keyes, Daniel. *Flowers for Algernon.* New York: Harcourt Brace Jovanovich, 1966.

Kjelgaard, James Arthur. *Big Red.* New York: Holiday House, 1956.

Klein, Norma. *Sunshine.* New York: Avon Books, 1971.

Konigsburg, E. L. *From the Mixed-Up Files of Mrs. Basil E. Frankweiler.* New York: Atheneum Publishers, 1967.

Lipsyte, Robert. *The Contender.* New York: Harper & Row, Publishers, 1967.

Logan, Jane. *The Very Nearest Room.* New York: Charles Scribner's Sons, 1973.

McCall, Dan. *Jack the Bear.* Garden City New York: Doubleday & Co., 1974.

McCullers, Carson. *The Heart Is a Lonely Hunter.* Boston: Houghton Mifflin Co., 1940.

Mathis, Sharon Bell. *Teacup Full of Roses.* New York: Avon Books, 1973.

Marshall, Catherine. *Julie's Heritage.* New York: Scholastic Book Services, 1969.

Marshall, James Vance. *Walkabout.* Garden City, N.Y.: Doubleday & Co., 1961.

Minahan, John. *Jeremy.* New York: Bantam Books, 1973.

Momaday, N. Scott. *House Made of Dawn.* New York: The New American Library, 1969.

Narayan, R. K. *The Vendor of Sweets.* New York: The Viking Press, 1967.

Neville, Emily. *It's Like This, Cat.* New York: Harper & Row, Publishers, 1963.

Nordhoff, Charles B., and Hall, James H. *Mutiny on the Bounty.* Boston: Little, Brown and Co., 1932.

Paige, Harry. *Wade's Place.* New York: Scholastic Book Services, 1973.

Peck, Robert Newton. *A Day No Pigs Would Die.* New York: Alfred A. Knopf, 1973.

Plath, Sylvia. *The Bell Jar.* New York: Harper & Row, Publishers, 1971.

Potok, Chaim. *The Chosen.* New York: Simon & Schuster, 1967.

Rabe, Bernice. *Rass.* New York: Thomas Nelson, 1973.

Rabin, Gil. *Changes.* New York: Harper & Row, Publishers, 1973.

Rawlings, Marjorie. *The Yearling.* New York: Charles Scribner's Sons, 1938.

Remarque, Erich M. *All Quiet on the Western Front.* Boston: Little, Brown and Co., 1929.

Richard, Adrienne. *The Accomplice.* Boston: Little, Brown and Co., 1973.

Richard, Adrienne. *Pistol.* New York: Dell Publishing Co., 1970.

Richter, Conrad. *The Light in the Forest.* New York: Alfred A. Knopf, 1953.

Richter, Hans Peter. *I Was There.* New York: Dell Publishing Co., 1973.

Rolvaag, Ole E. *Giants in the Earth.* New York: Harper & Row, Publishers, 1929.

Roth, Henry. *Call It Sleep.* New York: Avon Books, 1964.

Rulfo, Juan. *Pedro Páramo.* Translated by Lysander Kemp. New York: Grove Press, 1959.

Russell, Charles E. *A Birthday Present for Katheryn Kenyalta.* New York: McGraw-Hill Book Co., 1970.

Saroyan, William. *The Human Comedy.* New York: Harcourt Brace Jovanovich, 1943.

Segal, Erich W. *Love Story.* New York: Harper & Row, Publishers, 1970.

Sherburne, Zoa. *Too Bad about the Haines Girl.* New York: William Morrow & Co., 1967.

Snyder, Gary. *Regarding Wave.* New York: New Directions Publishing Corp., 1970.

Sommerfelt, Aimée. *Miriam.* New York: Scholastic Book Services, 1972.

Sperry, Armstrong. *Call It Courage.* New York: The Macmillan Co., 1940.

Steinbeck, John. *Grapes of Wrath.* New York: The Viking Press, 1939.

Stolz, Mary. *Leap before You Look.* New York: Dell Publishing Co., 1972.

_____. *Ready or Not.* New York: Scholastic Book Services, 1969.

Summers, James L. *The Long Ride Home.* Philadelphia: The Westminster Press, 1966.

_____. *You Can't Make It by Bus.* Philadelphia: The Westminster Press, 1969.

Swarthout, Glendon. *Bless the Beasts & The Children.* New York: Pocket Books, 1970.

Tunis, John R. *His Enemy, His Friend.* New York: William Morrow & Co., 1967.

Wagner, Jane, and Parks, Gordon. *J. T.* New York: Dell Publishing Co., 1971.

Wersba, Barbara. *Run Softly, Go Fast.* New York: Bantam Books, 1972.

Wiggin, Kate Douglas (Smith). *Rebecca of Sunnybrook Farm.* Boston: Houghton Mifflin Co., 1925.

Windsor, Patricia. *The Summer Before.* Harper & Row, Publishers, 1973.

Wojciechowska, Maia. *Don't Play Dead before You Have To.* New York: Dell Publishing Co., 1971.

_____. *The Single Light.* New York: Bantam Books, 1971.

Yates, Elizabeth. *Amos Fortune, Free Man.* New York: Dell Publishing Co., 1971.

Zindel, Paul. *The Pigman.* New York: Dell Publishing Co., 1970.

Chapter Five

Engaging in Drama

For the study of drama to be most effective, it must include improvisation as well as a consideration of the playwright's works. Many educators stress the importance of improvisation, but most of them concentrate on this process in the classroom experience of the young child. Few deal with the importance of improvisation in the lives of adolescents; not many recognize its importance in the study of drama; a few, especially the British educators, do recognize its relationship to the process of thinking.

Courtney points out that when a child improvises, he is engaged in an imaginative experience. This is "based on memory which, in itself, is based on observation—exactly the same process as that involved in abstract thought. . . . The dramatic imagination lies behind all human learning. . . . It is the way in which man relates himself to life. . . . It teaches us to think, to examine and explore, to test hypotheses and to discover truth."[1]

The sequence which was developed by a number of teachers under the guidance of the author recognizes the centrality of improvisation and the need for systematic experiences, each succeeding one depending on the previous. There was provision for comparison and contrast and for opportunities to interpret data, to predict events and consequences, and to explain new circumstances. The sequence was an endeavor to recognize with Courtney that "dramatic action is also the basis for later sensitivity and artistic experience, for the appreciation of the conditions of existence and of human needs."[2]

Acting Out and Writing Down Drama

There was no preliminary consideration of the question, What is drama? Rather, students were plunged almost immediately into the act of improvisation. They initially discussed ideas about incidents they could recall which held possibilities for dramatizing. This pooling of ideas gave students concrete events with which to work, led to primitive understandings of the meaning of "dramatic," and revealed the fact that some incidents could be staged while others could not. Thus, the students became aware of the fact that dramatists have limitations under which they work.

Students then wrote a paragraph describing an incident which would satisfy the criteria set up by them. In one classroom these criteria included the following: There must be conflict ("You can't just have someone sitting there shaking her head for a half hour"); the possibility of dialogue is essential ("Having two guys come out on stage for a fist fight wouldn't necessarily have meaning"); the conflict must be important to the persons involved, and it must reveal something about those persons.

The next day the teacher grouped the students in such a way so that every paragraph would be read by at least five peers. Each group selected the one they thought would have the greatest possibilities for dramatization. The three or four papers that were chosen were read and elaborated by the students who wrote them, in order to permit contributors to provide further background for the audience. The discussion which followed helped the whole class gain insights into the ingredients necessary for dramatization. An excerpt from an eighth-grade discussion is indicative of the level at which classes tended to function:

Teacher: Which of these paragraphs hold a story you think would be best for dramatization?

Sara: The one about the lady who tried to return some cards she bought. She had fifteen cards and she was trying to aggravate the shopkeeper. That could easily be acted, and you could see what she's like.

Sima: I like the one about arguments about what the family is going to watch on TV. It's typical of every family.

As soon as each author of the chosen paragraphs elaborated upon the behavior of the characters and answered the questions directed to him by class members and the teacher, he chose classmates to help him with the role playing. The groups were assigned to different corners of the room to make preparatory decisions about dialogue and characterization.

There were certain ground rules for role playing which had to be established. For example, no one could play himself because he was responsible for explaining to others how he felt, how he acted, why he felt and acted that way. This freed him to be someone else involved in the particular situation being portrayed. This also freed the class to criticize the portrayal without criticizing the student himself.

Usually, at least one of the three or four scenes fell flat. Usually, too, the teacher had the task of helping pupils differentiate between failure because of lack of experience in acting and flatness because of a lack of necessary ingredients in the composition of the scene. In any case the teacher assumed the responsibility for cutting off the performance when the aim had been attained. He did this by starting the applause which was immediately picked up by the "audience."

The role playing was followed by a teacher-led discussion, first directed to the players and then opened up to the full class. The teacher asked the actors questions such as, "How did you feel?" "Did you feel like the father?" "Did you feel like the teen-ager?" He then directed the questions to the class: "Did you feel that Jimmy acted like a real father?" "Since Jimmy is not actually the father, what could be done to make you think he was a father?" As this discussion proceeded, the teacher led the students to understand that these situations are drawn from life but they are not life. Drama must be made to seem real, but it is not real. Why? The dialogue itself was newly created in class; the players were not themselves, and even the situation did not occur exactly that way. When it was necessary, this third concept was reinforced by having two or three performances of the same incident. In one class a particular incident had occurred when the pupils were with another teacher, so all the pupils knew something of what had happened.

Teacher: Jerry, how did you feel when you played Mr. Wiley?

Jerry: I really felt mad because these kids are in an S.P. class* and they are intelligent enough to know that what they are doing is wrong.

Mattie: Even his facial expression showed his anger.

Allen: And the way he jumped and loosened his collar. . . .

George: He should have taken ten points off his mark.

Jim: It was good the way he said it's all very expensive equipment that's being misused.

Bob: It was not realistic the way they did it, but it was more dramatic than actually happened.

Sara: That's much too exaggerated.

Ed: I think it's o.k. to exaggerate somewhat, but if it's too much it spoils the whole thing.

Dan: All the plays I've known have been based on something realistic.

Sandy: You can't do it just exactly the way it happened, so it's not real; it's more like a carbon copy.

Mattie: No, it's not a carbon copy. Really, the incident gets changed.

Ed: But it is realistic just the same because it might have happened.

The same incident was then dramatized by three groups of students, each carrying through its own version of the situation.

Teacher: Which of the three versions was the most exciting to you?

Sara: The one where the teacher gets so mad he jumps on the desk.

George: But that's not even believable!

Ed: If we did the thing exactly as it happened, it wouldn't be interesting to the people who were there. You have to add something new to it.

From the above excerpts it is evident that students were evolving a concept of drama. Such a process was far more enlightening than any definition a teacher could offer.

Teachers modified the preceding procedures in accordance with the ability of the class and their own personal affinities. For example, some teachers dispensed with the

---

*S.P. means "Special Progress." Students in these classes complete the junior high school program in two years.

group work and selected the paragraphs to be read and dramatized. Others felt that a consideration of "What is drama?" should follow rather than precede an initial consideration of the basic content concepts to be evolved. Therefore, they focused the initial activity around one of the concepts.

The basis for selecting concepts was the awareness that the drama is uniquely suited for a consideration of motivations involved in human behavior. It was important for teachers to articulate the specific concepts about motivation on which they wished to focus. The sequence was developed around four concepts or ideas:

1. There are underlying motivations in the things people say and do.
2. People's basic needs and desires are closely related to their motivations.
3. People's motivations are affected by their environment.
4. People's motivations and actions affect those around them.

Those teachers who preferred to begin with a consideration of the concepts presented the first assignment to achieve this purpose. They asked students to write about an incident which revealed to them something previously unknown about another person. The role playing and discussions focused on the motivational aspects.

·   The last excerpt illustrates the students' readiness to consider the concept that drama is taken from life but is not life. They also needed further experiences in recognizing the importance of (1) dialogue in developing a picture of the characters, especially with respect to motivation, and (2) the setting in which the scene takes place. Therefore, they were given the assignment to eavesdrop upon a conversation which they thought had possibilities of being staged. The use of conversation from their own families or by people they knew was prohibited. They could listen in places such as the bakery, the laundry, the game rooms of their apartment houses, subways, bus stops, buses, or supermarkets.

They were instructed to write up their scene, giving the following information:

1. Setting, with a drawing of the stage setting and hypothesis about why the characters chose this setting.
2. Conversation written as dialogue.
3. Paragraph on "what you learned about the observed people as human beings."

The purpose of this last paragraph was to help students to see at a later time how much or how little one can learn about people from what they say and do in a brief encounter. The same paragraph was also a preliminary step in the consideration of characters and their motivations.

Next day, the class met again in small groups to select three or four scenes which could be staged easily. From these few, the class and teacher together selected one. An excerpt* from one such scene follows. Although the scene appears to violate the regulation prohibiting eavesdropping upon families, this scene was accepted because its use was sanctioned by the parents.

---

*Excerpts for this sequence were contributed by Elinor Weinreich Joseph.

Leslie: Mine takes place in the family living room. It's Sunday and relatives have come to visit. (Shows plan of living room and where each character sits or stands.)

Mother (turning to her husband): Shall I tell them?

Father (nods): Yes.

Mother: I'm going to have another baby.

Family: Congratulations! Great! That's wonderful! It's good to rear your family while you are young! etc. etc.

Father (smiling): The doctor thinks it will be twins.

Family: Oh no! For heaven's sake! How will you manage?

Grandmother: I'll help her. She'll manage. And Harry is good with children; he likes to do things for them.

Grandfather: In a way it's good. You'll have two children for the price of one!

Family: But where will they get two cribs? And how will you manage when both of them are sick? etc. etc.

The discussion that ensued led the class to analyze what could be learned from the dialogue alone. The reader must recognize that the above is only an excerpt; students have seen and heard considerably more.

Teacher: Can you gather anything about the family from the dialogue alone?

Sherry: The husband and wife are very happy . . . and the family itself seems very close.

Alan: I also get the feeling that it's a very close family because the grandparents are sticking close to the children and they come over every day.

Barbara: It's not a rich family; maybe middle class. . . .

John: It is a close family, but they have their own opinions. Some think it's going to be a mess · and I had the feeling they wouldn't want to baby-sit too often. But the grandparents would always be there when needed.

Steve: In one way some members of the family were discouraging. If it's twins, what can the parents do? They made it sound as if it was a tragedy!

The fact that there was a difference of opinion gave the teacher the opportunity to stress that some judgments could be made in a brief encounter and audience reactions may differ for a variety of reasons. The discussion then turned to what could *not* be known about the characters from this dialogue and what information would still be needed in order to cue in the audience on the motivations of each one of the people in that scene.

Ellen: . . . there's not enough action and there's no broad idea to really make a scene and to understand all the characters.

Steve: Yes, but you can branch out from this and get a lot of things into it.

Teacher: What would your "branching out" consist of?

Alan: There could be a scene where the wife figures how she's first going to tell her husband that she's going to have a baby. Maybe she knows he'll be worried about money.

Robert: And then when she tells him, he's either nice to her or upset, depending on the kind of person he is and maybe whether he likes children.

One way to achieve the understanding that a play may be taken from real life, but is not real, was to project the next scene. Scene 1 was real to the degree that the eavesdropper could recall the precise dialogue and tone of voice. Scene 2 was to be created by each pupil according to a predetermined idea he wanted to reveal.

Teacher: If this were a part of a play, what do you think would happen next?

Barbara: I think the family will be close, but because of the baby they'd drift apart and as the baby grows older they'd argue over what school he should go to and things like that.

Alan: I pictured the father thinking it's going to be a boy and he starts buying boxing gloves and a football and he can't wait . . . and then he gets twin daughters. He'll feel bad even if he still loves them, but everything will work out all right.

Ellen: If you borrow Barbara's idea you could have the next scene take place 3 months later, after the woman already has the baby (pupils correct the "three months"). O.k., *thirteen* months later (yells of "It doesn't take that long!"). Anyway, the father isn't grinning anymore because he sees all the work he'll have to do and he has to get up in the middle of the night to give the child the bottle and he isn't so happy about it.

Robert: Yes, but she said "another baby," so he probably knows what it's like.

Mattie: I'd change it a little. They have five girls and now she has twin girls and the man gets upset. He's the only man and his whole world falls apart.

Teacher: We have a variety of possible endings. How will you decide which one of these will be scene 2?

(Pupils discuss a number of "wrong baby switches" they have seen on TV.)

Ellen: In all of these there's great exaggeration. They have to exaggerate to make it funny.

Laura: You have to select one that is believable. A few are. I know, because when my mother had a baby, I saw some pretty nutty things happen, like my father had to go someplace and I was with him and my mother thought she was going to have the baby that day and I never saw my father so nervous. Then he said he'd call her and give her the number of the place he was at so she could call him. He keeps dialing and gets a busy signal the whole time so he gets very worried. Then he looks and sees he's dialing the number of the phone he's calling from. Such things do happen.

Peter: Some real things seem like exaggeration. Where my father works, this man's wife was going to have a baby. So, a few weeks before she was expecting, he went out to try to find different ways of going to the hospital. When it finally came around, he up and left without her. It's a true story (laughter).

(Pupils tell stories of newspaper items they remember pertinent to the topic.)

Teacher: We said that Leslie's real scene can be developed in a number of different plays. What you decide upon for scene 2 will depend upon the big idea you want to say to the audience. What are some possibilities?

Robert: You might want to show that they don't really want a baby and what happens to everybody in that case. Or maybe they want a boy but get a girl and that will affect all of them in some way. Or maybe it's a sick baby and he needs lots of care and saps all the money to keep him alive.

Teacher: Once you have settled on your big idea you want to put across, then you can decide on incidents. Tonight, put down in writing the idea with which you are concerned and then the incidents that will fit. We all have Leslie's scene 1, the real scene she saw, but we don't have a play. We don't know what comes next. Each of you will write what you think scene 2 will be. Do that after you have listed your main idea.

In most cases it was necessary to spend much time on the questions: What do you think happened before the scene opened? What do you think could happen next? and Why do you think this could happen? The purpose of such deliberation was not only to gather many possible ideas for scene 2 but to help students understand that clues given in the real scene could be used in creating the playwright's purpose. In addition, the process of making a list of ideas also helped them see that incidents chosen must match the idea of the play. Then, too, with this list the teacher led the students to the realization that the enacted scene was taken from real life but the projected scenes to follow could not be real but must be ordered to illuminate the purpose.

Some classes were able to handle a consideration of what might have happened before the eavesdrop scene. Usually, this task is difficult for students, unless the scene offers adequate inferences. Speculating about situations that might have occurred before the play or between scenes offers opportunities for high-level cognitive functioning. Students work increasingly in the world of possibility. They must make inferences from what they see and hear, they are encouraged to predict consequences and perceive relationships between cause and consequence; they must go beyond the data given and develop ideas; they evaluate occurrences and draw conclusions about their significance; they differentiate between the relevant and irrelevant. Repeatedly the teacher asks, "What made you think so?" Repeatedly, students are urged to defend their position. The process of projecting scenes and the sequence that followed it encouraged divergent rather than convergent thinking.

Students briefly explained the main idea they wanted to portray in accordance with their interpretation of the real-life scene, described the setting, and wrote scene 2. Their creations provided ample opportunity to enlarge upon the concept that what characters do and say must develop the basic idea. Some students were not ready to consider the relation between the main idea and characters' behaviors. Teachers preferred to spend time building the concept that events in plays are ordered, not "carbon copies" of life. One student's demonstration of her understanding was representative:

Marsha: I wanted to portray the husband because he let the family do all the talking in Scene I and he didn't seem worried about little things like cribs. But he's right on the button with important things when the big moment comes, and so is she. So, they will manage.

My scene 2 takes place in the kitchen nine months later. The husband and wife are eating breakfast. He is serving it.

Wife: The doctor says today.

Husband: That means it will be over soon. How do you feel?

Wife: Just fine.

Husband: Don't be nervous.

Wife: Don't you be nervous.

Husband: Is everything ready?

Wife: Yes. The suitcase is on my bed and my coat is in the hall closet.

Husband: Don't worry. I won't forget anything.

Wife: Is the car ready?

Husband: Yes. I'll drive it out of the garage and leave it on the street.

Wife: Do you have your keys?

Husband: Yes. Right here in my pocket.

Wife: Hurry. I think it's time.

Husband: Just sit still and don't worry.

Other students wrote about abnormal babies being born, fathers rebelling at having to do dishes and change diapers, relatives tormenting the older child with questions about whether he'd like a new sister or brother, and the mother revolting against no help from the father and leaving him for a week to handle the children alone.

As several versions of scene 2 were discussed, the class came to realize that each one was different, depending upon the author's concept of the character and his motivations. As each stage setting was examined for suitability and as comparisons were made, there began to grow a deeper awareness that the projected scene 2 should be a sharpened effect of some aspect of life.

Within the discussion of new scenes came a simplified analysis of what characters do, say, and think. If the author's purpose was to show how an ostensibly weak and yielding character can manipulate those about him, would he have his character say, "get out of here!" or would he behave differently? How would the people in the play influence the events, including the ending? How would events influence them in turn? How would the characters help the author tell the world about human motivation and behavior? Implicit in these questions were complex concepts; it was no easy task to teach them. Teachers often neglect to fill in the gaps in student's understanding, that is, to offer the kinds of experiences necessary to achieve the understandings. The experiences cited here were efforts to fill the gaps.

It may be argued that the entire process described is too time-consuming. It does take time, but the level of involvement and participation, the sheer amount students learn about drama, the degree to which the "stage is set," and the background laid for new learnings make it possible to proceed with depth study at a level of understanding not usually attained.

A number of educators have written recently about the relationship between drama and thinking. Not least in importance is the notion inherent in Courtney's statement: "If the process of social learning is inherently dramatic, and through the impersonation of roles we all adjust to society, the whole process of thought itself is related to the dramatic imagination."[3] Moffett sees dialogue as "the major means of developing thought and language" and stresses that "discourse does not just convey thought, it also forges it."[4] Alington suggests, "We learn to think by practicing thinking, and one of the best ways to practice thinking is to make plans about something which interests us; and one of the most interesting kinds of plan to make is a plan for future [imaginative] action."[5]

Students may make observations and record ideas and questions about subjects that concern or puzzle them. The observations and ideas they are encouraged to record in their notebooks must be used continuously in the classroom. The teacher must help students examine their recorded ideas frequently in order to determine how well they are related to the new understandings which are being gained.

Through the study of professional plays, the teacher helps students to analyze the contents of their notebooks for strengths and weaknesses. In turn, the analysis of their findings about plays and people helps pupils to bring richer insights to each new piece of drama. The discussion of each play should be related directly to the ideas the students are struggling to express and to clarify.

The recorded items are examined carefully to help the student decide what they mean in terms of his interests and in terms of possible purposes for his play. Even when the student has articulated his purpose, he must be helped to keep it in the forefront. As the student arrives at the point of decision making with respect to his own creative work, he engages in the very same process of harmonizing incidents and purpose; he assesses incidents to determine whether they enhance the characterization.

As they made plans for their own creations, many students found it comfortable to begin with a concrete ending. More students had ideas for the ending than for the opening of their play. In a sense students seemed to be working backwards when they made decisions about the concrete incidents first and then evolved a purpose. However, abstract ideas are evolved originally from the concrete; therefore, the process is a sound one. Certainly, the process helped students to share ideas.

Linda: I have an idea of showing a child who was blind and never could see. She has an operation and I want to show how she feels seeing because she doesn't know what people are going to look like. Yet, she's excited.

Barbara: That's a good idea because she has fear and anticipation of things you don't know about. She's afraid, but she wants to see. There's conflict within herself.

Teacher: So, she has mixed feelings about an impending new experience.

Michael: That happens a lot. I wanted to go on the roller coaster and I was scared but I wanted to go.

Robert: It's like the first time you go to camp. I was petrified, but I wanted to go so badly.

Teacher: Then, Linda's idea of mixed feelings about something which will be a new experience is a very common one which has meaning for all of us, though our specific situations are not the same. The idea, then, is universal.

Mattie: I read a book about a little girl whose mother died and father remarried. She resented the new mother because she had to share the father's affection.
Teacher: Are there other situations in life which revolve around rivalry for love?
Leslie: When a new child is born and the other one feels very left alone.
Barbara: It can be with brother and sister of the same age where the parents favor one over the other.

Barbara: I think Mattie could write a play where the girl is unwilling to show any love to the new mother and her sister. She wanted everybody to show her love but she was unwilling to give any.
Anne: Mine is going to be about a teen-ager whose parents are going away for the weekend and she wants to prove how grown-up she is. Her aunt who lives close by wants to take care of her and her brother, but the girl insists the aunt take care of them only one night. She wants to do it the rest of the weekend to prove she is grown-up.

Allen: I have an idea of a boy who moves into a new neighborhood and it's kind of a rough one and he either has to join this rough neighborhood or else he has nothing to do. He joins but he knows it's wrong.
Teacher: In planning this, what will you demonstrate?
Allen: The struggle between the right thing and the wrong one.
Teacher: In your problem, do you think joining the gang would definitely be wrong?
Allen: I am going to exaggerate the gang, and it will definitely be wrong.*

An analysis of the roles played by the teacher in the preceding excerpt is illuminating. In effect, the teacher used students' ideas to help students formulate purpose, which is in essence a generalization or a universalization. Teachers were aware of the fact that one specific is not adequate for generalization.

Through procedures such as those described, students engaged in verbal collaboration that is so important to the thinking process. They were propelled into a situation requiring them to use their data in writing. They had to make choices of characters, setting, and events. They made fiction out of fact and arranged in new ways events they had observed. An awareness grew that it is necessary to infer what goes on between acts and what took place before a play opens. It was essential for students to learn to recognize those clues which would aid them in the important task of inference making. Every activity involved thinking, planning, choice making, analyzing, discriminating, and generalizing.

Reading One-Act Plays

Generally, teachers moved rapidly into the reading of one-act plays. Appropriate one-act plays are still not easy to find for all levels of adolescent development. However, their availability, especially in paperback, is increasing, and even literature anthologies

---

*These excerpts were contributed by Elinor Weinreich Joseph.

are devoting greater attention to them since the Dartmouth Conference of 1966. The one-act play lends itself to the achievement of certain aims. Its brevity permits the introduction of a number of new ideas.

Since students already had considered the setting and since this is a relatively simple factor for them to understand, a number of teachers found this to be a satisfying focus for early study. *Thursday Evening* by Morley and *Trifles* by Glaspell were often used for this purpose. Students and teachers read stage directions noting the explicit directions for furnishing the stage and the description of the appearance of the characters. Students hypothesized about what the play's action might be in such a setting and what the mood would be. In some instances they made drawings of the stage setting, which helped them envision the action of the play as they proceeded with the reading and which were referred to for a variety of reasons during and after the reading and performance. Why does the playwright furnish the stage with these particular objects? Is there any significance to the particular location of each object? Are there any objects not mentioned in the initial stage directions which do play a significant role? How do you account for this delayed focus upon the object?

Students considered the appearance and overt behavior of characters: How does each character look? How does the playwright describe his appearance? Precisely what does he do when he first appears? What is the significance of these actions? What is the order of the appearance of each character? Is there any significance in this order? Focusing on particular objects and behaviors of characters helps to concretize the difficult transition to intelligent reading of plays and leads to a consideration of character, theme, and motivations underlying human behavior. Focusing on the concrete makes it possible for inexperienced students to uncover the basic meaning of the play. How students moved from an examination of concrete objects and events to greater abstraction in one discussion period is apparent from the following excerpts taken from a transcript of an eighth-grade class discussion of *Thursday Evening.**

Linda: The idea is that people appreciate what they have when they are about to lose it.

Bob: I think he's saying people fight because fighting is universal.

Debbie: He's showing that in-laws should not be stereotyped. They can do good for a married couple.

Richard: But they create the tension in the first place!

Teacher: If you believe as Linda does that people appreciate what they have only when they are in danger of losing it, why did Morley need the in-laws?

Richard: I don't think he did. I think he'd be better off without them.

Gary: He had to have them to show that people can influence others. They realized that Laura and Gordon were tense about them and they decided to play a game which would help the husband and wife relax.

Linda: I think they could have come together again without the in-laws. The author didn't need the in-laws. Gordon and Laura loved each other anyway. And if the parents didn't appear, there would be no tension to begin with.

*Excerpts contributed by Elinor Weinreich Joseph.

Teacher: Is it possible that we haven't yet discovered the real purpose if the playwright included the in-laws and we find them superfluous?

Howard: It could be he included them to make it humorous and to show up Gordon and Laura to themselves, to show themselves how silly they are.

Paula: Laura's mother keeps bringing up how horrible it is for Laura to live in this run-down house. Way down deep she means it even though she's making a joke of it now.

Bunny: They represent two different worlds: Laura's mother cares about material things, and Gordon's about the intellectual things. She says he's very intellectual and he'd become something if he wasn't tied down to a family.

Gary: I think we're missing the whole point. This is supposed to be a *humorous* play.

Teacher: Have you ever "carried on" without meaning what you said? Why did you do it and how did you feel?

Reading one-act plays was often alternated with acting out short stories. In some cases, creative dramatizations preceded reading the one-act play and constituted the transition from introductory activities to play reading. There is an important reason for acting out stories, besides the fact that most students enjoy the activity. Moffett explains one relationship between drama and narrative:

> The action of a narrative is not ongoing; it *has* gone on; it is reported action. As such it is a resume of some previous drama—summarized and abstracted by somebody . . . if the events are unrolling before his eyes—ongoing—they are being coded for the first time by someone who is *attending* them. . . . His coding of events is a first-order abstraction. . . . Whereas narrative summarizes drama, drama elaborates narrative.[6]

Moffett's statement pinpoints the abstract nature of the coding process that is essential in the intelligent viewing of drama. To help students grasp how drama is created from narrative, the creative dramatization of stories is of major importance. Drama requires that the players as well as the viewers fill in the gaps. Exploration of physical movements necessary to portray something described in narrative, but impossible to describe in drama, is one instance of filling in the gaps. A number of students take the role in spontaneous dramatization until the basic meaning of a particular event or the intrinsic nature of a character is explored. The exploration comes not only through the enactment but through the discussion following it, which focuses on the differences in interpretation as these differences came through to the audience.

Creative dramatization of stories also involves students in script writing, a process which reinforces their understanding of the relationship between narrative and drama. The very discussion in which the students engage is also dialogue, when it is a real discussion. Conversation in itself can be most dramatic and can be used to introduce the concept of dramatic dialogue as a gap filler essential in translating narrative to drama. There are a number of stories which lend themselves to gap filling with dialogue created by students. Teachers found particularly useful stories such as Björnsen's "The Father," Tolstoi's "How Much Land Does a Man Need?" Kleihauer's "The Cub," Hemingway's "The Killers," Cather's "Paul's Case," Saroyan's "The Shepherd's Daughter," and Faulkner's "Barn Burning."

Enactment of a story with improvised dialogue serves a variety of purposes. It helps students' personal development through language, and it gives them a sense of the immediacy of drama in contrast to the reporting element of the narrative. Also, with improvisation, the student has an opportunity to use his creative imagination. Courtney sees the relationship between creative imagination and drama: *"The creative imagination is essentially dramatic in its character.* It is the ability to see imaginative possibilities, to comprehend the relationships between two concepts, and to see the dynamic force between them."[7] To improvise appropriate dialogue is no easy task, for it requires that students perceive a number of interrelated concepts. For example, they must sense the relationship between a character and what he would be apt to say; they must recognize the conflict and its effect upon the characters; they must feel the importance of a certain event in the affairs of the characters.

Through creative dramatization, students gain new understanding about the fact that dialogue is the basic means through which the playwright delineates character. When they read one-act plays, they discover character through reading dialogue and gathering inferences from what people say and do as well as from what is said about them and to them.

In some instances, each one-act play was dramatized in part so that the discussions of purpose and character as inferred from dialogue were highly motivated. Pupils performed certain key scenes over and over in an attempt to convey the author's purpose with respect to the kind of persons he was intending to portray. One class that read Haughton's *The Dear Departed* was intrigued by the title and used it to discuss several aspects of the play, including development of character. In another class, the function of the child, Victoria, provided a fruitful field for indirect analysis of character development through dialogue and for analysis of the author's purpose.

Whatever path teachers chose in order to arrive at an understanding of character through things people do and say, there was an emphasis on the concept that every word is important in developing the reader's image of the personality and the reader's insight into the character's motivation. What do others say to him? Why do they say these things? Does he say one thing and mean another? What does he really mean? Everybody wants something in a play. What does he want? What does he say he wants? What does he want that he doesn't even speak about? Does he know he wants it? Why doesn't he mention it?

For a considerable time it is necessary for the teacher to concentrate on the main character and the ways in which the author used the other characters to contribute to the reader's feelings about the main one and understandings of his behavior. Students do not usually perceive deep motives until the teacher takes steps to help them. Pupils do not see the role of minor characters in the development of the main one until they are led by the teacher who makes a conscious effort to achieve the understanding. "Why is Victoria included?" "What does the author achieve in creating her?" "What would happen if he did not include her?" Often the decision as to who *is* the main character and a discussion of the question, What makes you think so? are the vehicles for achieving the goal. An examination of the questions, How does the author feel about him? and How do you know? is a more sophisticated focus for discussion.

Fortified with new understandings, students read four or five one-act plays. In some classes they continued to explore roles through role playing a telling scene. In other classes they discussed which play was best for revealing motivation for behavior, intensity of conflict, and character portrayal. They compared plays with respect to pertinence of title, revelation of "what the characters looked like," importance of stage setting, and depth of central meaning. In a third group of classes, students arranged plays in rank order according to a criterion chosen by teacher or students. In cases where students discussed possible criteria and then worked in groups arranged according to the criteria selected, the results were fruitful because there was a number of foci for discussion: Which criterion was most appropriate in the final analysis? What problems did the group encounter as they attempted to rank order? In certain classes, students worked independently on specific criteria before meeting in groups. They considered questions such as What are the main ideas in each play? Which of these ideas appeals most to you? To what extent do you think these ideas are true in real life? What makes you think so? What are the chief motivations of the main characters? Which main character appeals most to you? By what means did the playwright manage to get his motivation across to you? Then the students stacked the cards according to the appeal that the play held for them. In general, the last question was so difficult that teachers encouraged pupils to think about it rather than to respond in writing. The other questions initially received only brief responses in order to serve as reminders and stimulants for thinking. These questions later formed the focus for class discussions and more detailed writing. Discussions inspired students to raise their own questions about particular plays, especially as the teacher moved into evaluating plays.

The teacher may ask students to note the two plays they like most and the one they like least. If a committee is appointed to tally the information about classmates' opinions, the results may become the subject of heated discussions. Out of the discussion grows a depth of conceptual thinking and generalization which is not often achieved otherwise. Assessing the ideas which have the greatest appeal and those which fail to capture students, verbalizing the relationship between these ideas and real life, and articulating the beneath-the-surface significance of human behavior are activities intriguing to young adolescents. Students are meeting the playwright on their own terms: They select the plays of significance to them; they decide the "most and least;" they make the connections between the playwright's ideas and the vicarious or actual experiences of adolescents; they make the judgments about human behavior. This is not to say that the teacher plays no role, nor is it to say that anyone's opinion is as good as any other. There is a framework within which one learns to make judgments. Students are asked to give evidence; it is not a case of anything goes. They are encouraged to think about their own judgments and how they are related to the totality portrayed by the playwright; they are prompted to compare their judgments with the evaluations made by peers, for pupils experience the play on different levels.

It is necessary for some groups to begin the evaluations on a simple level. Each student may make charts based on the reading of a few one-act plays and rate five or six items on a four- or-five-point scale. The scale may range from excellent to unacceptable, and the items may be framed as questions:

a.   Was the stage setting best for the author's purpose?
b.   Did the events suit his purpose?
c.   Was the characters' behavior appropriate to the purpose?

    d.   Were their motivations in tune with the complexity or simplicity of the charac-
        ters portrayed?
        A portion of one student's chart will serve as an illustration.

Rating: 4 stands for "excellent," 3 "good," 2 "fair," 1 "poor."

Name of Play:	*The Undercurrent*	*The Lottery*
Purpose of Author:	One family member can hurt another to a dangerous degree.	It is destructive for people to follow blindly tradition or superstition.
(a) Setting	3	3
(b) Events	4	4
(c) Behavior	4	4
(d) Motivations	2	4
Total Score	13	15
Rank Order	5	1

    In one class after a discussion of reasons for student ratings of five one-act plays, the teacher introduced briefly *Where the Cross Is Made* by O'Neill. She permitted the class to enact the play at sight. Upon completion of this activity, the teacher pretended that she assumed all pupils understood the play. "All right. That's enough work on this play. Now let's go on to the next one." The spontaneous roar of protest that came in answer was not exactly unexpected. The teacher pretended she had no questions to ask them; therefore, why waste time on the same play just talking? The upshot of the matter was the group's assumption of the responsibility to raise the questions they wanted to ask because of admitted gaps in their understanding. They wrote questions on the board and led their own discussion using the teacher only as a resource person. It is interesting to note that a few of the elements that puzzled them were aspects with which most teachers do not concern themselves because they take it for granted that bright children know.

    1.   Was Nat crazy or not?
    2.   Were they ghosts or were they real?
    3.   Where did he get the map?

Of course, there were other questions that demonstrated great depth of understanding, but the above came first.

    When a class experiences satisfaction in thinking and planning together, when they feel they learn from each other as well as from the teacher, they are not prone to be satisfied with cursory treatment of a piece of literature. Nor are they satisfied with a line-by-line analysis which bears little significance for most adolescents.

    The one-act plays which were reported by teachers to be most fruitful for classroom use were Fletcher's *Sorry, Wrong Number,* Glaspell's *Trifles,* Ehlert's *The Undercur-*

rent, Tarkington's *The Trysting Place,* O'Neill's *Where the Cross is Made,* Gilbert's *Trial by Jury,* and Wilder's *The Happy Journey to Trenton and Camden.* Undoubtedly, these choices were influenced by availability of plays.

Writing Plays to Understand Drama

One procedure which encouraged students to review a play in order to see how the motivations of a character were revealed was to add a character, remove one, or cause one to behave differently from the way in which the author portrayed him. If an additional character was created, the problem became, What would he have to do in order to serve the author's purpose? Usually, the class decided there was little he could do, but not before many inappropriate suggestions had been made and discussed. If a character was removed, the problem was, What functions did he perform, and can the purpose be achieved without those functions? If a character was to behave differently, the question became, Can the other characters continue to behave as they had and still push the author's purpose forward? Through such analysis students were able to perceive how the playwright reveals motivation for characters' behaviors. For example, in a discussion of *The Finger of God* by Wilde, one class became involved in the role of the girl as a factor that could not be eliminated.

Allen: Strickland wanted to stop stealing, but his will was not strong enough and the girl came and gave man's will an extra push.

Ellen: . . . . He imagined the girl. I don't think she was there in flesh and blood. . . . She's his conscience. He didn't steal because of his conscience. The author can't eliminate a man's conscience if he has one. That was his fate. He was trying to show himself that he could steal again and fight off his conscience.

Barbara: He hated himself so much that he thought, "I'm pretty rotten. I must have been born to steal."

Linda: . . . . If he couldn't be anything else, he'd be a thief. He showed them all.

Laura: . . . . He stole a long time ago and was so guilt-ridden about it that he believed it was fated for him to steal and so the desire for money obsessed him.

Arnie: But he's been a broker for over twenty years. He's probably honest if people trusted him that long.

Sandy: He has a good reputation. The lady gave him the money to invest for her.

Charles: He's already been imagining things. He's ready to go off his mind. The girl vanishes and leaves no trace. He loses the timetable before he got to the office and then it suddenly shows up on his desk. . . . A secretary wouldn't just rummage through his things when he's not there.

Larry: She says she brought the letter because she knew he wouldn't be there next day. Strickland asks her how she knew. He denies that he was taking a train to Chicago.

Laura: The secretary brought his unimportant mail and he said the clerks usually take care of that. If she was his personal secretary, she'd have known that and she wouldn't have brought the mail. He's imagining that she is saying, "I'm the girl who answers when you ring three times." She was not there. Three rings are a bad omen and she's his conscience. She's there when he's about to do something he doesn't want to do. At such times he gives the button three rings and she comes to the rescue. She's his conscience. She's not flesh and blood. She stands for his conscience.

Mattie: He's panic-stricken when he finds her gone. The window has never been opened, but she's gone.

Laura: . . . . He didn't recognize her. She didn't tell who she was because she wasn't there! He was telling how they caught him in twenty-four hours, and she thinks it's funny, and she says, "You've been honest ever since." It's the conscience working and reassuring him.

Sherry: He says, "You're too late. Not even the finger of God could stop me." Later he says he'll stay and face the music. Now, if she didn't exist, she couldn't have changed his mind.

Barbara: Just because the play said the girl entered doesn't mean you have to take it literally. If it said a ghost enters, would that mean a real one enters?

Linda: Sherry said the girl reserved a stateroom for Mr. Strickland. It could have been anyone. Even Strickland himself could have done it because he is so excited and nervous. He could have done it and checked again and found he had done it. You can't take everything literally in a play like this because the truth lies beyond it.*

Controversial questions and issues are a crucial agent in propelling group thinking and sharing of ideas about the behavior of human beings. One teacher raised the question, "Is this a serious play?" The ideas which students developed in an attempt to solve this problem were on a level as high as the excerpts above. The same question was raised again in connection with Tarkington's *The Trysting Place.* If *The Trysting Place* is not a serious play, how would the incidents have to be changed in order to make it so? Would the present characters serve the purpose? Would their motivation remain the same?

Throughout the process of uncovering motivations, pupils need to be directed to seek from their environment examples of concealed motivations or whatever aspect of human motivations was being considered at any particular time. A natural outgrowth of one discussion on pertinent elements in their own environment led one class to decide to ask parents, "How did you meet and how did you decide to marry?" The fact that they consulted each parent separately provided fodder for further consideration when it transpired that the two versions were often quite different.

Allen: My mother said she was pretty scared. This was at the beginning of the war and my father was in the Army. . . . My mother's friend gave my father's friend my mother's address and my father's friend gave him my mother's address and he wrote to my mother. . . . When he was on furlough, they met and dated and they kept corresponding during the war. . . . Then one day he proposed in the ice-cream parlor and my mother said "o.k." and that was the end.

---

*Excerpts were contributed by Elinor Weinreich Joseph.

Sandy: After my mother met my father, she went to California to think things over. She became a secretary and my father was in New York and he called her up and proposed over the phone and she came back.

Then the students wrote the dialogue they imagined to have taken place during the proposal. Several such suggestions for observations and for out-of-school conversations gave tangible assistance to those students who were still floundering and seeking a focus for their play. The suggestions offered to all students new areas for discovering new ideas about relationships. One student who had twin sisters used incidents she observed and permitted herself the luxury of imagining what *might* happen as a consequence of some of the incidents. Again, these were concrete events and incidents that were examined for a variety of reasons, depending on students' needs as they tried to shape their plays.

As students began to write their plays, the teacher again directed them to professional productions which would help them with their particular problems. For example, *The Trysting Place* was used as a guide for format. Teachers need to lose fear of using a play more than once. Since the purpose is changed with each use, the rereading of parts provides for depth of study without complaints of boredom. It is acceptable because it is purposeful with respect to students' goals. Students need a second look and a third in order to proceed with the work involved in their own creation. Thus, they see the relationship of each element in the professional play to the one they wish to create.

Assistance with seeing relationships was fed into the students' creations of the mother-father proposal scene and others. It is difficult for young people to create a situation in which what the characters say reveals their motives. They need a great many experiences with literature and with looking at life. Some literary works which are suitable for this purpose are Chayefsky's *The Mother,* Miller's *The Rabbit Trap,* and Aurthur's *Man on the Mountaintop.* The study of plays in conjunction with creative writing bore fruit as was evidenced in many students' works. Students selected a variety of topics. Among them was a heavy concentration on black-white, boy-girl relationships. In general the ideas were in accordance with the stereotyped situation so prevalent in TV drama. Others selected areas such as politics, with scenes illustrating the fact that "the good guy doesn't necessarily win." One boy whose brother had recently been drafted into the service was concerned with the loneliness and rejection that is possible when young men are wrenched from their familiar surroundings. His creation, *The Recruit,* a crude first attempt by a young adolescent, nevertheless demonstrated many things that were learned. The description of the setting is worded with some finesse and a kind of empathy for Barney comes through to the reader. Character development and motivations for behavior are lacking. The dialogue as a means of portraying character is weak. Nevertheless, the creation shows evidence of some elemental understandings of the genre. The original play is reproduced here so that the reader may gain some idea of what can and cannot be expected of young adolescents working on a piece of writing as complex as a drama.

THE RECRUIT

Setting: The setting is a brightly lighted bunk house. There are three double beds spaced evenly about eight feet apart. Suitcases are scattered around each bed. The double bed in the center particularly catches the eye because clothes are spread all over the top bed and a rather dumb-looking person is up there unpacking. The room, otherwise, is quite orderly as an Army bunkhouse should be.

(*As we look in we see* Tom Rubin, *a man about twenty years old. He has blond hair and an evil look in his eye. He enters and takes his bunk below* Barney Bugle. Barney *is a boy eighteen years old with black hair combed down over his face in bangs. He is tall and lanky.*)

TOM:	Hey, jerk! What are you doing?
BARNEY:	I's just unpacking here.
TOM:	Well, do you mind getting your underwear out of my face?
BARNEY:	Why, sure, anything you say. Say you haven't told me your name yet. I'll tell you mine. My name is Barney Bugle. That's spelt B-U-G-L-E.
TOM:	(*Sarcastically*) That's fine. My name is Tom Rubin and I don't know how to spell it.
BARNEY:	Gee, that's funny. I ain't too smart and I know how to spell my name.
TOM:	(*Muttering to himself*) Oh, my goodness.

(*Entering now is* Sgt. Meany. *He is a fairly short but well-built man with a mean look on his face. Entering with him are* Howie Green *and* Joe Martis. *Both are ordinary men twenty or twenty-one years of age.*)

MEANY:	O.K. you four. Line up here.
BARNEY:	Heya Sarge. Am I gonna be in the Army like you?
MEANY:	(*Angrily*) Shut up!
BARNEY:	(*Shyly*) O.K. Sarge.
MEANY:	Now listen, you men. The colonel is coming to check on the new recruits, so I want you all to polish your shoes and look half-decent. (*Loudly*) You hear?

(*They all look quite nervous and scared now except for* Barney.)

BARNEY:	Sarge, can I say something?
MEANY:	No!
BARNEY:	But Sarge.
MEANY:	That's all!

(*He exits. The men all go to their respective bunks.* Barney *goes to the top one in the middle;* Tom *underneath him.* Howie Green *goes to the right and* Joe *to the left.*)

TOM:	(*Whispering to Howie*) What a nut up there.
HOWIE:	Yeah! He sounds like he never even went to school.
TOM:	(*Still whispering*) I think he was raised in the mountain or something.

(Joe *walks over now and the three all huddle together by* Howie's *bed.*)

JOE:	I guess you were talking about it up there.
TOM:	Yeah!
JOE:	Boy, it's going to be tough to live with him for two years.
HOWIE:	Maybe we won't have to.
JOE:	What d'ya mean?

HOWIE:	It's like this. The colonel is coming to check over the new recruits, right?
TOM:	Yeah, so?
HOWIE:	We'll fix it so as soon as the colonel takes a look at him it'll be the last time he'll ever see the inside of an Army post.
JOE:	I see what you mean.
TOM:	That's not a bad idea.
HOWIE:	Do we shake on it?
JOE and TOM:	You bet! *(They do and the curtain closes.)*

(As the curtain opens again, Barney *is on his bunk polishing his shoes. The other three are at* Tom's *bed thinking.)*

JOE:	What can we do to foul this guy up?
TOM:	Shut up, I'm thinking.
HOWIE:	Listen, this is what we'll do. We'll all get dressed the worst way we know how. Even though he dresses terribly, we'll have to dress even worse.
JOE:	Shhh, keep it down. He'll hear us.
HOWIE:	O.K. Like I was saying, we'll have to dress even worse. We'll tell him that's the way you're supposed to dress in the Army.
TOM:	Yeah, I've got a pair of these holey dungarees with me.
JOE:	I'll find something.
HOWIE:	O.K. Let's get to work.
BARNEY:	Boy, I hope I can pass inspection. I'm gonna try my best to polish these shoes. (Barney *now jumps down from the bunk and sees* Tom *putting on those holey dungarees.)* Say, that's no way to pass inspection.
TOM:	Why, sure it is. How else are you going to fight Japs? In your best Sunday suit?
BARNEY:	Are you sure that's how the sarge wants us to dress?

(The others all finished dressing in their bad clothes. All crowd around now.)

TOM:	Why, sure. Look at Howie and Joe *(He points.)* See how they're dressed?
BARNEY:	Uh-Hu.
TOM:	Well then why would we be dressing like this if we weren't sure?
BARNEY:	I guess you're right.

(Just then they hear footsteps approaching.)

HOWIE:	Holy mackeral! It's the sarge.
JOE:	What are we going to do? He can't catch us in these clothes.
TOM:	Quick! Under the beds!

(They quickly dash under the beds and Barney *is left there all alone, bewildered, and dazed. The sergeant enters.)*

MEANY: No, no Barney. That's not how we dress in the Army. Fix that tie. Put your shirt in your pants. Stand up straight! Look like a man.

(Barney *does each of the things he says.*)

MEANY: All right now. You look presentable. The colonel will be here soon and I want you all to pass inspection. Wait a minute! Where are the others?

BARNEY: Well, Sarge, the strangest thing happened. They heard you comin' and they all went and ran under the beds.

MEANY: *(Roaring)* Under the beds? Have you been drinking?

BARNEY: Honest Injun, Sarge. See for yourself.

(Meany *looks under the bed* Tom *is under and pulls him out.*)

MEANY: O.K. What's the meaning of this?

(The others have come out now.)

TOM: Well—you see, er, Sarge, it's er, well—

MEANY: Never mind! (He starts to look them over and sees the clothes they're dressed in.) What the—Where do you men think you are—at a dude ranch?

(*They hear footsteps again and this time* Col. Smith *enters.*)

MEANY: Attention!

(*Everyone snaps to attention.* Col. Smith *takes a look at the four men. The colonel is an elderly man sixty years old. He has a mustache and a trace of an English accent.*)

COL.:   Pitiful! Just pitiful! Listen you three, I'm giving you one more chance. If I ever see a display like this again, you'll be punished severely. Meany, what do you know about this?

MEANY: Well, you see sir. . . .

COL.:   Never mind. I know what I see. Remember what I say, you three. By the way (*pointing to* Barney) very nice, you.

BARNEY: Thank you, Col.

COL.:   Carry on, Meany.

MEANY: Yes, sir!

(They salute and the colonel exits.)

MEANY: You men are lucky. Now if I ever catch you pulling a stunt like that again, it'll be two months K.P. duty. As for you, Bugle, well . . .

BARNEY: Yes, Sarge.

MEANY: Well, all I can say is I'm proud of you, boy.

BARNEY: *(With a lot of emotion)* Gee, thanks, Sarge.

MEANY: Carry on, men. *(He exits.)*

BARNEY: Gee, I'm in the Army now.

*(The others have all gone to their bunks, faces in their pillows, and hands over their ears. The curtain closes.)**

The End

Reading, enacting, evaluating, and discussing plays gave direct help to students in the writing of their own plays because these activities furnished them with a variety of ideas. Students often became so intrigued by a new idea that they scrapped their first attempts and began all over again. As teachers and peers helped students with the writing of their plays, other aspects of the genre which pupils needed to know were uncovered. For example, one teacher discovered that the element of conflict had not received sufficient attention in her teaching. Another teacher realized that the role of exaggeration in building up the conflict was inadequately conceived by some students. A third found that it was necessary to give pupils a new view of the interpretation of a character with emphasis on what he says and does. On occasion roles played by repetition, contrast, and foreshadowing needed to be stressed.

Teachers must keep uppermost in mind the purposes of encouraging students to engage in play writing. They are not seeking professional playwrights. Just as art and music are for the enjoyment of all pupils and for the enrichment of their lives, just so is play writing and acting. Educators can learn much from children's spontaneous activities. When children engage in play writing, they learn to appreciate the art itself. More than that, play writing involves students in a creative cognitive act in which there is an opportunity to think together as well as individually. It requires careful observation of life.

The Full-length Play

It is through the full-length play that the teacher has the opportunity to develop a concept of the relationship between the characters and the audience. A productive focus for understanding that relationship is the idea of the "impending future." Langer draws clearly the contrast between human understanding of the future in daily life and audience reaction to it as the drama on stage unfolds. "In actual life the impending future is very vaguely felt . . . we do not usually have any idea of the future as a total experience which is coming because of our past and present acts. . . . In drama, however, this sense of destiny is paramount. It is what makes the present action seem like an integral part of the future, howbeit the future has not unfolded yet. . . . Even before one has any idea of what the conflict is to be . . . one feels the tension developing."[8]

The fact that the audience unfolds the future created in drama makes it mandatory that students be taught how to function as an intelligent audience. It is the audience who perceives the conflict and realizes there will be far-reaching consequences. Students need to learn that they know things the characters performing in front of them do not sense. The characters are presumably as unaware of the future as we are in our daily

---

*From the classroom of Elinor Weinreich Joseph.

lives. The full-length play has a greater opportunity to develop a vision of ordered reality than does the one-act play.

The theme of the impending future is not the only one that will sustain the reading of a full-length play. There is music in the words and phrases, the ideas, and the harmony of people and events that are in plays. Most teachers found that an all-encompassing activity which grew out of the particular play itself helped to sustain student participation and cognitive functioning. For example, students read Shaw's *Pygmalion* and selected lines and phrases which had not been used by Lerner and Loewe in *My Fair Lady*, but which in their opinion would make an equally good musical. The musical they proposed to create had to be in keeping with the spirit of Shaw. Usually, the students completed the first reading of the play in one or two sittings and were ready with their suggestions. Their combined suggestions constituted a formidable list from which to select the focus of songs. A small portion of one such list included

> "It's a fearful strain."
> "Don't you be so saucy."
> "For I'm a thinking man."
> "Besides, she's useful."
> "We're always talking, Eliza."
> "You're not bad looking."
> "I was happy. I was free."
> "That middle-class morality."
> "She doesn't belong to him."
> "I want a little kindness."

The task of deciding which phrases to keep and which to eliminate is a discriminatory function, for it means evaluating and selecting the relevant or the most relevant. The students must carefully consider all aspects of Shaw's *Pygmalion* in making these decisions. Then comes the equally exacting task of deciding which phrases will fall into each act, determining what the plot will be, and ascertaining how it will be apportioned into acts. Once these decisions are made, students can work in groups to make up their own musical.

In more than one class there were exciting discussions about why Lerner and Loewe did not make use of certain phrases which the students felt to be of great significance. For example, one class chose the phrase, "It's a fearful strain," which they believed characterized Higgins' actions as well as any other phrase. "Sit down!" and "Won't you sit down?" to contrast Higgins and Pickering were favorites. Students searched the play over and over to find reinforcement for their concept of contrasting characters. "It's no use talking to her like that" was chosen by some pupils who thought the musical neglected the importance of Mrs. Pearce. "She's so deliciously low" was an expression they "just loved" and one group used the line for one of the lyrics despite the fact that there was much dispute about its significance. There was controversy also about "Wrap her up in brown paper."

The preparation required to create lyrics was far greater than teachers anticipated. However, pupils didn't regard it as a requirement. This was an intriguing assignment and one which offered them vast empires for creativity. One boy claimed he read the play nine times and some parts of it well over that to seek the lines he wanted for his lyric. He needed lines which appealed to the ear, described the character, and meshed with the theme of the play.

During this activity it was not necessary for the teacher to ask detailed questions. Students themselves debated the issue, "Why didn't Lerner and Loewe use Mrs. Pearce?" They initially raised that problem when they discovered, "You must be reasonable, Mr. Higgins," "But what's to become of her?" and "You must look ahead a little." These issues were crucial to the play as was Mrs. Pearce, they thought. Their defense of their position left little to be desired. One boy felt that Shaw "packs a wallop in every line. It's such a little play and it says so much." When pupils come to such conclusions because the teacher has created a situation which permits them to learn, they examine a play on their own terms and for their own ends. The students make the analysis because they need to do so.

The reader must not mistake the intent of the activity of creating new lyrics and music. The intent is not to make playwrights and composers, though this would not be unacceptable to many. Rather, the purpose is to permit students to seek and find elements in the drama which have meaning for them.

Individual students compared the play *My Fair Lady* with Shaw's *Pygmalion*. They asked, "Why does act 1 scene 2 make Doolittle such a central character?" "In act 1 scene 3 are the behaviors of Pickering and Higgins true to Shaw?" In similar fashion they made a comparative study of *Pygmalion* and its musical adaptation. This whole comparative activity was originated by a few students who carried it through to the end on their own terms. They also carried many of their classmates and their teacher along with them. They spent hours examining the two versions, raised questions, and brought them into class for group thinking and illumination.

Some teachers did not ask students to create the new musical they planned. Rather, students used the knowledge gained from planning a musical to read another play which had never been the inspiration for a professional musical. Ibsen's *An Enemy of the People* was such a play. Before teachers decided to use it as a focus for a musical, there was much heated discussion among them about whether a serious play like this could or should be a musical. Arguments ran from "It is a serious play which would be killed by a musical" to "Well, what about *West Side Story?* Didn't that have serious elements to it?" Those teachers who dared to work with a play like *The Enemy of the People* found that students who usually disliked the play because it was "boring" now studied it with enthusiasm. This time the students were to create the musical and put on a performance for themselves.

One teacher reported:

> They picked out about nine thousand ideas and then we had to eliminate the silly ideas and pick out the most appropriate ones. There was a discussion of why this or that would be important. That night kids went home and came back the next day with songs already written. I didn't even assign it. I didn't have to teach the rest of the play, that's the way the whole thing went. I had them in committees to create the music. They rented two guitars. I was pretty impressed with the whole thing.
>
> Mike was on a committee with two boys who sang in monotones. They made up a song called "On the Town." While Mike sang accompanied by his guitar, the two boys said,

"Uptown, Downtown, Uptown, Downtown," in the background. The main idea was pollution spreading uptown, downtown. It was really very well done.

I felt using a serious play for a musical was a marvelous idea. It brought the whole point across. Students pointed out that people were not able to recognize what was good for them. This man had a sense of responsibility to his community and to his people and he was not going to run away. I asked them, "If you were writing the play, would you make the hero leave?" People threw rocks in the window at him and his family. For the first time Michael stood up and shouted, "Stay!" Michael is a black boy who is very bright and very frightened. He won't do anything unless he knows absolutely that it's going to be perfect. He has a big loud voice and he only whispers. I'm very concerned about Mike, but this was the first time that he struck out according to the way he really felt. Alan said he wouldn't stay if his children were in jeopardy. The community doesn't deserve it. "Why should I stay, and I don't think it's practical to believe anyone would stay." Then we talked about whether there are any people who do stay and we mentioned the Albert Schweitzers, the James Merediths, and the Dr. Kings.

In their songs, characterization came out tremendously. We had to pick out which ideas would be best to show that particular character. They established why his brother went against him, his brother being a follower, the conformer, and sang about how his brother tells him, "You've always been different." He was afraid of his brother's difference and they brought that out as well as the fact that he denied himself things and was afraid to live. He drank tea, whereas his brother had a passion for life. He was a man who loved life, loved his wife; he was a beautiful man. He loved his children, he could express his feeling, he loved being a doctor, he was involved with writing and with doing.

When other teachers taught the play, just plain taught it, the children didn't like it in the eighth grade, but these children did. They were singing it. They were thinking about it; they were involved in it. They no longer saw the play as taking place in Scandinavia fifty years ago. It hit home and they translated it in terms of the racial situation today: people who are trying to stop housing for lower-class black citizens. There were black children in each of the classes and this made it more real.

We discussed why the main character couldn't succeed in making the people see what was in their best interest. You would certainly see what was in your best interest. We decided we would have that meeting right here in class and each one was going to have the right to go to that meeting. "You may speak for him or you may speak against him." We would see if we could change the outcome of that scene. So each one took parts: "You are the doctor and you will write into the play what you would say, not what the doctor really said." Others took the uncle's part and rewrote that according to what they wanted. The speeches were very good. Kevin did a beautiful job. He got up and was convincing the people not to think reasonably. The main characters got together and got people who would support them and cheer for them. Other people got together; they were going to see that the doctor never got his speech said. The town meeting was their own town meeting, not the one in the play. Another way would be to write the act that would take place after the real play ends. What would happen? Would people come to be taught by him? Would he be able to teach them to think? Or he could stay and become like everyone else and stop thinking.*

A third activity for depth study began with the teacher's reading of two or three critics' brief comments that were challenging and puzzling. The students then searched

---

*This account was recorded by Elinor Weinrich Joseph.

for additional comments and reconsidered plays they had read, in the light of the specific comments. Checking critics' comments carried great appeal for academically superior students.

Students who had seen a professional performance on or off Broadway were usually inspired to read the play they had seen as well as to read *Act One*. Students who attended a professional performance after reviewing critics' comments and rereading the play invariably remarked that their study affected how they viewed the play. Parents who were theatergoers followed their children's school activity and reported not only their own involvement in it but also the fact that the caliber of their participation as an audience was changed to a large degree by new knowledge disseminated by their offspring.

Students debated informally whether a particular play was or was not a tragedy (or a comedy). The teacher duplicated brief quotations such as Heilman's reason for defining Synge's *Riders to the Sea* as literature of disaster rather than tragedy.

> In disaster, what happens comes from without; in tragedy, from within. In disaster, we are victims; in tragedy, we make victims, of ourselves or others.[9]

There are also Miller's argument in defense of the existence of modern tragedy and Krutch's denial of that existence. From Miller come these inclinations:

> As a general rule . . . I think the tragic feeling is evoked in us when we are in the presence of a character who is ready to lay down life, if need be, to secure one thing—his sense of personal dignity. . . . The flaw, or crack, in the character is really nothing—and need be nothing, but his inherent unwillingness to remain passive in the face of what he conceives to be a challenge to his dignity . . . from this total questioning of what has previously been unquestioned, we learn. And such a process is not beyond the common man.

And Miller adds,
> . . . tragedy implies more optimism in its author than does comedy . . .

for only in tragedy

> . . . lies the belief—optimistic, if you will, in the perfectibility of man.[10]

On the other hand, Krutch says that modern "tragedies" are misnomers because they "produce in the reader a sense of depression which is the exact opposite of that elation generated when the spirit of a Shakespeare rises joyously superior to the outward calamities which he recounts and celebrates the greatness of the human spirit whose travail he describes." Tragedies, says Krutch, are no longer written "because we have come, willy-nilly, to see the soul of man as commonplace and its emotions as mean." He adds, ". . . no man can conceive it [tragedy] unless he is capable of believing in the greatness and importance of man . . . it is only in calamity that the human spirit has the opportunity to reveal itself triumphant over the outward universe which fails to conquer it. . . ."[11]

Teachers also found quotations that explained the aspects of comedy. For example, there was one to the effect that repetition is an important element in comedy because the stock character keeps repeating himself.[12] He fails to assume the appropriate behavior that is necessary for a person who differentiates between situations. Such differentiation is necessary if a person is to assess what each situation demands.

Teachers did not go into technical definitions or discussions of tragedy or comedy. They had had disastrous experiences with this kind of procedure for years and now knew better. Statements such as the preceding ones were a challenge for students and gave them reasons for reexamining a play they were reading or had attended.

In almost all cases, the quotations used could readily be applied to daily life, and students did so. The disaster versus tragedy idea was so appealing that students began using their new ideas to analyze dramatic newspaper events. They also began to listen more intently to how adults used the terms "tragedy" and "disaster" and to involve those adults in reexamining the situations they were describing. The repetition-in-comic-character idea was also a subject of conversation throughout the year, in an infinite number of contexts. Interestingly enough, these conversations were quite serious. Students saw the buffoon in their lives in a new light, for they saw repetitious acts in their own behavior and gained a new insight into the very real difficulties involved in assessing the demands of new situations and in behaving appropriately. Later, repetitious acts became the subject of many original essays.

Another process which encouraged depth study of a play was comparing the play with the novel or narrative upon which it was based. Teachers found *Life with Father, The Member of the Wedding,* or *Mama's Bank Account (I Remember Mama)* to be useful for this study. When students read the narrative first, they had an opportunity to assess the changes made by the dramatist. In some classes it was helpful for students to decide what they would do with the narrative if they were to create a play from it. What would be included in each act? Which characters would they emphasize? Which motivations? When students read *The Diary of Anne Frank* by Goodrich and Hackett, they can appreciate, even if they are hostile to, some of the character changes and changes of events made by the playwright. For example, the dramatists open the play with the revelation that Anne is captured. Then, why read the play if you know this at the very start? Why bother attending a professional performance? Why did the dramatists make such a drastic change?

Playwrights must build conflict and reveal emotions quickly. Every scene is selected to perform a definite function. Which character is revealed in a particular scene? What is disclosed about him? What behaviors accomplish the disclosure? One character paces nervously, another tenderly fondles a fur coat. How do these actions compare with the diary? How do the dramatists use contrast to bring emotions out quickly and forcefully? There is love and hate, violence and tenderness, in the same scenes. Why do the playwrights pack a scene so full? How do playwrights portray the precarious nature of the incarcerated existence?

Dramatists may change fundamental things. For example, Anne feels tenderness for Peter in the final scenes, just before the onslaught of the Nazis. Why did the playwrights take the liberty to make this change? When students juxtapose specific parts of the diary with the play, they acquire a sense of the art of both genres. They have a focus for discussing the content including the emotions, motivations, and sensitivities of the characters. Further, the differences in meanings can be emphasized. Then, too, students should consider why the dramatists omitted certain incidents that seem important in the diary. The greater the number of sharp contrasts the students examine, the better the opportunity for depth study and cognitive functioning.

Another procedure consists of the students listening to short excerpts from recordings of plays, after watching peers perform those scenes. For example, a number of class successfully used the recording, *The Barretts of Wimpole Street.* Students were split into teams to decide on gestures to be used and on emphases for particular words and phrases. There were two "players' teams" who took direction from the two "directors' teams" and who were ultimately judged by the "evaluators' teams." The responsibility for the interpretation was on the shoulders of the directors as well as the players. The evaluation was never in terms of "best." Rather, it was presented as an analysis by the evaluators' team which was required to present a very specific analysis. The team structure made it mandatory that all groups study the part of the play which was to be performed. The outside-of-school time and thought pupils put into the preparation for such an activity was great. One factor that pleased students was the opportunity to select a role from three types of groups. The three-team performance constituted motivation for the required preparation for listening together to "real actors." The activity was highly valued by pupils. The procedure described here for *The Barretts of Wimpole Street* served well for parts of *Cyrano, Pygmalion, Romeo and Juliet,* and *I Remember Mama.* Often, advance notices of TV and radio performances were kept in mind so that the class could use these rather than recordings.

One of the chief advantages of the team procedure is that students learn how much decision-making responsibility the dramatist leaves up to directors, performers, and theatre artists. Students begin to appreciate that drama is unique in many ways, including the fact that it is visual as well as auditory, and its performance requires the teamwork of many types of artists. Rosenheim says, ". . . in his characterization, however profound and complicated it may be, the playwright tends, unlike the narrative writer, to be circumspect in his prescriptions concerning the appearance and mannerisms of his characters."[13] The actor's bodily actions can even change the meaning of the dialogue. The actor can distort the play. As Nathan points out, ". . . anyone who has seen two different groups present the same play knows that the dramatist's reins on the play are indeed loose."[14] Because actors and directors make crucial decisions, students must understand what the dramatist does to indicate to the actor the inherent qualities of the character he is portraying. The dramatist's intent must be clear, even while he depends on the actor to do a certain amount of interpretation of the character.

There are a number of team arrangements that can be used in connection with performing parts of plays. The arrangements selected depend upon the objective of the activity. For example, *The Member of the Wedding* by McCullers lends itself to the teaching of various interpretations of words, phrases, and sentences (e.g. how one says, as Frankie does, "I wish the whole world would die," or "I wouldn't do a kid thing like that."). When different students, each emphasizing different words, have a chance to read these or other selected lines, there is an opportunity to discuss the meanings of words in the context of a whole play. Differences of opinion create lively discussion and thinking and result in deeper understanding. As each student who is working on a particular scene explains his reasons for emphasizing a certain word or words, a type of referee is needed to help resolve the differences. Therefore the "author" is present in the shape of a committee of three. These three are students who have read, discussed, and studied the play independently, except for a few guides from the teacher. They have researched the play and the author. Whenever the group meets an impasse, the "author" is called upon. He gives his interpretation and tells how this line is related to the character and the author's purpose.

A few teachers tried to use a recording of a professional performance as an introduction to the study of a play. In general, this procedure was less successful than the one described above. In the first place, the mechanical instrument restricts the intimacy which arises between teacher and students when parts of a play are performed in the classroom. In the second place, the motivation that is inherent in pupils' performance of the play is lacking. The excitement of comparing themselves with professionals does not exist.

The procedure a teacher selects might well be checked against Bentley's statement that "a play presents a vision of life, and to the idea of vision the idea of wisdom naturally adheres. To share this vision and this wisdom . . . is not to receive information or counsel but rather to have a momentous experience."[15]

Producing a Play

Few teachers who are charged with the responsibility for play production are prepared for the task. Morgan [16] cites an AETA survey which indicates that less than one-third of the teachers assigned to play production and to instruction of theatre courses studied theatre in college. In fact, two-thirds of the teachers cast in the role of teacher-director have not studied theatre even for twelve college credit hours. Yet, play production in the secondary school has unique and significant educational roles to achieve.

One of the benefits lies in the social experience play production offers students. Smith ascribes these powers to it:

> . . . no individual can practice the art of the theatre all by himself. It requires and coordinates a multitude of activities. . . . It is as all-embracing as life itself, for it involves at times the practice of all the other arts and all the other crafts . . . the theatre offers an opportunity to test all these practices by performance, and in the process of doing so, it builds up a socialized situation equalled by few of the other tools of education."[17]

An allied educational function of play production is that the self-image of students is heightened through participation in a successful venture. McCaslin reveals the ingredients: "There is probably nothing that binds a group together more closely than the production of a play, and no joy more lasting than the memory of a play, in which all the contributions of all the participants have dovetailed so well that each has had a share in its success."[18] McCaslin moves on to clarify the relationship between enjoyment, discipline, and high-level performance: "Older children delight in the sharing of an activity and enjoy the discipline required to bring the performance to a high level."[19] The goal of "successful communication with an audience,"[20] as McCaslin sees it, is primary. It is the realization of this success that alerts students to the fact that they have performed on a high level. It is this success that makes the effort they have expended worthwhile.

Producing a play is fun and should be precisely that. However, fun and a free-for-all are two distinctly different things. As Miller cautions, "The fun is the joy of the play itself, the laughs, the good fellowship, the amusing things that happen."[21] Spolin puts it another way: "Creative freedom does not mean doing away with discipline. It is implicit in true creativity that a free person, working in an art form, must be highly disciplined."[22]

Another benefit of play production lies in the realm of the cognitive domain. Because the act of production provides a tremendous motivation for learning, students can be asked to study the play in far more depth than under almost any other circumstances. Fall is concerned with this relective advantage, even when plays are not to be produced for an outside audience: "By dramatizing the story, the child is led through the techniques of reflection, criticism, and relation in ways that appeal directly to his understanding and perception."[23] He will even expend the effort needed to understand the "truth" of the play, since he cannot portray his character accurately without that understanding. He must comprehend why the character does what he does; therein lies the theme. Siks points out that "the theme is the truth of a play. It is what a play says in terms of human, universal truth. . . ."[24] Furthermore, selecting a play is a cognitive experience. When students have read a number of plays and have discussed the plays' strengths and weaknesses in the light of possible performance, the results constitute a critique of each play. The act of production, of playmaking, implies a creative cognitive experience. The students re-create the play as they work at producing it. As Smith says:

> . . . the drama or the story written down in a manuscript or printed in a book, the lines to be spoken and the stage directions to be carried out, are not in the truest sense a play at all. . . . They become a play by being played, in the same way that a song comes into existence only as the printed words and notes are sung. . . . [A play is] a story presented by actors on a stage before an audience. . . . An unproduced play is not a play . . . it is only a script.[25]

SELECTING THE PLAY

Students generally cannot be held responsible for all the work involved in selecting a play, but neither can the teacher force upon them his own choice and expect maximum benefits to accrue. Students must delight in the play itself in order to hold up under what can be an endurance course ahead of them, and in order to gain maximum satisfaction from the work they put into the production. When students are set free to read many plays of their own choosing, they are able to help the teacher make a suitable choice.

Needless to say, the play must be an appropriate one for the developmental level of the players and the audience and must be suitable to the occasion. It should be a lively play, which moves quickly and which avoids lengthy scenes. It is important to select a play that bears repeated performances and still does not wear thin the interest of the performers. It must be worth the effort. The play must meet the educational needs of students. If students are prepared to focus their attention on an audience, to prepare for a high-level production, to be concerned about the playwrights' ideas rather than their own, then the literary play may be selected. In such case it is the result that is of primary importance. If students have been deprived of an opportunity to be creative and to express their own ideas and if the process rather than the result is of primary importance, then improvising a play based on a story may serve significant educational purposes.

The play should be such as to make use of the entire class in one way or another. There are many tasks to be performed: costume making, prop making, prompting, publicizing, and acting. A stage manager and call boys can be profitably accommodated. All need to contribute to the success of the venture.

Usually, one-act or short plays should be chosen or created for performance by younger adolescents and by students inexperienced in play production. The higher level performance toward which the group works usually does not permit too long a production. Since the budget of most schools does not include payment of royalties, it may be necessary to select an older play whose royalties have expired. Alertness to such detail is part of the educational growth of students.

CASTING

There are few if any "best" practices for casting a play. The teacher must take into account a number of complex educational considerations before deciding on casting procedures. His knowledge of the needs of a particular student or students will play an important role in the practices he adopts. Ward recognizes the complexity of the necessary considerations:

> The most democratic procedure is to choose the casts from those who volunteer for the parts. If we make it a privilege to play, not urging anyone who does not feel inclined to take part, we keep the spirit of fun in our playing. We are careful, however, to choose a few children with ability to carry the scene so that it will go well and give the group a feeling of success.[26]

As Ward suggests, casting is virtually an aspect of rehearsals. Because several groups of students read a particular scene, "every member of the class is thoroughly familiar with all of the characters before the casting is done. Each has had many chances to play the various parts, and the class has virtually learned the lines, so often has the play been reread."[27] By the time the casting is finished, all the students are familiar with the play. Further, when many students play one character, the role is more easily assigned to the student who seemed to be most comfortable with it.

Many teachers use double casting; each cast has an opportunity to perform, each for a different audience. The audiences may be peer classes. Double casting permits sought-after roles to be widely distributed and is an insurance against the last-minute illness of a major character.

REHEARSALS

Perhaps the most important guideline in the first stages of rehearsal is improvisation. After students read the first scene, they improvise it using no script. Ward elaborates the reason for a student's improvisation at this point:

It forces him to think, to know his character, to imagine how he feels and what he does. . . . Characterization . . . is the significant thing to be achieved just now, and evidence of insight into character is to be commended above exact representation of the scene.[28]

The class then discusses the performance and makes suggestions about how the characters would act. Other players repeat the scene and again the play is discussed. Different groups perform the same scene to acquire a sense of what it really is made of and to see how they can extract from it the fullest possible meanings. McCaslin agrees with this procedure, adding that, "improvisation helps the players become familiar with the plot, get acquainted with the character, and remain free in their movements."[29] Improvisation is used in later rehearsals whenever a player needs help in interpreting his character.

Another guideline is concerned with the persons who shall interpret how a character behaves. The ideas of students are used freely, but not indiscriminately. Students need to understand that the playwright had a theme, that the characters were created in harmony with the theme, and that the playwright must be accorded equal rights with, let us say, the composer of music. The composer's interpretation is written into the music to a certain degree; the musician is not permitted to interpret that music solely as he wishes, without regard for the composer's ideas. Those students who have already considered the keys to interpreting a novel may be aware that writers do have a degree of conscious intent. A very brief analysis of a critical scene or character by the whole class does serve to set limits to the interpretation which any actor may make. It is during the early rehearsals that the teacher helps students understand the purpose of the play and why it was written. It is important for students to understand the purpose if their individual performances are to contribute to what the playwright hoped to accomplish.

Two reading rehearsals are usually necessary. Their purpose is to have players go through the whole play using scripts. These rehearsals provide an opportunity to view the sustained roles students will soon adopt. Students are not permitted to act at this point. The emphasis is on interpreting the play. The big ideas are the focus of attention. Dodd and Hickson stress the importance of reading the whole play.

To begin with, each actor should be encouraged to read and study the whole play, forgetting, so far as possible, his own part. Then, with this general view at the back of his mind, he can look at the appearances of the character he is to play, the situations in which the character appears, what he does and says in those situations, always asking himself why the character behaves as he does.[30]

The reading rehearsals give students a sense of the play as a whole and give the teacher an opportunity to correct faulty interpretations. The reading may be interrupted to discuss the play line and the characters.

Then students "walk through" the whole play twice, with action and specific stage plan. The purpose here is to sustain characterization. Players go through the movements of standing, sitting, entering, and exiting in order to connect movement and dialogue as quickly as possible. It is one thing for a student to know how the weak old grandfather sits and stands for a few moments; it is quite another to sustain those movements for forty minutes. Students need to be placed in the position of appreciating the task very early in the rehearsals.

After the "walk-through" rehearsals, students should memorize parts not already memorized as a natural consequence of the work already done. Ward explains, "Lines should never be memorized until they are associated with the action, and then no time should be wasted in becoming line perfect. None of the finer business can be done satisfactorily until the players are free from their manuscripts."[31] The line rehearsal follows the memorization. Players go through the whole play twice if possible, and from memory. Some teacher-directors believe that teachers should prompt freely at this rehearsal in order to instill confidence and maintain the wholeness of the play. Others feel too much prompting releases the players from the task of memorizing early in the game, and also from the need to relate their lines to the main action of the play. Whichever the case, the teachers are aware that students require much encouragement and praise at this point. Whether the teacher decides to prompt or not, the script should be discarded so that the players learn early to carry on a conversation. Scripts are not permitted at this rehearsal or at succeeding ones, except for very special purposes.

The succeeding rehearsals all have predetermined emphases. A character rehearsal may be needed in which the players practice carefully how people being portrayed sit, stand, and walk. A property rehearsal is often necessary; there is one devoted to polishing the performance, another to maintaining optimum tempo. If the performance is to be public, two dress rehearsals are needed.

During the dress rehearsals, a small audience sits with the teacher-director in the audience. From this vantage point the teacher can call upon the players to project voices, to be attuned to the reactions of the audience, to hold the dialogue during laughter of the audience, and to sit at such an angle as to permit the audience to see all players. Rehearsals should not be inordinately long.

THE PERFORMANCE

Most teachers prefer to be backstage for any emergencies and usually call upon a colleague to assist them during the performance. The players need a relaxed teacher who can offer a word of encouragement. If the performance is for the whole school, the orchestra plays while the audience assembles. The music enhances the occasion, helps relax the players, and dispels last-minute worries about details that can no longer be remedied.

No matter what happens, no student should end the big day with the feeling that he has failed his teacher, his parents, his school, or himself. The players need praise from the teacher, parents, and peers. The teacher-director needs to "set the stage" for this reaction from the very moment the curtain makes its final descent. He circulates among students, bearing generous words of a complimentary nature. He offers praise to the students in the presence of parents. This occasion is an unforgettable one. The memories of this day must be marked only by the truly great opportunity it offered students to "*be* somebody."

The Special Case of Shakespeare

Producing for a peer audience a carefully selected scene from Shakespeare furnishes high motivation for involving students in a Shakespearean play. It is helpful if students have read at least one Greek play in translation such as Sophocles' *Antigone,* for the structure and language are simpler and more direct than Shakespeare's; also, students have an opportunity to become familiar with elements such as the role of the chorus and poetic style.

Most students cannot handle the reading of Shakespeare independently. When teachers assign scenes or whole acts for the student to read for homework, they defeat the purpose of including Shakespeare in the curriculum. The procedures suggested here are helpful for the teaching of all drama but imperative for students' reading of Shakespeare. They are suggestive, not prescriptive. Teachers should select those which meet the needs of their classes and which are suitable for particular plays.

The teacher should read much of the play to the class. He can carry the meaning of strange words, phrases, and structure by his inflection and gestures. By no means does it lessen interest in the play for students to know something about it before reading it, for it must be kept in mind that students are not totally unaware of the plots of some Shakespearean plays. In fact, knowing something about the play—not its historical background—can eliminate a hurdle and, if appealingly presented, can be motivational. The knowledge can furnish the cognitive stimulus for assimilation and accommodation. There are a number of means of providing the stimulus. For example, Chute's[32] brief essays on the plays to be read are usually enthusiastically received by students. The essays pinpoint crucial incidents and issues which can be used as focal points for another involving activity, that is, dramatizing a central situation before reading a play.

When pupils study Shakespeare, they need to talk about ideas and events which occur in the play before they read the play. For example, students may dramatize spontaneously, before they read it, the situation from *King Lear* in which Lear is testing his three daughters' love for him. Or they may dramatize the attempts of Cassius in *Julius Caesar* to get Brutus to join the conspiracy. Students dramatize a variety of ways in which characters might act; then a discussion is focused on the *why* of these behaviors. Meantime, students are gathering a fair idea of what the play is about. After the discussion the teacher reads the actual scene from Shakespeare; students follow the reading in their books. There should be no problem understanding the scene, the language, or the play itself. The students are already involved. They have tried to portray a cental issue on their own terms; then they meet that issue on Shakespeare's terms and are ready to compare and evaluate. It matters not at all that they "began to read the play in the middle of it." It is involvement, understanding, grasp of meaning, enjoyment, and appreciation that count. All teachers who tried this approach with enthusiasm reported success with the preliminary role play of a scene. Some classes went on to read the entire play and to enact other scenes as they considered why the play has lived through the years and why it is known to literate peoples in all lands. Others were able to read only with the teacher and to enact certain select scenes. The teacher used the read-and-tell method to help them experience the satisfaction of completing the reading of the play, enjoying it, and gaining new insights.

In some classes, after the teacher read Chute's essay on *Julius Caesar* and parts of the play, the students made up their own *Julius Caesar* using Shakespeare's language and events as their guide. This activity encouraged high motivation for reading and rereading particular sections of the play. There was a number of discussions about whether to keep expressions such as "Friends, Romans, countrymen, lend me your ears," or change them to "Friends and fellow citizens, listen to me." Teachers often wondered at the number of times Shakespeare's expressions were preferred. They need not have wondered. The fact that teachers were willing to permit students to become acquainted with the bard on their own terms, that students were not forced to analyze him line by line, and that they were given an opportunity to become acquainted with him as a focus for their creativity gave Shakespeare his chance to meet them where they were. The students' decision in favor of Shakespeare's lines bore out Bentley's statement:

The arts are compensatory. For the bad writing of everyday, literature provides good writing to astonish and delight. For the bad talk of everyday, the drama provides good talk to astonish and delight.[33]

This project cannot be a long drawn-out affair. Students will probably study the bard again and on equally good terms.

The use of movies and television productions in the absence of, or in conjunction with, the legitimate theater held a number of possibilities. Teachers were sometimes disturbed by modern portrayals of Shakespeare's plays. However, when they attended a showing at a local movie house during a Saturday matinee and watched the audience of young teen-agers alternatively sobbing and holding its breath for fear of missing a word, the teachers were forced to reconsider. They watched young adolescents sliding deep into their seats with the emotional impact of what they were experiencing. Teachers heard the teen-agers crying, "no, no," when tragedy was imminent, and murmuring, "Stay away, don't go near," when a favorite character was in danger. These teachers came to the conclusion that no authoritative production of Shakespeare existed and that each generation must mold the performance to its own vision of life and of the play. They knew then that "creative" productions do not annihilate Shakespeare but rather assure his everlasting influence and give testimony to his enduring import.

Another procedure was to use a newspaper story to write a play in the Shakespearean mode. For example, one class detected that royalty played a role in Shakespeare's cast. They selected Hussein and his struggle with Jordanian guerillas, created characters, sketched out the plot, and arranged for each act to be written by a different group. Once the acts were assigned, most of the work was done outside of class. Students needed time in class to present problems they encountered and to coordinate the work so that they would end up with one unified play rather than five separate ones. This class was reading *Julius Caesar;* they read and reread many lines which they decided to "steal" because they were so appropriate.

Perhaps the most productive procedure was to conduct a trial of a major Shakespearean character. Central to practically every Shakespearean tragedy is some character who can readily be placed on trial. For example, students placed Brutus on trial for the murder of Caesar. Students knew even before they began the first reading of the play that they would conduct such a trial. Soon the rules were laid down. For instance, no testimony could be presented in court which was not taken directly from the play. The trial was an open-book performance. Every member of the class had a role to play: judge, jury, prosecuting attorney, witness, etc. Students usually have watched so many courtroom scenes on television shows that they need no guidance about how to play the various roles. In fact, their collective information may be far greater than the teacher's. They do need the teacher's assistance in interpreting the characters of Brutus, Cassius, Mark Anthony, and Caesar.

The courtroom activity is inherently involving, adds an element of concreteness to a most abstract task, and encourages serious examination of the play to cull from it a large measure of inference about characters. The participants need many possible interpretations of particular statements by or about the character or about relevant events. The fact that each student has a specific role to play concretizes the study. The courtroom drama met enthusiastic response from virtually every teacher and class who gave it a serious try. One or two teachers tended to overdo the activity rather than to reserve it for specially needed and appropriate occasions. But in general, they were cautious about its use. The extent to which preparation for the courtroom scene encouraged eighth-grade students to grow in awareness is apparent in the following excerpts:*

Defense Attorney: Why didn't you want the conspirators to take an oath?
Brutus: We felt that as Romans we wouldn't have to. We didn't want this to seem like a revolution, only a disposition of local power.

Defense Attorney: Weren't you afraid that Marc Antony would turn the mob when you let him make that oration?
Cassius: I felt that Antony was like a son to Caesar, that he felt he was next in line and could take power, and I thought if he made the speech he'd be playing on the emotions of the mob which was very fickle and he could drive them to revolution. But Brutus wanted him to have this chance.

Defense Attorney: Will you explain your comparison of Caesar to Colossus?
Cassius: In ancient times there was a giant Colossus that towered over the harbor, and I feel that Caesar towered above the people in Rome. They were like little ants crawling under his legs. Whatever his wishes were, they had to carry them out.
Prosecuting Attorney: Caesar once said that you were lean and hungry. What did he mean?
Cassius: I didn't say that; Caesar said that.

The carefully thought-out preparation of the prosecuting attorney in this class was clear in his summation. The entire class was very much moved by his statement; as a matter of fact, the silence was broken only later as his peers warmly congratulated him. Excerpts from the summation follow:

The time has come for you to arrive at a decision. It is not a difficult one; it is merely a question of right or wrong, true or false, black or white, patriotism or murder. It would

---

*These excerpts and those that follow were from discussions and papers of an eighth-grade class taught by Elinor Weinreich Joseph.

be ridiculous to deny that Caesar was ambitious. But is it right to kill a great leader? . . . What were the real motives of the conspirators? We know of Brutus, the noblest, who would die for liberty. We also know of Cassius—Cassius the instigator of the plot to kill Caesar, Cassius the jealous one, Cassius the schemer, Cassius the "lean and hungry" one, Cassius the murderer. These men are not on trial; their motives are. Look at them as individuals, for that is what they are: mortal men, as Caesar was. They have ambitions as surely as every one of us do. But can you as responsible and intelligent individuals allow the cold murder of the greatest leader of this nation to be forgiven or forgotten because it is under the false cloak of patriotism? Members of the jury, for the good of freedom-loving people throughout the globe, do not allow yourself to be deceived. It was just a step for Cassius in the fulfillment of his ambitions. This was murder.

The reader can see in the following excerpts from students' papers written after the "trial" something of the level of thinking that learners had reached.

The people around him represented mere tools and steps to be used by Cassius in his climb toward his goal. He didn't look upon Brutus as a friend or a man but as something noble, something he needed, and thus something he used. The mob, instead of representing Romans he could help, represented tools by which he could gain power.

He looked upon people and events with the question, What can this do to help me? . . . His purpose thus changed his entire outlook . . . persuading Brutus to join the plot, letting Casca throw rocks at Brutus' window, organizing the plot to kill Caesar. . . . Inevitably these acts affected the people of Rome.
    . . . Cassius was very insecure and his need for affection and respect caused him to lose good judgment. His need to advance from his present position and the jealousy he suffers because of it is shown in a speech in which he tells Brutus that Caesar is . . . no more deserving of the rule of Rome than any of them. He feels jealous that a man like Caesar, who has many faults, should have gained the position of greatness which he feels he deserves. . . .
    Cassius is a weak individual who is unsure of himself and of his moves. . . . He takes the advice of others in order to gain respect. . . . Cassius' need for affection is shown in the argument with Brutus. He often cries, "You love me not," in this scene. . . . His need for respect and affection causes him to carry out the poor advice of Brutus.

    The play also demonstrates the many chasms and crevasses which men are lured into when motivated by the needs for power, glory, and even honor.
    Caesar and Cassius were men, and they both hungered for power and authority, as did Hitler, Mussolini, Trotsky, Nixon, and General Spinola; in each case the person was destroyed, just as their destroyers were or may be. The rise and destruction of power is a continuous cycle fed by the forces of opposition arising from the same ultimate goal. . . . Then, too, there are those like Brutus with a noble, selfless goal, but rather cross-eyed vision. . . . Inevitably, Brutus' scheme backfired.

The writing of these papers was followed by a discussion which had as its purpose the analysis of findings about the aspirations of the major characters in the play and the effect of these aspirations on others. The discussion also served as a summation of the ideas formulated thus far.

One teacher brought in a record of the complete *Julius Caesar,* after having chosen selections which would mirror the portions earlier selected by the students. There was so much interest in the varying interpretations that could be carried by the human voice that the class resisted discussing the selections and pleaded to hear the full *Julius Caesar.*

For some classes the confrontation with challenging issues is exciting. For example, is Brutus the central character, or is it Caesar? If the group thinks it is Brutus, then why did Shakespeare call his play *Julius Caesar?* How do Shakespeare's men regard the opposite sex? How does Caesar regard his wife? And Brutus? Macbeth? Students must, of course, present an appropriate defense of the position they take. Through the kind of thinking students do together about Shakespearean tragedies, they arrive at the understanding that an individual can use his personal power to make a momentous impact, positively or negatively, upon the society in which he lives.

Some Controversial Issues

Should Shakespeare be taught? The question was a manifestation of the inappropriate methods used. As teachers learned to permit Shakespeare to address those students who were developmentally ready and as teachers learned to adopt appropriate procedures, many students did find new meaning in the bard. In no way is this to say that all students were ready at a given stage or age for a Shakespearean experience.

Shall students attend a professional performance of a play before or after they read it? Teachers rarely found a middle ground on this issue, nor did they offer any rationale for their position except, "That's what worked for me," or "The students enjoyed it more," or "The students got more out of it." The same arguments were used for opposing positions. There was little attempt to define what was meant by "it worked;" teachers had no evidence to present that students did in fact learn more one way or the other.

Among the experts the difference of opinion is equally great, and perhaps even more intense. For example, Evans proclaims, "But to see the play and then to read it is not even as good as merely to read it." To see a play first and then to read it "is to damage the experience of reading it" because "the imagination is temporarily rendered inactive."[34] Hoetker[35] concluded, on the other hand, after making some attempts at a pilot study, that it depends upon the play. For example, students who had read O'Casey's *Red Roses for Me* before seeing it liked the performance better than those with no preparation, but students who were prepared for *Macbeth* liked it less than those with no preparation. With respect to knowledge gained from attending a performance, classes who had done no classroom work beforehand gained more than classes specifically prepared to attend the plays. Hoetker also found that teachers preferred to have students study a play before the performance. On the other hand, the actors felt that those aspects of a play upon which teachers tend to concentrate would hinder spontaneity of reaction. "The teachers thought that students had to be taught things so that they could understand plays; the actors thought the plays themselves could teach things."[36] Bentley, in skirting the argument, managed to advance a point of view that permitted teachers to continue to communicate about the issue, and perhaps eventually to take some steps to research creatively the answers to their own questions: "One is not forced into any choice between literature and theatre, and to know *Hamlet* or any great play should be to know it from stage and study, both."[37]

How much should students study historical background and stagecraft? Most educators agree that the study of historical background and stagecraft should be minimal. The plea is for teaching the work itself. Hoetker found that when background study of a play was brief, the students made higher scores on an appreciation test and on a *cognitive and desirable attitudes test.* [38] An increasing proportion of teachers now accept the fact that the concentration should be on the work itself, not on the background. Yet, many cannot resist the role of preparing a "good solid lecture" because "it will help students understand the play better."

How intensely should students analyze plays? The literature is replete with arguments such as that of Matthews: "Plays were written to be experienced—not studied."[39] If studying means "word by word, like translating Virgil at twenty lines a day," as Evans proposes, then it is better that plays not be studied. On the other hand, Evans argues in favor of eliminating fragmentary study that consumes weeks, because such a procedure sacrifices the "artistic impact."[40] Hoetker made some pilot research attempts to discover answers to this question of intensity of study. For example, he found that when there was intense study *after* the performance, the scores on tests were lower than when there was *brief* study of backgrounds following the performance. However, the results were not significant.[41] He found, too, that it made no difference whether brief study came before or after the performance, or intense study came before or after.[42] Intense study did yield one important advantage: students scored higher on the *thematic understandings* test. Hoetker hypothesized that this result may have been due to the fact that additional time for study made it more possible to touch on the issues pertinent to this factor.[43] In general, there seems to be some substantial agreement that line-by-line reading of the complete play bears few rewards for most secondary school students.

The problem seems to be that as educators we are still trying to solve complex questions with simplistic extremes for answers, that we all too rarely look to our basic educational objectives and philosophy for guidelines to our practices, and that all too often we have not clearly defined that philosophy and those objectives. Thus, on all levels of education we are confronted by our students with accusations of irrelevant education. In an interview reported by Howes, Arthur Miller made the following statement about his fears concerning what happens in secondary school classrooms: "The basic concern I have is the inevitable tendency to analyze rather than to wonder at and absorb literature nowadays. A play is a synthesis, after all, a dynamic and living *process.* . . . There is also a dehumanized, false emphasis on so-called technique. I don't write to exercise techniques but to convey some vision, and a certain joy in discovering invincible forces that go to make this animal human."[44]

NOTES

1. Richard Courtney, *Play, Drama and Thought* (London: Cassel & Co., 1968), pp. 55–56.
2. Ibid., p. 55.

3. Ibid., p. 222.

4. James Moffett, *Drama: What Is Happening?* (Champaign, Ill.: National Council of Teachers of English, 1967), pp. 12 and 15.

5. Argentine F. Alington, *Drama and Education* (Oxford: Basil Blackwell and Mott, 1961), p. 44.

6. Moffett, p. 2.

7. Courtney, p. 7.

8. Susanne K. Langer, *Feeling and Form* (New York: Charles Scribner's Sons, 1953), p. 308.

9. Robert B. Heilman, "Tragedy and Melodrama: Speculations on Generic Form," in *Perspectives on Drama,* ed. James L. Calderwood and Harold E. Toliver (New York: Oxford University Press, 1968), p. 154.

10. Arthur Miller, "Tragedy and the Common Man," in *Two Modern American Tragedies: Reviews and Criticism of Death of a Salesman and A Streetcar Named Desire,* ed. John D. Hurrell (New York: Charles Scribner's Sons, 1961), pp. 38–40.

11. Joseph Wood Krutch, "The Tragic Fallacy," in *Two Modern American Tragedies: Reviews and Criticism of Death of a Salesman and A Streetcar Named Desire,* ed. John D. Hurrell (New York: Charles Scribner's Sons, 1961), pp. 6–15.

12. James L. Calderwood and Harold E. Toliver, "Introduction to Comedy," in *Perspectives on Drama,* ed. James L. Calderwood and Harold E. Toliver (New York: Oxford University Press, 1968), p. 174.

13. Edward W. Rosenheim, *What Happens in Literature: A Student's Guide to Poetry, Drama, and Fiction* (Chicago: University of Chicago Press, 1960), p. 124.

14. Norman Nathan, "Shakespeare: 'The Play's The Thing,' " *English Journal* 56 (October 1967): 964.

15. Eric Bentley, *The Life of the Drama* (New York: Atheneum Publishers, 1964), p. 146.

16. Floyd T. Morgan, *Thespis in Academia,* 43rd Faculty Honor Lecture (Logan, Utah: Utah State University, 1971), p. 17.

17. Milton Smith, *Play Production for Little Theatres, Schools and Colleges* (New York: Appleton-Century-Crofts, 1948), p. 11.

18. Nellie McCaslin, *Creative Dramatics in the Classroom* (New York: David McKay Co., 1968), p. 145.

19. Ibid., p. 134.

20. Ibid., p. 130.

21. Helen Louise Miller, *Pointers on Producing the School Play* (Boston: Plays), p. 9.

22. Viola Spolin, *Improvisations for the Theatre: A Handbook of Teaching and Directing Techniques* (Evanston, Ill.: Northwestern University Press, 1963), p. 287.

23. Gregory A. Fall, Introduction to *Children's Literature for Dramatization: An Anthology,* by Geraldine Brain Siks (New York: Harper and Row, Publishers, 1964), p. 4.

24. Ibid., p. 97.

25. Smith, pp. 4–5.

26. Winifred Ward, *Playmaking with Children* (New York: Appleton-Century-Crofts, 1957), p. 134.

27. Ibid., p. 140.

28. Winifred Ward, *Creative Dramatics for the Upper Grades and Junior High School* (New York: Appleton-Century-Crofts, 1930), p. 139.

29. McCaslin, p. 134.

30. Nigel Dodd and Winifred Hickson, *Drama and Theatre in Education* (London: Heinemann Educational Books, 1971), p. 79.

31. Ward, *Creative Dramatics,* p. 164.

32. Marchette Chute, *Stories from Shakespeare* (New York: Mentor Books, 1959).

33. Bentley, p. 75.

34. Bertrand Evans, *Teaching Shakespeare in the High School* (New York: The Macmillan Co., 1966), pp. 80–81.

35. James Hoetker et al., *The Educational Laboratory Theatre Project: A Report on Its Operations* (St. Ann, Mo.: Central Midwestern Regional Educational Laboratory, September 1968 through August 1969), p. 103.

36. Ibid.

37. Bentley, p. 149.

38. Hoetker, p. 101.
39. Dorothy E. Matthews, "The Teaching of Drama in High School," *Illinois English Bulletin* 56 (February 1969): 16.
40. Evans, pp. 1 and 100–103.
41. Hoetker, p. 112.
42. Ibid., p. 113.
43. Ibid., p. 111.
44. Alan B. Howes, *Teaching Literature to Adolescents: Plays* (Chicago: Scott, Foresman and Co., 1968), p. 105.

References

Alington, Argentine F. *Drama and Education.* Oxford: Basil Blackwell and Mott, 1961.

Aurthur, Robert Alan. *Man on the Mountaintop.* In *Best Television Plays,* edited by Gore Vidal. New York: Ballantine Books, 1956.

Bentley, Eric. *The Life of the Drama.* New York: Atheneum Publishers, 1964.

Besier, Rudolf. *The Barretts of Wimpole Street.* In *Five Broadway Plays,* edited by J. Rodger Gow and Helen J. Hanlon. New York: Globe Book Co., 1948.

———. *The Barretts of Wimpole Street.* Caedmon Records # 1071.

Björnsen, Björnstjerne. *The Father.* In *75 Short Masterpieces: Stories from the World's Literature,* edited by Roger B. Goodman. New York: Bantam Books, 1961.

Cather, Willa. *Paul's Case.* In *Great Modern Short Stories,* edited by Bennett A. Cerf. New York: Random House, 1942.

Chayefsky, Paddy. *The Mother.* In *Best Television Plays,* edited by Gore Vidal. New York: Ballantine Books, 1956.

Chute, Marchette. *Stories from Shakespeare.* New York: Mentor Books, 1959.

Courtney, Richard. *Play, Drama and Thought.* London: Cassel & Co., 1968.

Dodd, Nigel, and Hickson, Winifred. *Drama and Theatre in Education.* London: Heinemann Educational Books, 1971.

Ehlert, Fay. *The Undercurrent.* In *15 American One-Act Plays,* edited by Paul Kozelka. New York: Washington Square Press, 1961.

Evans, Bertrand. *Teaching Shakespeare in the High School.* New York: The Macmillan Co., 1966.

Faulkner, William. *Barn Burning.* In *Stories,* edited by Frank G. Jennings and Charles J. Calitri. New York: Harcourt Brace Jovanovich, 1957.

Fletcher, Lucille. *Sorry, Wrong Number.* In *15 American One-Act Plays,* edited by Paul Kozelka. New York: Washington Square Press, 1961.

Gilbert, William S. *Trial by Jury.* In *15 International One-Act Plays,* edited by John Gassner and Mollie Gassner. New York: Washington Square Press, 1969.

Glaspell, Susan. *Trifles.* In *15 American One-Act Plays,* edited by Paul Kozelka. New York: Washington Square Press, 1961.

Goodrich, Frances, and Hackett, Albert. *The Diary of Anne Frank.* In *Best American Plays.* Supplementary Volume 1918–58, edited by J. Gassner. New York: Random House, 1956.

Greene, Maxine. "Literature and Human Understanding." *The Journal of Aesthetic Education* 2 (October 1968):11–12.

Hansberry, Lorraine. *A Raisin in the Sun.* New York: The New American Library, 1961.

Hart, Moss. *Act One.* New York: The New American Library, 1960.

Heilman, Robert B. "Tragedy and Melodrama: Speculations on Generic Form." In *Perspectives on Drama,* edited by James L. Calderwood and Harold E. Toliver. New York: Oxford University Press, 1968.

Hemingway, Ernest. "The Killers." In *Thirty-Eight Short Stories,* edited by Michael Timko and Clinton E. Oliver. New York: Alfred A. Knopf, 1968.

Hoetker, James et al. *The Educational Laboratory Theatre Project: A Report on Its Operations September 1968 through August 1969.* St. Ann, Mo.: Central Midwestern Regional Educational Laboratory.

Houghton, Stanley. *The Dear Departed.* In *Worlds to Explore,* edited by Matilda Bailey and Ullin Leavell. New York: American Book Co., 1951.

Howes, Alan B. *Teaching Literature to Adolescents: Plays.* Chicago, Ill.: Scott, Foresman and Co., 1968.

Hurrell, John D., ed. *Two Modern American Tragedies: Reviews and Criticism of Death of a Salesman and A Streetcar Named Desire.* New York: Charles Scribner's Sons, 1961.

Ibsen, Henrik J. *An Enemy of the People. Four Great Plays by Ibsen.* New York: Bantam Books, 1959.

Kleihauer, Lois D. *The Cub.* In *Best Short Shorts,* edited by Eric Berger. New York: Scholastic Book Services, 1958.

Langer, Susanne K. *Feeling and Form.* New York: Charles Scribner's Sons, 1953.

Lerner, Alan Jay. *My Fair Lady.* Music by Frederick Loewe. New York: The New American Library, 1962.

Lindsay, Howard, and Crouse, Russell. *Life with Father.* In *Three Comedies of American Family Life,* edited by Joseph E. Mersand. New York: Washington Square Press, 1965.

McCaslin, Nellie. *Creative Dramatics in the Classroom.* New York: David McKay Co., 1968.

McCullers, Carson. *The Member of the Wedding.* In *Famous American Plays of the 1940s,* edited by Henry Hewes. New York: Dell Publishing Co., 1960.

Matthews, Dorothy E. "The Teaching of Drama in High School." *Illinois English Bulletin* 56 (February 1969): 2-17.

Miller, Arthur. *All My Sons. Collected Plays.* New York: The Viking Press, 1957.

Miller, Helen Louise. *Pointers on Producing the School Play.* Boston: Plays, 1960.

Miller, J. P. *The Rabbit Trap.* In *Best Television Plays,* edited by Gore Vidal. New York: Ballantine Books, 1956.

Moffett, James. *Drama: What Is Happening?* Champaign, Ill.: National Council of Teachers of English, 1967.

Morgan, Floyd T. *Thespis in Academia.* 43rd Faculty Honor Lecture. Logan: Utah State University, 1971.

Morley, Christopher. *Thursday Evening.* In *15 American One-Act Plays,* edited by Paul Kozelka. Anta Series. New York: Washington Square Press, 1961.

Munro, John M. "Teaching English as a Foreign Literature." *The Educational Forum* 33 (March 1969):321–28.

Nathan, Norman. "Shakespeare: 'The Play's the Thing.'" *English Journal* 56 (October 1967): 964–69.

O'Casey, Sean. *Red Roses for Me.* In *Six Great Modern Plays.* Laurel Edition. New York: Dell Publishing Co., 1956.

O'Neill, Eugene. *Where the Cross Is Made.* In *Worlds to Explore,* edited by Matilda Bailey and Ullin Leavell. New York: American Book Co., 1951.

Rosenheim, Edward W. *What Happens in Literature: A Student's Guide to Poetry, Drama and Fiction.* Chicago: University of Chicago Press, 1960.

Saroyan, William. "The Shepherd's Daughter." In *75 Short Masterpieces: Stories from the World's Literature,* edited by Roger B. Goodman. New York: Bantam Books, 1961.

Shakespeare, William. *Julius Caesar.* In *The Complete Plays and Poems of William Shakespeare,* edited by William Allan Neilson and Charles Jarvis Hill. Boston: Houghton Mifflin Co., 1942.

———. *King Lear.* In *The Complete Plays and Poems of William Shakespeare,* edited by William Allan Neilson and Charles Jarvis Hill. Boston: Houghton Mifflin Co., 1942.

Shaw, Bernard: *Pygmalion.* Baltimore, Md.: Penguin Books, 1962.

Shulman, Irving. *West Side Story.* New York: Pocket Books, 1961.

Siks, Geraldine Brain. *Children's Literature for Dramatization: An Anthology.* New York: Harper & Row, Publishers, 1964.

Smith, Milton. *Play Production for Little Theatres, Schools and Colleges.* New York: Appleton-Century-Crofts, 1948.

Sophocles. *Antigone. The Oedipus Plays of Sophocles.* Translated by Paul Roche. New York: The New American Library, 1963.

Spolin, Viola. *Improvisation for the Theatre: A Handbook of Teaching and Directing Techniques.* Evanston, Ill.: Northwestern University Press, 1963.

Synge, John M. *Riders to the Sea. Five Great Irish Plays.* New York: The Modern Library, 1941.

Tarkington, Booth. *The Trysting Place.* In *15 American One-Act Plays,* edited by Paul Kozelka. Anta Series. New York: Washington Square Press, 1961.

Tolstoi, Leo. "How Much Land Does a Man Need?" In *A Book of Stories,* edited by Royal A. Gettmann and Bruce Harkness. New York: Holt, Rinehart & Co., 1955.

Van Druten, John. *I Remember Mama.* In *Three Comedies of American Family Life,* edited by Joseph E. Mersand. New York: Washington Square Press, 1965.

Ward, Winifred. *Creative Dramatics for the Upper Grades and Junior High School.* New York: Appleton-Century-Crofts, 1930.

———. *Playmaking with Children.* New York: Appleton-Century-Crofts, 1957.

Wilde, Percival. *The Finger of God.* In *Worlds to Explore,* edited by Matilda Bailey and Ullin Leavell. New York: American Book Co., 1951.

Wilder, Thornton. *The Happy Journey to Trenton & Camden.* In *10 Short Plays,* edited by M. Jerry Weiss. New York: Dell Publishing Co., 1963.

Suggested Plays

Apstein, Theodore. *Wetback Run.* In *Eight American Ethnic Plays,* edited by Francis Griffith and Joseph Mersand. New York: Charles Scribner's Sons, 1974.

Bass, George Houston. *Games.* In *An Introduction to Black Literature in America, from 1746 to Present.* New York: Publishers Co., The Association for the Study of Afro-American Life and History, 1968.

Carroll, Ellison. *Teacher, Teacher.* In *Electronic Drama: Television Plays for the Sixties,* edited by R. Averson and D. M. White. Boston: Beacon Press, 1971.

Chayefsky, Paddy. *The Big Deal.* In *Great Television Plays,* edited by William I. Kaufman. New York: Dell Publishing Co., 1972.

———. *Marty.* Reading Shelf I Series. New York: McGraw-Hill Book Co., 1968.

Chekhov, Anton. *The Proposal.* In *15 International One-Act Plays,* edited by John and Mollie Gassner. New York: Washington Square Press, 1969.

Chodorov, Jerome, and Fields, Joseph A. *Junior Miss.* In *Five Broadway Plays,* edited by J. Rodger Gow and Helen J. Hanlon. New York: Globe Book Co., 1948.

Davis, Hallie F. *The Curtain.* In *One-Act Plays for Today,* edited by Francis J. Griffith and Joseph Mersand. New York: Globe Book Co., 1945.

Finch, Robert, and Smith, Betty. *The Far-Distant Shore.* In *Modern One-Act Plays,* edited by Francis Griffith and Joseph Mersand. New York: Harcourt Brace Jovanovich, 1951.

Foote, Horton. *John Turner Davis.* In *Introduction to Drama,* edited by Louise G. Stevens. Wichita, Kans.: McCormick-Mathers Publishing Co., 1965.

Gilbert, William S. *Trial by Jury.* In *15 International One-Act Plays,* edited by John Gassner and Mollie Gassner. New York: Washington Square Press, 1969.

Glaspell, Susan. *Suppressed Desires.* In *10 Short Plays,* edited by M. Jerry Weiss. New York: Dell Publishing Co., 1963.

Green, Paul. *The No 'Count Boy.* In *One-Act Plays for Today,* edited by Francis J. Griffith and Joseph Mersand. New York: Globe Book Company, 1945.

———. *Quare Medicine.* In *10 Short Plays,* edited by M. Jerry Weiss. New York: Dell Publishing Co., 1963.

Gregory, Lady Augusta. *The Rising of the Moon.* In *The Mentor Book of Short Plays,* edited by Richard H. Goldstone and Abraham H. Lass. New York: The New American Library, 1969.

———. *Spreading the News.* In *Introduction to Literature,* edited by Edward J. Gordon. New York: Ginn and Co., 1964.

Hamner, Earl. *Appalachian Autumn. Appalachian Autumn and Other Plays.* Scope Play Series. New York: Scholastic Book Services, 1971.

Ibsen, Henrik J. *A Doll's House.* In *Four Great Plays by Ibsen.* New York: Bantam Books, 1959.

Jacobs, W. W. *The Monkey's Paw.* In *Seven Famous One-Act Plays,* edited by John Ferguson. Baltimore: Penguin Books, 1953.

Jacobs, W. W., and Rock, Charles. *The Ghost of Jerry Bundler.* In *Introduction to Literature,* edited by Edward J. Gordon. New York: Ginn and Co., 1964.

Jellicoe, Ann. *The Knack.* In *Laurel British Drama: The Twentieth Century,* edited by Robert W. Corrigan. New York: Dell Publishing Co., 1973.

Kaufman, Florence Aquino. *The Winner!* Scope Play Series. New York: Scholastic Book Services, 1971.

Kelly, George. *Craig's Wife.* In *Three Plays about Marriage,* edited by Joseph Mersand. The Anta Series. New York: Washington Square Press, 1962.

Kesselring, Joseph. *Arsenic and Old Lace. Three Plays about Crime and Criminals.* The Anta Series. New York: Washington Square Press, 1974.

Levin, Ira. *No Time for Sergeants. No Time for Sergeants and Other Plays.* New York: Scholastic Book Services, 1971.

Marqués, René. *The Oxcart*. In *Eight American Ethnic Plays*, edited by Francis Griffith and Joseph Mersand. New York: Charles Scribner's Sons, 1974.

Miller, Arthur. *The Crucible*. New York: Bantam Books, 1970.

———. *Death of a Salesman*. In *The Play: A Critical Anthology*, edited by Eric Bentley. Englewood Cliffs, N.J.: Prentice-Hall, 1951.

Milne, A. A. *The Ugly Duckling*. In *One-Act Plays for Our Times*, edited by Francis Griffith, Joseph Mersand, and Joseph B. Maggio. New York: Popular Library, 1973.

Mosel, Tad. *My Lost Saints*. In *Best Television Plays*, edited by Gore Vidal, New York: Ballantine Books, 1956.

Niggli, Josephine. *Sunday Costs Five Pesos*. In *15 International One-Act Plays*, edited by John Gassner and Mollie Gassner. New York: Washington Square Press, 1969.

Osborn, Paul. *On Borrowed Time*. In *Five Broadway Plays*, edited by J. Rodger Gow and Helen J. Hanlon. New York: Globe Book Co., 1948.

Perl, Arnold. *The High School*. In *One-Act Plays for Our Times*, edited by Francis Griffith, Joseph Mersand, and Joseph B. Maggio. New York: Popular Library , 1973.

Quintero, Serafín and Joaquin Álvarez. *A Sunny Morning*. In *Understanding Literature*, edited by Edward J. Gordon. New York: Ginn and Co., 1964.

Rattigan, Terence. *The Winslow Boy*. In *Favorite Modern Plays*, edited by Felix Sper. New York: Globe Book Co., 1958.

Rose, Reginald. *Dino*. *Dino and Other Plays*. Scope Play Series. New York: Scholastic Book Services, 1971.

———. *Thunder on Sycamore Street*. In *Best Television Plays*, edited by Gore Vidal. New York: Ballantine Books, 1956.

———. *Twelve Angry Men*. In *Great Television Plays*, edited by William I. Kaufman. New York: Dell Publishing Co., 1972.

Saroyan, William. *The Man with the Heart in the Highlands*. In *15 One-Act International Plays*, edited by John Gassner and Mollie Gassner. New York: Washington Square Press, 1969.

———. *The Time of Your Life*. In *Famous American Plays of the 1930s*, edited by Harold Clurman. New York: Dell Publishing Co., 1959.

Schary, Dore. *Sunrise at Campobello*. New York: The New American Library, 1961.

Seami. *Hogoromo*. In *The No Plays of Japan*, edited by Arthur Waley. New York: Grove Press, . 1957.

Sender, Ramon. *The Secret*. In *Drama I*, edited by Marjorie Wescott Barrows. New York: The Macmillan Co., 1962.

Serling, Rod. *Requiem for a Heavyweight*. In *Requiem for a Heavyweight and Other Plays*. Scope Play Series. New York: Scholastic Book Services, 1971.

Steele, Wilbur Daniel. *The Giant's Stair*. In *The Study of Literature*, edited by Edward J. Gordon. New York: Ginn and Co., 1964.

Stein, Joseph. *Fiddler on the Roof*. New York: Pocket Books, 1971.

Strindberg, August. *Miss Julie*. In *Drama, Principles and Plays*, edited by Theodore W. Hatlen. New York: Appleton-Century-Crofts, 1967.

Sutro, Alfred. *A Marriage Has Been Arranged*. In *Seven Famous One-Act Plays*, edited by John Ferguson. Baltimore: Penguin Books, 1953.

Tunick, Irve. *A Medal for Miss Walker*. In *Radio and Television Plays*, edited by Lawrence H. Feigenbaum. New York: Globe Book Co., 1956.

Ward, Douglas Turner. *Day of Absence.* In *Eight Ethnic Plays,* edited by Francis Griffith and Joseph Mersand. New York: Charles Scribner's Sons, 1974.

Williams, Tennessee. *The Case of the Crushed Petunias.* In *One-Act Plays for Our Times,* edited by Francis Griffith, Joseph Mersand, and Joseph B. Maggio. New York: Popular Library, 1973.

———. *The Glass Menagerie.* New York: Random House, 1945.

Chapter Six

Experiencing Poetry

Poetry is the first literary form children adopt as an integral part of the development of their communication process. Poetry offers experiences of sheer delight, for the child responds to its elements naturally. What, then, is the cause of the widespread rejection of contact with poetry by adolescents? Students offer some of the answers: "It's sissy stuff"; "It's all about love and things"; "Yech, you have to memorize it and put in all the commas and periods in the right places"; "I don't understand it"; "It's too hard"; "Nobody talks like that"; "What good does it do you, anyway?"

The poet makes many more suggestions than he does direct statements. He presents a small but very important segment of an idea in such a way that the reader or listener can perceive the entire idea. Poetry suggests and implies by means of the action within it. It is the process of suggesting rather than telling which makes poetry a stumbling block for so many adolescents. Poetry's compression and inversion of word order add to the difficulties. Yet, comparisons—metaphors and similes—play a role in the aesthetic pleasure poetry offers. In the view of Brooks and Warren, "A comparison may do more than wake up our imagination to the vividness of an image; it may make the imagination seize on certain ideas, and additional comparisons implied by the original comparison."[1]

The wealth of comparisons offered by poetry is, in Kenner's view, related to the development of taste in literature. "Taste is comparison performed with the certainty of habit."[2] "Comparison" is a key word here. Students must meet mediocre poetry in order to know the superior. "Certainty of habit" implies encounters with a wealth of poetry. Habits are not formed by tearing apart a few poems. Although this chapter explores the teaching of a limited number of poems, students' exposure to poetry was by and large simply that—exposure—and most often to those poems they themselves selected.

Somewhere along the line teachers have lost track of the chief purpose of introducing poetry: the joy of response to rhythm, repetition and rhyme, the sense of order, the imaginative elements. Poetry is for the joy of response to the surprises in the juxtaposition of seemingly unrelated things in a metaphor, the pace of the poem, the revelations that unfold, the melody, the harmony, the ambiguities, and the multiple meanings. We must help students recapture that joy; all the experiences teachers make possible must reinforce this goal.

Teachers can devise procedures which guide students into the study of poems without forcing them to accept the teacher's interpretations of the poet's meaning. The methods described in this chapter encourage the teacher to avoid rigid analysis and to establish an atmosphere of freedom and enjoyment. Such an atmosphere is especially important for young people whose previous experiences may have caused them to shy away from the reading of poetry. Avoiding a rigid analysis by no means implies that analysis is eliminated. On the contrary, more exciting and more creative analysis is achieved. In some cases, even deeper examination is made, resulting in greater appreciations than might otherwise be attained.

Basically, five or six methods which can be used profitably will be described: oral reading including dramatization, choral reading, setting poetry to music, illustrating poetry, and creative writing.

In general, methods of teaching poetry were unified with a common theme or concept. It must be emphasized that there was no poetry unit. The focusing ideas were considered and extended whenever they were appropriate to the poems. Poems were interspersed with the reading of other genre, though there were times in every grade when poetry was the chief concentration for a few class periods or even two weeks as students' interests dictated. A number of teachers selected three major concepts which had been planned in advance. It was felt that, though the concepts were applicable to all genre, they were suited to poetry in a unique way. The concepts are as follows:

1. There are certain emotions which are universal and the poet conveys them to us directly.
2. Emotions which to most people are commonplace are often highlighted by the poet.
3. The poet demonstrates deep concern for the human condition.

Brooks and Warren point out, however, that "the theme does not give the poem its force; the poem gives the theme its force."[3] Within these three basic ideas there were other subsidiary ones applicable to each chosen poem.

As teachers became familiar with the procedures described in this chapter, they turned their class periods into workshops to accommodate the needs, interests, and abilities of each student. Teachers did not abandon the notion that there is work to be done with the class as a whole. To explore each new procedure, the classes worked together with the teachers.

Interpretative Reading

Oral interpretation is of very special importance to poetry because, as Lee suggests, poetry "reaches its ultimate objective only when it is read aloud."[4] The emphasis in this book is on the creative nature of the interpretive act, for oral interpretation is the act of re-creating and communicating to others a literary work. When teachers are first confronted with this philosophy in practice, they often raise the objection: "But those two interpretations were so different! They made the poem mean almost different things." Geiger·offers some guidelines: "One good reading does not preclude another, even a strikingly different one, of the same poem. But each of these readings will be 'good' insofar as it reveals aspects of the poem. . . . The same oral interpreter may read the same poem in rather strikingly different ways. But the literary critic, too, may well change his stride significantly in his second essay on a given poet, and still have made sense in both essays."[5] Working with oral performance and the decision making about oral performance must inspire careful study and a deeper understanding of the work. The process is a highly motivational one and provides the reason for analysis which students can accept. It is the basis for pleasurable study. Analysis without performance is far less effective than analysis accomplished in conjunction with oral performance. Oral performance takes the student deeper into the work than can analysis alone because "our talk about a piece, even when it is highly critical talk, is not equivalent to the piece itself."[6] The chief purpose of oral interpretation is not to put on a polished performance, but to gain what Campbell calls "a quickened and deeper response to, and appreciation of, literature." Oral interpretation, says Campbell, is "oralizing litera-ture" during which process "the reader goes beyond analysis and creates the work anew."[7] For the recreation of the poem, no audience other than the reader himself is actually necessary. Bacon and Breen are also concerned with the "*full* response" to literature that can come only with oral performance. "We should hold that in certain respects oral performance is one of the best ways of insuring full response of students to literature, since it demands of the reader a considerably richer participation in the literary text than that ordinarily demanded by silent reading. Interpretation demands that literature *be experienced*—not simply, in some paraphrasable sense, 'under-stood.' "[8] Beloof goes even further in his plea for oral performance: "There is every indication, regarding understanding of a literary work of art, that full comprehension can come only through the participation of our bodies—that even the rational process itself is a special kind of emotional set which must be learned through a certain control of the body."[9]

BEGINNING STEPS

When students are first confronted with the act of oral interpretation, they often have difficulty differentiating between the speaker in the poem and the reader of the poem. Campbell offers some assistance with this problem: "The reader-speaker relationship is a relationship between a real person and an imaginary one. . . . The reader has created this person, the speaker, and he must react to, respond to, in a sense *become,* the speaker."[10] There is the real need for the oral reader to know who is the speaker in the poem and to whom he does the speaking. Burton defines the dramatic component: "In poetry, it is important that at the outset the reader establish the nature of the setting and characters, that he approach a poem as a kind of drama in which the 'speaker' may be the poet talking to himself, the poet addressing an audience of one or more persons, who may or may not speak in the poem. . . ."[11]

The presentation of the poem as a piece of drama is invaluable. One rarely finds an English teacher who demonstrates a grasp of this notion of a poem. The neglect is especially baffling when the fact is considered that so many textual critics explore the drama of poetry. Only a few will be cited here. Brower is emphatic: "Every poem is 'dramatic' in Frost's sense: someone is speaking to someone else. For a poem is a dramatic fiction no less than a play, and its speaker, like a character in a play, is no less a creation of words on the printed page. . . . It is important to remember that when we speak of the dramatic situation, we are thinking of all the relations implied between the fictional speaker and auditor in a poem. . . ."[12] Are they friends? Lovers? What are they doing? Is one listening to the other? In what manner is one speaking and the other listening? Is one bold, the other timid? Is one soft-spoken, the other attentive? Campbell supports Brower: "*All literature is dramatic discourse.* Or, more simply, there is a fundamental sense in which all literature is drama. . . . Every literary work is a statement that could be appropriately uttered by some 'person,' some 'speaker,' or 'speakers.' "[13] Drew reiterates, "In a sense all poetry has a dramatic element. The poet, directly or indirectly, is addressing someone else."[14]

Once teachers feel that students comprehend the dramatic orientation of poetry, they need to help them prepare for oral performance by developing an awareness that in every poem there is a speaker. Students require help in determining who he could possibly be. The speaker has a personality that can be explored. What can students determine about his personality? Is he old? Is he lonely? Does he like other people? What did the poet say to give them these notions? Also, the student must learn that the speaker is addressing himself to someone. To whom does the speaker address himself? Why? What is he saying? If this is a drama, there is a happening. Happenings go on in particular times and places. Where does this take place? At what time of day or year?

The teacher reads the poem in its entirety, usually more than once. The students will read it many times, as will be evident shortly, but at first it is the teacher's reading which makes it possible for students to overcome major obscurities. Perrine's analogy between poetry and music clarifies the need for many readings, but it is the students' preparation for performances which will ultimately make the difference: "A good poem will no more yield its full meaning on a single reading than will a Beethoven symphony on a single hearing. . . . One does not listen to a good piece of music once and forget it; one does not look at a good painting once and throw it away."[15]

The problem becomes one of structuring classroom experiences so that students' numerous contacts with the poem are natural and purposeful. The teacher informs students early in the game that there will be oral interpreting of the poem. A brief discussion follows in which the dramatic situation is explored, and the teacher reads parts of the poem again as needed. Questions such as those cited previously may be used as a discussion guide. In some cases it is helpful to students to consider what happened before the poem opened. Were the two people talking before this? About what? What is the relationship between these two? Do they like each other? Hate? How important is their conversation? What does it tell you? Excerpts from a tenth-grade discussion of Hardy's "The Man He Killed" reveal the importance of such an exploration:

Catherine: I think the speaker is a Vietnam veteran.
Joseph: It can't be. Thomas Hardy lived long ago. It's any war he means. The speaker is any soldier.
Patricia: I'd call him a mighty embittered soldier. . . .

Helene: Why do you think he's such an embittered soldier? There's nothing there to give you that idea. He's just stating a fact.
Patricia: Well, if he's not embittered, then he's surely disgruntled.

Michael: Anyway, we've established it's a soldier who's speaking.
Linda: A very disillusioned soldier.

Joseph: He's trying to say how ironic it all is. Except for the war, these two could very well be friends.

The class found it difficult to make a decision about the person or persons to whom the soldier was speaking. Some thought the soldier was "musing to himself"; others, "to his guilty conscience"; still others, "to the people who make wars," "to all humanity," "to some super patriot," "to the kin of the dead man in an attempt to justify his deed," "to a guy who's praising him for his bravery, but he's putting him down." Likewise, there was a number of proposals about time and place: "in an English pub," "in bed at night when he just can't sleep," "on the meadow shortly after the first shock of his deed had passed."

The purpose of the early class discussion was to perceive the poem as drama. Teachers need to feel comfortable about not doing too much teaching with any one poem. There must be a focus of one or two major points and a systematic buildup toward a broad goal as each succeeding poem is read. It is helpful for teachers to know that the excerpts of later discussions with the above-mentioned tenth-grade class demonstrated that in their preparation for performance students went beyond the teacher's focus.

Time is needed for deciding how the poem should be read. Certainly, thirty or thirty-five students cannot perform each poem before the whole class. Therefore, time-saving devices must be adopted. Decision making in small groups serves this purpose. It gives every student who is ready a chance to perform as well as to aid in the decision making. The outcome is the selection of one student from each group to give an oral rendition for full class consideration of that interpretation. During the group discussion much analysis has taken place and many ideas have been exchanged about meaning, stress, pauses, rhyme, and rhythm. Therefore, all students in the group have something at stake; the rendition represents their ideas. The most critical part of the teacher's task comes after the student performance. It takes skill to help the class discuss the interpretation without attacking the individual performer as a human being. Excerpts from the discussion by the same class cited above illustrate some of the problems and progress:

Karen: That "shot him dead"—I'd rather have him mulling it over. It needs a pause after the first "because," to show he's mulling it over.
Pamela: I think so too. That's why there's a dash after the first "because." And the second "because" starts a new line.
Richie: And then he starts to make excuses. "He's my foe; that's why I shot him."
John: "Just so" should be said bitterly. "Just so; that's the way it is."
Richie: I think he's questioning. For the first time he's questioning why he shot him.

Regina: You had him say, "I shot him dead because. . . ." and then, realizing why he shot him, "because he's my foe." For the first time he's realizing and questioning why he shot him. He didn't know why he shot him right off the bat.

Karen: Oh, no! He knew! He said, "If only we had met some other time in some other place."

Catherine: Perhaps it could be read as if it's the process of just coming into the realization.

Regina: I like the idea behind Billy's interpretation in terms of the rush of what he's done, then the pause and the reflectiveness—the alternating pace; rushing and saying, then grasping at straws and slow; rushing and then grasping at straws again, and slow.

Karen: Actually, it starts a little slowly; then it gets "Well, what could I do; he was my foe." Then it goes back again to the reflectiveness.

Catherine: The "quaint and curious" is meditative the way Billy's group did it.

Iona: I could never say it in a flippant manner. This is serious business. He doesn't mean "quaint and curious." He's sneering. He's bitter.

Joseph: When he uses those words "quaint and curious," it has a much more powerful effect on the listener than if he had used a very strong word. When we say the words, we're substituting "how horrible," not "quaint and curious." It was very ingenious of Hardy to use that type of tone.

Pamela: It came closest to what you would hear if you were overhearing a conversation sitting in a bar. I'm still not sure if he was explaining it to a fellow soldier or a child, you know. It felt like to himself, with just a twinge of guilt.

Marilyn: You read it once more like that, and I'll be in tears.

Michael: I think we do need the slowness. He's building up to the realization and to the negative "no other reason why." No other reason why he enlisted, no other reason why he killed him.

Linda: The tone—it sounds like the person would never think of saying it, who had had a half pint. It seems very sad.

Regina: I think though, the first stanza should be started off a little more lightly, to show that he's coming to have realization.

John: Yes, and the second stanza is "Well, I couldn't help myself; there he was and there I was." The third is the same way. The last has the real deep hidden feelings.

Teacher: The suppressed emotion you are feeling in the last stanza is closely allied to the bitterness you mentioned earlier.

These excerpts demonstrate the fact that oral interpretation sets the stage for uncovering meanings. Oral interpretation builds insights, interest, and mastery. Teachers are usually pleasantly surprised at the number of phrases and lines students can quote from memory after one such brief session; they are also amazed at the number of times students use these phrases in various contexts. "Quaint and curious" and "Because he was my foe, just so," when used out of context by two students, brought quick class response. The total experience built a new intimate language as the year rolled by and welded the class as a strong unit. It is true that sometimes the welding had a negative effect, for visitors or other teachers who were not aware that a particular phrase or line had taken on a special significance for this class felt left out or rather bewildered at student reactions. These brief excerpts make it apparent, too, that students are analyzing for a purpose. The poem has not been torn apart.

The performance-discussion procedure also lends itself to the enjoyment of learning. After engaging in it for two days with her high school students, one teacher commented,

"Never did I expect to see the day when *all* thirty-three of my students would enjoy poetry and beg for more. It happened."

Meantime, students have informally touched upon a number of poetic elements and have engaged in a variety of cognitive skills. They have transformed ideas from the printed page to oral performance. A range of inferences has been verbalized as students interpreted the poem and compared interpretations; the specific events of the poem have been transformed to the universal ideas suggested by the poet. Students have continuously peered into cause and effect as they weigh the impact of various aspects of each performance. The number of times they made hypotheses about syllables, words, or phrases that should be stressed and the number of times they predicted the effect of a pause have exceeded what students would tolerate if this process were formally directed by the teacher. They have even touched upon mood, as Brooks and Warren perceive mood: "A mood implies a certain attitude toward the world and may shade over imperceptibly into thought, into general statement, into whole systems of philosophy."[16] They have gained insight into the fact that poetry appeals to understanding as well as to the passions.

The level of the poem selected for the oral interpretation-discussion procedure needs to be carefully weighed. Some teachers protest that "The Man He Killed" and other poems of similar difficulty are not sufficiently difficult, have inadequate suggestive power, and lack the capacity to challenge bright students. Teachers often prefer a poem with more complex metaphors and ideas. There are a number of considerations that are in order. First, poems on the level of "The Man He Killed" are very satisfactory as an introduction to the kinds of procedures teachers will use throughout the secondary school years. Teachers who aim at enjoyment through quick involvement in the poem itself, through interchange of ideas among peers, and through oral performance select for initial study these poems which present few obstacles. It is not easy to learn all of the previously mentioned skills. These skills require experiences which stimulate assimilation and accommodation. These objectives cannot be achieved if the poem is too difficult.

A few additional story poems which serve the same purposes as Hardy's poem are "The Negro Woman" by Williams, "Four Little Foxes" by Sarett, "Out, Out" by Frost, "Abraham Lincoln Walks at Midnight" by Lindsay, "Annabel Lee" by Poe, "Silence" by Masters, "The Ballad of the Harp Weaver" by Millay, "Brass Spitoon" by Hughes, and "To a Small Boy Standing on My Shoes While I Am Wearing Them" by Nash. Teachers who encouraged their students to present a poem of their own choosing and then to select one for small group consideration were pleased with the degree of student involvement.

CHORAL READING

Through choral reading teachers can involve the whole class in a variation on the interpretative reading process; at the same time the process serves to interest a number of students who pursue this activity in a workshop setting. Frequently, teachers who have not worked with choral reading approach it with trepidation. This need not be so if they keep in mind the fact that the finished product is not of central importance. Performance is the motivating means towards the end result—enjoyment and deeper understanding.

Teachers who have engaged in the preparation of oral reading with their classes, as described in the preceding section, have far less fear of choral reading than they might otherwise have. They tend to possess a greater faith in what students can do, feel a sense of adventure and excitement in what they learn about students, and therefore are aware that they can throw to students the task of conducting the choral group.

After the teacher reads the poem to the students, there is again a brief discussion of the dramatic situation and the dramatic movement of the poem. If the poem is long, this discussion concludes with decisions about points at which the work naturally divides itself. Different groups may then work on the interpretation of particular portions. There is no such decision making about apportionment if the poem is divided into stanzas. This process of identifying natural divisions of the poem becomes the focus for interpreting it as a whole.

In one class students prepared "The Touch of the Master's Hand" by Welch. The first section was prepared by the whole class, with the discussion led by the teacher. At this time, the concerns centered around which words and lines were to be read by whom—a male voice, female, or chorus—and what to do with "he cried." Were the first four lines to be read by a mixed chorus or a single narrator different from the auctioneer? How do you know? The discussion may bore many students who are not interested in technicalities. The teacher's chief role is to encourage students to explore specific contents of the poem which give them clues. If the students merely offer, "A chorus should read this line," and neglect to explore clues, the session can become deadly. When each student has done some individual thinking about who should read certain lines, the sharing and decision making about performance are more productive.

At this point the teacher called upon five or six students to sit around a table in the center of the room and make decisions about a stanza, performing it for each other when this was needed as part of the decision making. Then, the whole class discussed how that group went about their preparation for the oral interpretation. What clues did they use? As they tried out various suggestions orally, how did they analyze the effects? What aspects of their group interaction were effective in shaping up the interpretation? In other words, the small group in effect was role playing a real situation which lent itself to on-the-spot analysis. From the role playing and discussion, the rest of the class could learn much about group behavior and preparation for performing poetry because the full attention, including the teacher's, could be centered upon a few individuals. Excerpts from such a role-playing session follow:

Janet: At least we're all agreed that the first four lines are narrative. Then there's a switch. There's a male solo for the auctioneer. Agree?

Ricky: Agree! But we're not agreed on who should read the first four lines.

Adam: Did anyone split it up after, "What am I bidden, good folks, he cried."

Eileen: I think a girl should say, "He cried."

Janet: I'm afraid it couldn't be done smoothly. That might give it an emphasis it shouldn't have. It might shift our attention.

Adam: That brings us down to "from the room."

Sandy: No it doesn't! "A dollar, a dollar" is not what the auctioneer is saying. Somebody in the crowd says that. Then he says, "Two dollars."

Janet: No! The punctuation is wrong if that's what it is. He doesn't say that. I would think a person in the crowd yells out, "A dollar, a dollar," and then someone else yells out, "Two," and then the auctioneer says, "Only two?"

Adam: So, we need bidders. You need two persons who yell out "a dollar" and then "two."

Ricky: Again, you're splitting it up too much. It's too distracting.

Eileen: Then you get complicated with having to bring back the narrator to get in just the word "Then."

Janet: Let's try it. Our ears will tell us whether we like it.

A brief discussion followed about roles students play in such group tasks and about new elements involved in the decision making and performance.

Teachers usually hesitated to break up this poem to distribute portions to different groups. Rather, they turned over the whole poem to groups, giving each an opportunity to perform. The final discussion centered around different interpretations that were revealed. One class concluded the full-group discussion with these ideas:

If you break it up too much, it gets complicated. We could give the chorus a greater possibility of variation. You can get different sound effects from the same chorus. It doesn't have to be one person for a softer sound.

There are things you can achieve with many voices that you cannot achieve with one.

The poem is half philosophical and half action. The philosophical parts should be read by a chorus representing many men, and the action parts should be solo.

It is important to stress that teachers do not conduct these activities one after the other. These are suggested procedures which have been found to be educationally productive. Teachers select what is appropriate for the students and for themselves. Not all teachers can conduct all activities equally well; not all teachers can conduct them equally well with all classes. New activities require practice on the part of the teacher and the students. Early in the semester the teacher may try one activity with two or three poems, or he may try two activities seriatim. The chief criteria are the degree to which students are involved in the poetry and are enjoying the contact with it.

For some teachers to stop teaching poetry by telling is no easy task. Some teachers have experienced no other type of procedure. They may be bothered by, even fearful of, the buzz of students' voices as they sit side by side discussing, practicing, or trying lines out for sound. Some teachers tolerate this aspect very comfortably, but fear the reaction of supervisors. However, in general, when supervisors feel confident that teachers are in control of the situation and that the buzz is purposeful, they too appreciate the active learning which is taking place. The teacher's function is to create a situation in which students can enjoy poetry. The teacher's initial reading of the poem gives students the opportunity to consider the whole piece at one session. Many teachers object to breaking up a poem and parceling out pieces for different groups to analyze and perform. However, other teachers feel that the wholeness is maintained since the entire poem is read, reread, and then discussed as an entity.

Guiding students in the evaluation of a performance presents a difficult problem. It is not the performance per se which is to be evaluated; rather, it is the interpretation which is open for discussion. It is not easy to separate these two elements. If performance is attacked, students regard criticism as a personal affront. The student with a flair for dramatics may carry the day, regardless of depth of interpretation. It helps matters to have the performers explain why they did what they did, how they decided on this, why they stressed certain words, and why they chose a chorus or solo for particular lines. When a group of eighth graders presented Johnson's "The Creation," the teacher for whom choral reading was a first experience managed to convey the stress on interpretation as is evident from students' increasingly objective comments. The first part of the discussion consisted of remarks such as the following:

Jeff: When he says, "That's good," it shouldn't be so solemn. It should be more jolly.
Paul: I like the way they read it. Each one tied right in with the one before, as if they looked up and saw the birds and then looked over there and saw the fishes. It should have been read like that because it tied in, one after another, as God wanted it.
Teacher: Do you mean that it all happened in such a short span of time that it should be read quickly?
Michael: Each thing happened one right after another.

Later in the same session, these comments were more typical, probably because the teacher's questions stressed the poem itself.

Richard: There are two things happening: One, he's lonely; and two, he then comes up with an idea. You need more than one voice to express this change.
Jeff: There are two parts in which God says something. One person can do it, changing his voice. It's the same person that's talking.
Vicki: There were two completely different thoughts: a sad and an exciting one. It's exciting when he says he'll make a man. We thought that needed two different voices.

In learning to evaluate their interpretation of a poem, students need to understand that the interpretation is acceptable only if every detail is in harmony with it. The better the interpretation, the more fully it throws light upon the details of the poem. Yet, it leaves no room for any one of the particulars to carry a meaning contrary to it. Students had an opportunity to compare their own performances with that on a record. When the teacher questioned the students' choices of voice and volume, he led them to examine the concept, "There are certain emotions that are universal." Students learned about the loneliness of man as seen through the character of God, the emptiness of human power, and the joy and satisfaction of achievement. The ideas of universality of emotions were expanded later through the use of other poems such as Robinson's "Richard Cory" and Dunbar's "Sympathy." Students began to gain a sense of Bone's philosophy though this was never presented to them. Bone observes that the poet "instructs us in the life of the emotions; he teaches us to recognize our murderous and self-destructive feelings, and to master them through form."[17] Clearly, there is wisdom in group thinking. When students try their hand at interpreting or reacting to a poem, the teacher on occasion can have responses summarized or excerpted, then reproduced so that each member of the class can consider the totality of peer reactions.

Oral interpretation combined with group thinking makes reliance on textual critics far less important than otherwise might be true. Geiger advances the status of the primary critic with the explanation that "in reproducing effects of the text itself, the oral interpreter approaches the literary work even more closely than the textual critic. . . . The interpreter . . . limits himself to the words presented by the author."[18] The interpreter is a "primary critic" because "while the textual critic can isolate and describe the 'tone' of the poem, the oral interpreter, as primary critic, can give the tone itself, in all its modifications."[19] One teacher whose class worked with Tennyson's "The Charge of the Light Brigade" in a choral reading endeavor reported:

> You really are getting at the meaning of this poem without the teacher talking so much and tearing it apart and asking a million questions. Nothing that I could do would ever be as effective in getting them to notice the punctuation and its relation to meaning. They were fussing with the fourth stanza until they noticed a colon and said, "It must be the same attitude before and after the colon." The kids did come up with talk about the repetition, how you handle the refrain, and how you handle the interpretation of each line. One group did it from the point of view of a woman left alone after her husband was killed in that battle. They used a ghostlike quality and a thin female voice because of the refrain repeating in every stanza. Another group did it from the point of view of a modern response to Vietnam: It's not theirs to do and die; the officers stood by and didn't get killed, and the one who made the "goof" didn't get killed. They knew in Tennyson's day people didn't protest and some felt the poem was full of satire. One group had someone very quietly saying in the background to a galloping speed and rhythm, "half a league, half a league, half a league onward."

One teacher who used this procedure summarized her experiences this way:

> The marvelous thing about this technique is it allows you to give the schmaltziest rendition you want and then split your class and let them argue. That's the experimental part of teaching. *That's* what they are involved with: the poem.
>
> It's civilized, because there's room for many points of view, and students find that comforting as well as enlightening.

A teacher of eighth-grade students who read "Lewis and Clark" by Benét evaluated his experiences with preparation for choral reading:

> All groups wanted to read before the class; the class was attentive to other groups, and as I was going around the room while they worked in groups, there was no fooling around —they were really working at it. During their free time, a few days later, I noticed some of the students reading their poem aloud together, just for the fun of it. . . . Whereas before they performed it, the reactions were, "It's silly," "I don't get it," "I don't understand what it's about," the later reactions were, "It's humorous," "I like it now," "The author took something serious and made it funny."

In this particular classroom a new workshop interest was born: the choral readers. The group of three girls was given its own cassette to have, so that whenever they were ready with a new rendition, the tape was waiting for them. If more voices were needed for a particular poem, it was up to them to secure interested participants. Before too many sessions were over, two boys joined the girls in their efforts to start a library of poetry tapes. They later added "Notes on————," a booklet about poems which caused conflict as they practiced reading them. The notes constituted explanations of reasons for settling on the interpretation in the final rendition.

Teachers reacted positively to using oral performance for teaching elements such as tone, pace, and rhythm; the students grappled with those elements of their own accord. Teachers felt that since in essence the students had dealt with those factors on their own terms, the role of the teacher was simply one of helping students recognize what they had uncovered. A tape recorder has a role to play here; teachers need to listen to class discussions in the silence of their homes and in the absence of the students. Thus, they gain perspective and determine needs. Also, students need to listen to themselves again, after a short lapse of time, to evaluate what they have uncovered and to determine next steps.

The poems the teacher or students select for choral reading must be intrinsically suitable for choral reading. Otherwise, the activity will not be effective, the poem will distorted in meaning, and the satisfactions to the students will be minimal.

Having students select poems encourages independent reading of many poems in preparation for the group's final choice. The satisfactions reaped from that selection process cannot be gained by continuous teacher selection of poems to be rendered. The criticism may be offered that students will select poems which are too easy. Rarely did students make selections which teachers silently questioned, and even then teachers felt the choices were justified on the grounds that "these students were the ones who needed to relax with poetry." One teacher reported that in such a group there were compensations because during the work session there was "much excitement, laughter, flair." Dunning offers teachers additional comfort: "Taste, the ability to judge a poem, develops from being involved and from careful consideration; it does not develop from being told what is good or bad."[20] In a few instances, students selected "solo" poems and tried to read them chorally.

The discussions which ensued, after their oral reading, proved to be good lessons in basic elements of poetry. Playing with new ways of rendering the same poems helped students "live into" them, a phenomenon Ciardi advocates.[21] The word "playing" is used advisedly. "Playing" with poetry is precisely what teachers need to help students do. Ciardi elaborates: "Learning to experience poetry is not a radically different process from that of learning any other kind of play. . . . And one of the real joys of the play impulse is in the sudden discovery that one is getting better at it than he had thought he would be."[22] Play is serious business; genuine play involves much work but no drudgery or boredom.

"The Creation" by Johnson was another favorite poem for choral reading as were Tennyson's "The Highwayman," Muir's "The Horses," Shapiro's "Doctor, Doctor, A Little of Your Love," Miller's "Columbus," Browning's "Incident of the French Camp," Dunbar's "We Wear the Mask," Frost's "The Runaway," Hughes' "Harlem," and Brooks' "We Real Cool."

DRAMATIZING THE BALLAD*

Many teachers prefer to begin oral interpretation of poetry with the dramatization of a ballad. Through the ballad, students can sense the poem as drama with relative ease.

---

*This section was written with Alice Fritsch Stollman.

In a ballad there are scenes corresponding to those in a play; there is dialogue in many ballads; the speaker is usually identified readily; future events, most often disastrous, are forecast in a fashion somewhat similar to a play. Ballads are concrete, as are all narrative poems, and students need to experience the concrete to arrive at the abstract.

Ballads tell of exciting events in a relatively uncomplicated manner. Each stanza adds a significant detail, even while it reflects most of the previous ones. This gradual addition combined with repetition alerts the listeners to the significance of each new detail. Ballads use memory-aiding devices such as rhyme. Rhyme also emphasizes the meaning. Since traditional ballads were rendered orally, devices such as repetition and rhyme were essential. Now these same devices offer a distinct advantage to the teacher in guiding the learning process in sequential steps. Robb observes, "It is well to remember that the oral presentation of poetry and prose precede all written literature and that man naturally tells stories and responds to rhythmical expressions of emotion."[23] Ballads also help students "respond imaginatively to things outside ourselves," which Bacon feels is an important role of literature. "Emotion means 'outward movement'; it is a physiological response to an outside stimulus."[24]

In considering the poem as drama, the teacher needs to help students deal with the plot of the poem. The dramatic movement is relatively easy to uncover in the ballad. Teachers felt that when they used the ballad for first experiences in looking at the poem as a play with a setting, characters, and plot, they were able to help students build a framework in which other elements of the poems became manageable.

A few teachers objected to the early use of the ballad because, "There's so much blood and guts." Beerbohm might reply to this: "Strange, when you come to think of it, that of all the countless folk who have lived before our time on this planet not one is known in history or in legend as having died of laughter."[25] Through the ballad, students can enjoy anew the beat of verse which Untermeyer feels is central in importance: "The beat of verse existed in the pulse before speech sprang to the lips. We breathe rhythmically; the tides regularly ebb and flow; day and night, light and darkness, the progress of the seasons, all have an ordered cycle. This measure of time begins in the very cradle—even before that period, when the child is rocked upon its mother's breast. From that time on rhythm dominates. The lullaby, the unworded tune, the brisk jingles of Mother Goose, awake an instant response from every child."[26] Through the ballad, students can move forward in the skills of interpretation and evaluation. These are two processes defined by Purves: "The child who wants the story read the same way over and over again both perceives and is engaged by form. The child who says, "Pooh is a funny bear," is moving towards interpretation, and the one who says, "That part is good because it's spooky," is evaluating. Engagement is in the child; so are perception, interpretation, and evaluation."[27]

Teachers encountered few problems with the dramatization of the ballad. One problem in particular did require some forethought: Are the students to take the roles of actors in this situation? Or are they to be readers? Aggert clarifies the basic difference between these two roles: "Interpretative reading is not acting. ... The actor uses complete impersonation, for he gives the impression of actually being the character he portrays. ... The actor attempts to make the audience see the character in himself; the reader attempts to make his listeners see the character in their own imaginations."[28]

As an introduction to the oral reading of ballads, one teacher presented a role-playing situation: "What happens when you come home late for dinner?" Two pairs of students

were given this problem as a preliminary assignment. Each couple was charged with
the responsibility of presenting a different reaction by the fictitious mother or father
to the situation. One couple was asked to present an angry parent and the other, a
worried one. As students played their roles, the teacher wrote on the board in large
letters the lines they used spontaneously which were the same or similar to those in
"Lord Randal." (The students had not yet been introduced to that ballad.) One line
was the universal question, Where have you been? and another was, Did you eat
supper? The angry parent bellowed, "Where have you been, you brat?" The worried
mother queried, "Where have you been, my baby? I was so worried." The repetition
of the same question in the role playing made a startling comparison with its echo in
"Lord Randal." The fact that the repetition in the role playing and the ballad had
different purposes and functions provided a focus for interpreting character and universal emotions.

The purpose of the role playing was to help present the idea of universality of
emotions, which was the main concept for this part of the poetry sequence taught along
with other genre. At this point, the teacher read "Lord Randal" to the students. There
was a short discussion in which the class expressed their initial feelings and ideas about
the poem. The teacher reread the poem as the students watched the text, and then they
discussed it in greater detail emphasizing the characters' motivation for what they said.
This ballad took place hundreds of years ago. The mother asked, "Where have you
been?" The connection between their own role playing and the situation which was
inherent in "Lord Randal" was obvious. Thus, students made their first verbalizations
of the concept of universality of emotions.

In the discussion, some young people refused to accept the fact that Lord Randal's
sweetheart poisoned him, and some could not see the relationship between the dead
dogs and the death of Lord Randal. One student attributed Randal's death to a broken
heart. He offered as evidence the fact that Lord Randal said, "I'm sick at the heart and
fain would lie down." The teacher went into a very brief explanation of the medieval
custom of dogs being fed scraps from the table and obtained a picture of a medieval
castle with the dogs lying near the table. She did this in an effort to help children see
that Lord Randal was poisoned because he ate the same food as the dogs had eaten.
One young student still protested that Lord Randal "just ate too much and had to lie
down."

The teacher read and then played a recording of another version[29] of the ballad
which contained more information: the eels were "speckled and spackled" and Lord
Randal's sweetheart had found the eels in a ditch of polluted water.[30] The never-ending
curiosity of well-instructed pupils led them to want more information about the different versions of a ballad, this one in particular. The teacher took the opportunity to point
out the fact that these ballads were not written down. Then she asked, "What happens
to a story that is not recorded?" The students were able to work out the answer to their
own question. The teacher then encouraged them to make a search for more variations
on this ballad. They had little difficulty since so many versions exist. In some classes
students became so involved that they continued the search long after the teacher
stopped mentioning the ballad, and in after-school groups they came together to "try
them out" and perfect performance. Inevitably, they brought the ballads to class. The
teacher used these occasions to help students discuss and analyze how content differ-

ences affect oral interpretation. In one class, the teacher used the "rumor clinic" technique to help students understand what happens to an idea which is passed orally from one person to another.

Some teachers felt it was necessary to make careful preparation for the dramatization. One class discussed what caused the sweetheart to take the action she did. Several suggestions were forthcoming: Lord Randal didn't have the money he promised her; he deceived her because he had another girlfriend; he had already made out his will and she killed him to get the money. The students were asked to prepare a dramatization at home, filling in the action between the lines, since the ballad is a skeleton of the plot. The teacher helped them prepare for this in a number of ways: (1) They formed groups according to the neighborhoods in which they lived so that arrangements for meetings would be possible. (2) The teacher helped students see that the setting had to be made evident through a narrator or through props to be obtained by the players. (3) She used pictures to lead them to visualize a medieval dining hall and discussed with them problems raised by the students such as, "This doesn't rhyme." "Soon" and "down" caused the chief difficulty. The teacher pointed out that this is a Scottish ballad. From there the students deduced that in those days "down" was "doun" and therefore rhymed with "soon."

The class was given two days in which to prepare their scripts and collect props. Every member of each group had a copy of his group's script. The props ranged from an anachronistic shotgun to plumed hats and capes. The scripts included creative dialogue, action, and setting in conjunction with some of the very lines in the ballad. One was written in colloquial English; another, in the attempted dialect of the period; and a third, in standard English. An excerpt from one of the scripts follows:

Scene 1

NARRATOR: As the scene opens, the sweetheart is in her house getting dinner for Lord Randal.

SWEETHEART (*to herself*): If all goes well, before long I will have all of Randal's gold. (*Aloud*) Come, Randal, your dinner is ready.

LORD RANDAL: Ah, boiled eels in broth. My favorite.

SWEETHEART: Yes, I made them specially for you

Scene 2

NARRATOR: After eating, Lord Randal goes home and is greeted by his mother.

LORD RANDAL: I had a wonderful supper tonight even though it was a little spicier than usual.

MOTHER: Lord Randal, my son. Are you sure you didn't have a little something extra to eat?

LORD RANDAL: Now that you mention it, I do feel a little sick.

MOTHER (*taking his temperature*): 105°!! You could die with a temperature like that.

Following each skit there was a short discussion of the different motivations and emotions inherent in the "drama." Dramatization is suited to the ballad for at least two reasons: The dialogue is dramatic and the ballad requires reading between the lines to discover motivations for each character's behavior. In one skit the motivation for the murder was that Lord Randall went fishing with another girl. In a second, the sweetheart said, "Well, dear, how much money have you set aside for me in your will?" In a third, Lord Randal killed his dogs because his girlfriend didn't like them. Students compared their scripts:

Teacher: Do you think this skit was an elaboration of the plot?
Marsha: Yes. The ballad told us his sweetheart poisoned him, but this skit gives the motivation.
Teacher: Was there an elaboration of the characters?
Shiela: Yes. The sweetheart was greedy. She wanted him to leave his fortune in his will to her.
John: Money means more to her than love. It was different in our skit. Lord Randal really committed suicide because his mother pushed him into marrying the gal. It was his mother's character that was elaborated.

Thus, dramatization helped the students to relive the ballad experience and to create their own imaginary situations which occurred behind the scenes.

For slower pupils one teacher taught several ballads, pairing the poems according to concrete themes. For example, there were the supernatural elements in "The Demon Lover" and "Proud Margaret" and the love motif in "Jay Gould's Daughter" and in "Barbara Allen." After discussing the ballads and the strong dramatic quality in them, the students were led to discover for themselves how the story was told. They saw the preponderance of question-and-answer dialogue, repetition, and refrain. In order to demonstrate that the ballad does influence their world, the teacher asked the students to listen to and bring in rock-and-roll records of songs they considered to be in the ballad form; they prepared to defend their choice.

During the time that her pupils were preparing the dramatizations outside of school, one teacher was making use of class periods for a consideration of another ballad, "Edward, Edward." In this poem the emotions are more subtle, but the ballad is similar to "Lord Randal" in the use of the question-and-answer technique. The discussion centered around the teacher's question, Why did Edward kill his father? There is nothing stated specifically in the ballad to answer this question, and the students could offer no immediate explanation. The teacher did not force an answer from the students; rather, she asked, "Why didn't he answer his mother's questions directly at first? Why was she forced to keep on questioning him into a corner?" The students caught the implication of guilt that must have been strong in Edward. "How do you know he felt so terribly guilty?" the teacher asked. The students understood that his plans for running away from the whole situation were implicit in the introduction of a boat. "Could the sailing on a boat mean something more drastic than merely flight?" The answer came, "It was a nice way of saying he was never coming back." The teacher went on with, "Was it a nice way of saying something even more drastic?" Then came, "Well, maybe it was a way of saying he would commit suicide." "Why did he say that he would leave his children the world's room and let them beg through life?" One boy decided, "He was afraid that his wife and children would betray him as he had betrayed them." Brief probing into the ballad with the class seemed to be necessary because "Edward, Edward" is shocking, and the students were unable to accept such a horrible deed. They felt a strong need to talk about the ballad after each performance. At last the consideration of the final line helped them understand that the mother had something to do with the tragedy.

> Larry: He's killing just about everyone—his father, himself, the curse on his mother, and his children and wife. He had something against his parents, because his children are part of his parents' blood.
> Christina: I think he wants to provoke one of his children to kill him.

> Larry: It seems the mother is the whole culprit. She might have hated her husband anyway.
> Nat: She's a very greedy mother, always looking after herself . . . and she's like a criminal who has others do the work for her, and she expects to get a reward.

This ballad, too, was dramatized in teams, this time with an emphasis on how to say particular lines to bring out a character's motivation for saying it. For example, the line, "And what will you leave to your own mother dear," was done in a witchlike, gleeful wringing-of-the-greedy-hands manner. Another group wove a portrait of a helpless mother, hand-on-breast fashion. In one class the students' reactions to peer dramatizations of the ballad helped clarify further the emotions and motivations implicit in the poem.

> Willis: I think Allen interpreted this part differently. He made you feel he had the whole thing planned out. He made you realize he knew what the mother was going to ask him.

The research the students did seemed almost endless. Daily they brought to school fascinating pieces of information that stirred the interest of the class.

> Stan: "The Cruel Brother" is a variation of "Edward, Edward." When they brought "Edward, Edward" to America, they thought it was too bloody for someone to kill his own father, so they changed it so that he killed his brother.
> David: I can't see that that makes it any better.
> Stan: The father is considered the absolute ruler of the household. It sounds better to kill the brother.
> Richard: Your brother is your equal.

The fascination with violence and death in the ballads was as strong as the denial of these phenomena and gave the teacher an opportunity to discuss the use of symbols of death. "Often in ballads there is no direct mention of dying, but the idea is conveyed in other ways, such as the floating hat Richard mentioned. Did you discover any others?" Responses came easily: "In 'Edward, Edward' he says he's going away to sea; in 'Lord Randall' he says, 'For I'm sick at the heart, and I fain would lie down'; in 'Barbara Allen' bells are 'knelling.'" The cognitive progression was evident; inferences were made which bring to mind Beardsley's statement about inference making: "To believe a statement because you think that it follows logically from another statement is to make an inference. And making inferences is what is meant by 'reasoning': to reason is just to take one statement as a reason for another."[31]

An analysis made in conjunction with dramatization added richness to the pupil's perceptions and insights and was heartily received by them. When the teacher brought in a recording of "Barbara Allen," the response was gratifying. The teacher thus built an awareness that ballads were sung and that in some cases even the music could be found. From this point on, the students searched for music to the ballads they knew, as well as for new ones. At this time the teacher became a learner along with the rest of the class. No teacher can compete with the knowledge of thirty avid researchers; these teachers made no attempt to do so.

By no means does the ballad sequence cited here take place in one class during one short space of time. In general, the sequence was interspersed with other pieces of literature dealing with motivation for human behavior. Other genre helped shed light on concepts students were evolving and added variety, gave focus for comparison, lent an awareness of universality of literary issues, and dispelled the tendency to consider one literary form too intensively. In some schools where teachers of various grades planned together, the sequence was distributed so that students studied ballads in at least two different grades.

Creating Ballads*

Writing ballads is an important and pleasurable activity for students. It offers an opportunity to play with ideas and sound effects made by the use of particular words and of word order, and it encourages the examination of elements of the ballad which were only lightly touched upon up to this point.

An encouraging first effort is the class endeavor, a ballad based upon a common experience which has some emotional implications. A favorite subject proved to be school; the title chosen was usually "The Ballad of (name of school)." In one case the class ballad followed the rhythm and rhyme pattern of "The Blue Tail Fly" and retained the refrain with a minor change. The class briefly considered "The Blue Tail Fly" for the main idea, ballad form, rhyme scheme, and meter. "What main idea would you like to convey in your ballad?" The answer was, "Frustrations of school life." "What specific frustrations would you consider?" There was no dearth of ideas! When all factors became common property through discussion, the students were paired for writing one stanza. As each pair completed its stanza, papers were exchanged for help from peers. At this point the teacher's aid was sought, especially when individuals disagreed about rhyme or meter. Now there was motivation for learning that a pattern of rhyme and meter appropriate to mood and meaning helps provide unity.

It was understood through illustration that no one given arrangement was the model for all ballads, but for class purposes argeement on some common elements like a-b-a-b and 4-3-4-3 was necessary. The class sang and recorded their ballad as a contribution to the library of tapes other students could use. Of course, there was much reaction to each stanza or group of stanzas before the final recording. One boy sang a few verses about homework. The interest was so high that if the class missed a word there was a spontaneous yell, "What???!" With no invitation they began to sing the performer's refrain, "Jimmy crack corn and I do care. . . ." Discussion of creations included topics

---

*This section was written with Alice F. Stollman.

such as the importance of the idea being conveyed and evaluation of whether or not the main theme really was conveyed. A student-initiated topic involved the differences found between boys and girls: "The boys went for the comedy side while the girls went for the dramatic."

Students were then thrown on their own to find ballads they enjoyed enough to recommend to classmates. They were invited to list the titles on a previously constructed chart. To be included on the chart were the various emotions, ideas, words, and techniques used in telling the ballad (e.g., question and answer, dialogue, or narrative). The teacher's purposes were to encourage students to open up for each other the world of ballads, to furnish them with ideas for creating their own ballads, and to have students discover how each aspect of the ballad or any work of art contributes to a unified creation. The selection of words and phrases was especially appealing to students, a fact which surprised the teacher.

After the ballads were charted, each pupil selected the one which he could most easily defend as a unified creation. In the discussion of their findings based on the charted information, the students discovered several aspects of the ballad that were basic: 1. In the poetic form of the ballad, certain fundamental universal human emotions are expressed. 2. The theme and plot are also primitive in that they often express violence and obvious tragic events. 3. The way in which emotions are revealed is far from complex because a simple question-and-answer or a narrative technique is employed. 4. The images of color in "blood red wine," "snow white pillow," "red ruby lips," "coal black coffin," and "milk white steed" are also uncomplicated expressions gleaned from the experiences of everyday life. 5. The simplicity of the rhyme scheme creates the feeling of the elemental organization of the ballad—the a-b-a-b rhyme scheme for example.

With their new perceptions students went back to the ballads they had read on their own to seek ideas they might like to consider in creating their own ballads. Many students had already written ballads with no suggestion from the teacher. They were encouraged to examine daily incidents which would be good subjects for the ballad. Suggestions were made by students and teacher as to places where a dramatic incident might be witnessed. Listed on the board were the subway, the basement of a not-too-elegant department store, the school yard, the gym locker, an auction, the beach, open air markets, the public parks, and the highway. Newspaper and television were other sources. The ballads created were much closer to the students' own lives (real or imaginary) than one might expect from these sources of ideas. One dealt with a wedding at which the bridegroom failed to show up; another was concerned with death, and a third, with a lost dog.

> O where is my Snoopy, friend Linus of mine
> O where is my Snoopy, my own faithful friend
> He's down by the dog house asleep on the top
> Or teasing the bird till he takes one good flop.

The ballad went on to detail the death of the dog, apparently an incident that did take place. Again, students exchanged their creations with other students and talked about how theirs differed from those they had read or heard on records.

As time progressed, a number of things occurred which revealed the impact of this work on the students. For example, one girl exclaimed, "I heard 'Early One Morning' in a TV Western. It's really real; it's really real." The ballad was the story of unrequited love, and she decided that it has relevance even today. A boy admitted in class, "You know, I have a poetry book at home and never looked at it until we started studying ballads." An important role of a teacher was thus accomplished: expanding students' interests, opening up new horizons. As a bonus, the act of creating ballads consolidated previous learnings. There appeared bits of evidence that students were beginning to learn to imply emotions in their creations. To suggest a sensation or emotion is a difficult cognitive task. It is one thing to say, "I hate to go to school," or "O beautiful Sabbath, a respite from school." It is quite another to create the sensation by designing an action which implies these feelings.

Best of all, the students enjoyed the writing tremendously, largely because the teachers did not force this as a solitary task. Rather, those who wanted to form "partnerships" did so; those who preferred to work alone had that option. A number of classrooms became workshops at this point, with an opportunity to tune in on individual needs and interests.

The transition from ballads to other narrative poetry was usually relatively smooth. There were scores of narrative poems available to students, so all kinds of interests and all levels of ability could be accommodated. Teachers were able at this point to free themselves and their students, so students could select not only the poems they liked, but also the activity they preferred. Some simply read to chosen peers; others grouped themselves to dramatize; still others used a tape recorder. A fourth activity was writing their own narrative poem after reading a number of them. One seventh-grade boy in an extremely disadvantaged neighborhood school submitted the following as one of many he created:

> Cornered in a Parking Lot, for a Shakedown
> I felt like I was trap
> By a family of lions
> In the weeds, and
> I had not a thing to fight them off
> No help around.
> I was like a cat running from a dog.
> There were too many.
> No sticks or rocks to help myself fight them off
> My body trembled
> Like there was an Earth Quake inside of me
> No place to hide, to run.

Poetry and Music

The transition from studying ballads to playing with music in poetry can be as uncomplicated as the transition to writing other forms of narrative poetry. This does not mean that teachers moved immediately from one fairly intensive mode of study to the next. It does mean that when students were ready for new experiences with poetry, "poetry to music" was a natural next step. Students had already sung ballads and listened to recordings of modern ballads.

Combining music with poetry achieved a number of positive results. First of all, it enhanced students' enjoyment of contact with poetry. It avoided engaging students in the activity Sweetkind called "tearing a passion to tatters"[32] because the experience of relating these two art forms made the "tearing" unnecessary. Poetry to music made memorization of poetry a natural part of students' lives. Just as certain pieces of music "hum in our heads" because we've heard them over and over again and because we enjoy the combination of sounds, so did students begin to hear poems in their heads. Students' experiences bore out Fowler's observation about memorizing poetry: "As the sound of great music haunts memory's ear long after the sound waves are stilled, so the music of great poetry remains in the mind of readers who have loved it."[33]

Poetry to music offers students an opportunity to sense more broadly the role of rhythm and repetition and to build on their inherent love of rhythm. As Untermeyer points out, ". . . rhythm is recurrence of certain sounds."[34] The vendor's "song" or "cry" of yesterday was strong in rhythm and rhyme to aid the public's memory. Advertisements today are also strong in rhythm and rhyme to aid memory, for rhyme too is a kind of repetition of sound. Repetition emphasizes and reinforces meaning. Where the rhythm changes, the reader or listener must be alerted to new shades of meaning. What is the poet calling to our attention at this point? What is the musician telling us to notice at this point? Rhythm's importance is elaborated by Aloian: "Rhythm in a poem is like hypnosis; it puts the reader into a receptive mood. . . . Once the main rhythm is established, the variations and departures from it help the reader to notice words and phrases to which the poet is giving special emphasis."[35]

In one class the teacher found students receptive to very brief explorations of rhythm and rhyme through two or three vendors' cries (street cries). Several students became so intrigued with the cries that their primary attention was devoted for a time to discovering new ones. The study of street cries by a few students opened up the whole panorama of folklore for the whole class. Students experienced a real sense of achievement when they uncovered street cries the teacher had never heard or read and when classmates became intrigued by their findings. The cries were so colorful that students made trips to other ethnic areas to try to "hear the real thing." Unfortunately, disappointment was usually the result, but they did listen carefully to vendors at open market stands and to those who had illegally laid out their wares (mostly jewelry) on the city's sidewalks. Students were struck by the similarity of familiar cries to those they discovered in books. The content, the rhythm and rhyme, and the repetition were outstanding features in almost all. Students made up their own tune for selling their wares. When students hunted down their own collections the teacher was surprised that such a wealth did exist in print.

In another class it was "The Poetry of Rope Skipping" that fascinated a few students who made this this their special interest. Originally, it was inspired by an article from the *New York Times* brought in by the teacher. The results were similar to those gained during the independent study of vendors' cries by a different group of students. Folklorists have researched folk poetry and rhyme games. Everyone was delighted to rediscover favorites such as

>In and out the windows,
>In and out the windows;
>In and out the windows,
>As we have done before.[36]

and another old rhyme

>Naughty girl, she won't come out,
> She won't come out, she won't come out.
>Naughty girl, she won't come out,
> To see the ladies dancing.[37]

Folklorists have researched such categories as marriage and funeral games, games of skill and chance, harvest, ghost, penalty, guessing, hide-and-seek, leap-frog, ball-games, and circle and line games.

The study of children's games has been the subject of serious attempts to uncover the history of life and customs in ages past. Gomme sets forth the thesis that children's games as a branch of folklore "contribute to the results which folklore is daily producing toward elucidating many unrecorded facts in the early history of civilized man." For one of her illustrations Gomme uses the primitive aspect of the game of "Touch": selecting the player by drawing lots. "It is possible that the game of 'Touch' has developed from the practice of choosing a victim by lot. . . ."[38] Students may make rich comparisons between Shirley Jackson's "The Lottery" and games of choosing by lot, with their historical implications.

Marriage games comprise another captivating category, to which Gomme devotes some time ". . . for these games offer evidence of the existence of customs obtaining in primitive marriage." Such customs include "marriage by capture, marriage by purchase, marriage by consent of other than those principally concerned, in other words, marriage between comparative strangers. . . ."[39]

Students can do their own research on games played by children in the streets of the city or the towns and compare the activities of children for similarities and differences among ethnic groups. They can try to discover the degree of truth in Gomme's statement: "There must be some strong force inherent in these games that has allowed them to be continued from generation to generation, a force potent enough to almost compel their continuance and to prevent their decay." This force is "the dramatic faculty inherent in mankind."[40] Other students who have acquired an interest in drama can experience the delight of uncovering more about the drama in children's games, using Gomme's intriguing disclosure: "These traditional games are valuable, therefore, for the information they afford in a direction not hitherto thought of, namely, in the study of early drama. If the drama can be seen in its infancy anywhere, surely it can be seen in these children's plays."[41]

Newell has additional surprises for students interested in the poetry and history of children's games. For example, there is a widespread notion that rhyme games are inferior and originate with socially inferior classes. Newell studied American children's games and poetry with the following conclusion:

It is altogether a mistake to suppose that these games (or, indeed, popular lore of any description) orginated with peasants, or describe the life of peasants. The tradition, on the contrary, invariably came from above, from the intelligent class. If these usages seem rustic, it is only because the country retained what the city forgot, in consequence of the change of manners to which it was sooner exposed. Such customs were, at no remote date, the pleasures of courts and palaces.[42]

In Newell's collection teachers and students can find rhyme games such as: "Little Sally Waters," "As We Go Around the Mulberry Bush," "Here We Come Gathering Nuts in May," "Soldier, Soldier, Will You Marry Me," "Lazy Mary, Will You Get Up," "Rich Man, Poor Man, Beggar-man, Thief," "Ring a Ring a Rosie," "The Farmer in the Dell," "Put Your Right Elbow In," "I Tisket, I Tasket," "Kittie Put the Kettle On," "London Bridge Is Falling Down," "On Dixie's Land I'll Take My Stand."

The works of Iona and Peter Opie deal with the psychological as well as the sociological elements of children's rhyme games and lore. "The scraps of lore which children learn from each other are at once more real, more immediately serviceable, and more vastly entertaining to them than anything which they learn from grown-ups. . . . The school rhyme circulates simply from child to child, usually outside the home, and beyond the influence of the family circle. . . . The school-child's verses are not intended for adult ears. In fact, part of their fun is the thought, usually correct, that adults know nothing about them."[43] Opie espouses the importance of permitting children their out-of-sight play. "We have overlooked that the most precious gift we can give the young is social space: the necessary space—or privacy—in which to become human beings."[44] "The rhymes are more than playthings to children," Opie explains. "They seem to be one of their means of communication with each other. Language is still new to them, and they find difficulty in expressing themselves. When on their own they burst into rhyme, of not recognizable relevancy, as a cover in unexpected situations, to pass off an awkward meeting, to fill a silence, to hide a deeply felt emotion, or to gasp in excitement. And through these ready-made formulas the ridiculousness of life is underlined, the absurdity of the adult world and their teachers proclaimed, danger and death mocked, and the curiosity of language itself is savored."[45] Any aspect of art that can fulfill all of these various roles and can add a bonus of sheer joy is one that should not be neglected by the schools.

It is important that collections of poetry be available in the classroom library and that these volumes cover a wide range of types and content. Today there are scores of paperbacks.[46] When the collection is gathered by teachers and students, there is little problem finding at least fifty books. Furthermore, the cooperative selection insures greater variety as well as appeal to student interests.

Unforeseen problems do present themselves, as is true of any aspect of teaching. In one case, a few students brought in college anthologies owned by parents. The fact that they were unsuitable for young people could not be accepted by the class. They could not surrender the books although almost every poem was beyond them. Finally, one by one, the teacher was able to introduce poems from other sources which appealed to individuals who in turn shared their own enthusiasms. The college texts remained available for those few students who were genuinely challenged by a particular poem.

Each student searched through the collections in order to discover poems which could be put to music. The search was motivated by the promise that everyone would have a chance to give a rendition to music of his chosen poem though not necessarily to the whole class. With the availability of inexpensive lightweight portable tape recorders and cassettes, the teacher can record student performances for use by next year's class as well as this one. There is high motivation in the knowledge that the taped performance is to be used now and in the future.

Competitive students often select a poem rendered by last year's class and attempt to outdo the performer. Others who are threatened by high competition can engage in this activity safely by rendering a poem not yet taped to music. The only students who expressed no interest in this activity were those who had no records or recorder at home. It is the obligation of the school to equalize educational opportunities by providing such facilities for all students and by making it possible for them to take the time within the school day to listen to records and to read poetry on their own terms.

At the end of the school year several students requested that their earlier renditions be erased because they now liked a different poem better, found more appropriate music, or felt the poem differently. Needless to say such requests were always honored, just so long as students were careful not to erase the work of a peer.

Meantime, teachers also chose poems which would demonstrate the way the activity could be done. One teacher taped her reading of Wylie's "Sea Lullaby" to Rachmaninoff's Symphony no. 2 and also to the first movement of Beethoven's Fifth Symphony. She played the renditions for the class and asked her students to try to determine why she chose this music for that particular poem. At first the students were surprised at the bombastic quality of the music, the poem, and the reading. Together, they discussed briefly the meaning of the poem in order to make a judgment as to the appropriateness of the music. Gradually, the pupils began to demonstrate some new understandings, such as that the Beethoven opening theme in its ominous quality foreshadowed in sound and emotion the tragic death of the boy in the poem. Later, the class saw that the death tragedy of the boy was foreshadowed within the first lines of the poem itself. The fact that the first lines of the poem and the first theme in the music foreshadow death became a vivid realization. Thus, the music was used as a vehicle for a closer examination of the meaning and the mood of the poem.

David: The music sort of sets the scenery for what's going to happen in the poem. It shows the darkness and the night.
Teacher: We call this "foreshadowing"; You are helped to feel what is going to happen later.
Myron: It mentions "blood" so you know there's a tragedy.
Marion: In each stanza where it was at the eerie part, the music got louder.
Robin: When it gets louder and softer, it gives the impression of the tide coming up and back.
Jay: The first three lines have it all: her clothes, and she choked him and beat him.
Teacher: Who did?
Jay: The sea.
Teacher: Yes, the poet gives the sea human characteristics, as you indicated when you said "her clothes." When he does this, we call it "personification." Can you figure out why he does this?
David: It says, "The child of the village was murdered today." It's the idea of human hands that killed him and that makes it more terrible.

Harold: And she shouted for joy, and that made the murder even worse.

Marion: She strangled him with one hand. She didn't even have to try hard.

Robin: In the third stanza it says the "prey." When I'm on the beach, I don't think of the sea that way.

Marc: When we read "Mother in Mannville," the first part told about the orphanage and the isolation from the world and even though it's not personification the author did fore-shadow and give you a feeling.

Jerry: In "Sea Lullaby" there's that description of the long fingernails.

Ira: She's a witch!

Nat: She sounds like a woman who just escaped from a madhouse. When she's strangling the boy, she's laughing [demonstrates the style of laughter].

Teacher: The poet also says she has teeth white as milk and has bright locks.

Adena: She might have been a beautiful woman but hate turns her to something treacherous and awful.

Martin: She's a smoothie; it says "beguile."

Judy: At night she creeps around and changes.

Michael: She sounds like Dr. Jekyl and Mr. Hyde. She changes day and night.

Jill: When you go to the beach you think of the sea as something nice and you never suspect it can be treacherous. At night you have a feeling of the bad side and that the sea isn't all good.

Gary: The music tells you right away that all is not well, with that bom-bom-bom-bom.

Nat: It's an ominous feeling—the music with that first stanza.

Jill: Rachmaninoff's music got lower when she was strangling him, and it should get louder.

Marc: I like Rachmaninoff's music. It foreshadowed more.

Larry: At one point Beethoven was a little voice, skipping along, and had no feeling of power.

Joyce: Yes, almost like people dancing.

Allen: Rachmaninoff was all slow; Beethoven kept building up until it was very loud and matched the poem that was building up.

Jay: Beethoven was like the sea slapping against the rocks.

Robert: Beethoven showed the struggle for life; he still had a chance of living. When it got softer, I had the feeling the boy was dead already.*

When the students finally understood the relationship between the poem and the music, they were able to discuss intelligently the teacher's reading. The major flaw, they discovered, was that the teacher permitted the music to control the performance rather than to provide a background to reinforce the poem's mood. They realized that the teacher changed pauses and punctuation to suit the music. Basically, the music was too strong for the poem. Some suggested that a lullaby be substituted but soon recalled that it was a nightmare lullaby. Several volunteered to bring in music which they thought more suitable, to practice it, and to present it to the class.

The students' performances and the discussion which followed each one added more insight into the poem.

Larry: When Steven read, "A child was murdered today," there were cymbals and it sounded like someone was hitting the child.

---

*Excerpts contributed by Alice F. Stollman.

Elliot: Steve's was very good because he stopped between stanzas and let the music enforce the meaning of the words, especially when the sea went up to meet him and he had the trumpets blowing.

Gary: Sherry's music sounds like a little ship sailing the ocean. It needs to be wild, with waves crashing down and with screaming.

Pat: When the murder happens, the music should be more violent. When you retell it, it's more sad than violent. The poet is retelling.

Michael: It should be said because it already happened. That's what I was trying to say before.

Monica: It's as if the sea is rubbing her hands together gloating over what is to come. The author thinks the sea is a villain.

Pat: Yes, the sea looks beautiful but the author is telling an incident to show it is evil underneath.

Teacher: You mean the sea covers its evil with beauty?

Students came to sense, in their own way, the beginnings of what Perrine postulates: "A correct interpretation, if the poem is a successful one, must be able to account satisfactorily for any detail of the poem."[47]

One emphasis was on the fact that not only could music be used as a background to a poem but that the poem itself has musical qualities. Students realized that the heavy stress and light stress, repeated, were an imitation of the waves breaking on the shore and then receding. To arrive at the concept that there is music inherent in the poem, the teacher selected a point in the discussion when the pupils were in conflict about an issue: "Is there music in the poem itself which would help you decide that?" In one case the clarification came when the class was divided about the effectiveness of a classmate's performance: "There is the sound of *cloak* and *choke*. That's harsh and the music has no harshness; the beat is off, anyway. The beat in the music is altogether different from the beat in the poem" [demonstrates]. Thus, only briefly, did the teacher help students to help each other understand the importance of light and heavy stress in creating rhythm and mood. Long delabored discussions of these elements would destroy the purpose of the central activity, enjoyment. A closer examination of stress would be more appropriate at a later time when the class was engaged in writing poetry or in making their own selection of a poem to set to music. For the present, it was sufficient that they understood some elementary facets of the relationship of light and heavy stress to meaning, mood, and rhythm.

More important now was a broader function of music within the poem. The teacher managed to get at this with a seemingly simple question: "Why did Wylie call her poem 'Sea Lullaby'?"

Elliot: It's a good title. The music that's in the poem is flowing like a lullaby. Sometimes a lullaby is really sorrow.

David: It's not suitable for a title. A lullaby is usually sung when a child goes to sleep. This one would give him nightmares.

Teacher: So you think this might better be called "The Nightmare?"

Donna: No. Even though it's read flowingly, it gives you butterflies in your stomach.

Robert: Lullaby puts someone to sleep. This one put him to sleep for good.

Gary: I agree with Elliot. It's a very good title. The words flow and the rhythm flows like a lullaby. But the poem has harsh sounds too because he'll be put to sleep violently. You don't sing a peppy song with peppy words in a lullaby. It would keep the kid awake.

Thus, the class exploration of the basic idea of the poem—that something as beautiful as the sea can also be destructive—remained the focus of attention. At the same time, the consideration of the relationship of sound and "beat" to the basic idea was of such a nature that the content focus was not lost but rather was illuminated.

Teachers who encouraged students to select poems and then to experiment with juxtaposition of poetry and music found it difficult to drag them away from this activity. To save time, the tape recorder was made available before and after school. Individuals and groups recorded their renditions whenever they felt ready. Other groups of students were invited to listen outside of class time, whenever such class time was simply no longer available. Some classes elected a panel of judges to select those taped efforts to be used for class consideration. Again and again, they marveled at the surprises in a poem, uncovered by the music. "We Real Cool" by Brooks was a great favorite with almost every class that discovered it. One student whose teacher had heard it performed to "Scorpio" in a college class decided to try it too, and eventually recorded her rendition. The reaction of those who listened was so intense that they insisted it warranted class time. In virtually every classroom there was at least one experience in which poetry brought "emotions to life"; MacLeish feels this is its "human" usefulness. "The crime against life, the worst of all crimes, is *not* to feel. . . . If poetry can call our numbed emotions to life, its plain human usefulness needs no further demonstration."[48] Music seemed to work hand in hand with poetry in achieving MacLeish's aim.

There is a number of procedural devices which are necessary in order that many students be offered the opportunity to perform and that the greatest possible climate for enjoyment of learning be present. The following devices received the largest vote of confidence by teachers:

1. Students were instructed to write the title of the poem and the name of the poet on the board before presenting their reading, either in person or via the cassette. The name of the music was also written, and a copy of the poem was distributed. In general, a repeat performance was necessary before the class was ready to react verbally. The surprises were sometimes too much for them. For this reason, some teachers preferred that the poem be read aloud first without music. Other teachers felt the preliminary reading to be beneficial because it offered a means of comparison with the musical rendition. A third group found this unaccompanied reading unnecessary and less motivating for the listeners as a whole.
2. Teachers invited students during the second rendition to jot down reactions to specific points they wished to discuss. In such cases, students usually wanted a third "hearing."
3. During the discussion, the performer was given the initial opportunity to explain how he arrived at his combination of poetry and music, why he chose either or both, and what he had to do to achieve his effect. Usually this send-off was sufficient to involve others. Most important, the explanation played a large

role in preventing students from evaluating the performer as a person. The teacher's questions helped, too: What is revealed that you didn't notice before? What is the speaker hiding? Kenner's point is worth noting here: "As every teacher knows, enlightened discussion in the classroom is never misdirected so long as no one forgets that art does not exist to be argued about, but to be perceived and assimilated."[49]

4. Working in groups saves time. Students listened to each other in small groups after having heard at least one presentation to the whole class. The presentation and discussion helped groups know how to function without immediate teacher direction. Each group selected one member's poem, evaluated the rendition, and helped their performer to revise the presentation. The presentation was made to the class as a group project.

5. The presentation of one poem to several different pieces of music was an engrossing activity.

Individual presentations take much class time. Sometimes teachers were able to get away with small-group presentations. Sometimes, students would have none of that. In one case the teacher helped students arrange themselves in groups, but they refused to accept the suggestion that it was sufficient to present their work to their small group. Every student demanded a chance to be heard by the whole class. So, small-group arrangement as a time-saving device was buried for the time being.

It is interesting to note that despite the students' insightful criticism of one teacher's performance in letting the music control the reading of the poem, several of their own renditions were characterized by the same error. A girl read "Woodman do not fell that tree" from "Woodman, Spare that Tree" by Morris and had to wait for the music on the record to catch up. On the other hand, there were several instances in which the line of poetry and the music complemented each other. When one boy read "My Papa's Waltz" by Roethke to contrapuntal music, he explained that one melody was "merry, like the father hopping around." The second melody "represented the kid getting hit on the head, probably crying, and the music is crying underneath." An eleventh grader who had read another poem "at least a dozen times and listened to a dozen pieces of music" had this comment to offer: "Sometimes music suggests a new but appropriate way of phrasing a part of the poem." One classmate of his suggested, "You've created a unique combination. It is a creation because you created the poem anew." A twelfth-grade group presented Sanchez's "Small Comment" to various musical selections and drew the following comments from classmates:

David: It reminded me of a cafe scene with black jazzmen in the background and somebody says, "Anyone want to read poetry?" and someone says, "Yeah."
Lorraine: The author is saying something very ugly, but at the same time she's using all the fancy words.
Lois: There's kind of a "ha-ha-you-big-jerk, don't you see what's happening around you?"
Beth: There's a biting sarcasm.
Joseph: And when she ends, "you dig?" she wants it that way.

Almost invariably students concluded, "You understand better what you are reading when you put it to music." For example, there came this final statement in a discussion of Shelley's "Ozymandias" which was delivered with a musical pause before and after Oxymandias speaks:

> I was able to visualize an old man, a philosopher, walking through the desert, meeting this traveler. The two men alone. The philosopher speaks very slowly picking his words very carefully, and then ending it, and walking on. And then the music came in. Perfect.

Their teachers were equally enthusiastic. "We have experienced 'Wows' in the classroom, applause, and an 'I-feel-like-crying' feeling."

Illustrating Poetry

Illustrating poetry is a pleasurable activity for many students. If the teacher sets up the activity in ways that encourage students who feel incapable of expressing themselves in art, the activity can be a meaningful experience for all students. Illustrating poetry stimulates thoughtful examination of and response to the poem itself; it lures students into making close associations between two art forms; it develops a taste for careful attention to detail and offers a base for an appreciation of broader meanings. Comparisons leading to an understanding of elements such as symbolism and metaphor are encouraged. Illustrating poetry builds an awareness of tone, mood, and unity without belaboring these elements thoughgh lectures or lengthy discussions.

Because a large proportion of adolescents regard themselves as possessing no ability to draw, they may resist any attempt to make this a serious activity. Therefore, the teacher must first devise illustrative activities which can be acceptable to adolescents. A successful one is the montage. The montage does not require that students be able to draw. It is a cut-and-paste activity which nonetheless makes demands upon the students. Students select for the background a picture from a magazine that offers photos with distinct texture. Upon the picture background, students superimpose other pictures and selected portions of pictures which they have cut out because they "say" something students would like to express. The first montage does not necessarily have to be associated with any poem in particular, and it is helpful if students can see a simple one made by the teacher. A montage with a dreamlike quality helps them move away from the notion that things must be real. The only stipulation is that the end result be a unified creation. Their productions are then discussed: In what ways is this montage a unified creation? What elements give it unity? Color? Dark and light values? Line? Content? Mood?

Most teachers began with the representation of a specific poem through a montage, using a montage they had made. One of them introduced Stevens' "Tea" to an eleventh-grade class.

> Teacher: Does this montage make any sense to you as a representation of this poem? Would you do things differently? Please keep referring to the poem as you react.
> Susan: It needs the spreading quality of the lamplight.
> Theodore: That's true. You could paint it in yourself, right on the montage.
> Rona: I'd show more of a contrast in color—the gray of the rats, the shriveled leaves, the dark —and then focus on the soft gold of the lamplight, gleaming, shining. And Java—something very exotic.

Vivian: I see it in terms of shapes too—gloomy shapes of gray and brown—and then rich luscious pillows.

Adrian: There's a contrast from "When" to "rats" and then, "your lamplight fell." The color changes. It should change on the illustration.

⬥—⬥—⬥—⬥—⬥—⬥—⬥—⬥—⬥—⬥—⬥—⬥—⬥—⬥—⬥—⬥—⬥—⬥—⬥

Marianne: I have certain moods that drag me to a cup of tea. . . . And sometimes I find myself staring at a cup of tea—that shimmering. Tea for me is an invitation to daydream. Perhaps when he sits down with a cup of tea, he starts to feel what autumn means to him: the tea is brown, autumn, cold.

Robert: There's the autumny feeling—the coldness out there—and then the warmness inside. You have some of that in the montage.

Theodore: From the title and colors, I'd swear this fellow is "tripping."

Alisa: I see it as a man who is sitting with an old acquaintance over a cup of tea. He's not married to her or anything; he's just reminiscing. "This is what happened to us," he says.

Teacher: Who is the speaker?

Fred: It's a man. "Your lamplight fell," he says, speaking to a woman.

Theodore: He has to be talking to a woman. The audience is a woman. It's too round for a man—like umbrella, and Java shining.

⬥—⬥—⬥—⬥—⬥—⬥—⬥—⬥—⬥—⬥—⬥—⬥—⬥—⬥—⬥—⬥—⬥—⬥—⬥

Teacher: What's the occasion?

Greta: They've gotten together again after a very long time.

Jeff: No, he's alone. He's reminiscing about this day, this period in his life. It's past tense: shrivel*ed*.

Rona: There's a finality there. I think it's a farewell. He's saying, "Maybe I stopped caring for you then."

Jeff; I don't think so. She brought him happiness. It's a sad reminiscing. It's certainly not optimistic. He starts by using images of a shriveled elephant's ear.

Rona: Well, I didn't exactly say it's a come on.

A ninth grade teacher reported her first experience:

I made a montage first, showed it to my class, and asked them to write down the first thing which hit them. They immediately picked up the unreality, the "beyondness." They made up stories about what this montage could be portraying, things I never thought of when I was making it. They floored me, and I just stood there like an imbecile. Then I read to them "Beware, Do Not Read This Poem" by Reed, and we briefly discussed it. They made montages in class which were fantastic. I thought ninth graders would regard this as an infantile activity, but they really dug it. They didn't have to agree on what was to be portrayed, and that made them feel secure. Yet, most did agree it was not the mirror's fault; it was the individual's fault. That's how they saw it. And they saw the audience as someone being warned about vanity. This one is obviously someone being sucked in! Watch it! Here there's distortion in the mirror. Here's another with a chain of events, one causing the other. Here's another with the present and the past, and, the opposite in the mirror. She cut out a mirror and put something else in it, to give you an idea of what the old woman was looking at. They made up stories about this old woman and included the idea of the psychology of the poem, telling you not to come near it, yet the poem is sucking you in. One used a picture for background and painted in figures herself. . . . They amazed themselves by the number of lines of the poem they could quote from memory without even trying.

Some teachers were disappointed that the montages were not all artistic master-pieces. Not all students are equally capable of performing any given activity; nor are they equally interested. Besides, the purpose was not the finished product. If an activity captivates the majority of students and achieves the educational ends, this is all that can be demanded of it. In some instances, only a few students were involved at first but when the the teachers realized the importance of making materials available, the resistance on the part of others melted away. This is a distinctly individual activity and cannot be forced. Students do not need to engage in it, in order to learn. They can learn from what others present, especially in small groups where each offering can be dis-cussed in depth. They can still react to what others create. They may prefer a related activity such as using the camera to illustrate how a poem "feels" or making a filmstrip of a poem. The process of creating a montage for comparison with a poem helps students perceive new relationships. The student makes associations partly because the images he meets, as he seeks to create a unified representation, give him new and clearer notions of the depth of the metaphor. Beloof makes much of the importance of such comparisons: "All things in the world are unique, yet all things are related; this paradoxical truth lies behind mankind's ability to differentiate and to see similarities —in short to make comparisons. . . . For even in the simplest figure of speech, the reader must reconstruct, out of his own experience, the connection aimed at in the compari-son.[50]

Of course, there will be students who make a montage to represent the images in the poem literally because they are not ready to deal with the metaphors or the symbols. At the other extreme, there are students who create a montage filled with menace, danger, and dread.

Metaphors and symbols hold elements of surprise. "Did anything in this montage surprise you?" teachers asked. Students were intrigued by surprises and by the re-sponses which their classmates offered. Often, a student was not surprised because he did not even notice a particular word, event, or implication, and when surprise did come, it rested in his perception of himself and "how I could have missed that." Often, too, the students were blocked by their own habit of searching for the one correct interpretation. Breaking the old habit of convergent thinking in activities that call for divergent thinking takes time. To handle ambiguities requires divergent thinking. Once students rid themselves of their inclination to seek the correct interpretation or relation ship, they began to enjoy the ambiguity as they sensed that the poet uses words with multiple meanings.

Sandburg's "Grass," which was introduced to the class by a student, inspired a first attempt at representation through the montage by a small group of eleventh graders. The montages spanned a wide range of insight and interpretation.

Black Panthers in jail, kids at Willowbrook, large mouths. Death ends everything, but one doesn't have to be literally dead to feel dead. . . . The mouths show how dead people are inside . . . they don't really express themselves.

War, death, fear, and many eyes. The eyes are sad, the strange expressions are sad, the poem makes me feel sad—there's so much violence today. Here's a lady in black, mourning. Others are facing away from her; they forget death.

Black background, death. But here's a monkey surrounded by blue. He didn't die. He's left. There's grass all over. The Statue of Liberty made up of the faces of many different kinds of people stands for all the dead.

Grass is in the background; battles and murder in the foreground. Grass can't cover all the deaths.

Some montages were so captivating that classmates concluded, "You could almost write a poem from that montage." Then the class listened to Seeger sing Reynolds' "God Bless the Grass" and compared grass as a symbol of life and truth and of man's striving to become what is good with Sandburg's perception.

One class after working with montages to represent Frost's "An old Man's Winter Night" concluded, "No poem is that obvious that you can look at it and know it." They arrived at this conclusion with no aid from the teacher. Students who formerly resisted reading a poem even once were no longer content with two or three readings. Through the montages of their peers accompanied by explanations, they gained new insights into the poem and were amazed at the richness which lay there.

One seventh-grade student selected Hughes' "Mother to Son" to represent in a montage. The teacher reported: "Her father wants to bring the montage she made to his place of business. He thinks it's beautiful. She found pictures in *Ebony* magazine and was all excited about the project because she has a Langston Hughes' poetry collection at home. The whole class just loves this activity. Every time I try to do something other than poetry, they go, 'Ugh, when are we going back to poetry?' "

Several teachers permitted students to work together.

I enjoyed doing this with them, just watching *them* enjoy it. . . . Working together is good for them. They're not an easy class. But rather than fighting, they were learning.

Teachers developed their own techniques for handling large numbers of presentations. The report of one teacher's experience follows:

Those students who chose to illustrate a poem rather than to set it to music brought their illustrations to school on a predetermined day. These were hidden from other members of the class until the teacher displayed them around the room. Each student read his poem, and the class was asked to identify which illustration belonged to it. Then there was a short discussion on how they were able to identify the picture. They remembered particular images. Now the illustrators knew the importance of what many of them had done: They had read and reread the poem to find images which they would represent graphically, images that captured the essence of the emotion. The poems presented ranged from Nash's "The Sea Gull Is the Eagle" to Wordsworth's "I Wandered Lonely as a Cloud." There was some difficulty getting the students to leave ballads out of this part of their study since they felt very secure with ballads.

The montage is a "freeing" agent for those who need it. Students were encouraged to create their own crayon or paint representations. Several students were intrigued by the use of paint on a picture they found in a magazine for background and by a combination of pictures. A substantial number of students continued this kind of activity on their own, creating ways to represent poems they liked. They found pictures they enjoyed and thumbed through collections of poetry to discover a poem which would make the picture immortal. This latter twist was their own idea and was not discouraged.

The act of making a relationship between two art forms holds much promise. Students who cannot initially find their way into one may ultimately be lured because of an interest in the other. The act involves comparison, inference, and discovery. Students reported pleasant surprise when they compared how much they were able to perceive now with their previous perceptions. For some, it was an experience in genuine self-discovery. They found new talents within themselves. For others, a whole new medium for sheer enjoyment was born.

Writing Poems

"If poetry does no more than minister to leisure, refining and increasing the fun of life, it fulfills a high mission."[51] Creating one's own poems can "minister to leisure" quite as well as reading and performing poems already written. Education for leisure is one of the critical roles of the schools, which the schools have not accepted widely to date. Yet, we have known for decades that in our technological society leisure hours have been and are still being increased as the work day is shortened.

Writing poetry teaches students much about the genre itself. It helps them understand its precision, its compression, and its design. It encourages the use of the imagination.

The beginnings must be geared to the abilities of the students. There are literally scores of procedures which serve well as initial experiences by giving students a sense of mastery. For example, one trusty standby is the "cinquain" accompanied by specific "how-to-do's" for each line, such as the explanation which appeared in *Scholastic Scope*. "A cinquain has five lines. Here's how to write each line:

1. A word for the title
2. Two words to describe the title
3. Three words to express action
4. Four words to express feeling
5. The title again, or a word like it."[52]

A teacher presented his creation with the comment that teachers, too, like writing cinquains for fun:

>Watermelons
>Big, round
>Squish, squash, chomp
>Love that juicy feeling,
>Melons

A student wrote:

> Papa
> Tall, skinny
> Banging, leaving, coming
> Will he return soon?
> Pappoo

Remarked a teacher:

> I was surprised, amazed. Here are kids who can't write, can't spell, can't do anything. And
> they sat down and wrote five lines. We first listed various topics they thought they might
> like to write about: dogs, monkeys, cookies, mini-bikes. This is the first time 80 percent of
> the kids in the class turned something in. They still turn them in, though I introduced this
> months ago. (Robert Cappuccio, personal communication.)

Critics may argue that these are not true cinquains because the structured instructions are too restricting. However, the particular restrictions as an initial exercise
opened up more students in more classes than did most other writing activities. Students did not remain on the level of the restricted cinquain. Once they gained a feeling
of self-confidence, they moved on of their own accord when the teacher introduced new
experiences. Not all students moved ahead readily; but then, those who needed the
security of the cinquain activity were the very ones who had been doing little legitimate
school activity if any. At least a half-step had been taken.

Untermeyer[53] claims that it was Adelaide Crapsey, the Amercian poet, who worked
out the cinquain with two syllables for the first line, four for the second, six for the third,
eight for the fourth, and two for the fifth. From the early beginnings cited above,
students can advance to this structure.

A second pattern that appeals to students is the diamante, the diamond-shaped poem
with its movement in contrasts. Students may need help in finding contrasting nouns
before they begin; examples are peace-war, love-hate, marriage-divorce, child-man,
night-day, life-death, etc. Although the diamante technically begins with a noun and
moves to two adjectives, three participles, four contrasting nouns or a phrase about the
first noun, then down to three participles again, two adjectives and a concluding noun,
the terminology may block creativity rather than aid it. Teachers devised ways of
helping younger adolescents by merely line drawing the format and giving them an
illustration of the type of words to use. Peace and war were favorites as were love and
hate. A seventh grader's poem illustrates the format.

line 1:	Noun	War
line 2:	two adjectives	cold, hard
line 3:	three participles	training, running, sickening
line 4.	four nouns or phrase	weapons, fortress, blood, hell,
line 5:	three participles indicating change	praying, fighting, winning
line 6:	two adjectives	proud, warm
line 7:	contrasting noun	peace[54]

A third initiation into poetry writing can be through the medium of the haiku. Haiku suggests "the large by presenting the small—the immense reflected in the minute. . . ."[55] The usually unrhymed poems have seventeen syllables, five for the first line, seven for the second, and five for the third. Henderson clarifies other "rules": The poem makes reference to nature but deals with one moment of human emotion and a particular event rather than a generalization; that event is in the present, not the past. Equally important, as Henderson points out, there are differences between Japanese syllables and the English; the questions of feasibility of unfinished sentences must be noted, and the teacher must be aware of the lack of criteria for haiku in English which "cannot be exactly the same as Japanese haiku."[56] The third fact gives the teacher some flexibility in the use of haiku, for strict adherence to the five-seven-five syllable pattern leaves with students an erroneous notion that haiku is merely "pattern poetry." A number of educators recognize the virtues of using haiku with students. Moffett wrote: "Usually each poem is a single sentence. No other piece of writing, except maxims, offers such an opportunity to focus on the the smallest units of discourse—the word, the turn of phrase, the structure of the sentence."[57]

A student wrote:

> A car hit a bird
> it bounced off my front bumper
> and hit the hard ground.

A teacher wrote:

> In early autumn
> the earth swallows my tears and
> flowers bloom next spring.*

A fourth introduction to writing poems can readily be combined with haiku but may be used as an activity in its own right. Students first write a sentence or two at the most about a moment, usually an unforgettable one, in their lives. Students may need to do some preliminary talking first; the teacher may briefly relate such a moment in his life. Brevity is of the essence. Then students select one significant detail in their sentence and elaborate on the detail until the sentence suggests a universal idea or a relationship with nature. The students then examine each word in their sentence, underline the significant ones, rearrange words, and change words until they say more vividly what the student wants to convey and until the entire creation sounds more pleasing to the ear. Several teachers conducted the unforgettable-moment activity omitting the last step in which students change words and rearrange them. They felt their particular classes were not ready for this until work with diction preceded it. Other teachers worked with diction as a part of the whole process on an informal basis.

Students enjoyed not only the final products but perhaps even more the process itself. On the chalkboard a number of students wrote their original sentences, the significant detail step, and the final product. They were surprised and impressed with the deep

---

*Haiku written by Linda Tremml.

feelings that lay within themselves. An example of achievements that occurred in less than one class period follows:

> Thoughts turned to pain, then—
> into tears, sad memories
> Trickled down my cheek.

Teachers may wonder at what constitutes enjoyment of writing poems and should not be surprised that the subjects students select are not necessarily happy ones. In fact, they most often are not!

Some students needed assistance with their unforgettable moment. Was it like a terrible dream? Was it like being lost on an uncharted sea? Or was it a microscope focused on one small wondrous element? With such questions the teacher was helping prepare for an awareness of metaphor and simile. One teacher brought in a large piece of bark with an unusual shape, partly deteriorated in the center so that a crater was formed. In class students looked closely at the object, touched it, and then tried to write what they felt about it. Was it in any way familiar? Similar to a familiar object? The aim was to increase understanding of what goes into a poem. Other teachers concentrated on having students watch things such as the role of numbers, colors, or heat and cold in some poems. They looked for words that make an object seem like a person or for menacing words as in Frost's "Out, Out." Students brought in objects and lined them up on the window sills. Anyone could select a few objects and group them, using them as a focus for his poem. One teacher used simple photos such as Elkins' "Man on the Move" and Leavitt and Sohn's *Stop, Look, and Write* for this purpose. In their poems students were encouraged to build a climax and end with a surprise. One class made a list of words which they felt had emotional connotations; examples were drugs, acupuncture, hijack, yippies, joy, shadow, aloneness. Students worked in pairs to record their first response to each of the words. The ideas that were extracted provided the emphasis as well as the stimulus for a number of poems. They juxtaposed words that did not seem to belong together on the surface and then explored their similarities and contrasts to determine the possibilities that lay inherent in the pair.

Opportunities present themselves to teach metaphors and similes as individual students perfect their poems. For example, an object is selected, preferably from the student's poem. In one case it was a *phone.* The teacher gathered a group of four or five students interested in "relating the unrelated" so that their poem could offer surprises. They would need *two* objects, the phone being one. They evolved comparisons such as:

1. A *phone* is a piercing *sword* invading the peace of the soul.
2. A *phone* is a clobbering *intruder* slashing the mind of all thought.
3. A *phone* is a welcome *convoy* defending the spirit against loneliness.

Students gradually gain an awareness that "one function of metaphor is to discover truth—not merely illustrate truth in the sense of simplifying it."[58]

A few teachers enjoyed Koch's *Wishes, Lies, and Dreams* so much that they initiated the writing of poetry in their own classes with some of his ideas. Students took heartily to the "Dream" poem, and teachers took seriously Koch's suggestions that students' poems not be corrected by the teacher and "that dreams didn't usually make sense, so their poems needn't either."[59] The ideas helped to bring about a "freeing" experience for teachers and students.

Other opening exercises which proved successful in that they stimulated students to create poems included the following: (1) Students were asked to keep their eyes closed for a few minutes and to determine the most "silent sounds" they were able to hear: "the throb of the furnace several floors below"; "my own heart beating at my belly"; "human bodies trying not to move"; "the overworked paper clip bursting with too great a burden"; "the bare branches rolling with the breezes." (2) The "sounds of silence" in the previous activity became the focus for a class poem. Each student contributed one "sound." The class grouped sounds for content and then arranged the items in such a way that they were pleasing to the ear. Groups of three students worked independently on connecting links. Efforts were reproduced for full-class consideration, and a class poem was born. (3) A similar activity consisted of closing the eyes, opening them quickly, and jotting down something observed which the student had never observed before and which he felt no one else had ever noticed. "The uniform book jackets add to the dull drab prisonlike atmosphere." "The nose of the paper airplane on the floor is pointed toward the door, ready to take off." "The grain of wood on the teacher's desk is like splattered glass." "Those bumps in the ceiling look like a teddy bear." Class consciousness of the role of similes and metaphors was a natural outgrowth of this activity. (4) Teachers presented a very short poem, omitting one line. Students composed the missing line and discussed briefly the effect of three or four "compositions." "Sea Gypsy" by Hovey was one short poem used for a similar purpose; students compared notes about how they arrived at the correct line in each stanza when they were offered a choice of three lines.

Bertha: I said the three lines and the last line of each stanza before I could decide. I said each stanza three times. The rhythm is off; too many syllables, etc.
Rick: And the mood is off.
Gail: And the other one doesn't rhyme.
Bertha: With "wander thirst" you can't go looking for love.
Peter: The one about "mire" doesn't make sense. It's been a call to adventure; the ship stood for that. So, wallowing in the mire just doesn't go.
Rick: The next one has nothing to do with the whole thing. The rhythm is all off; the stress on the first syllable is wrong.

Each student then wrote a short verse and presented his creation minus one line. In small groups, students composed the missing line; the activity became a game to see which line was closest to the original. Advanced groups discussed the pros and cons of each, including the original. The final decision belonged to the creator of the poem. (5) Nonsense verse is a fairly common initial writing activity, but a brief reminder may be in order. Lear's verse is often an inspiration; the fact that deep philosophical thought is not required at this point helps to instill confidence and to make sheer fun possible. Students who wrote nonsense verse showed evidence of a real awareness of rhythm, rhyme, meaning, and mood. The discussion was punctuated with laughter and cries of "that's babyish" or "that's humorous." A few students became intrigued with the process and independently chose poems to use for testing the skill of classmates.

Students need a variety of ways to begin their creative writing of poetry because the process may start from an idea or as Warren indicates, "from a phrase, a scene, an image, or an incident." Warren believes that "the creation of a poem is as much a process of discovery as a process of making," that creating a poem is "the process of discovering what the idea 'means' to him [poet] in the light of his total being and his total experience." For the poet the process is one of "discovering why the item has caught his attention in the first place—which is simply another way of saying that he is trying to develop the symbolic potential." The poet "does not fully know what he 'intends' until the poem is fully composed" because "the only thing he, in the ordinary sense, may 'intent' is to make a poem." He does not have "a blueprint of intention."[60] In the poems students wrote, there was often something of the quality of discovery Warren describes.

THE "AUTHOR'S NOTEBOOK"

The "author's notebook" or "secret notebook" has been mentioned in an earlier chapter. In preparation for writing poems, one class recorded the subjects the poet uses: the supermarket, the subway, war, traffic, noises, love, death, loneliness. "A poet can make going to a supermarket sound like a milestone in your life," one boy recorded. "He makes mountains out of molehills." "Poets exaggerate everyday things and make them sound and feel like something." "Poets put a different light on things."

To help the class understand the "different light on things," the teacher asked, "Did you ever take a little child for his first ride on a subway or his first visit to a supermarket?" Then came the flood of stories: "What a pain in the neck my brother was in the supermarket. He kept touching things and pulling them down from the shelves." "On the subway, my kid brother wanted to walk but he couldn't because of the movement of the train and he screamed when I tried to hold him." As these stories were pooled, the teacher asked whether the poet and the child have anything in common. Students realized that the poet sees ordinary things as if he is looking at them and experiencing them for the first time and that this accounts in part for his emotional reaction to everyday life. This discussion was filled with so much excitement that for the next assignment many pupils voluntarily took a younger child to a five-and-dime store, went for a walk in the park or simply around the block, gave him a new toy, or read a story to him. They watched him with a keen eye and recorded his reactions in detail. The activity's purpose was to "record things you saw, felt and heard, that is, ideas that can be the subject of a poem." There was need for looking at everyday events as if they were being seen for the first time." The wondering eyes of a child and the poet's fresh view of commonplace events would help them look.

Instead of taking a child with them, some students took notebooks or tape recorders to familiar places and noted happenings in the beauty parlor, the doctor's office, or at a well-traveled street corner. They watched behaviors of truck drivers on the expressway, owners of cars stuck in the snow, animals cavorting, a child engrossed in solitary play, children in group play. They made observations of activities on the floor of the gymnasium or in the school cafeteria, a new supermarket, a model house, the assembly hall.

When students later used these details to make a poem, they learned that "poetry is concerned, not with emotions and large gestures, but with 'minute particulars'."[61]

Today I was watching the way my friends walked. It impressed me the way that the people who get mad easily and always screamed took short quick steps, while the quiet kinds took long slower steps. I also noticed that when a person is mad, his tendency is to move very fast and unevenly, while a person in a good mood moves more slowly and has an even rhythmic step.

Entries such as the above became the subjects of class discussion at the discretion of the "author." During this time, the pupils explored their own ideas with the help of their classmates.

Larry: I was playing ball and collided with my friend and got the wind knocked out of me. You can't talk for about half a minute. You feel helpless. So, I'd like to center on the feeling of helplessness and speechlessness.

Ronnie: I looked at a tree through venetian blinds, and it seemed like a design.

Ellie: You have to decide on the meaning of the design or the meaning of looking through the blinds. It has to have a special meaning. Last week I was playing stick ball and I couldn't see because of the sun, so I got the image that the sun is the master of the human race.

Teacher: I played tennis near the Hudson River under the George Washington Bridge, a very scenic spot. The bridge is very impressive, especially because you are close to it. I tried to think of an image for that pattern and thought "steel or iron lace." But I didn't want lace because I needed something more masculine.

Gail: Could you have Vulcan, the God?

Larry: Even though it's masculine, you still can have some lace, some femininity.

Steven: Vulcan was master of his art, but he wasn't physically strong. He made steel armor.*

The teacher, too, kept a poet's notebook. Each day there was a five-minute discussion of entries made by teacher and students. The fact that the teacher was carrying through the same assignment freed the class to ask questions and to subject their own ideas to class scrutiny. Before long, the teacher's entries became too important to the students, so she was forced to discontinue this contributing role. It had served its purpose.

As the class needed more knowledge of elements like rhyme scheme and metrical pattern, the teacher went somewhat more deeply into a consideration of those factors. Also, while students practiced using poetic elements to reword their recorded observations, there was much recall and reference to poems already familiar to the class. Koch's *Rose, Where Did You Get That Red?* can be of assistance to students at this point. Koch offers them a variety of ways to use great poetry, such as Blake's "The Tyger" as a catalyst for discovery. Says Koch, "The main question the poet asks is a question they often think about: How did something get the way it is?"[62] Students can ask themselves the same kinds of questions and discover their own answers.

Students generally gave evidence of new abilities to appreciate and handle simile and metaphor. One student recorded, "Cat pouring over a tattered old pulp magazine. His lips were moving silently as though he were reciting a litany." MacLeish calls the

---

*Excerpt from a class taught by Alice Fritsch Stollman.

cognitive process of making relationships the "mating and matching of what does not mate and match in the habitual mind. . . ."[63] He explains further, "In a symbol the one 'thing' partakes of the nature of the other. In coupled images the two 'things' are often as far apart as fleshless bone and bracelet of bright hair. But in both the means to meaning are the same. Both make sense of the world by showing us relationships we have not seen."[64] Herein lies the crux of a cognitive task for which poetry is uniquely suited. It is the reader or the listener who must now do the perceiving, make the relationship between the two "things," and thus "make sense" of his own world.

Students began to create their own poetry at different times. The workshop setting was a supportive base, with students sharing ideas, teacher offering suggestions and encouragement, and attractive collections of poems and poetry posters making inviting overtures. As mentioned in a previous chapter, the physical setting of the workshop is important.

Upon completion of the first draft of original poems, the pupils gathered in small groups or pairs to consider each one. They were asked to concentrate on the emotion expressed rather than on the mechanics, though these were interrelated factors and actually could not be separated. However, the teachers' tendency was to separate the factors and their caution to the students was a safeguard against the teacher's own possible misguided activity. Philosophical discussions came often: "Is a poem a poem because it is mechanically correct?" "Is it a poem because it communicates a personal or pronounced feeling which requires some technical skill?" Inevitably, too, came the problem of helping students uncover the meaning of the poem they were trying to write and the emotion they wanted to express. Classmates in the small groups were ready to help. The help they gave ultimately brought rewards to the givers. The discussions clarified their own ideas, opened up new areas of thought, and enriched their own potential.

The students' poems were submitted to the staff of the school magazine. The editors found it difficult to make choices because there were so many worthy ones. One of the poems selected speaks for itself. It speaks also for the work and the joy that went into these productions, and for the "hard," yet satisfying, teaching and learning that preceded and attended the achievements.

Death—
A veiled hand
Floating through eternity,
Lightly touching
Upon the brows of mortals,
Then brushed aside by a soft breeze;
But one forsaken day
A harsh wind will blow
Leaving the hand stiff and cold,
And soon as the fingers thaw
They slowly drop around a heart—
And finally, the black veil drops
Over an immortal body.

Poetry and Dance*

The dance is another art form which gives esthetic pleasure and which can be used with poetry, though teachers have much more difficulty learning to use the dance than they do the other arts described in this chapter.

Because of the humorous and light quality of the limerick as a poetic form, it provided a good introducton to using dance as another art form through which to view poetry. Since several students in a seventh-grade class could tap-dance and since the limericks are syncopated forms, tap dancing was a suitable means for communicating this form. While two or three students tap-danced to the rhythm of the following three limericks, the others tapped out the rhythm with their fingers on their desks: "There was a young lady of Lynn," "A gentleman dining at Crewe," and "A tutor who tooted a flute."[65] They counted out the number of taps in order to establish the metrical pattern and learned that it often was 8-8-5-5-8 though there were many other patterns. In classes where there were no tap dancers, pupils used bongo drums, drum sticks, or pencils. Other poems were then discovered for their appropriateness with respect to the dance form, but this time for reasons other than the metrical patterns. Meaning, movement, and action were now the focus of attention. "The Runaway" by Frost was among the many that captured the imagination of the students.

Teachers who knew much about poetry often knew little about dance. Therefore, they were fearful and insecure in their first attempts to relate the two arts. They worried about whether the boys would accept dance as a classroom experience; they were concerned about how they could help pupils be free enough to "take a chance." Arrangements were made for the teacher who was most interested in this "new" process to meet with a professor in a nearby college. The professor had impressed large numbers of college students because of her ability not only to dance but also to help students convey the beauty of this art form. In one hour she was able to help the teacher understand how to approach the subject of emotions through the use of the body: Joy is expressed by outgoing movements—forward, upward, and outward; the arms and head go up and out, the body forward. Fear is expressed by inward movements, backward and downward; the head is lowered, the arms come in toward the body; the shoulders are hunched. She provided the teacher with a professional drum for the boys as well as a reference book and an understanding of why the primitive earthy poem may have appeal for some boys when they understood the relationship between dance and primitive religious rites.

The teacher introduced the idea of the relationship between the two art forms by having students use their bodies to portray certain basic emotions like fear, hate, and gladness. There was no lack of participation; rather, students couldn't wait their turn to show spontaneously how these emotions might be expressed. The audience analyzed and described the movements until they were able to make generalizations about the relationship between certain emotions and bodily movements. The teacher presented concrete situations which characteristically impel certain types of human movement.

---

*This section was written with Alice Fritsch Stollman.

Teacher: There are certain basic movements in poetry which are very important to dance. Instead of telling you what they are, I'm going to ask someone to express an emotion with the body alone. The emotions and movements concern things you do every day. For example, when you walk, can you reveal an emotion just by the way you walk?

Allen: Yes. If you walk as if you are trying to get somewhere, you would walk in a hurry.

Adrian: You could express happiness or sadness in the way you walk. You walk at a pretty brisk pace if you are happy. If you are sad, you walk slowly and hang your head.

Teacher: Yes! Will someone walk around the room, showing that he is the only one in the class who has failed the social studies test? Nat, go ahead [laughter]. You may exaggerate the emotion so we can see [laughter as he performs].

Teacher: What do you think Nat was feeling?

It is interesting at this point to examine the philosophy of the art of dance from the viewpoint of Langer. She rejects the notion that dance is physical movement, musical rhythm, or a dramatic art. Movement may be a *dance motif;* pantomime may be *dance material.* But neither is the dance itself. To her, "All dance motion is gesture. . . . Gesture is vital movement." The necessary ingredient is imagination: art is not an expression of the artist's actual emotion; rather, the emotion is "something the artist *conceived* as he created the symbolic form to present it. . . ." Langer cites Wordsworth's definition that poetry is " 'emotion recollected in tranquillity' " and adds, "It is *imagined feeling* that governs the dance, not real emotional conditions. The dance *imagines* the feelings in their appropriate physical form."[66]

Gerald: He was sad. He was walking as if something was burdening him down.

Teacher: How could you tell that just from his movement?

Judy: He hung his head; he walked very slowly and dragged his feet.

Larry: He clomped around. He really didn't drag his feet and he should; he should take slow, low steps. He was moving his feet pretty high up.

Marc: Maybe he was angry and decided to let off a little steam, so he raises his feet. (At this point Nat was called upon to clarify his feelings.)

Teacher: Let's try to express another emotion by movement of our bodies—fear. If something frightens you, what do you do? Do you go toward the object? (John performs.) Think of what John did when he pantomimed for us.

Marty: You try to protect yourself. That's why your arms go up and around your head like this.

Teacher: Yes. When Marty's arms went up, what happened to his head?

Sheila: His head went down on his chest.

Teacher: That's one important movement—contraction. Yes, his head went down and *into* his chest.

Teacher: Did you notice in news photographs or on TV how racial demonstrators protect themselves? They are taught to roll themselves up into a ball to give maximum protection (shows photo). Can you describe what bodily movements are taking place here?

Other teachers used TV programs, movies, and magazine photos that portrayed emotions. A number of teachers asked students to observe joyful and fearful moments in the lives of young children and how these affected bodily movement. The explorations of movement as it is related to feelings released both children and teacher to pursue

movement and feelings in poetry in order to determine which poems lent themselves
to expression through dance. The most important result of this work was the awareness
of the strong relationship between poetry and movement. One poem, "The Bronco That
Would Not Be Broken" by Lindsay enchanted a large number of students, if not all.
The class examined its suitability for dance.

Marcia: It has movement in it because a lot happens to the bronco.

Sheila: There's emotion all the way, especially in the last stanza when he dies. We can express
the emotion the way we did sadness, fear, and happiness.

George: He has spirit and that's good for dance.

Adena: He was so wild. Then they put him in a harness, but he kept dancing. They tried to
break him, and he kept rebelling. We can do all that with body movements.

Lydia: The crows tell him to beware, but he doesn't.

Ronnie: They know something bad will happen, something ominous.

Teacher (reads part about butterflies): What feeling do you get here?

Larry: Everything is happy and content. Why should he worry?

Jay: (reads part about the smell of grass): It makes him forget he's supposed to quiet down.
It made him wilder. He just wanted to dance more and more.

Robert: He's feeling carefree. He's still in a trance. He's not afraid of what will happen.

Jay: Because he's of royal blood he thinks these people have no right to train him.

Judy: The poet is trying to express his sorrow and anger at people who stop the colt from
dancing.

Marty: The grasshoppers and the sparrows are enjoying themselves, and they are encouraging
the colt.

Elliot: When the snake came he could have run away, but he keeps on dancing.

Larry: It was unnecessary to kill a horse because he has spirit. It makes me feel anger.

Ira: The whip didn't work. They made him drag such a heavy burden the next day. That's
another part good for dance.

Elliot: He'll do anything to get rid of them all. He was even more disobedient now.

Sherry: He was running fast and the mules couldn't keep up. We could dance this with the
mules lagging behind.

Joel: The mules bit him, and the driver beat him with a pole.

Larry: There's plenty of hate there. We'd have to dance hate.

George: You feel pity for the horse all through the poem.

David: That poor horse. He is in torture and pain and can't do anything about it. I feel pity
for him, too.

Marian: It reminds me of a little boy who is trying to put up a front all this time and is trying
to get attention and he suddenly realizes he's putting up a losing battle. The horse tries to
keep it up because his animal friends are encouraging him. When he's beaten and the flies
get at him, he can't keep up the front any longer.

John: That colt is just going through agony.

After discovering a "thread that would help to keep all stanzas unified," the students
in groups tried to decide how they would portray the meaning and emotions of their
particular stanza in dance. They met a number of problems, some of which needed full

class consideration. For example, there were the problems of deciding "how to show the difference between capering, cantering, prancing, and contorting" and "how best to portray the mood of despair."

In one class, a boy appointed himself a free-lance composer. He went from group to group to decide which instruments he needed to help peers express their movements in the poem. On a sheet of music paper, he laid out the plan for each stanza.

The teacher assured the students that there was no expectation of professional performance and that pantomime was perfectly acceptable. The teacher later described the presentations as "organized chaos." At first the plan was to discuss the movements for each stanza with respect to meaning and mood, but the objection that "it destroys the mood" was overpowering. Some suggested that the feeling of wholeness could be maintained because the poet repeats the last line of each stanza. At first the class agreed upon this as a unifying force, but when they were on the brink of performing their own stanza, they decided that since each stanza expresses a different emotion, the last line takes on a different meaning. Here lies a strong piece of evidence of the degree to which students were experiencing not only this poem, but poetry.

The teacher finally settled for reading the poem in its entirety to put the class in the mood and then the groups performed in sequential order. The discussion further illuminated the meaning and the emotions of the poem.

Diane: The music is too bouncy, as in a dance. The poem didn't seem to me to be just a dance. In the last stanza it is very gory, and dancing music didn't fit.

Ian: It did fit. He died without any disgrace and kept on dancing to the very end.

John: Steven got the high dancing music in the piccolo, but there were a few parts such as when the mules bit him that needed big basses going really hard.

Teacher: In the last stanza, what does the poet mean by, "And the merciful men, their religion enhancing, stopped the red reaper to give you a chance"?

John: The poet wants me to be a little sympathetic.

Allen: Cruelty to animals is still going on and the poet wants us to cut cruelty.

Larry: Everyone is so cruel to people, like now with the school-busing violence. They do one thing to clear their conscience. Then they can say, "I didn't do anything so bad; look at this that I did."

Lena: They tried to break a horse in one of the most cruel ways I ever heard of—ruining the horse, punishing him for acting natural.

Doris: The horse's ancestors danced. He had it in his blood, but the men didn't realize that.

Teacher: Are there any questions you'd like to ask about the poem?

Allen: Are they trying to show they are free and the horse isn't? There must be a reason for putting in butterflies and grasshoppers—to tell him, "beware."

Teacher: Do you think the colt lost dignity?

Lydia: Yes. He came from a well-known family. The way they treated him was a loss to his dignity.

John: I disagree because it says he scorned all disgraces. He died because he didn't want to be broken and he wanted to keep up his pride.

Robert: The poem says, "With snake whips advancing." At that point the horse stops still, stands firm. Then the line after that he went back at them.

Jay: We were doing it for the line before; the horse had so much pride. He wasn't going to give in, and we showed him standing firm. In the last part he jumps at the horse whippers which makes them more angry at him.

Marian: When you were in that circle, I didn't understand what you were supposed to be.
Jay: When one hand went down, it was supposed to symbolize that the horse was broken but still wanted to dance, so we lifted up our hands to show that even though we started to break a little, we were dancing. We didn't give up.
Larry: This stanza symbolized the beginning of the end of the horse. We went down and then came up again to show there was still hope. Later, of course, when the end came, there was no getting up again.

Instead of performing the dance, one group of older students taught the poem to ten year olds in their neighborhood and filmed their performance using an 8 mm camera; another sought the cooperation of a dancing teacher at a neighboring YMCA and the class made an after-school trip to watch the performance which furnished the subject of discussion the next day.

Several classes that had experienced poetry through dance as well as with music, illustration, and other stimuli for oral performance were asked to present favorite poems by whatever means each student felt most appropriate. There was a wide variety of poems including Housman's "When I was One-and-Twenty," Thomas' "A Refusal to Mourn the Death, by Fire, of a Child in London," Dickinson's "I Should Not Dare to Leave My Friend," "I'm Nobody, Who Are You?" and "Because I Could Not Stop for Death." The results were interesting: No student chose dance, though pantomime was used by several. By far the greatest number set the poem to music in one class; in others, the writing of original poems won out. The third most appealing medium was the illustration.

The Cognitive Connection

From the work of Nathan Isaacs, Piagetian scholar, one can gain insights into the cognitive functions which are closely related to experiencing poetry, although Isaacs himself does not discuss this particular relationship. Just as the young child "watches and finds more to watch, follows and finds more to follow, turns toward sounds and sees as well as hears . . . manipulates and produces effects which then prompt him to repeat his action till he can produce them at will,"[67] the contacts of the older child with his environment bring about corresponding types of cognitive growth. The sounds he hears in poetry cause him to "turn toward them," now in the sense of being attracted to those that please him and excite him. The more he hears such sounds, the more he finds to hear; the more he produces such sounds, the more he finds to produce.

The same kind of learning effects cannot be gained by verbal explanations because "verbal communication can only become a source of real knowledge and understanding where children have already done so much living learning that they can meet verbal explanations three-quarters of the way."[68] By and large, students have not engaged in the kind of "direct living learning" necessary for understanding verbal explanations of poetry. Attempts at explaining it cannot take the place of permitting the poem to be.

The "direct living learning" can be approached through permitting the poem to perform . . . through music, illustration, choral work, writing, and dramatization. "Effective thinking," says Isaacs, "needs the kinds of full-bodied meanings and ideas which can only emerge from the activities of living learning, worked over themselves with the help of language."[69]

Experiencing poetry through "direct living learning" satisfies the conditions prescribed by Isaacs for the verbal teaching stage, the time when the "chalk-and-talk" method of teaching may be started gradually in early adolescence. He stresses that "a steady accompaniment both of actual direct experience and of free discussion should be maintained throughout."[70] The various types of action contacts with poetry satisfy the learning conditions of the student since "he is constantly impelled from within towards action, and then carried on by the interest and satisfactions which this action brings to him."[71] Thus, he gains mastery which is the motivating force toward further learning.

Furthermore, poetry can open enduring interests as has been indicated in this chapter. The building of interests is an intellectual concern of Isaacs in his effort to protect students from being "plunged into the world without anchorage or compass." Without such interests students "risk becoming the victims of a chronic boredom which makes them a heavy burden to themselves as well as to society."[72] On the other hand, genuine interests developed through direct living learning can insure "a real, meaningful share of their own in our vast and varied contemporary world—some forward-facing interests which they could keep on pursuing with active zest and restimulating rewards."[73] Without such rewards, cognitive growth is obstructed.

NOTES

1. Cleanth Brooks and Robert Penn Warren, *Understanding Poetry* (New York: Holt, Rinehart & Winston, 1960), p. 83.
2. Hugh Kenner, *The Art of Poetry* (New York: Holt, Rinehart & Winston, 1959), p. 219.
3. Brooks and Warren, p. 46.
4. Charlotte I. Lee, *Oral Interpretation* (Boston: Houghton Mifflin Co., 1959), p. 357.
5. Don Geiger, *The Sound, Sense, and Performance of Literature* (Chicago: Scott, Foresman and Co., 1963), pp. 52, 54.
6. Ibid., p. 18.
7. Paul Campbell, *The Speaking and the Speakers of Literature* (Belmont, Cal.: Dickenson Publishing Co., 1967), p. 10.
8. Wallace A. Bacon and Robert S. Breen, *Literature as Experience* (New York: McGraw-Hill Book Co., 1959), p. viii.
9. Robert Beloof, *The Performing Voice in Literature* (Boston: Little, Brown and Co., 1966), p. 9.
10. Campbell, p. 104.
11. Dwight L. Burton, "Teaching Students to Read Imaginative Literature," in *Teaching English in Today's High Schools; Selected Readings,* ed. Dwight L. Burton and John S. Simmons (New York: Holt, Rinehart & Winston, 1965), p. 118.
12. Reuben Arthur Brower, *The Fields of Light: An Experiment in Critical Reading* (New York: Oxford University Press, 1951), pp. 19, 22.
13. Campbell, p. 14.

14. Elizabeth Drew, *Poetry: A Modern Guide to Its Understanding and Enjoyment* (New York: W. W. Norton & Co., 1959), p. 74.

15. Laurence Perrine, *Sound and Sense: An Introduction to Poetry,* 2d ed. (New York: Harcourt Brace Jovanovich, 1963), p. 18.

16. Brooks and Warren, p. 79.

17. Robert Bone, "American Negro Poetry: On the Stage and in the Schools," *Teachers College Record* 68 (February 1968): 440.

18. Geiger, p. 2.

19. Ibid., p. 10.

20. Stephen Dunning, *Teaching Literature to Adolescents; Poetry* (Chicago: Scott, Foresman and Co., 1966), p. 94.

21. John Ciardi, *How Does a Poem Mean?* (Boston: Houghton Mifflin Co., 1959), p. 666.

22. Ibid., p. 669.

23. Mary Margaret Robb, *Oral Interpretation of Literature in American Colleges and Universities,* rev. ed. (New York and London: Johnson Reprint Corp., 1968), p. 232.

24. Wallace A. Bacon, *The Art of Interpretation* (New York: Holt, Rinehart & Winston, 1966), p. 8.

25. Otis J. Aggert and Elbert R. Bower, *Communicative Reading,* 2d ed. (New York: The Macmillan Co., 1970), p. 195.

26. Louis Untermeyer, *Modern American and British Poetry* (New York: Harcourt Brace Jovanovich, 1935), p. 426.

27. Alan C. Purves with Victoria Rippere, *Elements of Writing about a Literary Work: A Study of Response to Literature* (Champaign, Ill.: National Council of Teachers of English, 1969), p. 64.

28. Aggert and Bower, p. 8.

29. Burl Ives, *The Burl Ives Song Book* (New York: Ballantine Books, 1953).

30. There are a goodly number of recordings which are readily available. Among them are Harry Belafonte's rendition (RCA Victor L 203; LPM 1022) and Buffy Sainte Marie's (Vanguard VRS-9250).

31. Monroe C. Beardsley, *Practical Logic* (Englewood Cliffs, N.J.: Prentice-Hall, 1950), p. 9.

32. Morris Sweetkind, *Teaching Poetry in the High School* (New York: The Macmillan Co., 1964), p. 5.

33. Mary Elizabeth Fowler, *Teaching Language, Composition and Literature* (New York: McGraw-Hill Book Co., 1965), p. 274.

34. Louis Untermeyer, *Doorways to Poetry* (New York: Harcourt Brace Jovanovich, 1938), p. 74.

35. David Aloian, *Poems and Poets* (New York: McGraw-Hill Book Co., 1965), p. 31.

36. Alice Bertha Gomme, *The Traditional Games of England, Scotland, and Ireland,* vol. 2 (New York: Dover Publications, Inc., 1964), p. 269.

37. Ibid., p. 270.

38. Ibid., p. 473.

39. Ibid., p. 488.

40. Ibid., p. 514.

41. Ibid., p. 530.

42. William Welk Newell, *Games and Songs of American Children* (New York: Dover Publications, 1963), p. 7.

43. Iona Opie and Peter Opie, *The Lore and Language of Schoolchildren* (Oxford: The Clarendon Press, 1959), p. 1.

44. Iona Opie and Peter Opie, *Children's Games in Street and Playground* (Oxford: The Clarendon Press, 1969), p. 14.

45. Ibid., p. 18.

46. The volumes cited above by Gomme and by Newell are available in paperback. There is a section on children's games in Oscar Williams, ed., *The Silver Treasury of Light Verse* (New York: Mentor Books, 1961).

47. Laurence Perrine, "The Nature of Proof in the Interpretation of Poetry," in *Teaching English in Today's High Schools,* 2d ed., ed. Dwight L. Burton and John L. Simmons (New York: Holt, Rinehart & Winston, 1970), p. 107.

48. Archibald McLeish, *Poetry and Experience* (Boston: Houghton Mifflin Co., 1960), p. 66.

49. Kenner, p. xviii.
50. Beloof, p. 275.
51. Earl Daniels, *The Art of Reading Poetry* (New York: Farrar, Straus & Giroux, 1941), p. 69.
52. *Scholastic Scope* 13 (September 1970): 19.
53. Untermeyer, *Doorways to Poetry,* p. 395.
54. For additional illustrations, see Anne Wescott Dodd, *Write Now! Insights into Creative Writing* (New York: Globe Book Co., 1973), p. 85.
55. Untermeyer, *Doorways to Poetry,* p. 140.
56. Harold H. Henderson, *Haiku in English* (Rutland, Vt.: Charles E. Tuttle Co., 1968), p. 28.
57. James Moffett, *A Student-Centered Language Arts Curriculum, Grades K–13: A Handbook for Teachers* (Boston: Houghton Mifflin Co., 1968), p. 361.
58. Brooks and Warren, p. 270.
59. Kenneth Koch, *Wishes, Lies, and Dreams: Teaching Children to Write Poetry* (New York: Chelsea House Publishers, 1970), p. 11.
60. Robert Penn Warren, "A Poem of Pure Imagination: An Experiment in Reading," in *Selected Essays,* ed. Robert Penn Warren (New York: Random House, 1951), pp. 268–69.
61. Stephen Spender, *The Making of a Poem* (London: Hamish Hamilton, 1955), p. 10.
62. Kenneth Koch, *Rose, Where Did You Get That Red? Teaching Great Poetry to Children* (New York: Random House, 1973), p. 35.
63. McLeish, p. 87.
64. Ibid., p. 80.
65. Elizabeth O'Daly, Egbert Nieman, and Herbert Potell, eds., *Adventures for Readers, Book I* (New York: Harcourt Brace Jovanovich, 1958), pp. 90–91. All three limericks are included in this volume.
66. Susanne K. Langer, *Feeling and Form* (New York: Charles Scribner's Sons, 1953), pp. 172–81.
67. Mildred Hardeman, ed., *Children's Ways of Knowing: Nathan Isaacs on Education, Psychology, and Piaget* (New York: Teachers College Press, 1974), p. 136.
68. Ibid., p. 139.
69. Ibid.
70. Ibid., p. 156.
71. Ibid., p. 163.
72. Ibid., p. 174.
73. Ibid., p. 175.

References

Aggert, Otis J., and Bower, Elbert R. *Communicative Reading,* 2nd ed. New York: The Macmillan Co., 1970.

Aloian, David. *Poems and Poets.* New York: McGraw-Hill Book Co., 1965.

Bacon, Wallace A. *The Art of Interpretation.* New York: Holt, Rinehart & Winston, 1966.

Bacon, Wallace A., and Breen, Robert S. *Literature as Experience.* New York: McGraw-Hill Book Co., 1959.

"Barbara Allen." In *Stories in Verse,* edited by Max T. Hohn. New York: The Odyssey Press, 1943.

Beardsley, Monroe C. *Practical Logic.* Englewood Cliffs, N.J.: Prentice-Hall, 1950.

Beethoven, Ludwig Van. Fifth Symphony. Columbia M–31634.

Beloof, Robert. *The Performing Voice in Literature.* Boston: Little, Brown and co., 1966.

Benét, Stephen Vincent. "Lewis and Clark." In *The Reading of Poetry,* edited by William D. Sheldon, Nellie Lyons, and Polly Ronault. Boston: Allyn & Bacon, 1963.

"The Blue Tail Fly." *The Burl Ives Song Book.* New York: Ballatine Books, 1953.

Bone, Robert. "American Negro Poetry: On the Stage and in the Schools." *Teachers College Record* 68 (February 1968): 440.

Booth, Philip. "Was a Man." *The Islanders.* New York: The Viking Press, 1961.

Brooks, Cleanth, and Warren, Robert Penn. *Understanding Poetry.* New York: Holt, Rinehart & Winston, 1960.

Brooks, Gwendolyn. "We Real Cool." *3000 Years of Black Poetry.* Greenwich, Conn.: Fawcett Publications, 1970.

Brower, Reuben Arthur. *The Fields of Light: An Experiment in Critical Reading.* New York: Oxford University Press, 1951.

Browning, Robert. "Incident of the French Camp." In *Story Poems: An Anthology of Narrative Verse,* edited by Louis Untermeyer. New York: Pocket Books, 1957.

Burton, Dwight L. "Teaching Students to Read Imaginative Literature." In *Teaching English in Today's High Schools: Selected Readings,* edited by Dwight L. Burton and John S. Simmons. New York: Holt, Rinehart & Winston, 1965.

Butler, Francelina. "The Poetry of Rope Skipping." *The New York Times Magazine,* vol. 2. (December 16, 1973):90, 92, 93, 94.

Campbell, Paul. *The Speaking and the Speakers of Literature.* Belmont, Cal: Dickenson Publishing Co., 1967.

Ciardi, John. *How Does a Poem Mean?* Boston: Houghton Mifflin Co., 1959.

"The Cruel Brother." *The Oxford Book of Ballads.* London: Oxford University Press, 1969.

Daniels, Earl. *The Art of Reading Poetry.* New York: Farrar, Straus & Giroux, 1941.

"The Demon Lover." In *Tales in Verse,* edited by Lewis G. Sterner and Marcus Konick. New York: Globe Book Co., 1963.

Dickinson, Emily. "Because I Could Not Stop for Death." In *The Mentor Book of Major American Poets,* edited by Oscar Williams and Edwin Honig. New York: The New American Library, 1962.

————. "I'm Nobody, Who Are You?" In *The Mentor Book of Major American Poets,* edited by Oscar Williams and Edwin Honig. New York: The New American Library, 1962.

————. "I Should Not Dare to Leave My Friend." In *The Mentor Book of Major American Poets,* edited by Oscar Williams and Edwin Honig. New York: The New American Library, 1962.

Dodd, Anne Wescott. *Write Now! Insights into Creative Writing.* New York: Globe Book Co., 1973.

Drew, Elizabeth. *Poetry: A Modern Guide to Its Understanding and Enjoyment.* New York: W. W. Norton & Co., 1959.

Dunbar, Paul Laurence. "We Wear the Mask." In *3000 Years of Black Poetry,* edited by Alan Lomax and Raoul Aboul. Greenwich, Conn.: Fawcett Publications, 1970.

Dunning, Stephen. *Teaching Literature to Adolescents; Poetry.* Chicago: Scott, Foresman and Co., 1966.

"Edward, Edward." In *Stories in Verse,* edited by Max T. Hohn. New York: The Odyssey Press, 1943.

Elkins, Deborah. "Man on the Move." Photos and Manual. New York: Franklin Watts Publishing Co., 1970.

Fowler, Mary Elizabeth. *Teaching Language Composition and Literature.* New York: McGraw-Hill Book Co., 1965.

Frost, Robert. "An Old Man's Winter Night." *Robert Frost's Poems.* New York: Pocket Books, 1954.

_____. "Out, Out." In *Stories in Verse,* edited by Max T. Hohn. New York: The Odyssey Press, 1943.

_____. "The Runaway." In *The Golden Treasury of Poetry,* edited by Louis Untermeyer. New York: Golden Press, 1959.

Geiger, Don. *The Sound, Sense, and Performance of Literature.* Chicago: Scott, Foresman and Co., 1963.

Gomme, Alice Bertha. *The Traditional Games of England, Scotland and Ireland,* vol. 2. New York: Dover Publications, 1964.

Hardeman, Mildred, ed. *Children's Ways of Knowing: Nathan Isaacs on Education, Psychology, and Piaget.* New York: Teachers College Press, 1974.

Hardy, Thomas. "The Man He Killed." In *Story Poems: An Anthology of Narrative Verse,* edited by Louis Untermeyer. New York: Pocket Books, 1957.

Henderson, Harold H. *Haiku in English.* Rutland, Vt: Charles E. Tuttle Co., 1968.

Housman, A. E. "When I Was One-and-Twenty." In *Great English and American Poems: The Pocket Book of Verse,* edited by M. E. Speare. New York: Pocket Books, 1956.

Hovey, Richard. "The Sea Gypsy." In *The Reading of Poetry,* edited by William D. Sheldon, Nellie Lyons, and Polly Ronault. Boston: Allyn & Bacon, 1963.

Hughes, Langston. "Brass Spittoon." In *The Book of American Negro Poetry,* edited by James W. Johnson. New York: Harcourt Brace Jovanovich, 1959.

_____. "Harlem." In *Black Voices: An Anthology of Afro-American Literature,* edited by Abraham Chapman. New York: The New American Library, 1968.

_____. "Mother to Son." In *Poetry Festival,* edited by John Bettenbender. New York: Dell Publishing Co., 1966.

Ives, Burl. *The Burl Ives Song Book.* New York: Ballantine Books, 1953.

"Jay Gould's Daughter." In *Something to Sing About,* edited by Milton Okun. New York: The Macmillan Co., 1968.

Johnson, James W. "The Creation." In *Black Voices: An Anthology of Afro-American Literature,* edited by Abraham Chapman. New York: The New American Library, 1968.

Kenner, Hugh. *The Art of Poetry.* New York: Holt, Rinehart & Winston, 1959.

Koch, Kenneth. *Rose, Where Did You Get That Red? Teaching Great Poetry to Children.* New York: Random House, 1973.

_____. *Wishes, Lies, and Dreams: Teaching Children to Write Poetry.* New York: Chelsea House Publishers, 1970.

Langer, Susanne K. *Feeling and Form.* New York: Charles Scribner's Sons, 1953.

Lear, Edward. *Edward Lear's Nonsense Books.* New York: Dover Publications, 1951.

Leavitt, Hart Day, and Sohn, David A. *Stop, Look and Write.* New York: Bantam Books, 1964.

Lee, Charlotte I. *Oral Interpretation.* Boston: Houghton Mifflin Co., 1959.

Lindsay, Vachel. "Abraham Lincoln Walks at Midnight." In *Great English and American Poems: The Pocket Book of Verse,* edited by M. E. Speare. New York: Pocket Books, 1956.

_____. "The Bronco That Would Not Be Broken." In *Adventures for Readers, Book I,* edited by Elizabeth C. O'Daly, Egbert W. Nieman, and Herbert Potell. New York: Harcourt Brace Jovanovich, 1958.

"Lord Randal." In *Story Poems: An Anthology of Narrative Verse,* edited by Louis Untermeyer. New York: Pocket Books, 1957.

Masters, Edgar Lee. "Silence." In *The New Poetry: An Anthology of Twentieth Century Verse in English,* edited by H. Monroe. New York: The Macmillan Co., 1930.

McLeish, Archibald. *Poetry and Experience.* Boston: Houghton Mifflin Co., 1960.

Millay, Edna St. Vincent. "The Ballad of the Harp Weaver." In *Tales in Verse,* edited by Lewis G. Sterner and Marcus Konick. New York: Globe Book Co., 1963.

Miller, Joaquin. "Columbus." In *Tales in Verse,* edited by Lewis G. Sterner and Marcus Konick. New York: Globe Book Co., 1963.

Moffett, James. *A Student-Centered Language Arts Curriculum, Grades K–13: A Handbook for Teachers.* Boston: Houghton Mifflin Co., 1968.

Morris, George Perkins. "Woodman, Spare That Tree." In *Highdays and Holidays,* edited by F. Adams and E. McCarrick. New York: E. P. Dutton & Co., 1927.

Muir, Edwin. "The Horses." *Sound and Sense, An Introduction to Poetry.* New York: Harcourt Brace Jovanovich, 1963.

Nash, Ogden. "The Sea Gull." *Verses from 1929 On.* Boston: Little, Brown and Co., 1952.

_____. "To a Small Boy Standing on My Shoes While I Am Wearing Them." In *Anthology of Light Verse,* edited by Louis Kronenberger. New York: The Modern Library, 1935.

Newell, William Welk. *Games and Songs of American Children.* New York: Dover Publications, 1963.

O'Daly, Elizabeth; Nieman, Egbert; and Potell, Herbert, eds. *Adventures for Readers, Book I.* New York: Harcourt Brace Jovanovich, 1958.

Opie, Iona, and Opie, Peter. *Children's Games in Street and Playground.* Oxford: The Clarendon Press, 1969.

_____. *The Lore and Language of Schoolchildren.* Oxford: The Clarendon Press, 1959.

Perrine, Laurence. "The Nature of Proof in the Interpretation of Poetry." In *Teaching English in Today's High Schools.* 2d ed., edited by Dwight L. Burton and John L. Simmons. New York: Holt, Rinehart & Winston, 1970.

_____. *Sound and Sense: An Introduction to Poetry.* 2d ed. New York: Harcourt Brace Jovanovich, 1963.

Poe, Edgar Allen. "Annabel Lee." In *Great English and American Poems: The Pocket Book of Verse,* edited by M. E. Speare. New York: The Pocket Library, 1956.

"Proud Margaret." In *The Oxford Book of Ballads,* edited by James Kinsley. London: Oxford University Press, 1969.

Purves, Alan C. with Rippere, Victoria. *Elements of Writing about a Literary Work: A Study of Response to Literature.* Champaign, Ill.: National Council of Teachers of English, 1969.

Rachmaninoff, Sergei. Symphony no. 2. RCA Victor. LM–2106.

Reed, Ishmael. "Beware, Do Not Read This Poem." In *The Black Poets,* edited by Dudley Randall. New York: Bantam Books, 1971.

Reynolds, Malvina. "God Bless the Grass." *Broadside* 64. (November 15, 1965):

Robb, Mary Margaret. *Oral Interpretation of Literature in American Colleges and Universities.* rev. ed. New York and London: Johnson Reprint Corp., 1968.

Roethke, Theodore. "My Papa's Waltz." In *Sounds and Silences,* edited by Richard Peck. New York: The Delacorte Press, 1970.

"Round and Round the Village." In *The Traditional Games of England.* vol. 2, by Alice Bertha Gomme. New York: Dover Publications, 1964.

Sanchez, Sonia. "Small Comment." *Home Coming: Poems.* Detroit: Broadside Press Publications, 1968.

Sandburg, Carl. "Grass." *Modern American and British Poetry.* New York: Harcourt Brace Jovanovich, 1935.

Sarett, Lew. "Four Little Foxes." In *Reflections on a Gift of Watermelon Pickle and Other Modern Verse,* compiled by Stephen Dunning, Edward Lueders, and Hugh Smith. Glenview, Ill.: Scott, Foresman and Co., 1966.

Scholastic Scope. New York: Scholastic Magazines, 13 (September 1970).

"Scorpio." Detroit Guitar Band. No longer available.

Shapiro, Karl. "Auto Wreck." In *Sounds and Silences,* edited by Richard Peck. New York: The Delacorte Press, 1970.

————. "Doctor, Doctor, A Little of Your Love." In *Sound and Sense, An Introduction to Poetry,* ed. Laurence Perrine. New York: Harcourt Brace Jovanovich, 1963.

Shelley, Percy Bysshe. "Ozymandias." In *Sound and Sense, An Introduction to Poetry,* ed. Laurence Perrine. New York: Harcourt Brace Jovanovich, 1963.

Spender, *The Making of a Poem.* London: Hamish Hamilton, 1955.

Stevens, Wallace. "Tea." In *The College Anthology of British and American Poetry,* edited by A. Kent Hieatt and William Park. Boston: Allyn & Bacon, 1972.

"Sweet Potato Man." In *An Introduction to Black Literature in America,* edited by Lindsay Patterson. New York: Publishers Company, 1968.

Sweetkind, Morris. *Teaching Poetry in the High School.* New York: The Macmillan Co., 1964.

Tennyson, Lord Alfred. "The Charge of the Light Brigade." In *Story Poems: An Anthology of Narrative Verse,* edited by Louis Untermeyer. New York: Pocket Books, 1957.

————. "The Highwayman." In *Story Poems: An Anthology of Narrative Verse,* edited by Louis Untermeyer. New York: Pocket Books, 1957.

Thomas, Dylan. "A Refusal to Mourn the Death, by Fire, of a Child in London." In *The Golden Treasury of the Best Songs and Lyrical Poems,* edited by F. T. Palgrave. Brought up to date by Oscar Williams. New York: The New American Library, 1961.

Untermeyer, Louis. *Modern American and British Poetry.* New York: Harcourt Brace Jovanovich, 1935.

————. *Doorways to Poetry.* New York: Harcourt Jovanovich, 1938.

Warren, Robert Penn. "A Poem of Pure Imagination: An Experiment in Reading." In *Selected Essays,* edited by Robert Penn Warren. New York: Random House, 1951.

Welch, Myra Brooks. "The Touch of the Master's Hand." In *The Pocket Book of Popular Verse,* edited by Ted Malone. New York: Pocket Books, 1945.

Williams, William Carlos. "The Negro Woman." In *Poetry in English,* edited by Warren Taylor and Donald Hall. New York: The Macmillan Co., 1970.

Wordsworth, William. "I Wandered Lonely as a Cloud." In *Great English and American Poems: The Pocket Book of Verse,* edited by M. E. Speare. New York: Pocket Books, 1956.

Wylie, Elinor. "Sea Lullaby." In *Adventures in American Literature,* edited by Rewey B. Inglis et al. New York: Harcourt Brace Jovanovich, 1952.

Suggested Poems

Auden, W. H. "The Unknown Citizen." In *Sounds and Silences,* edited by Richard Peck. New York: The Delacorte Press, 1970.

Baker, Karle Wilson. "Let Me Grow Lovely." In *Pocket Book of Popular Verse,* edited by Ted Malone. New York: Pocket Books, 1945.

Bellac, Hilaire. "Matilda, Who told Lies and Was Burned to Death." In *Stories in Verse,* edited by Max T. Hohn. New York: The Odyssey Press, 1943.

Blake, William. "The Sick Rose." In *Poems: An Anthology,* edited by Burton Raffel. New York: The New American Library, 1971.

―――. "The Tiger." In *Poetry Festival,* edited by John Bettenbender. New York: Dell Publishing Co., 1966.

Brautigan, Richard. "The Chinese Checker Players." In *Man in Action,* edited by Hannah B. Haupt, Lilla Heston, Jay Littell, and Sarah Solotaroff. Evanston, Ill.: McDougal, Littell & Co., 1972.

Brooks, Gwendolyn. "A Song in the Front Yard." In *I Am the Darker Brother,* edited by Arnold Adoff. New York: The Macmillan Co., 1968.

Browning, Elizabeth Barrett. "How Do I Love Thee?" In *Poetry Festival,* edited by John Bettenbender. New York: Dell Publishing Co., 1966.

Browning, Robert. "My Last Duchess." In *Tales in Verse,* edited by Lewis G. Sterner and Marcus Konick. New York: Globe Book Co., 1963.

Carroll, Lewis. "Jabberwocky." In *The Silver Treasury of Light Verse,* edited by Oscar Williams. New York: The New American LIbrary, 1957.

―――. "Father William." In *The Silver Treasury of Light Verse,* edited by Oscar Williams. New York: The New American Library, 1957.

Coatsworth, Elizabeth. "Swift Things Are Beautiful." In *Reflections on a Gift of Watermelon Pickle and Other Modern Verse,* edited by Stephen Dunning, Edward Lueders, and Hugh Smith. Glenview, Ill.: Scott, Foresman and Co., 1966.

Crapsey, Adelaide. "Susanna and the Elders." *Verse.* New York: Alfred A. Knopf, 1934.

Cullen, Countee. "Incident." In *I Am the Darker Brother,* edited by Arnold Adoff. New York: The Macmillan Co., 1968.

―――. "A Song of Praise (For One Who Praised His Lady's Being Fair)." In *Black Voices: An Anthology of Afro-American Literature,* edited by Abraham Chapman. New York: The New American Library, 1968.

Cummings, E. E. "In Just ―――." In *Reflections on a Gift of Watermelon Pickle and Other Modern Verse,* edited by Stephen Dunning, Edward Lueders, and Hugh Smith. Glenview, Ill.: Scott, Foresman and Co., 1966.

―――. "Spring Is Like a Perhaps Hand." In *The Mentor Book of Major American Poets,* edited by Oscar Williams and Edwin Honig. New York: The New American Library, 1962.

Cuney, Waring. "My Lord, What a Morning." In *3000 Years of Black Poetry,* edited by Alan Lomax and Raoul Aboul. Greenwich, Conn.: Fawcett Publications, 1970.

"The Death and Burial of Cock Robin." In *The Silver Treasury of Light Verse,* edited by Oscar Williams. New York: The New American Library, 1957.

Dunbar, Paul Laurence. "Sympathy." In *I Am the Darker Brother,* edited by Arnold Adoff. New York: The Macmillan Co., 1968.

————. "We Wear the Mask." In *3000 Years of Black Poetry*, edited by Alan Lomax and Raoul Aboul. Greenwich, Conn.: Fawcett Publications, 1970.

Eliot, T. S. "Macavity: The Mystery Cat." In *The Reading of Poetry*, edited by William D. Sheldon, Nellie Lyons, and Polly Ronault. Boston: Allyn & Bacon, 1963.

Evans, Mari. "The Rebel." In *I Am the Darker Brother*, edited by Arnold Adoff. New York: The Macmillan Co., 1968.

Farjeon, Eleanor. "Strawberries." *Poems for Children*. Philadelphia: J. B. Lippincott Co., 1951.

————. "Who'll Bury My Valley Lillies?" *Poems for Children*. Philadelphia: J. B. Lippincott Co., 1951.

"Frankie and Johnny." In *Poetry Festival*, edited by John Bettenbender. New York: Dell Publishing Co., 1966.

Frost, Robert. "The Death of the Hired Man." In *Tales in Verse*, edited by Lewis G. Sterner and Marcus Konick. New York: Globe Book Co., 1963.

————. "Mending Wall." In *Great English and American Poems: The Pocket Book of Verse*, edited by M. E. Speare. New York: The Pocket Library, 1956.

————. "Stopping by Woods on a Snowy Evening." In *Poetry Festival*, edited by John Bettenbender. New York: Dell Publishing Co., 1966.

Goldsmith, Oliver. "Elegy on the Death of a Mad Dog." In *The Pocket Book of Popular Verse*, edited by Ted Malone. New York: Pocket Books, 1945.

Hayden, Robert. "The Whipping." In *I Am the Darker Brother*, edited by Arnold Adoff. New York: The Macmillan Co., 1968.

Herrick, Robert. "Delight in Disorder." In *Great English and American Poems: The Pocket Book of Verse*, edited by M. E. Speare. New York: The Pocket Library, 1956.

Holmes, Oliver W. "The Height of the Ridiculous." *The Silver Treasury of Light Verse*. New York: The New American Library, 1961.

Hood, Thomas. "The Song of the Shirt." In *Great English and American Poems: The Pocket Book of Verse*, edited by M. E. Speare. New York: The Pocket Library, 1956.

Hughes, Langston. "As I Grew Older." In *Black Voices: An Anthology of Afro-American Literature*, edited by Abraham Chapman. New York: The New American Library, 1968.

————. "I, Too, Sing America." In *I Am the Darker Brother*, edited by Arnold Adoff. New York: The Macmillan Co., 1968.

————. "The Negro Speaks of Rivers." In *American Negro Poetry*, edited by Arna Bontemps. New York: Hill & Wang, 1963.

————. "Too Blue." In *Reflections on a Gift of Watermelon Pickle*, edited by Stephen Dunning, Edward Lueders, and Hugh Smith. Glenview, Ill.: Scott, Foresman and Co., 1966.

Jenkins, Brooks. "Loneliness." In *Reflections on a Gift of Watermelon Pickle*, edited by Stephen Dunning, Edward Lueders, and Hugh Smith. Glenview, Ill.: Scott, Foresman and Co., 1966.

"John Henry." In *Poetry Festival*, edited by John Bettenbender. New York: Dell Publishing Co., 1966.

Johnson, Fenton. "A Negro Peddler's Song." In *Black Voices: An Anthology of Afro-American Literature*, edited by Abraham Chapman. New York: The New American Library, 1968.

Jordan, A. C. "You Tell Me to Sit Quiet." In *Man in the Poetic Mode*, edited by Jay Zweigler. Evanston, Ill.: McDouglas, Littell & Co., 1970.

Justice, Donald. "The Missing Person." In *Sounds of Silence*, edited by Betsy Ryan. New York: Scholastic Book Services, 1972.

Leigh, Henry S. "The Twins." In *Tales in Verse,* edited by Lewis G. Sterner and Marcus Konick. New York: Globe Book Co., 1963.

Markham, Edwin. "A Creed." In *Poetry Festival,* edited by John Bettenbender. New York: Dell Publishing Co., 1966.

Merriam, Eve. "How to Eat a Poem." In *How to Eat a Poem and Other Morsels,* edited by Rose H. Agree. New York: Random House, 1967.

Millay, Edna St. Vincent. "Afternoon on a Hill." In *The Sound of Poetry,* edited by Mary C. Austin and Queenie B. Mills. Boston: Allyn & Bacon, 1963.

_____. "Ballad of the Harp Weaver." In *Tales in Verse,* edited by Lewis G. Sterner and Marcus Konick. New York: Globe Book Co., 1963.

Moore, Marianne. "Silence." *The Complete Poems of Marianne Moore.* New York: The Macmillan Co., 1967.

Moore, Rosalie. "Catalogue." In *Reflections on a Gift of Watermelon Pickle,* edited by Stephen Dunning, Edward Lueders, and Hugh Smith. Glenview, Ill.: Scott, Foresman and Co., 1966.

Parker, Dorothy. "Resumé." In *Reflections on a Gift of Watermelon Pickle,* edited by Stephen Dunning, Edward Lueders, and Hugh Smith. Glenview, Ill.: Scott, Foresman and Co., 1966.

Po-Chu-i. "Losing a Slave-girl." In *Poems: An Anthology,* edited by Burton Raffel. New York: The New American Library, 1971.

"Poor Old Lady." In *The Sound of Poetry,* edited by Mary C. Austin and Queenie B. Mills. Boston: Allyn & Bacon, 1963.

Pound, Ezra. "Meditation." In *Reflections on a Gift of Watermelon Pickle,* edited by Stephen Dunning, Edward Lueders, and Hugh Smith. Glenview, Ill.: Scott, Foresman and Co., 1966.

Robinson, Edwin Arlington. "Miniver Cheevy." In *Tales in Verse,* edited by Lewis G. Sterner and Marcus Konick. New York: Globe Book Co., 1963.

_____. "Richard Cory." In *Tales in Verse,* edited by Lewis G. Sterner and Marcus Konick. New York: Globe Book Co., 1963.

Scott, Sir Walter. "Breathes There the Man with Soul So Dead." In *Poetry Festival,* edited by John Bettenbender. New York: Dell Publishing Co., 1966.

Service, Robert W. "The Cremation of Sam McGee." In *Tales in Verse,* edited by Lewis G. Sterner and Marcus Konick. New York: Globe Book Co., 1963.

Shapiro, Karl. "Doctor, Doctor, A Little of Your Love." In *Sound and Sense,* by Laurence Perrine. New York: Harcourt Brace Jovanovich, 1963.

"Sir Patrick Spence." In *Tales in Verse,* edited by Lewis G. Sterner and Marcus Konick. New York: Globe Book Co., 1963.

Stafford, William. "Fifteen." In *Reflections on a Gift of Watermelon Pickle,* edited by Stephen Dunning, Edward Lueders, and Hugh Smith. Glenview, Ill.: Scott, Foresman and Co., 1966.

Teasdale, Sara. "Faces." In *On City Streets,* edited by Nancy Larrick. New York: Bantam Books, 1968.

Thayer, Ernest Lawrence. "Casey at the Bat." In *Tales in Verse,* edited by Lewis G. Sterner and Marcus Konick. New York: Globe Book Co., 1963.

Whitman, Walt. "Come Up from the Fields, Father." In *Poetry Festival,* edited by John Bettenbender. New York: Dell Publishing Co., 1966.

Whittier, John Greenleaf. "Barbara Frietchie." In *Poetry Festival,* edited by John Bettenbender. New York: Dell Publishing Co., 1966.

"Whoopee Ti Yi Yo, Git Along Little Dogies." In *Time for Poetry,* edited by May Hill Arbuthnot. New York: Scott, Foresman and Co., 1952.

Wilcox, Ella Wheeler. "Laugh, and the World Laughs with You." In *Poetry Festival,* edited by John Bettenbender. New York: Dell Publishing Co., 1966.

Williams, William Carlos. "Smell!" In *Being Alive,* edited by Hannah B. Haupt, Lilla Heston, Joy Littell, and Sarah Solotaroff. Evanston, Ill.: McDougal, Littell & Co., 1972.

————. "The Term." In *Reflections on a Gift of Watermelon Pickle,* edited by Stephen Dunning, Edward Lueders, and Hugh Smith. Glenview. Ill.: Scott, Foresman and Co., 1966.

Wylie, Elinor. "Velvet Shoes." In *The Sound of Poetry,* edited by Mary C. Austin and Queenie B. Mills. Boston: Allyn & Bacon, 1963.

Chapter Seven

Coping with the Essay and Exploring the Biography

The essay is often regarded as being a minor genre. Yet, it is of major importance because it includes articles and editorials which comprise a large portion of the materials we read. For reasons which will become apparent as this chapter unfolds, the concentration here will be on the literary essay and the familiar essay in particular.

Although the essay is the genre in which the author speaks directly to the reader, students are frequently unable to approach the essay and converse with the author on his terms. They need a wealth of observational, conversational, and research experiences either in preparation for reading the essay or as a follow-up. These experiences enable students to comprehend the essence and importance of the essay and to share the process through which the essayist arrived at his point of view. The same process may lead them to a view that is opposite from the essayists. Appropriate concrete experiences with the genre will develop an ability to handle essays on an abstract level.

Bacon's statement serves more or less as an aim when one is dealing with the immature reader: "Rather than creating a world of its own, as the literary work does, it [essay] tends to join the reader in the actual world to talk about something in which narrator and reader have a common interest—to create one side of a dialogue in which the reader supplies the other half."[1] The teacher cannot assume that the narrator and reader have a common interest. Rather, the teacher's task is to help build those interests, so that as the student matures he is able to supply the other half of the dialogue.

The essay is perhaps the most neglected genre in the secondary school. Teachers frankly admit, "I avoid it like the plague." The reasons offered usually are "We read essays in college and they were dull, boring, and difficult." However, Burton is aware that "what has become almost archaic in commercial usage is only the word *essay* itself. The form is as up-to-date as this morning's newspaper or this week's magazine."[2] Once teachers understand how to select essays, become aware of the tremendous variety of types, and learn how to handle them in the classroom, their attitude toward the genre changes radically. They learn how to take advantage of a fact Bernstein cites: ". . . the essay's merit is uneventfulness. . . . In biography events occur without climax. In the essay, ideas occur, but occurrences do not."[3] Teachers need to understand and make use of the fact that "the essay is more like a chat, a one-man bull session, beginning somewhere and ending somewhere else, and often indecisively."[4] Those which do end indecisively give the teacher and students an extraordinary opportunity to argue issues with the author. Teachers find some students most uncomfortable with indecision. Such students seek the right answer to an issue or a point of view presented by the essayist. For these students the study is perhaps more necessary than for those who are comfortable with delayed decisions and who enjoy taking part in making those decisions.

Essays and Cognitive Development

The proper handling of essays encourages cognitive growth. Although they speak directly to the reader, they are often deceptively simple. For one thing, they present an attitude. An attitude is usually not directly expressed, forcing the student to uncover it beneath a maze of illustrations and detail. Essays present an evaluation. The process of evaluating is a complex one; to comprehend fully the import of the evaluation requires understanding the relationship among the details and the illustrations leading to the final appraisal by the essayist. Furthermore, the main issue is not always directly stated. As Bernstein concludes, "Essays are deceptive. Even the personal, ingratiating one that doesn't seem to have a debatable issue anywhere in sight will have one lurking there, never fear. If you can't locate it, don't teach the bore."[5]

Still another challenging aspect of the essay is the personality of the essayist. Boas points out, "The essay is always the expression of a personality; unless it reveals the personality which inspired it, it is an editorial, an article, or a report."[6] To detect personality through what a writer says about a given topic calls for complex inference making.

Brashers adds another facet, "The familiar essay allows us to conceive the generalities of life by perceiving particular instances, usually anecdotes, about it."[7] He goes on to point out what amounts to cognitive problems for the reader. "Anecdotes in familiar essays are typical structural metaphors."[8] Whether metaphors appear in poems or in essays, they require equal ability to see relationships. "It is often said that it is virtually impossible to exhaust the implications and comparisons in a good metaphor; just so, the structural metaphor builds upon the reader's common knowledge to expand an anecdote into a subject much larger than the anecdote. . . . The juxtaposition of the anecdote against the larger subject allows the perception and entertainment of the larger subject to come through."[9]

The relationship between the cognitive domain and the affective domain is vital, too. Unless the students' contacts with the essay bring enjoyment and satisfaction, they will avoid the essay and be deprived of the pleasures and challenges it holds. Their reaction will depend in large measure on the particular works to which they are introduced and upon the experiences teachers permit the essay to offer them.

"Conversing" with the Essayist

There are various elements in the familiar essay which are appropriate for secondary school students. One lies in the fact that a writer is not always under obligation to cover every aspect of his subject. It is consoling for students to know this as they approach their own writing, and it gives them an opportunity to continue the "conversation" where the essayist left off. "Like no other writer, he [essayist] addresses his reader directly, companionably," writes Wagenknecht. "The essay is closer to good talk than any other kind of writing. . . . He chooses a theme because it interests him, and simply because he feels no obligation to achieve a complete, comprehensive, or definitive coverage of it, he is relaxed as no other writer is relaxed."[10] As a matter of fact, says Highet, "Essays are intended not to exhaust the subject—which usually means exhausting the reader—but rather to say a few good things about it and to give readers the pleasure of continuing the author's thought along their own channels."[11] Boas and Smith take pains to clarify the issue of incompleteness:

> The essay is usually incomplete. This does not mean that it is unfinished. Any essay is complete in itself, but it does not begin to exhaust the possibilities of its subject matter or even of its author's reactions to that subject matter. It gives us a complete idea of the way the author wishes us to look at his subject within the limits of space and time at his disposal.[12]

To tell students the facts inherent in the preceding comments is one thing; to have them learn is another. Those teachers who worked on new ways to approach the essay and who were interested in helping students to converse with the author, to enjoy the incompleteness, and yet to wish to participate in completing it, soon realized students needed to engage in a process similar to that in which the essayist probably engaged. Through such process, the students could gain insights that would enable them to make the essayist's subject a new topic for their own conversation, oral and written.

One of the most successful introductory essays used was Smith's "Coping with the Compliment." It proved its capacity to break down negative attitudes on the part of teachers as well as of students. It was as enthusiastically received in the twelfth as in the seventh grades. Undoubtedly, one of the chief ingredients making for its effectiveness with students was its humor. Lewis and Sisk point out that "lighter informal essays can lead to appreciation of humor, delight in originality and clever expression and, as the author's own personality is revealed, interest in human nature."[13] However, an analysis of what makes Smith's essay humorous will not achieve the desired end. It will do nothing but destroy the intent of the essay itself as well as the purpose of teaching it.

All students have had some experience with compliments—giving or receiving them or observing the effect upon a recipient when another person bestows a compliment. Therefore, there is mutual interest between the essayist and the reader. However, teachers must be aware that although compliments constitute an area students have observed, they may not have given much thought to their observations. The introduction the teacher selects will depend upon his multiple purposes and upon the maturity of his students.

Most teachers found it sufficient to start reading the essay to the class, followed by students completing it independently. A few teachers turned on a tape recorder to catch the initially stifled laughter which quickly turned into freer explosions. When students finished the essay, the teacher played back the tape so the classes could hear their own reactions, and the discussion was on! "What were you laughing at?" seemed to be all that was needed to start the discussion.

Now came the task of offering students experiences which would make it possible to "converse" with the essayist. Teachers assigned students the task of paying a genuine compliment to a peer, an adult, a younger child, or in some cases all three. They were to jot down the compliment paid, the person to whom it was directed, and the response. This note-taking was to be done as soon as the object of their attention was out of sight. Invariably, teachers expressed surprise that so many students engaged in the activity and participated eagerly in the ensuing discussion.

There are cautions worth mentioning. Students may use this experience to play jokes on others. Students should be instructed to give the compliment only if they mean it.

During class time next day, at first there was a mere recounting of what had happened. This mere recounting of experiences and information is crucial for a base upon which to build higher cognitive levels. Interestingly enough, the caliber and content of compliment as well as responses remained much the same in grades seven through twelve. Comments from a tenth-grade class were as follows:

Sharon: I told a girl I like her hair, and she said I must be crazy.
Alice: I told one of my friends I liked her shoes, and she started to name all the other people who had the same shoes.
Edward: I told this guy he looks nice today, and he said he looks nice every day.
Bertha: I told a friend she looks pretty, and she said she sure tries.
Frank: I told one of my teachers she looks nice, and she said I really made her day.
George: I told a teacher that I liked his shirt and he began to tell me how he washes it, where he bought it, and in what other colors it comes, and other garbage like that.

It is interesting to note the people to whom students turned in carrying out this assignment. Out of fifty compliments given by one class, twenty-seven went to friends, eleven to siblings, five to mothers, one to a father, and the remainder to uncles, young children, neighbors, or local merchants. The contents of compliments was somewhat anticipated by the teacher who did not discuss this beforehand with students. Thirty compliments were related to clothing, eleven to general appearance and/or grooming, seven to skills and intelligence, and two were miscellaneous.

The particulars of the responses were difficult to categorize, but as has been brought out in earlier chapters, the process of categorization is essential for cognitive growth. The responses were classified into seven categories as follows:

1. Disbelief—14
   "Are you kidding?"
   "I can't draw."
   "Yeah, sure!"
   "What the hell is wrong with you?"
2. Blasé response—12
   "They're mine."
   "Don't I sound good all the time?"
   "It's o.k." "It's there."

"I know; that's why I bought them."

"It ought to be."

"I like them too."

"I try."

"And they're comfortable too."

3. Suspicion of motives—10

"What do you mean?"

"Yeah, o.k. I'll do the dishes; you don't have to butter me up."

"Why? Do you want to wear it?"

"Why did you say that?"

"You think you're funny."

"I'm not in the mood to play games."

4. Need for reassurance—7

"Really? Do you really think so?"

"This?"

5. Witty remark—3

"I'm glad. I've been wearing it since I was eight."

"I may not always be right, but I'm never wrong."

6. Acceptance—2

"Thank you."

"I'm glad you like it."

7. Miscellaneous—2.

The discussion then rose to another level as a result of the categorization process. The students were now able to hypothesize and to make some tentative generalizations. The teacher reminded students that their aim was to "complete" Smith's essay.

Evelyn: Hardly anyone said a plain, "Thank you." Smith is right! And everybody's parents taught them to say, "Thank you," from the time they could talk!

Vick: It was mainly teachers who answered compliments by saying something positive or witty or by being grateful. Maybe they know how to handle themselves better. We're better at ranking each other out.

Evelyn: A few adults did say, "Thank you." Maybe it means that a lot of people do feel inferior. Or maybe they think if they say, "Thank you," others might think they know they're great, and they seem conceited.

Billy: And most people would rather seem modest than conceited.

Other students met with experiences which caused them to draw different conclusions.

Sally: Older people are afraid of muggers, so if you say something nice, immediately they act afraid.

You don't usually have to compliment a friend because a smile or a facial expression will show your compliment.

Ben: If you compliment a person who turns out to be exceptionally lonely, don't be surprised if you get a history on what you complimented him on.

Cathy: The surprising thing is the number of hostile responses. I thought it was something I did wrong when that kind of response came, but I see many others had the same thing happen.

Bill: We unearthed something not in Smith's essay: We're more comfortable with our friends than with our families where compliments are concerned. We don't *have* to say, "Thank you." We can say, "Screw you." So, if we were conversing with Smith, we'd tell him that. He's left out the whole teen-age bit. Maybe he doesn't know about it.

Lisa: He left out the fact that compliments are a social asset and shouldn't be taken too seriously. Compliments are good icebreakers, good ways of making friends.

Joan: We're so used to putting each other down and insulting each other so that people were suspicious and they were amazed when they received a compliment and were trying to figure out why.

John: My conclusion is that Smith is too conceited. He thinks he knows all about compliments and does not give you the feeling he knows there are other factors and situations calling for other answers.

These were bare beginnings in hypothesizing about behavior.

Now the teachers sent the students back to the essay. One class focused on the question, How would you like Smith as a friend? Others discussed what aspects of human reaction to the compliment were omitted by Smith or treated too lightly. What did this tell about him? Was he a good observer of human behavior? What evidence is there in his essay? The vast majority of teachers reported that as students left the room they jokingly complimented one another.

Writing an Essay: Beginnings*

If students are thrown on their own to write an essay simply because they have the data, the efforts can bear negative results. They need to know how to organize their thoughts using the data as a springboard. As students reviewed their categories and Smith's essay, they listed topics on which they'd like to concentrate: family reactions, young children's behavior, witticisms, humility versus conceit, social expectations, banishing the compliment, and teenage alternatives. Students had to be assured that their essay did not have to be witty, sarcastic, or ironic. They were told that it could be serious, should reflect their experiences and how they felt about them, and should mirror their own personalities, not Smith's. Cook's statement offered reassurance at this point:

A successful essay says a thing clearly and memorably. It is required to do no more. An essayist does not have to be inspired as does a poet; he does not have to encompass mankind as does a novelist. He only has to have a thing to say, and even that may be only tentative.[14]

Teachers demonstrated that in any conversation between two or more people, the attitudes, feelings, and modes of expression differ. Some teachers played a minute or two of a taped conversation from a TV program; others played back a previous discussion by the students themselves on a controversial issue. They did this so students

*This section was written with Lola Cronacher.

could feel assured that differences in personality reflection were not only acceptable but essential.

The first essays were usually written in class, often in pairs. In some cases, teachers asked students to take their essays home for a bit of polishing. Either way, the literary results were far from enchanting. In all classes, most students gave evidence that they clearly understood the need for illustrating and supporting detail for the main idea they were trying to convey. Most of them still did not grasp the concept that the kind of "conversation" a writer holds with his audience is different from the continual participation characteristic of face-to-face conversation. They didn't yet know how to "compensate for the loss of their listener."[15] Some excerpts follow; they demonstrate that students did enjoy writing together.

Know Your Relatives by the Compliments
They Accept

Mothers are the suspicious type. When you give them a compliment, they always think you want something. If you say, "Hey, ma, you look nice," she replies, "How much do you want?" This shows the suspicious nature of mothers. . . . Fathers are the acceptable type and receive compliments in good taste. "You look sharp!" I tell him. He replies, "Thank you! I try."

Compliments Don't Always Work

Sometimes even little children are sarcastic. I was baby-sitting once. The little boy was a complete angel until his mother left. The first words he utters are, "I want my mommy." Great as you are with little kids, remarks such as, "You're a good boy," don't work. Or you can use, "Big boys don't cry," only to get the reply, "Get lost."

Compliments in the Family Circle

If there's one thing I can't stand, it's going to my family's family circle meetings. Now don't get me wrong. I love my family, even my Aunt Harriet who weighs 374 pounds and insists it's only baby fat. What I don't like about these chaotic reunions is the bull . . . these clichéish relatives hand out.

In less than one-half hour I'm told I look like seventeen different relatives. My Aunt Sadie insists I, (being so attractive) find a nice mate and get married. My Uncle Arthur wants me to go to his home town college because with my brains I could get far in the business world.

These were the "best" excerpts from papers of students who were classified as being average academically. The essays and the discussions illustrate the students' lack of in-depth experience with conversation, thinking, and writing about issues of interest to them. Yet, the students declared, "This was the best assignment you ever gave us." At least, here was something on which to build.

Hypothesizing with the Essayist

A unit on the essay is not recommended, even for the twelfth grade. The essay should be read in conjunction with other genre for comparative purposes. If the class is considering a theme such as "Sex Roles in Society" and reading a variety of materials, several essays can be read on the same theme so that points of view may be compared.

Themes like "Sex Roles" or "Human Protest" are suitable because they are of intrinsic interest to adolescents and because a wide variety of essays are to be found on them. Ample materials permit the teachers to help students assess the difference between pure exposition and the literary essay, and the comparisons aid in understanding the essential hypothetical nature of the essay. Boas explains, "The real essay is never pure exposition, because pure exposition is an attempt to substitute knowledge for relative ignorance. . . . Many contemporary discussions of economics, history, science, and literature are wrongly called essays because, when their information has been extracted, they have no more worth . . . the real essay, being interesting in itself, can never be outdated."[16]

The essayist hypothesizes. Says Cook, "He offers not final truths, but hypotheses. He sets up his ideas as challenges to the minds of his readers . . . while he may want to illustrate his point in order to render it clearer, he need not prove it. . . . We believe or accept not because we are argued into submission but because the essayists have confronted us with their personal formulations and have tacitly challenged us to propose better."[17] Cook's hypothetical aspect of the essay combined with Boas' explanation makes for another important focus in teaching the essay. Boas explains, "The real essay is never pure argument. Argument aims at conviction. . . . The writer of pamphlets or sermons is fighting a battle. Victory is his goal. His writing is his ammunition, and . . . once it is fired, it is spent. The essay, however, is never mere ammunition. The essay is its own excuse for being."[18]

Several teachers who were working with a sequence on "Sex Roles" decided to use Broun's "Holding a Baby" as one central essay. They selected it because of its humor and because it lent itself to investigation. Teachers created an interview schedule, with the help of students, for the students to use in gathering information on specific areas of daily activity. To each question the interviewee would be asked to answer "man," "woman," or "both," and if he wished, he would give some explanation of his choice. A few teachers duplicated the schedule for student use. Some sample questions follow:

Who should	man	woman	both	comment

1. Go shopping for food
2. Do the cooking
3. Wash the dishes
4. Take out the garbage
5. Change the baby's diapers
6. Do the gardening
7. Wheel the baby carriage
8. Drive the car
9. Sign the checks
10. Discipline the children
11. Repair household items

Before making the assignment, one teacher administered her questionnaire to family and friends, in order to evaluate the questions and to anticipate some problems students might encounter. She reported the results as being fascinating. She found the following:

> When parents are perfectly matched, they brainwash each other and agree on everything: Dishes, a woman's job; laundry, a woman's job; changing diapers, a woman's job; staying up at night with the baby, either; garbage, a man's job, wheel the carriage, a woman's job. That was an older couple. A young couple I interviewed had an outburst over this. The man wanted to wheel the baby carriage when they are together because he has equal rights, but the wife said it's a woman's task. She said, "It's a man's job to take out the garbage," and he said, "Forget it!" By the way, he takes out the garbage. On the subject of changing diapers, she said, "Either." He yelled, "No!" And he doesn't. Shopping for food? He wanted to go, but she said "It's a woman's job." Preparing meals? She said, "My husband"; he said she should do that. Driving the car? She said, "The man," even though she has a driver's license. . . .
>
> Well, I couldn't stop. I was fascinated. So, I interviewed teen-agers too—a boy and a girl together. In every case, when it comes to writing checks, they thought the man should do it. . . .
>
> When I asked how they came to these decisions, tradition won out over discussion. . . .

In doing this preliminary work, the teacher realized students would have problems with note-taking as well as approaching people. Therefore, she decided to set up three or four role-playing situations in which students would receive practice in handling the assignment. At first, she served as the person being interviewed. After that, students took on the two roles. She found it necessary not only to teach note-taking and approaches to people but also to explore with the students why they were doing this type of assignment. They knew the topic of study; they knew they were preparing to read an essay; they had already engaged in one "action research" project and were aware of its benefits. Now they explored the importance of listening to what people say as well as how they say it; gathering primary data before drawing opinions about democratic structure in families versus tradition in societal role assignment; observing people's attitudes toward their roles as exhibited in facial expressions, humorous response, or the way they address each other; assessing value structure in one specific area of their lives. This exploration was significant because it gave students a wide variety of foci to use as they approached subjects of different ages and different relationships to them. It helped put the student at ease, and in turn he was able to put his interviewee at ease.

Some teachers preferred to have students interview each other in pairs during class time after the class had arrived at two or three hypotheses about what they would discover. They felt they and the students could handle the data more readily with a tighter, more limited field. For teachers and students who need this type of security, such a procedure is most beneficial. Eventually, these teachers were able to widen the field so that students could converse with people of various age levels and in a range of relationships to them.

After the students conducted their interviews, they reported their findings to the class and tallied their results. In the interest of saving time, one teacher wanted to arrange his class in small groups. However, each student wanted the whole class to hear his report. The class, understanding the teacher's viewpoint, met in small groups during lunch and after school and tallied their results.

This was a solution to the time versus interest problem for this class. It should be mentioned here, however, that for many classes the reporting and exchange of experiences is a perfectly legitimate use of school time. In every English curriculum bulletin there is mention of oral work. What better conversation piece can there be than that in which students have become so involved that they can't be stopped? They are also building ideas, gaining insights, examining attitudes, and becoming involved in a problem which affects their whole lives. Furthermore, they are gathering energy, motivation, and materials for writing.

Now the students had a wide perspective with which to approach "Holding a Baby." Without the wide perspective, the larger issues in the essay are lost to most students. The whole idea of the male's incapability in areas of child rearing is Broun's concern as is what fathers are missing when they do not claim their "half share." The fact that students have collected much data on relevant issues makes the hypothesis inherent in Broun's essay most apparent.

In some cases, teachers read the essay to the class, with the students following their copies. In other instances, students read it after the teacher read the first five paragraphs. If teachers keep in mind the main purpose of reading informal essays—enjoyment—they do not resist turning the essay over to the students only at the point where they can handle it independently.

More than one teacher brought in a doll to introduce the essay. One tenth-grade teacher reported:

> I brought in a rag doll. I picked out the biggest boy in the class and threw it to him, so that he was forced to hold the doll. "Not me!" he cried, and handed it to the next one. First the boys handed the doll around, then the girls. They all concluded the boys don't know how to hold the baby and the girls do.

In such an instance the introduction takes only five or ten minutes. But, what have the students learned? In what way does it prepare them for understanding the basic issues of the essay? How does it help build a broad perspective in which to set the essay? This kind of motivation does not build mastery through understanding. Inherent in motivation is mastery. If the activity does not do this, then it must fall under the category of being a gimmick. It matters not that the students enjoy it. If the teacher wishes to introduce such an activity purely for enjoyment, that is purposeful, but he should be under no illusion that this is motivation or that it advances cognitive development.

Intelligent, fruitful, and pleasurable discussion of the essay requires that the teacher have prepared questions which focus on the central issue as well as on the language and structure of the essay. These questions must be prepared with students as well as the essay in mind. Following is a sequence of questions, though in many instances the teacher need not verbalize them. Some of them may already inherent in what students say as a consequence of a previous question or of an issue they have raised. Students need to be taught to present proof by citing specific sentences in the essay as they initially attempt to grapple with a question. "Proving" helps enhance alertness to language as well as clarification of the issue. Bernstein says, "Send them after answers

to questions raised by the essay. . . . Essays tend to be mild, but you want conten-
tiousness."[19]

1. Do you think the author is a man or a woman? What makes you think so?
2. What is his attitude toward his own sex?
3. If this were a speech, would it be more suitable if it were delivered to a men's club or a women's club? Why? How would men react? Women?
4. Does Broun like children? What evidence can you provide?
5. Is he a good observer of children? Provide evidence.
6. Do you think he has had his "half share?" Provide evidence.
7. What is his hypothesis?
8. What surprises are there?

This kind of question sequence helps students attack the essay directly. These questions permit students to grapple with the author without too much interference from the teacher and to sense the hypothesis posed by the essayist. Questions that call forth controversy inherent in the essay help students understand its essence.

Broun's essay is deceptively simple, especially for younger adolescents who tend to interpret every word literally and are confused by the mood and meaning in satire. Eighth graders thought the author was female because

In the second paragraph it sounds like the author is making fun of men; they can't even sew on a button. Then he says men can't even wash a baby's face.

It wasn't until the teacher introduced the question about whether the idea would best be the subject of a speech before a men's club or a women's club that the heart of the matter could be explored. Then the students practiced saying certain expressions from the essay in a number of ways. Even then, the evidence was clear that the cognitive structure of a number of students was simply not developed sufficiently to accommodate the subtleties of the content and that much work remained to be done.

Joan: He'd definitely tell this to a women's club. In spite of what he says about women enjoying their roles, I think they would welcome the idea of having some help from their husbands.

Rona: Well, he's trying to get men to participate in caring for their children, and it's not going to do much good to tell it to women.

Roco: I think it's something both men and women should hear because he says, "Probably men alone could never have maintained the fallacy of masculine incapacity without the aid of women."

Kitty: I don't understand. Doesn't that just mean that men would be nowhere without women?

Roco: Women support the idea that a man shouldn't hold a baby because they really want to do it all by themselves. It makes them feel important. . . .

Stewart: He observed that men neglected to take part in caring for children, while mothers monopolize the responsibility.

Max: If he wanted to teach people how to hold a baby, this isn't the way to do it. All he needed was to write a manual with pictures showing where to put the hands.

In classes where students had already read at least one previous essay, teachers asked that they examine their primary data again and examine Broun's essay. The purpose was to decide upon an hypothesis he had not handled or about which they had fresh evidence. Some teachers found students enjoyed being paired for this work—one boy and one girl. Broun had made a particular hypothesis. In pairs, the students were prepared to check his or to make others. Some students who still felt unprepared for this activity took a trip to the park to note who was playing with young children, precisely what the adults were doing with them, and whether the adult was male or female.

The kind of essay that permitted this checking of hypotheses and creation of new hypotheses involved students emotionally in the issue and insured enjoyment. Other essays which were suitable for the hypothesizing were Swift's "A Modest Proposal," Benchley's "Now That You're Tanned—What?" and Buchwald's "Don't Be a Pal to Your Son."

Becoming Aware of the Writer's Personality

A third focus for participating in the exploration of the essay is the writer's personality. As Lee stresses, "the writer of an essay is less concerned with presenting facts than with developing ideas and sharing his personal opinions . . . and his attitude toward his subject is of primary importance. . . . The writer's personality and his personal set of values are reflected in the facts and concrete objects which he selects to set up associations."[20] Boas gives strong support to Lee's position, "Chiefly . . . the value of an essay depends upon the personality which it reveals. . . . We value them [great essays] for the most precious of gifts, the revelation of personality . . . the essay gives us the best reflection of what Emerson called God's noblest creation . . . 'man thinking'."[21]

Oral performance is the key to discovering the writer's personality. To discuss the writer's style as the means to this end is relatively fruitless since style involves complexities such as tone, metaphor, irony, and other subtleties. It is oral performance that helps bring out the qualities of which E. O. Shakespeare writes: "The essay, at its best, is superb writing, an art so subtle in structure and language that it appears to be artless. Besides making its point, it gives the intelligent reader all sorts of 'fringe benefits,' the subtle delights of perception and insight that only the best authors seem capable of bringing to light with just the right literary turn of phrase."[22] Oral reading is enriched by the understanding that in former times actors wore masks to depict a character, that such a mask was called a *persona,* and that today we use *persona* to refer to the "mask" with which a writer adorns himself when he writes. With this knowledge, Thurber's and other informal essayists' "performances" become more meaningful. Brasher attempts to unmask the importance of the persona:

> The writer's persona is the imagined speaker, the voice in the words. . . . Informal style . . . has a highly developed persona or sense of the author. . . . Our sense of the author is heard as a voice. Writing always has a voice in it; informal style emphasizes the personal in that voice. . . . Writing is a form of speaking.[23]

Thus, the essay is drama of a sort. The "mask" helps depict how the author feels about his subject. The illustrations he offers are ingredients of the "voice." Is he an "either-or" man or does he hold to the middle ground? What do you gather about his temperament? his intolerances? his understanding of people? his observations?

The availability of Thurber's essays and the brevity and consistency of style and format within certain groupings of his essays made the teaching of the personality factor through his works a rewarding enterprise in most instances. Thurber was a favorite of teachers who attempted to deal with the personality revelation of the essayist. "The Shrike and the Chipmunks" and "The Peacelike Mongoose" were read by more classes than were any other Thurber essays. The former permitted students to continue the topic of "Sex Roles" in those classes where interest still ran high.

The fact that Thurber appealed to students does not mean that the implications in Thurber's essays are easily grasped. For example, after students in a ninth-grade class performed "The Shrike and the Chipmunks," a brief discussion revealed some of the causes of misinterpretations.

Gloria: That's a short story, not an essay.
Herbert: An essay is supposed to give an opinion. This is an opinion, but a kind of paradox on it. It gives a moral, so it's a fable.

Gloria: There are characters in here and there's a plot. Now, to me, as soon as you have characters and plot, you no longer have an essay.

At this point the teacher explained the diversity of form of the genre.

Teacher: When you read the essay, you made me feel most sorry for the female chipmunk. Is that how you felt?
Catherine: Yes, because her husband was such a lazy good-for-nothing slob.
Paul: But she was so pushy, always on his back to do this and that. I bet he was sick of her and wanted to rebel.
Edward: I'm not sure I understand the whole point of it. Everything you expect to go right goes wrong, and everything you expect to go wrong goes right.
Teacher: Could you be more specific?
Edward: When the chipmunk can't find his studs and stuff, you expect that something bad will happen since he couldn't go to the banquet, but instead it saves his life.
Paul: And it was a good thing the doorway got clogged with laundry and dirty dishes.

To help students examine more closely the central idea of the essay, the teacher asked them to list all events as they occurred, to write the letter M if it happened to the male and F if it happened to the female, and to suggest whether Thurber meant each occurrence to be positive or negative (P or N). One group listed the following specifics:

The male arranged nuts artistically.	M	P
The female wanted many piled up.	F	N
She told him to do it her way and be wealthy.	F	N
He refused to let her interfere.	M	P
She flew into a rage and left him.	F	N
She threatened, "The shrike will get you."	F	N
She called him helpless.	F	N
He can't find his studs.	M	?

He can't go to the banquet.	M	?
He remains alive.	M	P
The shrike can't get into the clogged doorway.	M	P
Chipmunk slept all day.	M	?
He had breakfast after dark.	M	?
He went out for air after dark.	M	P
The shrike got bumped and killed.	M	P
Female returned.	F	?
She saw the mess in the house.	F	?
She shook her husband.	F	N
She said, "What would you do without me?"	F	N
"I'd go on living," he said.	M	P
"You wouldn't last five days."	F	N
She cleaned the house.	F	P
She got him up.	F	?
She said he needs exercise.	F	?
She took him for a walk in the sun.	F	N
They are killed.	F	N

Then they examined the full-class "data" to decide Thurber's values and attitude toward the battle of the sexes.

> Janice: He's a male chauvinist. I've read other things he wrote, and he has a really crummy opinion of women.
> Teacher: Do you think that crummy opinion comes through to the reader in this essay?
> Janice: Sure. The female chipmunk is like a typical middle-class wife who works her husband really hard so that she can live in luxury. Her husband just wants to be left alone.
> Teacher: But that's not the way you read it. Does Thurber find fault only with the female? Look at your chart.
> Godfrey: He knows that the husband was stupid for letting the wife push him around.
> Paul: That's probably why they both get killed at the end. They're both fools.
> Cynthia: Maybe Thurber thinks the tragedy never would have happened if the male was in more control.

Instead of making a chart, after their oral reading some students drew creatures to represent Mr. and Mrs. Chipmunk. Each student explained why he made his creature this way; the class concentrated on whether they thought Thurber would agree and how they knew this.

> Helen: Isn't that an illustration of the shrike up there? And the male and female chipmunks have little paws? She's got long eyelashes. She's pink. It's humorous and light, like the essay.
> Debbie: She's blue in the face. She's the *blue* one.

> Teacher: Pick out words from the essay that reveal the hardness underneath and the seeming innocence and softness of "Once upon a time."

> Carl: She seems the superior one, but Thurber doesn't sound so fond of women, so I think it's tongue in cheek.

Helen: He's a male chauvinist pig.
Mike: She's set on making him work, by gosh.
Helen: He can choose!
Mike: Oh, can he? That's debatable.
Helen: He did choose not to let her interrupt his designs. He's not that much of a weakling.

Jean: Nobody gets a name but *Stoop*. It's interesting. It's for *stupid*. It's a hard word. Thurber likes those words. *Stoop* is named because he's symbolic of all the stupid things that happen to all the unnamed people of the world.

Carl: There's premonition here too. He says, I'll go on living, I guess. He guesses!

They discussed why Thurber used the fable as a medium, what effect it had, and what it revealed about Thurber.

Helen: Thurber sure masks himself. He doesn't dare come out and say, Look how harsh women are; poor little meek long-suffering men.

Additional Thurber essays that were well received by students studying sex roles or other topics such as conformity in modern society or dehumanization in the modern world were "The Unicorn in the Garden,"[24] "Courtship through the Ages," "The Very Proper Gander," and "The Rabbits Who Caused All the Trouble." Each one lends itself to oral performance for the discovery of the persona.

EXAMINING STRUCTURE

The organization of an essay is part and parcel of the persona. Students learn much about the author from discovering for themselves his organization, even while they learn to use such an essay as a model for their own writing. A tenth-grade class used cartoons or diagrams to highlight the organization of Thurber's "The Peacelike Mongoose." One boy drew a series of buildings surrounding his peacelike mongoose—a public building representing tradition, the mongoose's house in which lived the family, a motel to house the strangers, and a courthouse. Out of each window stared eyes, all in the mongoose's direction; and mouths were obvious, each having its own comment. Other students drew actual diagrams with lines, blocks, or circles, or lines and triangles, each accounting for different incidents and showing the relationship to the main theme. Still others tried a tree with trunk, branches, and twigs. Some even included roots.

Regardless of the format, the activity caused careful reading and rereading, as well as analysis of relationship between main idea and details. Perhaps most important was the students' grasp of a sense of style which is an integral part of the author's personality. Evidence of their understanding lies in comments students made about their diagrams.

Eleanor: Thurber's essay starts out like a fairy tale so that if I didn't read the rest, I would have thought it would end like a fairy tale. That shift in feeling is a surprise, and I had trouble making a simple consistent diagram. That's why I used partly curvy soft lines and then hard blocks.

Fay: Fairy tales usually end with, "They lived happily ever after," but here that's not what happened at the end, so I tried to use pastels and harsh colors in my diagram.

Grace: It has an innocent, childlike flavor at first. It has animals like in children's books and everything just happened to happen. That's why I diagrammed mine in the form of a book.

Herbert: The satire is there right in the beginning. He has to kill cobras. It's like Vietnam. It's your duty to go and kill or be killed. So, I used a series of bomber planes dropping bombs on the poor little mongoose, and the way I arranged them shows the structure.

Gloria: His "why" is like ours, the younger people. We're questioning and challenging the traditional ideas. Why should generals be adorned for fighting and killing? Why is it an honor to die fighting? So I had emblems for each of his critics and a chain on the corner of them tied to him.

Parker: Thurber is angry. The animals who talk provide a contrast and actually show up his anger. He's angry at society for maintaining its stupid traditions and forcing everyone into a mold. So, my diagram is Thurber. He's yelling. Each yell is one after another at the people who are abusing the mongoose.

Students had no difficulty with the satire in the essay, nor the juxtaposition of harshness and innocence. As a matter of fact, teachers found this essay one of the best for teaching the "voice" of the essayist.

Thurber's "The Trouble with Man Is Man" was used successfully to help students gain an appreciation of metaphor and simile. The students enjoyed his use of animals in statements such as "The human being says the beast in him has been aroused. . . ."; "It is our species, and not any other, that goes out on wildcat strikes"; "the cock-and-bull story was not invented by the cock and the bull"; "The detective smells a rat and begins pussyfooting around." One teacher introduced the essay by asking students to recall expressions in which animals are used to describe people. "You smell like a skunk," "She eats like a bird," "He eats like a pig," "She's fat as a horse," "She's a bird brain" were among those offered by students. Students enjoyed the essay largely because it gave them a new slant on a familiar phenomenon. In addition, they were intrigued with attempts to explain why people use particular animals to inflate "the already inflated human ego by easy denigration of the other species." They asked, "Why is it a shark that is used in the expression loan shark?" Why "cocksure," "rat race," "dog eat dog"? What is the meaning of each of these expressions? What is the characteristic of the animal that causes people to use him in this way? Thus, focusing on animals in metaphor helped to uncover structure.

Thurber's "How the Kooks Crumble," an "indictment of radio" for reveling "in news items of horror, terror, catastrophe, and calamity" and for having commercials "read by the reporters in exactly the same tone as the calamities, thus giving the listener the spooky feeling that the deaths of scores of persons in an air crash are no more important than a new candy bar . . ." was another favorite. A number of teachers introduced this essay with a prior assignment for students to listen to a fifteen-minute news broadcast. Students listed the items reported and noted briefly in writing their feelings as these items were reported. In some classes, the listening was done during class time, using a taped program. In other cases, teachers asked students to bring in newspapers so that the reports could be compared with the radio broadcasts.

After the oral reading of the essay, a discussion was held about the central idea. One ninth-grade class felt Thurber was concerned with brainwashing.

Stanley: Brainwashing is a really serious matter.

Tom: Brainwashing is as bad as guerilla warfare. Why was this written in such a funny manner? It's tragic, not funny.

Susan: If someone says something in a serious way, you don't listen. If you get him to laugh, you may get to him.

Vivian: It's like the ads against cancer. They used to show the diseased skin on TV. People couldn't bear it. So, the advertisers switched to "kick the habit" because people listen to light stuff. They block out horrors.

After some discussion, students categorized their findings into optimistic and pessimistic news items and tried to assess the difference in sheer volume. Then they went back to Thurber's essay to compare their findings and feelings with his. In several classes, teachers asked students to cut out ten major new items from the newspaper and to arrange them into positive and negative piles. The difference in volume was astonishing, all in favor of the negative.

Teachers discussed the results of their teaching of "How the Kooks Crumble."

Thurber hits this subject hard. Students hear so much bad news they become oblivious to it, as with the tragedies in Vietnam and Cambodia.

Or they are instilled with fear. There's an all over fear, a nameless fear. Thurber didn't express this, but they did as they compared his persona with their own.

Apathy is the bad thing. It comes from so much bad news. They can't conceive of it. The enormity of it is just beyond conception. They cannot conceive of that kind of catastrophe [Vietnam and Cambodia].

We decided to make up a program and broadcast it on closed circuit. We called it "no news is good news." Students proposed ways they wanted news reported. They cited parts of Thurber's essay as they introduced their program, and the school was all agog.

There's a program on channel 7 which includes awful things that go on in hospitals; yet they are always clowning around, and I can't figure out for myself whether it's good to make things light against such horrible incidents, or whether it's bad because things are so serious.

I was sometimes baffled about how to guide students reading Thurber. Really, what are his values? When he juxtaposes these things so closely, you don't know which is the calamity. The same tone and voice and the closeness of the various items on radio take away from the disastrous feeling. The same is true with Thurber. He desensitizes. We are all so jaded, bitter, and concerned with the negative aspects of society and of life. Where is the optimism?

White has a reply to the concerns of these teachers:

There is a deep vein of melancholy running through everyone's life and . . . the humorist, perhaps more sensible of it than some others, compensates for it actively and positively.

Humorists fatten on trouble. They have always made trouble pay. . . . The world likes humor, but it treats it patronizingly. . . . It feels that if a thing is funny it can be presumed to be something less than great, because if it were truly great it would be wholly serious."[25]

Thus, a study of contrasting elements in an essay not only revealed something of its structure but also raised new questions in the minds of teachers.

One method of analyzing structure is through the use of the cartoon. Teachers used a "Peanuts" cartoon in which "Sweetie" expounds on the injustices of the school's marking system. It didn't take students long to recognize that the cartoon is virtually an essay. Some teachers used it as a means of examining the structure and organization of an essay they were studying. Students enjoyed tremendously the use of the cartoon with Thurber's essays. The teacher suggested the use of stick figures so that those who couldn't draw were not frightened away from the activity. With the cartoon they had little trouble portraying the "wolf-in-sheep's-clothing" language and were also able to analyze relationships between details and main idea.

More Writing

Thurber's fablelike essays are excellent as models for writing, and writing does wonders for understanding structure. Students have problems differentiating the traditional school composition from the essay. Thurber's essays are short and yet use tremendous amounts of detail to illustrate a point. Once students have the experience of modeling their essay after one of his, they tend to be freed from the old habit of plunging themselves into a composition consisting of a series of generalizations.

Students checked the newspaper to gather articles in which animals are used as Thurber noted and created cartoon-essays for those articles that could be catalysts for neo-Thurber essays. One article was headed "New Watchdog on Oil Spills." Although the students lived on the shore and were aware of the great number of oil spills, the headlines made no sense to them without the teacher's assistance in interpretation.

The Thurber enthusiasts also tended to read many more of his essays than were introduced by the teacher. When they fashioned their creations after him, they conveyed to the reader the distinct feeling that the writing was a thoroughly enjoyable experience. A ninth grader wrote:

Once upon a time a rabette found she was pregnant and tried to unearth a place where she could have an abortion. Word spread around that she didn't want to give birth to her baby. "But," said the Elders, "it is the duty of every rabette to have the baby once conceived, or be banished."

"Why?" asked the rabette. "Rabet doesn't want to be his father, and he doesn't want to be my husband, and I don't want to be his wife, and I don't want any Rabettini's."

"She's a tramp," cried Rabette's father.

"She's pregnant," cried her mother.

"She's a fetus killer," shouted her brother.

"She's prolific," whispered her sister.

Strangers who knew nothing about her wrote her up in the newspapers and said they had seen her plotting against the religion of the State.

"My body is my own business, and I have the right to bear only *wanted* children," argued Rabette.

"Right is four-fifths the same as might," said a neighbor.

"Right is five-thirteenths of responsibility," said another.

"Right is five-sixths murder."

Finally, the rumor spread that Rabette had influence on other teen-agers and if she were permitted to go on, the whole fabric of society would become corrupt. So, she was tried, convicted by a show of traditions, and condemned to carry—the battle of the fetus into the next generation.

Moral: The bearer knows best where the fetus hurts.

There were other essays and fables students enjoyed at different intervals in their secondary school career. Students read Aesop's fables and considered questions such as, How are animals used to explain human actions? and Why does Aesop use animals in this way? White's "About Myself" is also suitable for the creative discovery of structure and as a model for student writing. Older adolescents enjoy conversing with White as they write essays in his manner. Additional favorites as writing models were Benchley's "My Face" and "Take the Witness!" Buchwald's "The Children Are Restless," "Richard the Third (With No Apologies to Shakespeare)," and Orwell's "Shooting an Elephant," all of which inspired a number of complementary essays. Thurber's "Courtship through the Ages" appealed to older students as a model but did not interest most younger ones. Thurber's "University Days" and Day's "Father Opens My Mail" provoked a good deal of student reaction in writing within all grades on the secondary level.

Buchwald's "Don't Be a Pal to Your Son" was responsible for a number of creative challenges entitled "Don't Be a Son to Your Father." His "Politeness Is Not Dead"[26] stirred a group of seventh graders in an inner-city school to keep a record of what happened when they behaved politely. The astonished teacher discovered that the majority thought politeness meant doing a kind deed for someone. They listed things such as "not yelling at my mother," "helping with packages," "staying with a friend when she was crying," "asking Grandmother if she needed anything at the store," and "taking the dog out." It is certainly a fact that every new experience for students was an eye-opener for teachers and thus served as a diagnostic technique for those teachers who were interested in determining what were the next steps in the cognitive development of students.

Photographic "essays," too, proved worthy when students sought ways of expressing their ideas. For this purpose Leavitt and Sohn's *Stop, Look and Write!* was useful because it is inexpensive and contains photos in sequence as well as photos which challenge thought. Elkins' "Man on the Move" served the same purpose and offered the advantage of photos large enough for several students to examine simultaneously.

The fact that students are not able to read well is no reason whatsoever for depriving them of experiences in literature which they are able to appreciate and enjoy. Teachers devised ways of handling individual differences, especially in classrooms where reading skills were a deterrent. The tape recorder in this case provided what virtually constituted a second teacher. Students listened to the essay while their eyes followed the words in print. Later, they taped their own brief reactions. The teacher was freed to work with other students who still had not reached this degree of independence in learning, while a third group was collecting data for an essay on "Coping with the Cafeteria." A fourth group was working on "Peanuts" cartoons, trying to determine which ones offered the best possibilities for their own essays. One student was writing a Thurber-like essay about a *verk*.

After experiencing the processes described in this chapter, most students eventually were able to handle appropriate essays without the direct concrete experiences of interviewing or paying compliments. They called upon their previous experiences through memory and imagination. Such a result was a long-term achievement for both teachers and students.

Teachers need to know that it is noneducative to push for the main idea of an essay until the students have explored what happened in the essay. When the teacher reads to students, he can assist them in overcoming comprehension problems created by authors' innuendos and unfamiliar language. Students on all levels need the kinds of concrete experiences described in this chapter, so they can converse with the essayist and create essays of their own. There exist essays which students can enjoy thoroughly so long as teachers are aware of Highet's caution about an essay having "two purposes —to interest its readers and to inform them; but it is far more important that it should interest them."[27]

Essay writing gave the student a sense of his own worth; he learned he had ideas that were good enough for a conversation with the essayist. He did not feel pressured to be creative in the same sense that a short story or a play demands creativity. He had only to hold a point of view and to make a case for it. The highest compliment to the procedures that inspired writing came from a tenth-grade boy who, having read his essay on "Fact and Opinion" to a group of peers, commented that this was his "first self-satisfying essay."

Biography

In many instances there were students who preferred the biography over any other genre. The very first book one group of inner-city students read voluntarily was a "skinny" biography of Dr. Martin Luther King. "Is it true?" and "Did it really happen?" were the criteria for the selection of the follow-up works. Wagenknecht's observations support the notion of the increasing popularity of the biography. "But if our times have given the deathblow to the essay, they have, on the other hand, made biography more popular than it has ever been before."[28]

For evidence that the biography is of increasing interest today, one need only to examine any issue of *The New York Times Book Review* or the shelves of the biography section of a public library or a well-stocked paperback bookstore. Yet, surprisingly, one can flip through a half dozen consecutive issues of the *English Journal* and find not one article on biography.

IS IT LITERATURE?

The issue of whether biography is literature or history has been raised by teachers and pursued by critics. Brooks, Purser, and Warren take the position that because "the decisive element here is not the mere use of facts," because the biographer must "order his facts into a pattern" in order to "make them fit into a logic growing out of the character of the man," and because "his picture of the man is arrived at . . . by an act of the imagination," biography is "beyond ordinary history." It "tends to give a more complete and coherent picture of character in action and invites . . . an imaginative involvement that makes for dramatic tension." Thus, "the story tends to be, in the emotional sense, rounder, the problems of human values more fully explored." It is the biographer's process of interpretation of facts and his use of imagination, despite the requirement of accuracy, which "brings us into the realm of literary values."[29]

Sauer takes a different view: "Biography is not a literary type. Actually, it is a form of history made somewhat literary by the author's selection and interpretation of the events he includes in his work and, in the case of some biographers, by the manner of his writing style."[30] Wagenknecht[31] agrees with Sauer about the ordinary biography being out of the realm of literature, but he recognizes that it is still an important genre.

Woolf makes a very strong case for the biography as art, though she recognizes the restricted nature of this genre. "Yet on that lower level the work of the biographer is invaluable; we cannot thank him sufficiently for what he does for us. For we are incapable of living wholly in the intense world of the imagination." "Sober fact" is the "proper food" for "the tired imagination."[32] Bernstein supports her with his thesis that "you are not asking students to feel or emphathize, but to *know.*"[33]

Thrall and Hibbard appear to take a stand on the middle ground. The biography in their view must be "an accurate history" and yet "must make some effort to interpret these facts in such a way as to present character and habits of mind . . . it must emphasize personality. And this personality must be the central thesis of the book." When the biographer uses anecdotes or letters, he must use only those which "reflect this central conception of personality."[34]

Here lies an important focus in teaching the biography: How can it be that two biographers writing about the same person present two different perspectives on the man? Lewis and Sisk agree that this seeming dilemma presents a "plus" to the teacher. The intricacies of character become the central issue for student examination, discovery, and appreciation. "Their good qualities are there for admiration, their bad qualities for wonder. Here is occasion to make students aware of the strange and contrasting strands of character that exist within human beings."[35]

BEGINNINGS: THE AUTOBIOGRAPHY

Before complexities of character and comparisons between biographies can be made, the teacher has much building to do despite the fact that Sauer believes one cannot teach the biography. "In a way there is no such thing as the *teaching* of biography. We read biographies and share our pleasure with others as we relay exciting stories about the people of whose lives we read accounts."[36] Perhaps other educators agree, judging from the scant elaboration of procedures in methods books for teachers.

Actually, teaching the biography presents unique problems and opportunities for enjoyment and cognitive development. As with the essay, the biography requires that students engage in processes similar to those of the biographer. First, of course, is the autobiography, with the diary being a suitable starter. The teacher should read excerpts from *Anne Frank: The Diary of a Young Girl* or *Go Ask Alice* to highlight not only their relationship to biography but also the importance of primary documents. When students become acquainted with excerpts from diaries of adolescents, their own attempts to set down events and reactions to events gain significance and dignity. What shall go into them? These are secret documents. Why does the writer keep them under lock and key?

When students keep diaries, their confidentiality must be respected by the teacher and by peers. Some students choose not to surrender their diaries, even to the teacher. Students should know beforehand that if they feel this way about whatever happens to them in the four days of diary keeping (two school days and a weekend), their wish *not* to turn in the diary will be honored. A four-day diary offers quite sufficient data for teacher's and students' purposes. Anything longer than that can become tiresome. Some students need help in structuring the content. For example, they can focus on an aspect of their lives which is of great concern to them. Other students require a time structure rather than a thematic one. For those, the division of the day gives confidence in finding their way into a diary: What did you do as soon as you woke up and until you arrived at school? During the lunch hour? After school until supper time? After supper until you went to bed? Often students needed reminders of the types of detail that should be appropriate: With whom did you do these things? Did you enjoy them? Wish they'd happen again? Wish they'd never happened? Did you enjoy talking with anyone that day? What made you feel that way? The diary helps students to become involved in biography as a genre, gives them a feeling for the kind of detail that is needed to reveal a personality, and helps them with later understandings. They learn later that even famous men may not have spent a childhood much different from theirs. That thought is a morale booster.

Some students permitted teachers to read aloud excerpts from their diaries, often anonymously. These were used to give peers an opportunity to assess whether personality was revealed in the style and in the incidents related. Teachers read the diaries and prepared a list of topics which anonymous students were concerned with as revealed by the diaries. The list was presented to the students. They wondered at the tremendous range of topics. "You are a pretty interesting class!" remarked one teacher and led them to decide for themselves which aspects they would be interested in looking for when they read biographies. The teacher then read another excerpt from an anonymous diary and patterns of writing were discussed. What would you still like to know about this person? A host of questions bubbled forth. What purpose would the answers to these questions serve? Students categorized the questions, and patterns were thus revealed.

The teacher introduced excerpts from biographies. Especially appropriate at this point were Parks' *A Choice of Weapons,* Morris' *Brian Piccolo: A Short Season* and Killilea's *With Love from Karen.* These biographies describe human beings with joys as well as problems of loneliness, stresses, and strains of one kind or another. In these three instances the details were known personally to the author because the account was either autobiographical or written by someone in a close relationship to the person.

Some teachers introduced the autobiography by setting up a series of topics of great moment to the students: "My Room," "A Half Hour with Pop," "Supper at My House," "When My Family Goes on an Outing," "The TV Crisis," "That Dog of Mine," "I Wish," "My Worries," "What I Like about Me," "What Others Like about Me," "A Moment of Hope," "Fears," "Being Somebody," and a host of other open-ended topics. Students selected those of greatest significance for them and wrote accounts which, when put together, reflected something about their lives and constituted the beginnings of an autobiography. The thematic account was successful in that it avoided the usual starter, "I was born in Halcyon Hospital on April 15, 1961." It gave structure to the autobiography and yet permitted each student to include what was of interest to him. It provided opportunity for combining incidents and ideas in such a way as to give meaning and wholeness to the final work. The teacher's chief task at this point seemed to be to help students understand that the incidents they reveal are those which make it possible for the author to know himself; he is in fact conversing with himself. "Talking to myself" became an intriguing project from which grew a class biography in one instance complete with photos and cartoons. The process of making a table of contents, a foreword, a preface, and an index took students into biographical collections like Kieszak's *Turning Point.* The students' book was entitled *Who's Who,* although *We're Leaving* and *Look Us Up Ten Years from Now* were close competitors for the title.

The project raised issues such as, How much should a biographer tell? Why do people want to know about other people? If the person is still living, does that make a difference in what is revealed? *Should* it make a difference? The students were working on the autobiography but moved easily back and forth in their thinking and questioning between the biography and the autobiography.

PLAYING THE ROLE OF BIOGRAPHER

Another problem students needed to undertake was, How does a biographer secure information about a person whom he knows well, but not well enough? Students assumed the role of a biographer. This was achieved in a number of different ways. In one class each student wrote a true sentence about "The time I _____," with the aim of writing something that would attract attention when it was read to other students. Students grouped themselves around the classmates whose escapades they wanted to know more about, and in groups interviewed that person for whom they wanted to play biographer. At first the questions asked were solely those that happened to come to mind at the spur of the moment. As a result students had difficulty writing their account about the life of the chosen person. Questions were then structured with the help of the teacher and a second round of interviews was held.

There was much to write. Students were interested in their chosen character and only technical writing difficulties were encountered. The procedure is fraught with problems. Unless the teacher knows the sociometric setup of the group, some students who have offered themselves as "subjects" will have no biographers. Some teachers simply grouped students sociometrically for this activity; others selected the one outstanding experience and, with the consent of the author, used it as the subject while the rest of the class played biographer.

The writing served a number of purposes. Most important was the fact that no two biographers saw the "subject" in the same light. Each highlighted a different incident or placed a different interpretation upon a particular incident. This fact drew mixed feelings from students. "How did you get that from what he said?" One class drew the conclusion that they simply didn't know enough; therefore, they were reading into a particular incident. As a result of playing biographer to their peers, students had these reactions:

Daphne: I learned many new and wonderful things about new and wonderful people.

Michael: None of us put everything down. It must be that all biographies are biased because you can't put everything down.

Carmen: I didn't know there was that much to tell about myself! They kept asking questions, and I kept talking and talking.

Darlene: I'd rather listen to her than write!

Carl: That could be a chapter in a book. All the incidents could be a separate chapter, especially the one about the phone call.

Mirtha: I don't think our group was very selective in what we wanted. So, we didn't ask the right questions. Ours could have been as interesting as theirs, but we didn't ask the right questions. When Jack wrote his autobiography, we could see that. He could choose, because he had endless resources. He knew what to select, because he knew what happened to himself. But we didn't.

Lucille: I don't agree with that. A biography is different; it's not supposed to be an autobiography. The people who write autobiographies were more emotional.

Michael: You get caught up in what the autobiographies were saying. The people who wrote biographies have to dig deep to really get to know the person so they have the goods.

Pamela: You have to dig deep to find out about yourself sometimes.

Mirtha: Our questionnaire wasn't good enough. We really didn't know what we were after. We have to decide.

Peter: Even so, everyone had their own beginning. Mine was like an introduction to a person's life. Gladys did hers chronologically, and Beth did an interpretation.

Beth: That's how I got into trouble.

Lois: The information you gave was wrong. I didn't say what you said.

Beth: I was reading Thorne's *Madame Curie* and I'm sure the things that were written about her childhood weren't real facts. Maybe they were based in facts, but they were interpretations.

Lois: That's OK. But not about where someone was born.

Jeffrey: Well, she said her relatives were from Ireland, so Beth figured her parents were from Ireland, but they weren't.

David: Mine was more earthy than the others. I concentrated on the conflict she had in her childhood.

Eloise: She was fun to write about because she picked out little incidents which tell a lot about herself. It's very human—how she bathes her baby brother and accepts her younger sister.

Helen: It was really good. It was unified as she told it. It begins with the perfect child and ends up in a glory of the imperfect. It's like what we said about biography—there's bad and there's good in everybody.

Ed: I had the feeling that in the biography of Albert Schweitzer, the author was twisting facts to make them fit his point of view. I had the feeling some people were doing that in this class, too.

Beth: There's always a bias in biography. You can't put everything down. When you pick something and skip something else, you are showing your bias.

Thus, students were evolving for themselves a number of ingredients in a good biography. They were on the threshold of understanding what critics have had to say about biography.

1. "The biographer should avoid building up his central figure as a logical being. There is no logic in life or in living persons."[37]
2. "A biographer is not a court record nor a legal document. He is a human being, and his temperament, his own point of view, and his frame of reference are unconsciously imposed upon the man he is writing about . . . there is no such thing as a completely objective human being. . . . You will never succeed in getting at the truth if you think you know ahead of time, what the truth ought to be."[38]
3. "The chief disadvantage that all biographers share, I think, is ignorance, ignorance of what actually took place in the hero's life. . . . Some of the jars and accidents of the hero's daily life we may know, but what about the inspirations and sudden insights that enabled him to rise above them? the subject himself can seldom recall the answers. . . ."[39]

The students' first biographies were by no means spectacular works of art, but there were a number of spirited ones. Typical was the biography of Robert, a tenth grader who knew the school classified him as "an average student":

Bang! bang! boom!! go the firecrackers and ash cans, whiz go the sky rockets, it's always very noisy on the 4th of July. The only place there is peace and quiet is in a hospital. As a matter of fact in 1962 on the 4th of July in Central General Hospital a baby boy was born to Mr. & Mrs. Penya, who already had a two-year-old girl, Philomena. The Penyas named this baby Robert. Since the day Robert was born he always had accidents, for example at the age of three Robert slid down the slidingpond head first, not knowing he cut himself bad he ran into the house to tell his mother about his great trick. When she saw the blood all over Robert's head she almost fainted, she rushed Robert to the doctor and the doctor fixed it all up. Another accident happened when he was at his four-year-old birthday party. Robert and his friends were watching television when his mother called out, "Does anybody want soda?" He ran into the kitchen where his father was sitting on a stool with a lit cigarette, he ran right into the cigarette, Robert was rushed to the hospital right away. The doctor put a patch on his eye, he had to wear the patch a couple of months.

From the first day of school Robert had many problems. In kindergarten he was the smallest boy in his class, so when they were graduating kindergarten Robert was the first on line, he led the boys the wrong way and messed the whole ceremony up. In the first grade Robert had kidney problems, he always went to the bathroom in his pants, but he got over that in a few months. In the second and third grade Robert had these two teachers who were very mean, so he didn't really learn anything because the teachers were always too busy yelling at the boys and girls. In the fourth grade Robert could not learn anything because he was in love with his teacher. In the fifth grade all the way up to the ninth grade Robert fooled around a lot. In the ninth and tenth grade Robert's marks started getting better because he liked the school, Central High, very much. Robert is now in the middle of the tenth grade.

....His intentions are to get married and have two kids, he only wants two kids because when he and his wife die there will only be two kids, this way he doesn't add to the population explosion. He wants to go into the movie business and become an actor. . . . That is Robert's life up to today, who knows what he will be or what he will do in the future.

In one class a college professor who was a poet in his own right was invited to be the "subject" of student biographies and to be subjected to the class interview. There was a flurry of activity in preparation for his visit. One activity was creating an interview schedule. It is interesting to note the questions that concern young adolescents:

1. What stories did your parents tell about the memorable things that happened to mark your birth?
2. Did your mother and father always fuss over you? Did they think you were a cute baby?
3. Did your own parents raise you or were you raised by someone else?
4. What is the full name your parents gave you? Do you use your full name?
5. Did you have a tough childhood?
6. Where were your parents from?
7. What one event in your childhood do you remember best?
8. Do you have the same personality you had as a child? How have you changed?
9. In school, were you an average student?
10. What was your best subject in high school?
11. What is your religion? Do you practice your religion?
12. Do you have many friends? Do they bother you when you try to make up poems?
13. Are you married? Do you have any children?
14. Who was the person that influenced you most to write poetry?
15. How old were you when you began to write poetry?
16. Do you have any pets?
17. When you were our age, did you have any hobbies? Sports?
18. Have you ever tried pot, wacky weed, or any drug?
19. What is the thing you wish for most?

Teachers found it necessary to help students try out answers to questions. If questions did not elicit anything but a bare fact, or a "yes" or "no" reply, were students satisfied? Were they seeking incidents? Then what questions would elicit the recounting of happenings? The teacher read incidents from the life of Gandhi or Father Damien, and students tried to word questions to which these incidents were virtual answers.

Other teachers made the procedure even simpler. They asked students to enlist the aid of parents who contacted local celebrities they knew. Community people on the whole were willing to take three students into their home or office and to permit them to interview a relative or a secretary. They helped students to gain a sense of an hour in a typical day and permitted them to read clippings from the local newspaper about them.

One teacher used himself as the subject of the students' biographies, answering students' questions, bringing in photos of himself at various stages in his life, and letting them read articles by and about him from previous editions of the school newspaper. He made it possible for one small group to interview his mother, another his wife, a third his son, a fourth former students, a fifth other teachers. Actually, the work on the teacher's biography was far more rewarding for students than the activity of bringing in an outside resource person.

READING BIOGRAPHY

Student findings gleaned from their diaries or their peer biographics were categorized and tallied. The resulting summary formed the basis of a discussion to determine the focus on which students would like to concentrate as they read biographies of their own choosing. A number of students were already deeply engrossed in reading a biography that the teacher had introduced incidentally. A few of the most successful themes included "Man against the Odds," "Success and Failure," "I Have a Dream," "A Choice of Weapons," "Man in All His Complexity," "I'm a Unique Man," "I Want to Be Somebody," and "A Break with Tradition." The thematic approach was necessary. The topic chosen was broad enough for the teacher to give students relatively free reign not only to make their own selection of a biography but to decide how and with whom they would share these. Since all of these topics were evolved from their diaries, the connection between the introductory experiences and the individual readings was firm, and thus aided the grasp of new materials.

Through the biographies they read, students discovered concepts such as "there are many factors which contribute to the making of a great man"; "there are many stresses and strains an individual endures before he arrives"; "there arc scores of people and happenings which influence a character"; "no individual is all good or all evil and even great men have weaknesses"; "what one individual regards as success may not be an aspiration of another individual"; "all human beings have aspirations which when thwarted show an effect in their behavior"; "a person's values can be detected in what he does and in what he wants." These discoveries were not stated in this manner by students, but students gave evidence that these generalizations had been formulated. Almost all of the biographies they read elaborated these generalizations, especially *Choice of Weapons* by Parks, *My Lord, What a Morning* by Anderson and *With Love from Karen* by Kellilea.

The thematic approach permitted thirty-five students who were reading almost thirty-five different books to meet on common ground. When students were considering the topic "A Choice of Weapons," they and the teacher formulated questions to be considered in panel discussions: What "weapons" did the character have at his disposal? Which ones gave him the strongest push toward greatness—the physical or the psychological weapons? Who were the people in his life that gave him strength? What incidents in his life provided psychological weapons? What was there within him that made him a unique man? Which of all the "weapons" does the biographer seem to feel was most responsible for his outstanding achievements? With such a sequence of questions students who had read Preston's *Martin Luther King,* Parks' *Choice of Weapons,* Bryan's *Susan B. Anthony* and Dooley's *The Edge of Tomorrow* could comfortably discuss common issues in a panel presentation and discussion. When the presentation was concluded, all students could contribute their offerings of new insights about the same issues, because all books held these issues in common. In addition, even before the panel discussions, the teacher could stimulate thought about what students were reading. When the teacher brought in brief biographical sketches of Marilyn Monroe, Cassius Clay, or Albert Schweitzer, all of which raised questions pertaining to "weapons," she asked, "As far as you've read in your book, do things seem to be happening in a similar way, or are they turning out differently?" Thus, students were constantly feeding information to the group, with a daily sense of achievement because each one was the sole possessor of that particular piece of information.

In a number of instances teachers were able to secure filmstrips of famous people with coordinated recording of music and oral account of his life. Martin Luther King was a favorite. Students often chose to read biographies of people about whom audio-visual materials could be secured. They read the biography, in small groups previewed the filmstrips, and then decided together what important incidents in or aspects of his life had been omitted by the filmstrip. Their own account focused on the omissions. Usually, students were delighted with themselves. The tales they told were more interesting than those on the recording in most instances, and in some cases they dramatized situations from the life of their subject. In other words, they used the film for their own information and as a stimulus for creative presentation. Only four or five minutes of class time were devoted to watching the filmstrip and listening to the recording. The biographies they read had far more fascinating tales to tell, and they as a group had more creative ideas for presentation.

In another class a few students used a 16 mm movie. The group who had read the biography spent long periods after school watching the movie over and over to decide how they could substitute themselves for the sound track. When the day arrived for their report to the class, they presented the movie without "canned" sound; they were the sound track. It was a real performance, and, as the appreciative classmates evaluated it, was "almost like choral reading."

It should be clarified at this point that the preceding introductory procedures were appropriate and enjoyable for all students on all levels. But there came the time when some students were able to deal with more complex questions. For example, they read at least two biographies about a favorite character such as Martin Luther King, Marian Anderson, or Tom Dooley and tossed around questions such as, What did each biographer omit, neglect? Why? What might this tell you about the biographer? the subject? Did the biographer like the subject? What induced him to select that particular person? Did this biography cause you to change your mind about any ideas you held? Did it give you a new point of view about anything? Students were able to go on a hunt for principles such as oversimplification. Does the biographer imply that Marian Anderson became famous because Eleanor Roosevelt was her great friend or that JFK was assassinated because he was a Kennedy?

Students were able to juxtapose an essay and a biography, e.g. White's "Mary White" and Gunther's *Death Be Not Proud.* They found enjoyable the challenge of ferreting out biographer's biases as well as inconsistencies. They even discussed what notions their subjects held about "the good life," about how life should be lived. They found it possible to examine the complexities of the personality and to make judgments about which biography was too sanctimonious. When they discovered such a biography, they went on a search to see if the subject had any enemies and to read negative opinions of him.

The most intriguing problem of all for the academically apt student was, What is not explained? A biography raises questions about a personality; which ones are not satisfactorily answered? This problem presents one of the most challenging cognitive experiences. Was the biographer's omission intentional? What clues are there?

The biography is a suitable genre for students who are ready to function on a high cognitive level. Part of the reason lies in the fact that there is a relationship between incident and personality, which in effect is the relationship between the concrete and the abstract. Students must learn to construct a personality from the incidents in which he has involved himself.

There is one thing, however, that even academically superior students cannot be expected to do. They cannot check the accuracy of facts. Teachers who tried to focus in on this aspect invariably were frustrated as were the students. To check facts requires months and even years of study; there simply is not enough time, even in cases where one or two students may possess sustained interest.

When students become enthusiastic readers of biography, they are able to try on for size a number of adult situations, aspirations, values, and even aspects of adult personalities. They can reject those that do not appeal to them, and they can assimilate those that they are cognitively and affectively prepared to accept. Thus, their own lives are enriched as they learn from the goals, the deeds, and the reactions of great men and women.

Personality, according to Piaget, achieves its final form in adolescence. For the development of personality, the biography seems to be a uniquely suited genre. Piaget explains that personality is different from the self which is relatively primitive and characterized by egocentricity. A man "is said to have a strong personality when he incarnates an ideal or defends a cause with all his activity and will."[40] Biography offers content through which students can examine ideals and their effect upon an individual. Biographies often deal with the subject's aspirations and the ways and means he used to achieve them. This content is related to the task of adolescent personality development. Piaget writes, "One may say that personality exists as soon as a 'life plan' . . . which is both a source of discipline for the will and an instrument of cooperation, is formed."[41]

The adolescent responds to the realism in a biography, despite the fact that his concern is with reforming the world. "The adolescent in all modesty attributes to himself an essential role in the salvation of humanity and organizes his life plan accordingly."[42] It is when he tries to put his ideas into practice that "true adaptation to society comes automatically. . . ." It is then that he adapts to an "ever-widening reality."[43] Biography offers him an opportunity to explore that reality vicariously through the life of another human being and thus treats him to some previews of that "ever-widening reality."

NOTES

1. Wallace A. Bacon, *The Art of Interpretation* (New York: Holt, Rinehart & Winston, 1966), p. 366.
2. Dwight L. Burton, *Literature Study in the High Schools,* 3d ed. (New York: Holt, Rinehart & Winston, 1970), p. 196.
3. Abraham Bernstein, *Teaching English in High School* (New York: Random House, 1961), p. 256.
4. Ibid., p. 257.
5. Ibid.
6. Ralph Philip Boas, *The Study and Appreciation of Literature* (New York: Harcourt Brace Jovanovich, 1931), p. 215.
7. Howard C. Brashers, *The Structure of Essays* (Englewood Cliffs, N.J.: Prentice-Hall, 1972), p. 296.
8. Ibid., p. 286.
9. Ibid.
10. Edward Wagenknecht, *A Preface to Literature* (New York: Holt, Rinehart & Winston, 1969), p, 322.
11. Gilbert Highet, *Explorations* (New York: Oxford University Press, 1971), p. 306.
12. Ralph P. Boas and Edwin Smith, *Enjoyment of Literature* (New York: Harcourt Brace Jovanovich, 1937), p. 397.
13. John S. Lewis and Jean S. Sisk, *Teaching English 7–12* (New York: American Book Co., 1963), p. 265.
14. Don L. Cook, "On Teaching Essays," in *On Teaching Literature,* ed. Edward B. Jenkinson and Jane Stouder Hawley (Bloomington, Ind.: Indiana University Press, 1967), p. 137.
15. Brashers, p. 281.
16. Boas, p. 215.
17. Cook, pp. 138–39.
18. Boas, p. 215.
19. Bernstein, p. 260.
20. Charlotte I. Lee, *Oral Interpretation,* 3d ed. (Boston, Houghton Mifflin Co., 1965), pp. 136–37.
21. Boas, p. 238.
22. Edward O. Shakespeare, Peter H. Reinke, and Elliot W. Fenander, *Understanding the Essay* (New York: The Odyssey Press, 1966), p. xiii.
23. Brashers, pp. 277, 278.
24. See Chapter II for film reference bearing this title.
25. E. B. White, "Some Remarks on Humor," in *The Second Tree from the Corner,* ed. E. B. White (New York: Harper & Row, Publishers, 1954), p. 174.
26. *No longer available.*
27. Highet, p. 304.
28. Wagenknecht, p. 325.
29. Cleanth Brooks, John T. Purser, and Robert Penn Warren, *An Approach to Literature,* 4th ed. (New York: Appleton-Century-Crofts, 1964), pp. 561, 559, 560.
30. Edwin H. Sauer, *English in the Secondary School* (New York: Holt, Rinehart & Winston, 1961), p. 204.
31. Wagenknecht, p. 325.
32. Virginia Woolf, "The Art of Biography," in *The Types of Literature,* ed. Francis Connolly (New York: Harcourt Brace Jovanovich 1955), p. 641.
33. Bernstein, p. 264.
34. William F. Thrall and Addison Hibbard, *A Handbook to Literature* (New York: The Odyssey Press, 1936), pp. 51, 52.
35. John S. Lewis and Jean C. Sisk, p. 271.
36. Sauer, p. 203.
37. S. H. Steinberg, ed., *Cassell's Encyclopedia on World Literature,* vol. I (New York: Funk & Wagnalls, 1954), p. 61.
38. Marchette Chute, "Getting at the Truth," in *The Province of Prose,* 2d ed., ed. William R. Keast and Robert E. Streeter (New York: Harper & Row, Publishers, 1959), pp. 340–41.

39. Wilmarth S. Lewis, "The Difficult Art of Biography," in *The Province of Prose,* 2d ed. ed. William R. Keast and Robert E. Streeter (New York: Harper & Row, Publishers, 1959), p. 298.
40. Jean Piaget, *Six Psychological Studies* (New York: Vintage Books, 1968), p. 65.
41. Ibid.
42. Ibid., p. 67.
43. Ibid., pp. 68–69,

References

Anderson, Marion. *My Lord, What a Morning.* New York: The Viking Press, 1956.

Bacon, Wallace A. *The Art of Interpretation.* New York: Holt, Rinehart & Winston, 1966.

Benchley, Robert. "My Face." *The Benchley Roundup.* New York: Harper & Row, Publishers, 1954.

———. "Now That You're Tanned—What?" In *Pleasure in Literature.* edited by Egbert Nieman and George E. Salt. New York: Harcourt Brace Jovanovich, 1949.

———. "Take the Witness!" *My Ten Years in a Quandary and How They Grew.* New York: Harper & Row, Publishers, 1936.

Bernstein, Abraham. *Teaching English in High School.* New York: Random House, 1961.

Boas, Ralph P., and Smith, Edwin. *Enjoyment of Literature.* New York: Harcourt Brace Jovanovich, 1937.

Boas, Ralph Philip. *The Study and Appreciation of Literature.* New York: Harcourt Brace Jovanovich, 1931.

Brashers, Howard C. *The Structure of Essays.* Englewood Cliffs, N.J.: Prentice-Hall, 1972.

Brooks, Cleanth; Purser, John T.; and Warren, Robert Penn. *An Approach to Literature.* 4th ed. New York: Appleton-Century-Crofts, 1964.

Broun, Heywood Hale. "Holding a Baby." *Collected Edition of Heywood Broun.* New York: Harcourt Brace Jovanovich, 1941.

Bryan, Florence Horn. *Susan B. Anthony.* New York: Julian Messner, 1961.

Buchwald, Art. "The Children Are Restless." *Son of the Great Society.* New York: G. P. Putnam's Sons, 1965.

———. "Don't Be a Pal to Your Son." *Don't Forget to Write.* New York: The World Publishing Co., 1958.

———. "Richard the Third (With No Apologies to Shakespeare)." *I Never Danced at the White House.* New York: G. P. Putnam's Sons, 1973.

Burton, Dwight L. *Literature Study in the High Schools.* New York: Holt, Rinehart & Winston, 1970.

Chute, Marchette. "Getting at the Truth." In *The Province of Prose.* 2d ed., edited by William R. Keast and Robert E. Streeter. New York: Harper & Row, Publishers, 1959.

Cook, Don L. "On Teaching Essays." In *On Teaching Literature,* edited by Edward B. Jenkinson and Jane Stouder Hawley. Bloomington, Ind.: Indiana University Press, 1967.

Day, Clarence. "Father Opens My Mail." *Life with Father.* New York: Pocket Books, 1943.

Dooley, Tom. *The Edge of Tomorrow.* New York: Farrar, Straus & Giroux, 1958.

Elkins, Deborah. "Man on the Move." Photos and Teachers' Manual. New York: Franklin Watts, 1967.

Fowler, Mary E. *Teaching Language, Composition and Literature.* New York: McGraw-Hill Book Co., 1965.

Frank, Anne. *Anne Frank: The Diary of a Young Girl.* New York: Pocket Books, 1953.

Go Ask Alice. Englewood Cliffs, N.J.: Prentice-Hall, 1971.

Gunther, John. *Death Be Not Proud.* New York: Random House, 1953.

Highet, Gilbert. *Explorations.* New York: Oxford University Press, 1971.

Kieszak, Kenneth. *Turning Point: A Collection of Short Biographies.* New York: Globe Book Co., 1973.

Killilea, Marie. *With Love from Karen.* New York: Dell Publishing Co., 1964.

Leavitt, Hart Day, and Sohn, David A. *Stop, Look and Write!* New York: Bantam Books, 1964.

Lee, Charlotte I. *Oral Interpretation.* 3d ed. Boston: Houghton Mifflin Co., 1965.

Lewis, John S., and Sisk, Jean S. *Teaching English 7–12.* New York: American Book Co., 1963.

Lewis, Wilmarth S. "The Difficult Art of Biography." In *The Province of Prose.* 2d ed., edited by William R. Keast and Robert E. Streeter. New York: Harper & Row, Publishers, 1959.

Morris, Jeannie. *Brian Piccolo: A Short Season.* New York: Dell Publishing Co., 1972.

Orwell, George. "Shooting an Elephant." In *The Types of Literature,* edited by Francis Connolly. New York: Harcourt Brace Jovanovich, 1955.

Parks, Gordon. *A Choice of Weapons.* New York: Harper & Row, Publishers, 1973.

Piaget, Jean. *Six Psychological Studies.* New York: Vintage Books, 1968.

Preston, Edward. *Martin Luther King: Fighter for Freedom.* Garden City, N.Y.: Doubleday & Co., 1968.

Sauer, Edwin H. *English in the Secondary School.* New York: Holt, Rinehart & Winston, 1961.

Shakespeare, Edward O.: Reinke, Peter H.; and Fenander, Elliot W. *Understanding the Essay.* New York: The Odyssey Press, 1966.

Skapura, Robert J. "Lawsuits, Duels, and Burma-Shave: Nonfiction Works . . . If You Let It." *English Journal* 61 (September 1972):831–35, 842.

Smith, H. Allen. "Coping with the Compliment." *Essays for Modern Youth.* New York: Globe Book Co., 1960.

Steinberg, S. H. *Cassell's Encyclopedia on World Literature.* vol. I. New York: Funk & Wagnalls, 1954.

Swift, Jonathan. "A Modest Proposal." In *The Types of Literature,* edited by Francis Connolly. New York: Harcourt Brace Jovanovich, 1955.

Thorne, Alice. *The Story of Madame Curie.* New York: Scholastic Magazines, 1961.

Thrall, William F., and Hibbard, Addison. *A Handbook to Literature.* New York: The Odyssey Press, 1936.

Thurber, James. "Courtship through the Ages." *My World and Welcome to It.* New York: Harcourt Brace Jovanovich, 1942.

_____. "How the Kooks Crumble." *Lanterns and Lances.* New York; Harper & Row, Publishers, 1955.

_____. "The Peacelike Mongoose." *Further Fables for Our Time.* New York; Simon & Schuster, 1956.

_____. "The Shrike and the Chipmunks." *The Thurber Carnival.* New York: Dell Publishing Co., 1962.

_____. "The Trouble with Man Is Man." *Lanterns and Lances.* New York: Harper & Row, Publishers, 1955.

_____. "University Days." *The Thurber Carnival.* New York: Dell Publishing Co., 1962.

Wagenknecht, Edward. *A Preface to Literature.* New York: Holt, Rinehart & Winston, 1969.

White, E. B. "About Myself." *The Second Tree from the Corner.* New York: Harper and Row, Publishers, 1954.

_____. "Some Remarks on Humor." *The Second Tree from the Corner.* New York: Harper & Row, Publishers, 1954.

White, William Allen. "Mary White." In *Worlds to Explore,* edited by Matilda Bailey and Ullin W. Leavell. New York: American Book Co., 1951.

Woolf, Virginia. "The Art of Biography." In *The Types of Literature,* edited by Francis Connolly. New York: Harcourt Brace Jovanovich, 1955.

Suggested Essays and Collections

Alan, Jack. "How to Raise a Dog." In *How to Do Practically Anything,* edited by Jack Goodman and Alan Green. New York: Simon & Schuster, 1942.

Benchley, Robert. *My Ten Years in a Quandary and How They Grew.* New York: Harper and Row, Publishers, 1936.

_____. *Of All Things.* New York: Holt, Rinehart & Winston, 1921.

Bracken, Peg. *I Try to Behave Myself.* New York: Harcourt Brace Jovanovich, 1963.

Brooks, Cleanth, and Warren, Robert Penn. *Modern Rhetoric: Shorter Edition.* New York: Harcourt Brace Jovanovich, 1961.

Broun, Heywood Hale. "The Fifty-First Dragon." *Collected Edition of Heywood Broun.* New York: Harcourt Brace Jovanovich, 1941.

_____. "James Weldon Johnson." *Collected Edition of Heywood Broun.* New York: Harcourt Brace Jovanovich, 1941.

Buchwald, Art. "Coddling Victims of Crime." *The Establishment Is Alive and Well in Washington.* New York: G. P. Putnam's Sons, 1968.

Fadiman, Clifton. *Any Number Can Play.* New York: The World Publishing Co., 1957.

Feiffer, Jules. "Couch-as-Couch-Can." In *Understanding the Essay,* edited by Edward O. Shakespeare, Peter H. Reinke, and Elliot W. Fenander. New York: The Odyssey Press, 1966.

Golden, Harry. *Only in America.* New York: The World Publishing Co., 1958.

Greene, Jay E. *Essays for Modern Youth.* New York: Globe Book Co., 1960.

Gunther, John. "Some Texas Jokes." *Inside USA.* New York: Harper & Row, Publishers, 1947.

Hughes, Langston. *Simple's Uncle Sam.* American Century Series. New York: Hill & Wang, 1965.

Kazin, Alfred. *The Open Form: Essays for Our Time.* New York: Harcourt Brace Jovanovich, 1961.

Kerr, Jean. "Aunt Jean's Marshmallow Fudge Diet." *Please Don't Eat the Daisies.* Garden City, N.Y.: Doubleday & Co., 1957.

Leacock, Stephen. "The Awful Fate of Melpomenus Jones." *Literary Lapses.* New York: Dodd, Mead & Co., 1939.

_____. "How We Kept Mother's Day." *Laugh with Leacock.* New York: Dodd, Mead & Co., 1961.

_____. *Literary Lapses.* New York: Dodd, Mead & Co., 1939.

_____. "Wanted: A Goldfish." *Too Much College.* New York: Dodd, Mead & Co., 1939.

Littell, Robert. "Let There Be Ivy." *Read America First.* Freeport, N.Y.: Books for Libraries, 1968.

Parker, Elinor, ed. *I Was Just Thinking: A Book of Essays.* New York: Thomas Y. Crowell Co., 1959.

Peck, Richard, ed. *Leap into Reality: Essays for Now.* New York: Dell Publishing Co., 1973.

Repplier, Agnes. *Essays in Miniature.* St. Clair, Mich.: Scholarly Press, 1970.

Rosenthal, A. M. "No News from Auschwitz." In *Understanding the Essay,* edited by Edward O. Shakespeare, Peter H. Reinke, and Elliot W. Fenander. New York: The Odyssey Press, 1966.

Shaw, Charles B., ed. *American Essays.* New York: The New American Library, 1955.

Skinner, Cornelia Otis. *Our Hearts Were Young and Gay.* New York: Dodd, Mead & Co., 1942.

Thurber, James. *Credos and Curios.* New York: Harper & Row, Publishers, 1962.

_____. *Further Fables for Our Time.* New York: Simon & Schuster, 1956.

_____. *Lanterns and Lances.* New York: Harper & Row, Publishers, 1955.

_____. *My World and Welcome to It.* New York: Harcourt Brace Jovanovich, 1942.

_____. *The Thurber Carnival.* New York: Dell Publishing Co., 1962.

Vonnegut, Kurt. "Good Manners, Good Missiles, Good Night." *Welcome to the Monkey House.* New York: The Delacorte Press, 1968.

White, E. B. "Ghostwriting." *The Second Tree from the Corner.* New York: Harper & Row, Publishers, 1954.

_____. *Here Is New York.* New York: Harper & Row, Publishers, 1949.

_____. "Notes of Our Times" *The Second Tree from the Corner.* New York: Harper & Row, Publishers, 1954.

Zinsser, Hans. *As I Remember Him.* Boston: Little, Brown and Co., 1964.

Suggested Biographies

Adoff, Arnold. *Malcolm X.* New York: Thomas Y. Crowell Co., 1970.

Allen, Fred. *Much Ado about Me.* Boston: Little, Brown and Co., 1956.

Angelou, Maya. *I Know Why the Caged Bird Sings.* New York: Random House, 1969.

Arnothy, Christine. *I Am Fifteen and I Don't Want to Die.* New York: Scholastic Book Services, 1966.

Asinof, Eliot. *Craig and Joan: Two Lives for Peace.* New York: Dell Publishing Co., 1971.

Babb, Sanora. *An Owl on Every Post.* New York: The New American Library, 1972.

Baldwin, James. *Nobody Knows My Name.* New York: The Dial Press, 1961.

Baruch, Bernard. *Baruch: My Own Story.* New York: Holt, Rinehart Winston, 1957.

Beckhard, Arthur. *Albert Einstein.* New York: Avon Books, 1960.

Bigland, Eileen. *Helen Keller.* New York: S. G. Phillips, 1967.

Bishop, Jim. *A Day in the Life of President Kennedy.* New York: Random House, 1964.

Bontemps, Arna. *Young Booker.* New York: Dodd, Mead & Co., 1972.

Borland, Harold. *High, Wide, and Lonesome.* Philadelphia: J. B. Lippincott Co., 1956.

Carroll, Sara N. *The Search: A Biography of Leo Tolstoy.* New York: Harper & Row, Publishers, 1974.

Chapin, William. *Wasted: The Story of My Son's Drug Addiction.* New York: McGraw-Hill Book Co., 1972.

Colver, Anne. *Florence Nightingale, War Nurse.* New York: Dell Publishing Co., 1961.

Cousins, Norman. *Dr. Schweitzer of Lambarene.* Westport, Conn.: Greenwood Press, 1973.

Daley, Arthur. *Knute Rockne: Football Wizard of Notre Dame.* New York: P. J. Kenedy & Sons, 1960.

DeKruif, Paul. *Microbe Hunters.* New York: Pocket Books, 1940.

DeMille, Agnes. *Dance to the Piper.* New York: Grosset & Dunlap, 1952.

Dooley, Tom. *Deliver Us from Evil.* New York: Farrar, Straus & Giroux, 1956.

Doss, Helen. *The Family Nobody Wanted.* Boston: litle, Brown and Co., 1954.

Duncan, Isadora. *My Life.* New York: Liveright Publishing Corp., 1933.

Faber, Doris. *I Will Be Heard: The Life of William Lloyd Garrison.* New York: Lothrop, Lee & Shepard Co., 1970.

Fellings, Tom. *Black Pilgrimage.* New York: Lothrop, Lee & Shepard Co., 1972.

Frisbee, Lucy Post. *John F. Kennedy, Young Statesman.* Indianapolis: Bobbs-Merrill Co., 1964.

Frolick, S. J. *Once There Was a President.* New York: Kanrom, Inc., 1964.

Gergen, Joseph. *The Story of Dr. Julius Erving.* New York: Scholastic Book Services, 1975.

Gibson, Althea. *I Always Wanted to Be Somebody.* New York: Harper & Row, Publishers, 1958.

Gilbreth, Frank B., Jr., and Carey, Ernestine Gilbreth. *Belles on Their Toes.* New York: Thomas Y. Crowell Co., 1950.

Giovanni, Nikki. *Gemini.* Indianapolis: The Bobbs-Merrill Co., 1971.

Gollomb, Joseph. *Albert Schweitzer: Genius in the Jungle.* New York: Vanguard Press, 1949.

Griffin, John Howard. *Black Like Me.* Boston: Houghton Mifflin Co., 1960.

Harrison, Eddie, and Prather, Alfred V. J. *No Time for Dying.* Englewood Cliffs, N.J.: Prentice-Hall, 1973.

Haskins, James. *From Lew Alcindor to Kareem Abdul Jabbar.* New York: Lothrop, Lee & Shepard Co., 1972.

Hautzig, Esther. *The Endless Steppes: Growing Up in Siberia.* New York: Thomas Y. Crowell Co., 1968.

Hickok, Lorena A. *The Story of Helen Keller.* New York: Scholastic Book Services, 1960.

Keating, Bern. *Chaka, King of the Zulus.* New York: G. P. Putnam's Sons, 1968.

Keller, Helen. *The Story of My Life.* New York: Grosset & Dunlap, 1902.

Kennedy, John F. *Profiles in Courage.* Young Readers Memorial Edition. New York: Harper & Row, Publishers, 1964.

Killilea, Marie. *Karen.* New York: Dell Publishing Co., 1964.

Klaben, Helen. *Hey, I'm Alive!* New York: Scholastic Book Services, 1964.

Krents, Harold. *To Race the Wind.* New York: Bantam Books, 1973.

Mann, Peggy. *Clara Barton, Battlefield Nurse.* New York: Coward, McCann & Geoghegan, 1969.

Marshall, Catherine. *A Man Called Peter: The Story of Peter Marshall.* New York: McGraw-Hill Book Co., 1951.

Masani, Shakuntala. *Gandhi's Story.* New York: Oxford University Press, 1950.

Mayerson, Charlotte L., ed. *Two Blocks Apart.* New York: Avon Books, 1971.

Meaker, M. J. *Sudden Endings.* Garden City, N.Y.: Doubleday & Co., 1964.

Meigs, Cornelia. *Jane Addams.* Boston: Little, Brown & Co., 1970.

Merrett, John. *The True Story of Albert Schweitzer: Humanitarian.* Chicago: Childrens Press, 1964.

Merton, Thomas. *Seven Storey Mountain.* Garden City, N.Y.: Doubleday & Co., 1970.

Miers, Earl Schenck. *The Story of John F. Kennedy.* New York: Grosset & Dunlap, 1964.

Moore, Carman. *Somebody's Angel Child: The Story of Bessie Smith.* New York: Thomas Y. Crowell Co., 1969.

Newman, Shirlee P. *Marian Anderson: Lady from Philadelphia.* Philadelphia: The Westminster Press, 1966.

Nolan, Jeannette Covert. *The Story of Clara Barton of the Red Cross.* New York: Julian Messner, 1941.

Patterson, Floyd. *Victory over Myself.* New York: Scholastic Book Services, 1963.

Rau, Santha Rama. *Home to India.* New York: Scholastic Book Services, 1963.

Reid, P. R. *Escape from Colditz.* New York: The Berkley Publishing Corp., 1956.

Reiss, Johanna. *The Upstairs Room.* New York: Bantam Books, 1973.

Roeder, Bill. *Jackie Robinson.* New York: A. S. Barnes & Co., 1950.

Roos, Ann. *Man of Molokai: The Life of Father Damien.* Philadelphia: J. P. Lippincott Co., 1943.

Roosevelt, Eleanor. *On My Own.* New York: Harper & Row, Publishers, 1958.

Ruth, Babe. *The Babe Ruth Story.* New York: Scholastic Book Services, 1964.

Schoor, Gene. *Young Robert Kennedy.* New York: McGraw-Hill Book Co., 1969.

Shepard, Betty. *Mountain Man, Indian Chief: The Life and Adventures of Jim Beckworth.* New York: Harcourt Brace Jovanovich, 1968.

Skinner, Cornelia Otis. *That's Me All Over.* New York: Dodd, Mead & Co., 1948.

Strousse, Flora. *John Fitzgerald Kennedy, Man of Courage.* New York: P. J. Kenedy & Sons, 1964.

Terzian, James, and Cramer, Kathryn. *Mighty Hard Road: The Story of Cesar Chavez.* New York: Pocket Books, 1972.

Thomas, John. *The True Story of Lawrence of Arabia.* Chicago: Childrens Press, 1964.

Thompson, Thomas. *Richie.* New York: Bantam Books, 1974.

Thorne, Alice. *The Story of Madame Curie.* New York: Scholastic Book Services, 1961.

Van Riper, Jr., Guernsey. *Lou Gehrig: Boy of the Sand Lots.* Indianapolis: The Bobbs-Merrill Co., 1949.

Waite, Helen Elmira. *Make a Joyful Sound.* New York: Scholastic Book Services, 1964.

———. *Valiant Companions.* New York: Scholastic Book Services, 1959.

Wechsler, James. *In a Darkness.* New York: W. W. Norton & Co., 1972.

Whipple, Chandler. *Lt. John F. Kennedy—Expendable!* New York: Universal Publishing & Distributing Corp., 1964.

Withington, Alfreda. *Mine Eyes Have Seen: A Woman Doctor's Saga.* New York: E. P. Dutton & Co., 1941.

Wong, Jade Snow. *Fifth Chinese Daughter.* New York: Scholastic Book Services, 1963.

Wright, Richard. *Native Son.* New York: Harper & Row, Publishers, 1969.

Chapter Eight

Assessing the Attainment of Goals

Measurement and evaluation are primarily concerned with the improvement of instruction. Unless the teacher knows what happens to students as a result of his instruction, curriculum change is not likely to occur. This chapter does not discuss the measurement of student achievement or progress in order to assign a grade or stamp a label upon the student. Rather, it focuses on ways of assessing changes in students that can be related to the literature program, in order to measure the effectiveness of the curriculum with respect to the objectives set forth for it. Evaluation is "the process through which one judges the value of something," as Eisner phrases it.[1]

Since the objectives of teaching literature are broad, the measuring devices and processes must be diverse. No one measure is adequate. Evaluation is not a series of questions administered at the conclusion of a unit or learning sequence. Rather, it is an ongoing process and takes place when teachers make comments on students' papers, when they confer with students, and when students match themselves against their previous achievements rather than constantly against others' achievements. This last aspect gains importance from the facts that students read different materials, select individual projects, or engage in different qualities of experience. If students have helped to set the specific goals for their own learning, it is even more possible for them to evaluate their present performance against previous attempts. They need to know whether they are achieving the goals they set for their learning.

Schools which fail to offer students an opportunity for self-evaluation restrict their learning power. Evaluation is part and parcel of the learning process. By the same token, an evaluative instrument, device, or procedure is a learning situation. Appropriate evaluation procedures affect learning in positive ways. Such evaluation gives direction to new learning. When evaluation procedures are properly administered, students welcome and demand them.

Since enjoyment is a primary goal of teaching literature, measurement and evaluation procedures must do nothing to violate this objective. When measurement devices are also good teaching procedures, they do nothing to destroy enjoyment; as a matter of fact they enhance it. We constantly test ourselves and enjoy the act. For example, popular magazines often run "corny" questionnaires. Adults frequently spend many leisure moments answering these questions, comparing notes, and arguing over the universality of their responses. We test ourselves in many other ways: We race against our own typing speed; we match wits with friends about the subtleties of a movie; we match today's batting averages against yesterday's; we voluntarily test out our skill in swimming and we enter all kinds of competitions in many areas of life to assess our skills. We enjoy the rigors through which we put ourselves. That's the key: The testing is self-inflicted. We measure ourselves against ourselves or against someone else whose performance may be superior but who is a friendly competitor. We test ourselves in those areas we feel ready for testing. The decisions are not imposed upon us. Something of this quality of student involvement in the measurement program must be kept.

The procedures that are selected for evaluation must match the purposes of the program. For some objectives, informal devices may be far more appropriate than the formal. For example, one of the goals of teaching literature is to develop sensitivity and insight into other human beings as well as into one's own person. Sociometric tests administered at the end of the school year along with either oral or written interviews can be carefully compared to the first one for the content they reveal. Not only do individual students' offerings permit comparative analysis, but also the sociogram is studied for differences in the numbers of students who are highly rejected. The sociogram reveals differences in the lines of communication between students who have previously formed closed cliques.

Informal procedures such as the sociogram are not to be regarded as inconsequential. They may be the most effective. Standardized tests serve extremely limited purposes and cannot be used to fulfill the broad functions with which this book concerns itself.

The same informal procedures that were used for diagnostic purposes can be repeated in a new context for evaluating change. The sociometric test including sociometric interviews, responses to open-ended questions, diaries, and transcriptions of small-group and full-class discussions are among those devices which reveal changes in cognitive functioning and affective development. "Not all data, especially in art, need or can be quantified," writes Eisner.[2] But the changes that are symbolized in the differences in diaries, discussions, and open-ended responses can serve as a focus for evaluation.

The Sociometric Test and Interviews

The changes that take place as a consequence of sensitivity training through literature study can best be illustrated by the sociometric picture surrounding Ava, an eighth-grade girl in a lower-middle-class all-white neighborhood of a northern city. Ava lives with friends of the family, her father having died when she was very young and her mother having been institutionalized because of tuberculosis.

The admnistration of the sociogram should be followed by oral or written responses, but too often is not. In this instance the specifics were as follows:

1.   Each student wrote the names of the three classmates with whom he would most like to be seated in the literature class. Choices were to be held in

confidence by the teacher and students. The students were instructed to list the names in order of preference.

2.   The sociometric question was administered at approximately two-month intervals.

3.   After each sociometric question, students were either interviewed about their choices, in private, by the teacher or were asked to write in confidence about the reasons for their choices. The lead question for the interview was, How did you happen to choose _____?

Ava was an extremely shy and withdrawn student. The teacher administered the first sociogram in November, at which time Ava managed to speak in an interview with the teacher about Phyllis, her first choice:

> When we go to church we always hang around together. In school, too. And I walk home with her and we go to the library. I knew her when we were small. We used to go to visit Mrs. Pleasant together. I used to go over Phyllis' house. When she says something she doesn't hurt your feelings.

About her second choice (Evelyn), she used vague platitudes:

> I just like her, that's all. She's nice. I don't know. She just acts nice.

Her explanation for the third choice (Beatric Ann) added little to round out the picture.

An examination of these responses reveals several things. Phyllis was chosen on the basis of their past experiences together, and her inability to harm. Furthermore, churchgoing provided an emotional tie. Her choices were based on the help the girls offered her. One formulates an early hypothesis here of an adolescent who cannot extend herself, that is, who plays the role of a receiver of favors. Her need seems to be for others to extend themselves to her and to protect her. Her activities outside of school seem limited to walking to and from school and church.

An examination of the contents of reasons given by students who chose Ava can be of help in adding shape to the picture. Phyllis was the only person who extended a choice to her in November. However, since this was a mutual choice, it was a definite plus for Ava:

> Same like with Evelyn. She doesn't talk very much. She doesn't swoon over the boys. She has a sense of humor. She isn't loud. She isn't yelling all the time. When she does talk, she doesn't overdo it. She likes most of the things I do. She doesn't like boys, and Evelyn and I don't. We're more interested in schoolwork. We can have fun with her.

Phyllis's reasons accentuate the negative. It's what Ava doesn't do that attracts her. Yet, there is a hint of the positive—the sense of humor.

Two months later, in January, Ava again chose Phyllis, Evelyn, and Beatrice Ann. About Phyllis, she repeated substantially the November comments. This time, however, she verbalized the concept of being "in" with people. Further, she recognized that being able to sit and talk together was reason for choice.

> She's a lot of fun. She don't hurt your feelings. We used to play together when we were little. She and Evelyn are good friends, and I'm in with Evelyn as we all like each other. We go to confirmation class and sit together and talk about things that happen in school.

Her comments about Evelyn confirmed the hypothesis that her dependent behavior was useful to her:

> She helps me. Like in Social Studies I was afraid to get up and recite. So she checked my paper before class and said the answers were right and I shouldn't be afraid to say them. That's why I recite more. She's lots of fun in gym. We ask Miss Gene to be on the same team and she lets us. We walk home together too. She helps me pick the literature books, tells me which ones she thinks I'd like. When we went to Marie's house she came after me, and I didn't have to go alone.

Her statement reveals as much about Evelyn as it does about herself, which is often the case in interviews. But the fact that she can now relate clearly a concrete interpersonal incident is a far cry from the "she's nice" cliché. All her reasons are school related; apparently school was a place where a lonely withdrawn adolescent could find a few comfortable moments with another peer. The structure of the classroom activities gave nourishment to these relationships. When they went to Marie's house, it was to prepare for a panel discussion of a book these students had read.

Her reasons for choosing Beatrice Ann gave credence to the above hypothesis.

> She's full of fun too. We walk home because she lives the same way. She talks so fast sometimes you can't even get what she's saying but she makes you laugh. If the kids are going somewhere and I'm standing in the doorway, she'll always ask me to come along for a walk or something.

An examination of the responses on the other side of the coin—those who choose her—reveals that in January Evelyn chose Ava for the first time, explaining:

> First I felt sort of sorry for her because she was bashful, but now I like her so much. She's so nice. She's sort of innocent—I don't know. She never does anything wrong, whereas most of the girls do. She was scared to go to Marie's house about the panel so I went with her. She doesn't know Marie so well. I used to like the other kids more than I do now. They'd be thrilled if their mother let them out every single night. I wouldn't because I'd just as soon stay at home and read. She isn't always talking about boys. She can get silly with Phyllis and me. Not as silly as we are but just a little bit. She's always neat and clean.

Again, Ava was chosen partially for what she did not do. However, there was a definite indication that Ava was behaving more openly: she could get silly. As is often the case, the interview reflects much about the developmental pressures bearing down on both girls.

The contents of the last series of sociometric interviews given in March reveal further changes. Of Evelyn, Ava related a concrete incident to illustrate what she meant by the much used term "fun."

When I go with Phyllis, I go with her, too. All three of us go together. When I didn't know the words in spelling, she helps me. She's a lot of fun, too—her and Phyllis both. We got brown and white shoes. Evelyn doesn't polish hers, and I tried to get Phyllis to polish hers, but she says "No," because Evelyn thinks they look better not polished. Then I try to get her to polish them and she does. Then Evelyn gets her to leave them sloppy again.

This commentary indicated important changes in Ava. The circle had widened; there was a definite feeling of belonging to a group. Also, the most withdrawn of the girls now became comfortable enough with another person to tell her how to dress. While the focus of reasons for choice was still on school, there was a widening of activity indicated: Choice can be made because you can influence other people. It is not always necessary to remain dependent upon the goodwill of others. Further, the reasons for choice can contain a purely personal content, completely divorced from school. In March, Phyllis chose Ava again:

She's so changed. Now she's getting really silly. She was supposed to call her godfather and didn't and Mrs. A. [woman who takes care of Ava] made her go to bed at 7.30, but she laughed about it. Evelyn and I are a bad influence on her—she goes home saying 'snazzy' and 'putrid."

There's two girls in Fieldston. Joyce is white; her father is colored. She had a white mother who died, but now she has a stepmother who is colored. Mrs. A. didn't want Ava to play with her, but she was always dressed nice. She tells Evelyn and me stories about her, and all the fun she had.

Mrs. A always wraps Ava up in veils when she goes to see her mother. She's afraid she'll catch something.

She doesn't get along with Roseanna very well. She's stubborn and won't do anything.

So, by March Ava showed a few continuing signs of rebellion at home for causes established earlier, and a new self-assertiveness. Most important, Evelyn chose her for positive reasons, not solely for what she didn't do. There were signs of an increasing outgoingness.

She gets a lot sillier than she used to. I don't think she's jealous either. She never brags. Phyllis doesn't either. I don't like people who brag. She's getting more mischievous than she used to be. She's more alive. Didn't her hair look nice today?

If anyone ever asked her for anything, I think she'd give it to them. I think she's very sympathetic. She can be very stubborn, when she wants to be. I can't think of a particular instance, but I just have the feeling. She's very emotional. When her mother called up, she started crying.

Sometimes she looks as if her eyes are laughing, but she's really serious. Some people have such cold eyes but hers aren't.

She's very obedient. Mrs. A. told her not to eat anything because it would spoil her dinner. Phyllis and I were starved and had a hot dog. As usual we're starved. But she didn't buy anything. But we made her take a bite out of each of ours. We had to practically kill her to take it.

Although the teacher was concerned about Ava in the first weeks of the school year, there was evidence in the sociometric interviews that Ava was gaining strength to work through her problems. It was not possible to use discussion responses to measure change in her case; she said nothing throughout the entire year in a full-class discussion. Her diaries and her written reactions to stories and books were used to assess change in areas other than that revealed by the interviews.

A very significant thing that happened was her choice of Jill in March. Jill replaced Beatrice Ann as her third choice. Here she tells her reasons:

> She was on the panel discussing Canfield's *Understood Betsy.* She called and I told her about it. She was making me remember that when we were in the second grade I was in a play, and I was the crow. She said why don't I talk in school the way I do over the phone. She helped me in the panel with the questions, and she said she'd call me up sometime, but I guess she never got around to it. She asked me to go to the show with all the kids when they go. Vicki and Beatrice Ann take care of the children in church when their mothers are in church, and they tried to get me to go. The only time I see Beatrice Ann outside of school is when we take care of the nursery together.

There are indications here of a give-and-take relationship. Someone made a contact with Ava for the purpose of securing information, and Ava had it to give. In return she received help. Further, the conversation was satisfying enough to Jill that she paid Ava a backhanded compliment. The fact that Jill did not follow through on a promise did not deter Ava from choosing her. The significant factor is that she gave evidence of readiness to admit new people. However, she still had not surrendered her use of dependence on others for help.

The literature content per se was not responsible for the changes that took place in Ava.[3] It may have been the nonthreatening atmosphere of the literature classroom or the diverse activities from which students could select that was responsible. The facts that the books Ava and her friends chose to read did concern themselves with peer relationships and that the curriculum was pitched toward sensitivity training could have helped make the difference. The activities initiated in the classroom were followed through in situations with social overtones: going to the library together, meeting in classmates' homes for preparation of panel presentations, initiating telephone conversations about class activities and then extending those conversations to social areas.

Teachers can use sociometric data not only for the study of changes in individuals but also for the study of changes in entire groups. No teacher can possibly be aware of the quantity of change that is taking place in the lives of students within one year, unless there are aids for studying the phenomena attending the modifications. A similar statement can be made for the quality of that change. In Ava's class, an analysis of the March sociogram showed the lines of communication between students to be much longer than in November; more students deliberately included others in their activities. There was evidence that students consciously chose new people because they "wanted to know them better," because "the things he says in our discussion shows he's very smart," and because they were reading and recommending the same books. Mutual choices had increased in number, indicating that more students were finding a comfortable environment; closed cliques were virtually nonexistent. These were significant changes. Case study procedures such as those initiated with sociometric techniques offer potential for evaluation.

Using Class Discussions for Evaluation

Another significant informal means of evaluating what is happening to students is to create scoring categories for assessing responses in full-class discussions of a story, play, or poem. The same categories that are used to assess individual written comments can be used, especially if the material is to be quantified. One teacher used the following categories:

1. Makes generalizations
2. Explains behavior
3. Hypothesizes
4. Makes comparisons
5. Restates incidents
6. Makes self-references
7. Passes judgment
8. Distorts meaning of incident
9. Draws inference

At first the teacher encouraged students in a lower middle-income school to use their own experience in order to help them identify with the behavior of characters in the stories. As time passed, she reduced the calls for tales of personal experience to explain behavior of character. Some students continued to rely on such recollections; others were able to explain behavior without reference to themselves. At first the teacher asked repeatedly, "What would you do if you were _____?" This question was used in an attempt to help students identify with characters, and to reduce unsupported judgmental statements which were indicative of narrow cognitive and affective functioning. As students became involved in understanding and explaining behavior, less advice was given.

Students read self-selected books, formed panels, and presented issues. Well in advance, the date of the panel presentation was announced, so that anyone who wanted to read the book in order to enter into the discussion after the presentation was free to do so. Although the panels usually consisted of five or six students, the numbers who engaged in the discussions were far greater. One eighth-grade group presented *Sensible Kate* by Gates. This book is usually classified by the experts as being on the fifth-grade level. Fortunately, the experts' opinion was not available to these eighth graders who enjoyed the book. The question arose: Do you think your parents need you? The responses in a portion of the discussion which followed have been categorized.

Generalizes Hypothesizes	Evelyn: Yes. Having children gives them a certain responsibility in life. Without you, they'd wander around maybe. But children give them somebody to take care of.
Makes self-reference	Phyllis: Well, at home, my brother and I are awfully silly. We make my mother and father laugh. He does, anyway. But all I'm good for is talking. I nearly drive them nuts.

Generalizes
Makes
self-reference

Elaine: They love you so much. They have someone to love. I didn't understand that before, but I do now.

Generalizes
Makes
self-reference

Jill: It's easy to think you're not needed, especially when you put up a fuss when they ask you to do something. But when I take care of my sister for my mother, she really gets a thrill out of it. And so do I. And when she goes away, I know she misses me.

Generalizes
Makes
self-reference

Charles: I don't think it's so much the things you do that make the difference. It's that you miss each other so. Last summer I went to my grandmother's and my mother wrote to me every day, she missed me so much. I wrote to her too, every day.

In this discussion there was little opportunity for moralizing or for making judgments. The unusual number of self-references was due to the issue that arose or to the question raised. The students did not go back to the story until the teacher led them to do so. The question itself led them away from the story. If the teacher wanted to determine whether the students were still relying on self-reference, she compared their performance in October and May; she had to consider the particular circumstances of the discussion before quantifying took place and before meaningful comparisons could be made.

In February the same teacher read with the students Jackson's "After You, My Dear Alphonse" and opened the discussion with the question, "What do you think the story was trying to show?"

Distorts
meaning

Robert: That most blacks need clothes. (Chorus of "no's!")

Distorts
meaning

Virginia: All people have manners.

Generalizes

Peter: That black people can be equal to whites if you give them a chance. They can be polite, too.

Restates
incident

Elaine: That the little black boy didn't need the old clothes. He had just as good clothes.

Restates
incident
Generalizes

Janet: His sister is going to be a teacher. Some Negroes are just as educated as we are. It shows they aren't any dumber and can get a good position if they get a chance.

Explains
behavior

Harold: His mother acted funny when he said his father was a foreman. She didn't think he could get such a good job.

Restates
  incident
Explains
  behavior

Marie: She was surprised that they had money for clothes.

Generalizes

Evelyn: Feeling sorry for people is as bad as not liking them.
  Pitying them, I mean. Nobody likes to take charity.

Passes
  judgment

Rose
Marie: She should have sensed that he didn't need the clothes.

Generalizes
Explains
  behavior

Henry: That's racial discrimination, because if it wasn't she
  wouldn't be so shocked that he had as much money as her boy.

Explains
  behavior
Passes
  judgment

Janice: Mrs. Wilson was under the impression that all Negroes are
  poor. She's not really interested in them. If she were really
  interested and cared about people, she would know that some
  have already done O.K. in the world, and that all are not poor
  anymore. She acted very ignorant right there.

Explains
  behavior
Draws
  inference

Doris: She was always thinking Negroes should have
  hard-working jobs where they do the hard work. She couldn't
  believe that it was true that a Negro family should have enough
  money and enough to eat.

Passes
  judgment

Charles: I think she was nice. She didn't try to hurt his feelings.

Restates
  incident

Robert: She was surprised that his mother didn't work.

Restates
  incident

Henry: She was surprised that his sister went to college.

Passes
  judgment

Elaine: I think she was the rudest thing. She took the cake away
  and made him feel that he was lower.

Draws
  inference
Generalizes
Explains
  behavior

Harold: She felt as if Boyd was a slave.

Draws
  inference

Janice: When she saw Boyd carry the wood, she didn't want him
  to. Between children that was just as if he were another white.
  She thought Johnny made him do it, that he was treating him
  like a servant, because that was in her mind. She didn't want
  Johnny to think he was lower.

Draws inference	Evelyn: She thought this was the first time he had a good meal.
Restates incident	Janet: When he refused to take the clothes, she took the gingerbread away. She found out he had enough to eat, so she wasn't going to give him more.
Draws inference	Evelyn: She did that because they let her down.
Explains behavior	Elaine: She kept telling Boyd to take more and more and more. She thought he didn't have enough.
Draws inference	Betty: Johnny wanted Boyd's friendship even if he was black.
Draws inference	Marie: He didn't even think of his color.
Draws inference	Janet: He didn't even see it.
Draws inference	Doris: Oh, yes, he did!
Draws inference	Janet: I mean he did see it of course, but he just thought nothing of it.

Here, students were able to stay on course in a sustained fashion and to give serious thought to one experience until that experience was clarified and until concepts inherent in it began to develop. They attempted, without the aid of the teacher, to examine the situation from the point of view of each of the three characters in order to get a fuller comprehension of the story. There is evidence that they were grappling with causes and were making a few attempts at generalizing from experiences other than their own. There is evidence, too, of the great gaps in understanding that still remain.

If the teacher engages in this type of evaluation several times a year using whatever categories are appropriate to his aims, he can make reasonably good assessments about what changes in the class as a whole are taking place in the cognitive and affective domains with respect to responses in literature. He can assess how the cognitive and affective structure of each individual is developing. Does the student ever think ahead or make hypothesis on his own? Does he generalize at any time? Is he generalizing to a greater extent now than before? And are his generalizations on a higher plane? Does he identify with other characters? Can he interpret behavior increasingly without the aid of self-reference, or does he still need the concrete crutch of referring to himself before he can perceive relationships? Does he see that behavior is caused or motivated? Does he think in terms of multiple causation? Does he use generalizations that have no basis in concrete events? Does he think complex human problems have simple solutions or stem from simple causes? Does he make inferences?

From such analyses of discussions, the teacher can gain a sense of the way in which various topics affect different students. Which students are affected by the women's liberation focus, sibling rivalry, the problems of being left out, the impact of power or powerlessness, racial relationships? Who responds to diverse situations? These discussion analyses can also determine to what extent the group is effective in helping members think more maturely than they would if they attempted to respond without interaction. The effectiveness of the group can be seen if the teacher offers students an opportunity to respond first in writing before peer interaction and next in group discussion based on relatively open-ended questions about the same story.

Open-ended Responses to Stories

One phase of students' ability to make generalizations, draw implications, "feel with" other human beings, and comprehend the complexities of human behavior can be ascertained from written responses to a story that has been read to them by the teacher. The act of reading to students eliminates the danger of assessing skill in reading rather than comprehension of complex ideas. For students who have great difficulties with writing skills, the tape recorder may be used for evaluating cognitive and affective growth. A number of stories is appropriate for the purpose. Successfully used have been Deasy's "The High Hill," Jackson's "The Witch," Gibbs' "The Test," and Kreis' "Things Greater than He." The incidents in the story must be rich and varied enough to give students of widely different interests and orientations an opportunity to find their way into the story situation.

The responses of students in a class to a given story can be categorized in a number of ways. The teacher creates categories that pertain to the aims of teaching. Some useful categories already exist, such as those in Bloom's *Taxonomy* or "Levels of Understanding" by Bradfield and Moredock. The categories can be modified to suit the specific aims. Bradfield and Moredock describe levels that range from "imitating" and "repeating" what the author says (Level I) to "remembering, recalling, and classifying" (Level II), to "comparing, discriminating, and illustrating" (Level III), to "explaining, predicting, and drawing inferences" (Level IV) and finally to "creating, discovering, and reorganizing" (Level V). The problem with using categories created without reference to the particular activity in which students have engaged is that such categories fail to consider the uniqueness of responses. Furthermore, it is not always productive to try to determine whether a student's statement is Level II or III on a particular predetermined scale. Rather, the teacher needs descriptive categories derived from the responses themselves. As a teacher reads through a set of papers and senses that a number of them are replete with "should's" and "shouldn't's," with little or no interpretation, he realizes there is a gap in thinking as well as in affective development. Therefore, he lists this type of thinking as one category about which he needs to know more and in the area of which some indirect teaching may be necessary.

An eighth-grade class in a virtually all-white lower-middle-income community considered how people feel when they are put down by others for causes out of their control, how they react to being hurt, and how the author makes these things apparent through inference. In early November, the teacher wanted to determine to what degree students could harvest inferences and pinpoint causes for behavior, and to assess how much they could gather about the feelings of another human being. She read "Things Greater than He" by Bernardine Kreis to the class. It is the story of an "almost" nine-year-old Jonathan who is eager to visit his best friend Bob in order to give him a birthday gift, and Jonathan wants to go there by himself. "You've never traveled that far alone," says his mother, with sadness in her voice. Meantime, the murmur of his father's voice as he prepares the Sunday sermon is heard in the next room: "And the oak tree and the Cypress grew not in each other's shadow." Jonathan's house is at some distance from his school because his father wanted to succeed Jonathan's grandfather as minister of the church. Jonathan's mother reluctantly agrees to let her son go alone. Excitedly, he travels on the bus, unaccompanied for the first time. He enters Bob's apartment building which he thinks is like "a king's palace." In the hall there is a mirror from floor to ceiling, and Jonathan smiles at himself before he goes to Bob's apartment. Once there he discovers a birthday party for Bob in progress. All Bob's other classmates are there. As Jonathan stands outside the door, Bob's mother "herds" the very white sea of faces away from the door "deeper into the house, as though from a great danger." "And suddenly he knew. . . ." As Johathan ran down the stairs, he caught sight of himself in the mirror and "stared in surprise at his face."

Out of thirty-four students, one-third failed to grasp any of the implications of the story, even that Jonathan was black, despite the fact that Kreis specifically writes at the end, "The deep black of his own skin." This is not a subtle story, though it does have some subtleties. Perhaps the fact of oral presentation without a copy of the text was responsible for some of the misinterpretations. Certainly, the text should be in the hands of the students while the teacher reads, because the students who take a moment to think of something else while the teacher reads can miss significant parts. In such case, this is not a measure of growth in inference gathering, but in power to attend. The teacher had the feeling, however, that the ten or eleven students who failed to grasp the story were having difficulties with their own adjustment and simply were not ready to consider the problems of a black child. Kathleen's response is revealing of the cognitive and affective plane on which such students were functioning:

> In a way I liked the story and in a way I didn't. . . . I think that it shows you that if you do as your mother wants you to do you won't get in as much trouble. If he had paid attention to his mother and didn't go he wouldn't of had been as embarrassed as he was. By going to Bob's party when he wasn't invited.

Whether this girl recognized the racial overtones of the story is unclear. Certainly, if she did she was not willing to admit the existence of a problem and concentrated instead on the safe "mind your mother" focus, even though it was irrelevant to the main theme of the story. She found one safe aspect, distorted it to suit her own needs, and concentrated on it without regarding the implications of the story. Responses like hers are studied carefully for the creation of appropriate categories. In this case, three categories seemed to fit: "makes judgmental statements," "distorts central meaning," "rejects main character." To be helpful, categories must be descriptive, yet general enough to be inclusive. It is not sufficient to use a category like "fails to comprehend." That does not give direction to specific gaps in learning and is therefore not sufficiently helpful. The question is, what does he do with the material presented?

This instrument was administered after a relatively short period of work toward very long-term aims. After the individual written responses, the class held an open discussion led by the teacher, so that each student could "test" his response against the opinions and insights of others.

Aubrey, by far the "brightest" student in the class as measured by standardized intelligence tests, was highly rejected by her peers. Her rigid behavior caused her to suffer much at their hands. She, as well as Kathleen, found it difficult to accept the central thesis of the story.

> I would have liked it better if it had explained more at the end. Was he a Negro or an Indian from India? Did his parents have some Negro or Indian blood, and so he was black? . . . I think the story was rather indefinite. . . .
>
> Jonathan's mother is rather hard to understand. The way she said, "You've never gone that far alone, before." If Jonathan was a cripple, I could understand. Maybe nine is rather young, but why didn't she just say it, instead of saying it so sadly?
>
> When Jonathan saw that he was not invited to the party, he acted as though it was his first hurt. If he was Negro or Indian, it couldn't have been.

Aubrey made harsh judgments against the mother, against the author, against Jonathan. She wanted things stated as facts in bold print. She read a great deal but was uncomfortable during full-class literature discussions and small-group discussions. She was much happier during social studies discussions which permitted her to use facts she had gleaned to shed light on an issue. Literary men baffled, upset, and annoyed her. Yet, she read many novels and plays and claimed to enjoy them. The teacher assigned these categories to Aubrey's reaction: "makes judgmental statements," "ignores (avoids) central meaning." She suspected it would take a very long time to effect any significant change in Aubrey's cognitive and affective patterns. Meantime, it would be helpful to know whether the students who bypassed the racial issue would respond in the same way to another story about rejection, this time on a religious or ethnic basis rather than a racial one.

Kathleen's and Aubrey's responses are illustrative of students at one end of the spectrum. On the other end, students were right on target. Among these there was a great range in what students noticed about how people felt, the degree of sensitivity to other people's feeling, and the extent to which they could explain a behavioral phenomenon. Cathy wrote:

> I think the boy was black. Because if he wasn't asked to the party and Bob's mother seemed as if she didn't want Bob to talk to Jonathan. . . . I also think Jonathan's mother didn't want him to go alone to his friend's house because someone might start calling him names and he might feel bad. I think his mother was scared to let him go.

The teacher assigned two categories: "Explains behavior" and "interprets feelings."

Some students who did understand the central meaning of the story were unable to explain behavior. Rather, they offered a series of "should have's."

They should have been different to him because he's just like every other person. Mrs. Bascom should have invited him in. . . . The boys should have been friendly and played with him.

Although the focus of these statements was widely different from Kathleen's, the category nevertheless remains "makes judgmental statements."

In some instances students concentrated on one character only, attempting to explain behavior; others went down the line, dealing with interrelationships between characters. For example, Donald was bothered by Mrs. Bascom's behavior and focused in on her.

I think that John was a black boy, and Bob's mother had something against the Negro people. Mrs. Bascom told Bob to hurry up the conversation with John because she couldn't stand having her son associating with a Negro boy. She looked away when John looked at her in the doorway to make him feel that he was not wanted and hoped that he would leave . . .

On the other hand, Val was more concerned about the feelings of Jonathan's mother and the reasons for her behavior. However, she did not ignore Bob's mother and was one of the few students who noticed the earlier role of Bob himself. Yet, she did not question his failure to act in the new situation. By no means did Val perform in any outstanding way on a group intelligence test.

Johnny, the little boy was not invited or accepted to the party because of his colored skin. He was a Negro. Also, the reason I think that Johnny's mother was afraid to let him go alone was that all of his nine years he spent with her, and if he went someplace by himself someone might make fun of his color and he was young and probably did not realize that some people were ingrone [ignorant] [ingrown?] and might hurt his feelings. . . . Bob's mother was very mean and cruel to little Jonathan and that was when he really realized that people did not like him because of his color. Bob evidently never gave a hoot or even a thought about Jonathan's skin, for he seemed very nice and liked Johnny a lot.

Johnny's mother had a feeling of what might happen and therefore did not wish to cause her son unhappiness. But she probably figured he had to find out some day what some of the people thought of him.

Yet Val, with all her perceptiveness about Jonathan's mother and her alertness to the role of several characters never questioned that Jonathan must "find out some day," never challenged the status of things as they are, nor related the suffering of these characters to the larger societal issue.

None of the students made any attempt to uncover the meaning of the title; none of them were aware of the multiple inferences in "You've never traveled that far alone" though most students noted the sadness in the mother's voice. Nor did any of them absorb the implications of the father's sermon—admittedly an advanced concept—or question why the author inserted it. Only one student noticed that it was his father of whom he needed to ask so much, not his mother.

As a result of this kind of analysis, the teacher had a clearer notion than previously about the present posture of each student with respect to cognitive and affective reactions to story situations. The evaluation was diagnostic, as is every educational evaluation. The purpose was to improve instruction. The teacher knew that most responses were simply restatements of story events, that students could not make abstractions with any degree of comfort or facility, and that they needed help in examining the interrelationships and interactions of characters whose behavior affected the actions and emotions of others. Yet, there were clear indications that most students would be able to move ahead, given the appropriate literary materials and experiences.

How Do Students Enjoy Literature?

Teachers tried a number of devices to assess students' enjoyment of literature. One teacher asked them to tell her in writing how they felt about the reading they had done. It was June; the students understood that grades had already been recorded; there was a nonthreatening atmosphere, and students accepted the teacher's statement of the purpose of the task—to help her in planning for next year's class. A boy wrote:

> The thing I liked best was when ever there was a substitute we could read our own books when literature came around. Everything would be quiet and you could read with out any noise. Anyway it's more fun reading your own books instead of reading those big blue book with all different stories in it. Those big books when you read those big books 9 out of 10 your not going to like the stories but if you read your own books then you have something and you don't talk to anybody around you. Those stories you read Miss Edson are okey sometimes but not always. I'd still rather read my own books. Anyway's when you read your own books I think you learn alot more than reading the big blue book because when you read the big blue book you don't even lisson but when you read your own book it's a book you like and you learn alot out of it because you pay attetion to it.

The teacher found this excerpt to be an eloquent illustration of the principles of teaching literature: Encourage students to select their own reading matter; allow ample opportunity for involvement in a book; do not rely on class anthologies; involve students in the selection of stories and poems to be considered by the class or run the risk of their being judged "okey sometimes." The teacher had used "the big blue book" only four times, but it was never forgotten. She reasoned that the very presence of the uniform set of books standing on the shelf was a constant threat. Those books were not seen in her classroom again. Here, then, is a vivid example of what evaluation achieves: The teacher did discover how a student felt about reading; in turn, she improved her instruction to meet the demands of her objective.

Students indicated in a number of different ways the need for a sustained period of time in which to become involved with a book. A boy wrote:

> I think reading was easy this year because I enjoyed reading. You wouldn't have to read an hour each night you could just take home a book one night and read it. . . .

A girl's reaction was peculiarly reminiscent of Hunt's interpretation of Piaget (see Chapter Three, p. 68).

The more I read, the more I now, and the more I now, the better I like to read. The kinds of books that I like best are the ones about girls and boys of my own age.

Some reactions offered clues to the patterns of development of interest in reading through the grades. Students seem to recall quite clearly how they felt and what they did about reading from year to year. The teacher did not request this information; it came forth of the students' own accord. One girl wrote:

I liked to read ever since I first learned to read, but I never thought much about the library until I got in the fourth grade then, I read practicly all the books in the library for the fourth grade. Then I stopped and didn't read much until the eighth grade . . . I don't like to read about famous people or unusual people, just common people . . . When I read a book, I feel as though I were with that person and I understand just how they feel. When they are happy, I'm happy when they are sad I'm sad. . . . Every time I get into an arguement with someones, I remember a book that I read and a particular incident and tell them.

A second girl offered reasons for the difference in her attitude toward reading from one year to the next, while a third tried to explain the changes that took place in her feelings within the one academic year:

I like to read very much. I started to like it when I first began the eighth grade. Were we can choose the book we want, not the teacher to tell us to turn to page 10 and study.
    Last year I didn't read any book at all. To compare last year with this year, you'll find a 100% difference.
    At the beginning of this year I just dreaded to hear the word "read." But now I love to read. Even though I'm slow I like it very much. . . . This year we have panels and discussions and it makes you want to read the book the panel or discussioners are talking about. . . .

On the other end of the continuum were students for whom reading was certainly not an enjoyable activity:

I do not like to read and I can't keep still.
I like to read, but not very often.

And there were the students who had reservations about books in their lives, but who may have been affected in a positive way by what the school had done that year. At least they were able to offer advice to the teacher.

Anthony: It's O.K. to make us read because we can choose short exciting books that we like so much. They don't take long, and then we got to like to read. . . . Get rid of those girl books up there and get some books on horses and Indians and cowboys.

Geraldine: I'd like to find in books a better ending to some of them because some end flat when they could go on for another couple of pages.

Jonathan: No I don't like to read very well because I think it is borring. . . . When I was younger I never read a book until last Christmas . . . and I finished that but it took me an awful long time. . . . I told one of my friends that *His Own Where* was the best book I ever read. . . . I thought he would like it and I wanted to tell somebody because I liked it so much.

Karen: I like to read certain kinds of books only . . . about people of my own age. . . . I first began to like to read in the eighth grade. . . . If I was the teacher I would change absolutely nothing because I enjoyed every minute of the literature I did this year.

Since the teacher was making an effort to discover open-ended questions and topics that offer the most abundant clues to curriculum evaluation, she asked another class to respond to a different topic in writing. This writing was done in June under circumstances similar to those described above. "The Things I Liked Best This Year" encouraged response to a wider variety of experiences. Thus, the topic furnished feedback about several activities so that the teacher could assess how well each one held up under the scrutiny of the students. Furthermore, this topic gave students a chance to choose to mention an activity such as reading or to neglect it completely. Excerpts from one girl's response reveal that to her reading was important; discussions—in and out of school—also made a positive imprint.

Thing that I like best this year was the books we could read. In seventh grade we didn't have any books to read; and never before were they so good and about girls and boys your own age too! If I had my way, I'd like to have read every book in this room.

The next best thing I liked was discussions. I learned more about people this year than I ever learned in my whole life. Before I came into this room, I wasn't prejudiced about Negros and I wasn't friendly either. I just never gave it a thought. . . . I had an argument with my father about them and I won! I have a Negro friend too and . . . I like him better than most whites I met.

Students were able to identify the activities that gave them pleasure, and some were able to give reasons for their reaction. Reading, discussions, panels, role playing, group work, independent activities, and listening to stories were high on the list. Since the teacher indicated that their honest reactions would be helpful to her in planning for next year, students often addressed their responses to her. The following excerpts indicate once more the importance of student participation in planning.

One of the things that we did this year and I liked best was when you read us a story and let us make up our own questions and discuss it together. I liked it because I found it more interesting than having you make up the questions. I also liked it because you read the story and it was easier for us to follow than if each child read a paragraph. I also liked the way you had us work in a group quite often. I liked it because I think by working together you get to know people a little better and are able to understand them a little better. . . .

As did the previously mentioned class, students underlined their interest in books about teen-agers. They enjoyed reading "when there's nothing else to do," liked it because "it helps pass away the dull hours and we have some pretty good books." They appreciated the fact that "we had our pick of books and didn't have to all read the same book." They declared, "Reading is better than sitting all day with a textbook in your hand." When a boy who avoided reading earlier in the year can say, "Now I like very much to read when I have time and sometimes I make the time to read," the teacher has information with which to evaluate one effect of the program on that student.

Discussing stories and other literary genre was a favorite activity. Most students had had very little experience with open-ended "conversations"; this activity made a deep impression. One student wrote:

> What I like best was when you would read us a story and let us discuss it. . . . When we discuss some stories my ideas are different from somebody elses and it changes my ideas and sometimes puts me on the right track of things. It was also helpful to me because when we would discuss I would see just what other people thought. . . .

Role playing came next quantitatively in students' favor. They used the term "socio-drama" because the teacher used it. Two representative responses dealt with the feelings that were portrayed and the motivation inherent in such drama.

> The thing I really liked was the way we presented sociodrama. A person can present his or her problem in literature and can "just know" how they feel and what it would be like to be in his shoes.

> I liked sociodrama because it made learning interesting and also we saw what would happen in real life and not just make believe.

Panel discussions and preparation for them ranked next in students' favor. The social aspect was given equal importance with the intellectual.

> We came together in each others houses and in school. By getting together I got to know everybody in the room.
> How many things we had to learn! We talked over the book upside down and inside out. We had to decide what thoughts were most important and we had to make up good questions.

Individual projects and class projects came within the six highest chosen activities. One girl had studied the reactions of three children in a day-care center to four stories she read to them. She ranked it the most important thing she did all year.

> You learn to do things and you learn to conquer things you couldn't conquer before. You can make people understand what you mean. You can see how they feel. . . . You feel older.

The distribution of students' choices of activities reinforces the importance of varied experiences as well as of balance between intake and output activities. The study of literature cannot be solely an intake activity. Students who were not initially involved in reading did read because it made possible the satisfying participation in output activities with their peers. The students' reactions underscore once more the impact of the social arrangements on learning.

Informal contacts with students and the systematic observation of students yield information on the ways in which they enjoy literature. The teacher observes four or five students for one week and records observations daily; the following week she observes another four; this process is continued until there is a brief record of the pertinent behaviors of each student. The process is repeated three or four times a year. It alerts the teacher to the problems and progress of all students in the class. Patterns of learning and new needs can be uncovered in the course of the academic year.

Some excerpts from the files of one teacher indicated how much can be revealed by short accounts of the activities of students in one brief period. The diverse ways in which students use school activities for social purposes, the ways in which social contacts became motivation for academic learning, and the struggle for a sense of achievement are all in evidence. There is enjoyment and satisfaction in being able to cite *Mama's Bank Account* to give comfort to a friend, in sharing significant parts of a book, and in knowing it is possible to finish a book in two days.

Charles

When I entered the room Charles was sitting in front of Elaine and turning around to face her. They were engaged in a quiet serious conversation. Then Peter and Everett called to him to help them with a panel preparation. He went commenting, "They're supposed to be my friends. Why do they disturb me?" A few minutes later he came dashing up to me. "We need a girl for one part of something we're working on." I told him to get one. Without a moment's hesitation, he went up to Elaine and demanded that she come. Also without a moment's hesitation, she went.

Ed

Volunteered to act the part of the father in "Double Payment." The kids teased him about his high-pitched voice, but he took it good naturedly and still insisted on acting the part. The children went over their parts during the lunch hour and performed in the afternoon. I thought they might try to tease him again, but they became so interested in the story that they took him pretty much for granted, voice and all.

His mother stopped in after work. Said she hoped I thought Ed had made progress this year. She felt he had. Said she was most pleased that he had found courage enough to contribute orally in class. Formerly, he had never dared for fear someone would laugh at him. Said she was thrilled he was reading so much. She had had so much trouble trying to get him interested in books. Now he was "reading one right after another."

Evelyn

Read constantly, every spare minute. When she came across something she enjoyed, handed the book to Phyllis to enjoy it, too.

Elaine

The music teacher asked Elaine to leave her class today for some kind of misbehavior. She later, of her own account, went down to apologize. After school she told me it was the very first time she had ever been "thrown out of any class" and seemed genuinely disturbed about it. Doris answered, "Well, like it says in *Mama's Bank Account,* as long as you know you did wrong, and won't do it again, we can forgive you." Elaine smiled.

Mary

She proudly told me today that she had read *If I Love You Am I Trapped Forever?* in two days. It was her first day back after a week's absence. "I'm reading much faster now," she said, "and I understand faster."

If, along with the records of observations, teachers periodically keep samples of students' written work, there is additional information to aid in evaluating the program.

For example, two-day diaries that are recorded in the fall and two-day diaries recorded in May can reveal something of the positive or negative effects of the program on students.

Tests, Measurements, and Evaluation

Ebel defines measurement as "a quantitative description of how much a student has achieved." It is "objective and impersonal."[4] On the other hand, evaluation is a "qualitative judgment" of the degree to which the curriculum has enabled the student to perform satisfactorily. Measurements may form a partial basis for evaluation, but they are by no means the sole pieces of evidence. Certainly, a quantitative description of achievement will not suffice as a basis for evaluating a student's preparation for creative use of leisure time. Thus, measurement is not evaluation; there is no value placed upon the score; the score simply tells how much of the desired characteristic has been attained. The evaluation process is more complex. A value judgment is placed upon the performance.

There have been attempts to measure one aspect of the teaching of literature: appreciation, which has both affective and cognitive elements. Cooper reviews attempts to "get at appreciation of literature" through "content analysis of the oral or written response." He alerts the teacher to the pros and cons of content analysis. The response can be free, or it can be structured, in reply to a set of specific questions. This approach to measuring appreciation is very flexible. It has the additional attractive feature of being acceptable to teachers who doubt the validity of discrimination tests and objective tests; the material for study is a student's own written essay of response to a literary work. Its major disadvantage is that the analysis is extremely time-consuming. Coding each separate statement in a set of essays takes many hours."[5] However, there are ways of formalizing the content analysis, especially for transcribed discussions. One such method was used by Taba[6] for evaluating the use of literature to develop sensitivity. The author was the classroom teacher at the time of the Taba study and collected the data for the content analysis. Once the data were collected (in this case transcriptions of many classroom discussions about various literary works), they could be examined in a number of different ways to uncover various categories inherent in them. When teachers work together on the discovery of categories imbedded in the data and then analyze the responses, the findings can be an eye-opener to them.

The Interpretive Exercise

The purpose of this section is to call attention to another device through which the teacher can evaluate the role of the curriculum in developing divergent thinking. Gronlund believes that "the most promising form for measuring a variety of complex learning outcomes, in most school subjects, is the interpretive exercise."[7] It is well suited to some aims of literature study because its format is flexible and diverse. Ebel differentiates the interpretive exercise from the essay test.

> The essay test . . . asks, in effect, "What can you tell about this subject?" The prevalent types of objective test ask, in effect, "What do you know about this subject?" The interpretive

exercise asks, in effect, "What are you able to find out from this material?" or "What are you able to do with it as background?"[8]

The interpretive exercise moves away from the traditional demand that students reproduce old learnings. However, it is difficult to construct and time-consuming to score. Yet, "a skillful test constructor using interpretive exercises can measure most of the important outcomes of general education,"[9] whether they be general background, attitudes, values or cognitive skills of analysis, organization, and synthesis. Perhaps the greatest advantages of this type of device are that students enjoy them and appreciate the opportunity to match their present performance against their past performance. Also, the exercises are useful instructional devices. In no case should they be labeled "tests," at least not so long as that word carries a threatening connotation. The students have before them the story on which the exercise is based or may listen to it on tape. The purpose of the exercise is not to test recall; the teacher freely answers questions about the directions and the story. The test does not evaluate the student's ability to follow directions, nor is it to measure growth in reading skills or in recall unrelated to inference drawing. When teachers are clear about this fact, they are less apprehensive about assisting students with problems unrelated to achievement of the objective being appraised.

An interpretive exercise may ask students to predict how the character in a story will behave ten years later; it may ask them to consider three main characters in three stories and to decide which one they would most like for their friend. In all instances they explain their decisions and predictions. Students may be asked to decide which of two or three characters stands the best chance of leading a satisfying life or to predict how the experience related in the story will affect the behavior of the character immediately following the close of the story. The interpretive exercise may also be used to assess divergent thinking. Jackson's "The Witch" is unusually good for practice in divergent thinking, because it raises so many questions and leaves students with "an unfinished feeling." Students are reminded to consider carefully what is going on with all the characters in this story and then to write down as many questions as they can think of, about this story, that would help them understand what is going on with each character. Following are questions raised by twelfth graders:

Was the man joking throughout the conversation?
Why didn't the mother break off the conversation?
What was the boy looking at when he first saw the witch?
Where did the man come from?
Why did the man tell the boy this story?
Why does Johnny feel that strong adults will eat each other?
Did all of this really happen or was the whole thing Johnny's fantasy?
How does the boy say "Prob'ly" at the end of the story?
Why does the mother become so upset?
How is the man relating the story? What is his tone?
What is the connection between the lollipops in the man's story and the lollipops the boy is eating at the end?
Why didn't the man react more strongly to the mother's comments?
Why did the boy change from being the man's ally to being his mother's ally?

Why was eating so important in this story?
Why did the mother insist the old man leave when he had already told the story?
Who is the witch in this story?
Why does the old man juxtapose buying his little sister things and eating her?
Why does the mother answer all the questions that the old man poses to the boy?

Such an interpretive exercise not only assesses ability to think divergently but also encourages the process. Out of twenty-nine students, eight included at least five of the questions listed above. Some students mentioned others not listed here. When all questions are categorized, tallied, and used as a focus for group discussion, students become increasingly aware of the crucial nature of almost every detail in the story; they see the importance of every character and of being concerned about every character and event. They come to realize sharply that there was much they missed in the first reading; that a few of their peers asked original, perceptive, and pointed questions; and that without consideration of full data, their attempts to solve the problem of the tale leave much to be desired. They also become aware that even if they eventually should be able to settle upon a solution, they may not necessarily be right. Until all facets of all questions are brought to light, some doubts will linger.

This is not a comfortable situation for students who yearn for closure. Over substantial periods of time in which this type of activity is emphasized, students do find themselves able to observe in greater breadth and depth and to make more acute analyses. They can put more things together in a greater number of combinations and come up with something new. Loban, Ryan, and Squire emphasize the instructional role of testing: "The kind of evaluation a teacher uses has a strong influence on what pupils learn. From tests . . . the student can perceive whether his teacher is concerned with the depths or the superficialities of literature."[10] The exercise described here not only offers quantitative and qualitative data about students' ability to think divergently, but also furnishes a model for such thinking.

A second exercise for divergent thinking is also a key to another cognitive skill: predicting a character's behavior in a new situation. Prediction, which demands the drawing of a relationship between cause and consequence, is a cognitive skill to be encouraged. The cognitive skills are not discrete. Drawing inferences, making conclusions, seeing the relationship between cause and effect, and predicting are all interrelated. "The Test" by Gibbs lends itself to a test of ability to predict, as does Jackson's "After You, My Dear Alphonse." In the case of "The Test," the new situation usually selected by teachers centers around a new "test" crisis in which Mrs. Erickson does go with Marian to take the driver's test. Students are asked to describe what will happen and to explain their reasons for thinking so. Some students reject outright the notion that Mrs. Erickson would ever go with Marian and cite as their reason the fact that she was as prejudiced as the inspector but in a more subtle, less overtly brutal way. "She couldn't even talk with her about race and color." "She wasn't honest with her." "She couldn't face the truth. Instead of putting the issue squarely on race, where it belonged, she said, 'It's probably better to have someone a little older with you.' " "When Marian tries to bring up the issue of race, she says, 'Oh, I don't think it's that.' " More complete excerpts from a few eighth-grade students' papers give a flavor of students' feelings:

If she had gone she would have seen the truth, and it might have changed her whole personality. She didn't want to face the truth.

If she went and the inspector said something to hurt Marian, she probably wouldn't say anything to him.

She wouldn't go because she didn't want to know what would happen. If Marian failed, she didn't want to be a witness to the inspector's prejudice.

Maybe if a white lady was in the car, she would pass.

She would sit very still so she wouldn't make Marian nervous.

She wouldn't do anything. She'd want Marian to do it on her own.

The students' responses demonstrated the power of such an exercise to place students on a range of levels with respect to the ability to make predictions. A few students were highly sensitive and observant and pointed up issues worthy of the attention of the entire class. Others settled for "Mrs. Erickson is a thoughtful lady."

A tenth-grade teacher gave the same assignment but asked students to cite a direct quote from the story, which they considered influential in making their assessment, and then to give reasons for regarding this quotation of such significance. One student selected the following quotation: "It will be marvelous to have someone dependable to drive the kids to school." She reasoned thus:

Mrs. Erickson is a confusing character. This statement says that she trusts Marian with her children. However, even Mrs. Erickson does not trust Marian as an individual. Before anything, Marian is a "Negro." She is not an equal to Mrs. Erickson. She considers Marian as a person who is inferior, a servant who can be trusted. Mrs. Erickson is prejudiced and doesn't even know it.

Another student chose the same quotation from the story and commented:

Driving is a menial job to her and she feels it is below her status; she is therefore prejudiced like the inspector.

From a third student came the following statement:

This sounds very condescending. Mrs. Erickson is using Marian for everything she can. Now if Marian gets her license, she can drive the kids to school, too, besides everything else that she does.

The process of having students select appropriate and significant details has more than one advantage. For one thing, it is a test of whether they can separate the significant from the insignificant. Also, when teachers offered quotations from a story, they often failed to give a sufficiently long quotation for the student to be able to comprehend the problem. The basic information from which the inference was to be drawn was missing. Furthermore, students can select the passage they can talk about; in so doing they reveal something of the impact of the story upon them. The fact that such exercises can discriminate between those students whose inference making is weak or strong is evident from the responses of two boys who chose "Afternoon in the Jungle" by Maltz. The exercise required them to select three statements from the story which revealed the most about Charlie, put them in rank order, and explain why they felt their first choice was the most revealing. One boy simply wrote, "It shows the kind of person he is." The second commented in part:

> When he appeared to turn to stone, it was as if he had no feelings for anybody. And stone is gray, like the sidewalk was, and the gray day. And gray is not black and not white. It's like he can't win and he didn't know he lost. It's gray.

A third interpretive exercise for measuring ability to think divergently is for the students to concentrate on a problem the main character must solve. The students select the problem, raise questions leading to its solution, and answer each question until a solution is found. An example of the problem and questions for "Afternoon in the Jungle" follows:

> Problem:
> Will it ever be possible for Charlie to find his way out of the jungle?

> Questions:
> What are Charlie's aspirations?
> What makes him seem like a happy (or unhappy) person?
> What does he think about other people?
> Where are his friends?
> How does he spend his leisure time? Does he enjoy doing these things?
> What does Charlie know? What does he have to learn?
> Is he a "born loser?" How does the author feel about this?
> When he turned to "stone," is there anything that can make him human again?

This exercise appeals to only a relatively few students. Those who do select it find satisfaction when they can work with a partner to try out their questions and answers.

Transfer and Finding Similarities

Gronlund believes that proper evaluation procedures "can contribute to greater retention and transfer of learning by (1) focusing attention on those learning outcomes that are most permanent and most widely applicable, and (2) providing practice in applying previously learned skills and ideas in new situations."[11] He points out, too, that retention is far better with complex outcomes like applying principles than with the memorization of facts. Furthermore, "the ability to interpret new experiments actually increased during the year following instruction." Therefore, when teachers emphasize complex outcomes such as understanding concepts and interpreting materials, transfer should increase. "The use of tests and other evaluation instruments which specifically require the *application* of ideas and skills in new situations can also facilitate transfer. Evaluation of this type teaches pupils to anticipate transfer and to seek out the familiar elements in the new situation."[12] For example, students who read "The New Kid" can apply concepts they have considered in "Afternoon in the Jungle."

> How are the main ideas in the two stories similar?
> In what ways are the environments of the two boys alike?
> Are their contacts with other people similar in any way?
> Do you think Marty will "turn to stone?"

Once students are alerted to this kind of comparison, they begin to make similar comparisons for individually selected stories, build up higher levels of generalizations, and in turn, develop even greater opportunities for transfer.

Bloom points out that "the most reliable and valid measure of transfer would be the one that sought to find out what specific analogues one has incorporated from literature —whether he sees literary characters in the people he meets, whether he sees literary situations in the situations he encounters, whether he derives a part of his working morality from literature, and whether the comparison of literary and nonliterary events is a commonplace with him."[13]

Measuring Change in the Affective Domain

Because the affective and cognitive tasks are interrelated, devices to measure learning may be similar. There are, however, some devices which highlight the affective domain.

One device is for the students to set the stage for a dialogue between two characters; for example, Charlie of "Afternoon in the Jungle" meets Marty of "The New Kid" in the schoolyard. The student is to ask himself, "What will they say to each other?" The dialogue is then evaluated for a number of affective ingredients. With which of the two characters does the student identify? Which one does he draw more sympathetically? After the students complete their dialogue, the teacher offers a questionnaire of one or more items similar to the following suggestions:

1. Which boy started the conversation? Explain your reason for thinking he would be the first one to speak.
2. If you had to choose one of these two boys as your close friend, which one would you choose? What makes you feel this way?
3. Which boy would have more understanding of the feelings of the other one? Explain your reasons for thinking so.
4. If you were forced to trade places with Marty or Charlie, whose "boots" would you rather be in, Marty's or Charlie's? What makes you feel that way?
5. Which character would you like to know more about, Marty or Charlie? What would you like to know about him?

The assumption in the fifth item is, the more a student wants to know about a character, the more is he involved with that character. This assumption directs the teacher to another simpler device: Students select four or five characters from stories they have enjoyed. "Which one would you most like to know more about? What would you like to know about him? You may list as many things as you wish." Such questions give students an opportunity to engage in a device used by the whole class and yet to make their own selection of the characters and stories.

These devices do have the power to discriminate between students of high and low affective response as is evidenced from the following excerpts from senior high school students' papers about the father in Durham's "Home Again, Home Again." The teacher simply asked, "How do you feel about the character you selected?"

> Lois: I feel a little sorry for him because he's a sick, old man who had bad breaks all his life. He comes home because he's sick, and it's the only place he knows.
> Jeffrey: I feel bad for him because I think he had a purpose for leaving and regretted it. I think his daughter was too hard on him and made him feel worse. I think it was good that he finally came back to see her and still love her.
> Beth: This story makes me feel sorry for him. It makes me want to reach out, try to help him. Sympathy for rejection from his daughter. Sick old man, bending his pride, returning home after five years.
> Shelley: I wouldn't like him because he had just left the family. I would not let him back in the house again even if he was sick.
> Peter: I feel that he wasn't good enough to live with them before, but when he was old and half dead he all of a sudden wants his family to take him back again! He was just a drunkard and a bum.

There are other productive devices. The sociometric "test" when focused upon a literary activity can be revealing. Students are asked to choose three classmates with whom they would like to discuss the stories or poems being read, or with whom they would like to present a panel discussion of issues in a novel. The reasons they offer for their choice of person will be quite as important as the choices themselves. If three choices are permitted, the first one will be by far the most significant. The reasons usually carry cognitive as well as emotional overtones. Students who make their early choices on an affective basis solely but then graduate to include the cognitive as well are demonstrating a type of maturation. At least for the hour in which books are considered, they can forego the pleasure of having a best friend near them and substitute the intellectual pleasure of a stimulating session.

Open-ended questions such as the following can also provide information about student progress in the affective domain:

1. Which character would you like to change places with?
2. Which character would you like to help?
3. Which character could influence your life?
4. Which character is the luckiest person in all the stories and poems you know?
5. Which character is the most miserable person in all the stories and poems you know?

This type of open-ended topic can be created ad infinitum by teachers and students. For most classes, the teacher must spell out the information needed: "Why would you change places with this character?" "What is there about his life that makes you feel this way?" Then students follow the same kinds of questions when they create open-ended questions on their own.

Scoring Student Responses

The scoring of responses can be frustrating initially. It is necessary to discover an appropriate key already created or to create the categories. There are a few scales available for measuring the attainment of cognitive tasks. One which teachers find possible to use after they thrash out the meanings of terms, is Bradfield and Moredock's "Levels of Understanding"[24] which was described earlier.

The meanings of the particular terms used in the scale are best agreed upon when teachers examine together a few student responses in an attempt to categorize these responses. For example, one teacher used a new-situation test following the reading of "After You, My Dear Alphonse" by Jackson. In the new situation, Mrs. Wilson, the mother of the white boy, is on the school board and is asked by the president of the board to call Boyd's mother who has volunteered her services. One tenth-grade boy's response consisted in part of: "Mrs. Wilson would probably give her a job that didn't need too much intelligence. . . . She wouldn't ask her; she'd tell her, and in a way that would sound amiable enough but is actually a sugarcoating for her misconceptions." Teachers battled over this response in an attempt to assign a level to it. Some felt that a "reorganization" had taken place when the student projected "sugar-coating" behavior on the part of Mrs. Wilson toward Boyd's mother. Others felt it merely meant "recognizing" what had been said already. Some believed the statement, "Mrs. Wilson wouldn't ask her, she'd tell her," meant the student was "bringing in a new thing," using knowledge of the character to project a future act. Others challenged, "But what in the story leads us to believe that she'd tell her? She asked Boyd if he wanted the clothes and if he wanted to eat; she didn't tell him." This comment drew the reply, "She says, 'Other little boys would be grateful for clothes.' She tells, all the time. She's a preacher." Teachers came to some agreement that when a student catches Mrs. Wilson's perception of a black woman's intelligence despite the fact that there is no mention of intelligence, he is interjecting a new element and therefore reorganizing, because "the student takes all the information and incidents in the story, draws an inference, and says, 'She thinks all blacks are inferior.'" They decided, too, that "these arguments prove there's no such thing as objective marking because we bring our own prejudices; that is, "A teacher can't just make up a test and score it herself if she's going to use the results for real evaluation." They decided that their questions could become a pattern which students can use for testing themselves on self-selected stories. The responses could be evaluated using the same categories regardless of the story chosen.

Most teachers are not familiar with the problems of reliability between the individuals making judgments in the application of given criteria. They have not experienced the situation in which at least three peers sit down to evaluate independently a set of devices of any kind. They have not experienced the challenge of discussing the bases for scoring a student response about which none of them could agree. They have not experienced the satisfaction of revising and revamping the teacher-made scoring categories comprehensive enough to account for all the responses of the students. Nor have they ever created categories that are in accord with their own teaching objectives.

Other criteria for content analysis can be found in Bloom's *Taxonomy of Educational Objectives* written in two volumes focusing on the cognitive and the affective domains. The cognitive categories begin with *knowledge,* including knowledge of facts, classifications, principles, etc. Students demonstrate first-level categories of knowledge through recall. The second level is *comprehension,* including the ability to restate an idea or to paraphrase; to interpret, explain, or summarize ideas; and to extrapolate—a task which involves determining consequences and implications. The third is *application* in which the student can solve a new problem by selecting the appropriate idea. The fourth level is *analysis* in which the student demonstrates an ability to break content into its various elements in order to draw relationships between those elements; it also includes the ability to identify principles governing organization. The fifth is *synthesis* which involves combining content creatively (e.g., developing a plan to test an hypotheses). The sixth level is *evaluation* which encompasses making judgments about the value of materials.

Clark[14] illustrates these levels with examples from literary experiences especially of interest to the English teacher. She offers substantial assistance to teachers in defining Bloom's terms and in clarifying their meanings through examples.

Teachers find helpful the taxonomy of the affective domain since there is available little else for them to use for content analysis in this field. Even if they only discuss the meanings of the categories, they gain new insights about the levels of their students' responses. Krathwohl et al. list five major classifications or levels. In general, these categories were more useful in evaluating class discussions than individual written work. The first is *receiving* or attending which involves a simple awareness of a phenomenon as well as a willingness to tolerate and not to avoid the stimuli. The second level is *responding* which indicates a measure of involvement; the student engages willingly in activities related to the stimuli and even displays enjoyment in response. *Valuing* is the third category indicating a measure of internalization of the value which has worth to the student even in the face of conflicting values. He will even try to influence others to value his belief. *Organization* is fourth; the student tests his values in a number of ways, examines and refines them, and builds a hierarchy of values. The fifth level is *characterization by values* which signifies that the person lives by his hierarchy of values to the extent that he acts in accordance with them without having to make a conscious effort. The person who is truly characterized by such a hierarchy of values has a philosophy of life. These categories make it apparent that the cognitive and affective domains are related and have the additional advantage of removing the "emotional" domain from the restricting and limiting connotations of "sensitivity training."

Teachers who used Bloom's coding scheme or Bradfield and Moredock's were struck by the fact that a number of students previously "undiscovered" were performing on a high cognitive level. The transformation in the teachers' thinking about such students came largely from the fact that the categories force teachers to examine what students do know; the categories are descriptive, not punitive. It is interesting to note that when teachers begin to notice particular students, students' attitudes change toward school, toward literature, toward learning. Certainly, the teacher's new awareness of a given student is an intrinsic aspect of curriculum change. As academically superior students discovered a new challenge in literature through the new scoring devices and knowledge of coding, their esteem for the study of literature rose to new heights.

Once teachers became familiar with categories for levels of thought, some were concerned about the fact that they had given little attention to levels of difficulty in their creation of devices. They tried to set up tests in order of difficulty. For example, in using clues to detect characteristics or to support one's decisions about a character, one teacher arranged tests in the following order:

1. In the first test sequence, she gave a number of clues from which the students were to select.
2. In the next test sequence she asked them to find their own clues.
3. In the third, students selected their own clue and decided which one was the most important and which was the least important.

Interestingly enough, teachers' sincere efforts at arranging tasks in order of difficulty brought about what they considered great change in the improvement of their teaching. Now they were forced to assess how students learn cognitive tasks, which tasks must be learned before others, where gaps in teaching lay, and how these could best be filled. One teacher commented:

> This experience has made me aware of many new avenues available in the teaching of literature. I have discovered that, more often than not, I have been testing for entirely different objectives than those which I have been endeavoring to teach. Often I have been testing for a mere regurgitation of material which I have previously fed my class, at the expense of far more important goals . . . I discovered that the necessary tools require more preparation and greater insights on the part of the teacher than I have heretofore understood. However, there is also greater organization and a feeling of confidence in knowing that one has a clear-cut objective in mind, and that one is testing for this objective.

The feeling of security was often mentioned by teachers. The knowledge that some kind of order can be created in the teaching of literature was in large measure responsible for this security.

Summary

It is important that the testing format be varied. The main reasons are two-fold: (1) There is no one test that can reveal the achievements of objectives with any degree of certainty, and (2) the varied format itself holds a measure of learning motivation. One teacher remarked: They seemed intrigued by the format of the instruments themselves. They are accustomed to general essays, summarizes, or fill-in questions. For this reason the variety of each device helped to hold their interest. I had anticipated that some students would just not bother to hand in or complete the work since "It didn't count." However, all the students willingly completed all the work.

The kinds of exercises outlined in this chapter can provide motivation for learning if students understand clearly their own specific areas of strength and weakness. Gronlund suggests, "When pupils learn the qualities desired in a performance or a product and obtain experience in judging their own work in terms of these criteria, they are better able to provide their own immediate feedback. This type of self-reinforcement and self-correction of errors is basic to learning and an ultimate object of all education."[15] Periodic conferences with the teacher about the collection of diagnostic and evaluative data in students' folders are essential. Students must understand the precise function of each device so they can evaluate their own growth and use similar devices for self-instruction, wherever they find those devices useful. The sociometric test, however, is not the subject of an evaluative conference. Its function is entirely different from other devices. The information provided by the sociogram and the interviews is used solely by the teacher for the enhancement of group and individual learning. Before a sociometric test is administered, teachers should understand not only its functions but also its confidentiality. In most instances the same generalizations hold true for the students' diaries.

Like curriculum theory, evaluation procedures for the attainment of the complex goals of literature leave much to be desired. While evaluation in the arts receives the attention of the specialist, teachers can work at cutting the ties to meaningless testing. One teacher labeled the kinds of evaluation procedures described in this chapter "a many-splendored thing." It had forced her to stay on course with her objectives, to discover not only her students' strengths and weaknesses but her own, and to change emphasis in teaching procedures so that she and they "could come out with something worthwhile." Now she knew how to "not only measure and diagnose learning but to promote it."

Cooper has summed up the need for appropriate evaluative measures in literature:

> As we move into the era of the response-centered humanitarian curriculum in English, we will want to do more than assess comprehension of literature at the level of interpretation. As we renew our attempts to foster growth in appreciation of literature, we may want to assess that growth and also examine claims put forth for teaching methods designed to foster such growth. Administrators and national assessors may soon insist that we make these assessments, and teachers should be prepared for that day.

NOTES

1. Elliot W. Eisner, "How Can You Measure a Rainbow? Tactics for Evaluating the Teaching of Art," *Art Education* 24 (May 1971): p. 36.
2. *Ibid.*
3. Burton, citing the Purves-Beach report, states that "there is no clear evidence that people change behavior as a result of reading literature." See Dwight L. Burton, "Research in the Teaching of English: The Troubled Dream," *Research in the Teaching of English* 7 (Fall 1973): 180.
4. Robert L. Ebel, *Essentials of Educational Measurement* (Englewood Cliffs, N.J.: Prentice-Hall, 1972), p. 326.
5. Charles R. Cooper, "Measuring Appreciation of Literature: A Review of Attempts," *Research in the Teaching of English* 5 (Spring 1971): 19.
6. Hilda Taba, *With Perspective on Human Relations* (Washington, D.C.: American Council on Education, 1955), pp. 109–11.

7. Norman E. Gronlund, *Measurement and Evaluation in Teaching,* 2d ed. (New York: The Macmillan Co., 1971), p. 197.

8. Robert L. Ebel, "Writing the Test Item," in *Educational Measurement,* ed. E. F. Lindquist (Washington, D.C.: American Council on Education, 1951), p. 244.

9. Ibid., p. 246.

10. Walter Loban, Margaret Ryan, and James R. Squire, *Teaching Language and Literature* (New York: Harcourt Brace Jovanovich, 1969), p. 552.

11. Gronlund, p. 475.

12. Ibid., p. 276.

13. Benjamin S. Bloom, J. Thomas Hastings, and George F. Madaus, *Handbook on Formative and Summative Evaluation of Student Learning* (New York: McGraw-Hill Book Co., 1971), p. 758.

14. Sandra Clark, "Color Me Complete and Sequential," in *The Growing Edges of Secondary English,* ed. Charles Suhor, John Sawyer Mayher, and Frank J. D'Angelo (Champaign, Ill.: National Council of Teachers of English, 1968), pp. 47–49.

15. Gronlund, p. 474.

References

Bloom, Benjamin S., ed. *Taxonomy of Educational Objectives. Handbook I: Cognitive Domain.* New York: David McKay Co., 1956.

Bloom, Benjamin S.; Hastings, J. Thomas; and Madaus, George F. *Handbook on Formative and Summative Evaluation of Student Learning.* New York: McGraw-Hill Book Co., 1971.

Brackett, Peter. "Double Payment." In *Best Short Shorts,* edited by Eric Berger. New York: Scholastic Book Services, 1967.

Bradfield, James M., and Moredock, H. Stewart. *Measurement and Evaluation in Education.* New York: The Macmillan Co., 1957.

Burton, Dwight L. "Research in the Teaching of English: The Troubled Dream." *Research in the Teaching of English* 7 (Fall 1973): 180.

Canfield, Dorothy. *Understood Betsy.* New York: Scholastic Book Services, 1962.

Clark, Sandra. "Color Me Complete and Sequential." In *The Growing Edges of Secondary English,* edited by Charles Suhor, John Sawyer Mayher, and Frank J. D'Angelo. Champaign, Ill.: National Council of Teachers of English, 1968.

Cooper, Charles R. "Measuring Appreciation of Literature: A Review of Attempts." *Research in the Teaching of English* 5 (Spring 1971): 19.

Deasy, Mary. "The High Hill." *Harper's Magazine* 196 (February 1948):128–35.

Durham, John. "Home Again, Home Again." *The Long Haul and Other Stories.* New York: McGraw-Hill Book Co., 1968.

Ebel, Robert L. *Essentials of Educational Measurement.* Englewood Cliffs, N.J.: Prentice-Hall, 1972.

———. "Writing the Test Item." In *Educational Measurement,* edited by E. F. Lindquist. Washington, D.C.: American Council on Education, 1951.

Eisner, Elliot W. "How Can You Measure a Rainbow? Tactics for Evaluating the Teaching of Art." *Art Education* 24 (May 1971): 36.

Forbes, Kathryn. *Mama's Bank Account.* New York: Bantam Books, 1947.

Gates, Doris. *Sensible Kate.* New York: Scholastic Book Services, 1962.

Gibbs, Angelica. "The Test." In *75 Short Masterpieces: Stories from the World's Literature,* edited by Roger Godman. New York: Bantam Books, 1961.

Gronlund, Norman E. *Measurement and Evaluation in Teaching.* 2d ed. New York: The Macmillan Co., 1971.

Heyert, Murray. "The New Kid." In *The Study of Literature,* edited by Edward J. Gordon. New York: Ginn and Co., 1964.

Jackson, Shirley. "After You, My Dear Alphonse." *The Lottery.* New York: Avon Books, 1965.

————. "The Witch." *The Lottery.* New York: Avon Books, 1965.

Kerr, M. E. *If I Love You, Am I Trapped Forever?* New York: Dell Publishing Co., 1974.

Krathwohl, David R.; Bloom, Benjamin S.; and Masia, Bertram B. *Taxonomy of Educational Objectives, Handbook II: Affective Domain.* New York: David McKay Co., 1964.

Kreis, Bernadine. "Things Greater than He." *Senior Scholastic* 50 (1947):25–26.

Loban, Walter; Ryan, Margaret; and Squire, James R. *Teaching Language and Literature.* New York: Harcourt Brace Jovanovich, 1969.

Maltz, Albert. "Afternoon in the Jungle." In *Modern American Short Stories,* edited by Bennett Cerf. New York: The World Publishing Co., 1945.

Taba, Hilda. *With Perspective on Human Relations.* Washington, D.C.: American Council on Education, 1955.

Index